This study redefines relations between writing and playing in Shakespeare's theatre as marked by difference as well as integration in both the provenance and the production process of early modern stages. In his close readings in *Richard III*, *Midsummer Night's Dream*, *Hamlet*, *Troilus and Cressida*, *Macbeth*, *Timon of Athens* and other plays, the author traces contrariety but also liminality between the imaginary world-in-the-play and the visible, audible playing-in-the-world of the playhouse. Engaging both worlds, Shakespeare's stage projects verbal and performance practices each to "double business bound"; together they inform his theatre's most potent impulse then and, the author suggests, now, in our own theatre.

Robert Weimann is Professor of Drama at the University of California, Irvine, and member of the Berlin-Brandenburg Academy of Arts. In the field of Shakespeare and early modern studies, his most recent book-length study is *Authority and Representation in Early Modern Discourse* (1996).

Cambridge Studies in Renaissance Literature and Culture 39

Author's Pen and Actor's Voice

Author's Pen and Actor's Voice

Playing and Writing in Shakespeare's Theatre

Robert Weimann

edited by

Helen Higbee and William West

CAMBRIDGE UNIVERSITY PRESS

PUBLISHED BY THE PRESS SYNDICATE OF THE UNIVERSITY OF CAMBRIDGE
The Pitt Building, Trumpington Street, Cambridge, United Kingdom

CAMBRIDGE UNIVERSITY PRESS
The Edinburgh Building, Cambridge CB2 2RU, UK   www.cup.cam.ac.uk
40 West 20th Street, New York, NY 10011–4211, USA   www.cup.org
10 Stamford Road, Oakleigh, Melbourne 3166, Australia
Ruiz de Alarcón 13, 28014 Madrid, Spain

First published 2000

Printed in the United Kingdom at the University Press, Cambridge

Typeset in Times 10/12pt [VN]

A catalogue record for this book is available from the British Library

ISBN 0 521 781302 hardback
ISBN 0 521 787351 paperback

For Barrie Stavis,
American Playwright

Contents

Preface

If I may use old-fashioned tropological language that must seem recklessly at odds with the idea of authorship as set forth on these pages, then this book is an offspring that willfully and irresistibly upset a long established order of succession. According to this order, the present study was devised as a second, contextualizing chapter to a work in progress provisionally entitled, "Shakespeare and the Power of Performance: Authority and Representation in the Elizabethan Theatre." Sharing the fate of what originally was the Introduction thereto – now available under the title *Authority and Representation in Early Modern Discourse* (1996) – the present offshoot has grown up with an unforeseen dynamic all of its own. Caught up in the current upheaval in Shakespeare criticism, with its exhilarating rapprochement among textual scholarship, theatre history, and performance studies, this book owes its exposition and arrangement to an attempt to conjoin variegated perspectives on its subject. The deliberate criss-crossing between title and subtitle underlines the idea that, in Shakespeare's theatre, "author's pen" is in "actor's voice" just as players' voices and bodies, with all their contrariety, resonate in the writings of the pen. Hence, the result is no longer what, as in the case of the first volume, may be called a companion study but rather a self-contained sequel that henceforth will dictate some of the terms of the third and final volume in the project at large.

Genealogies tend to be perceived as tedious these days, but here I need to recapitulate at least part of the story of this project in order to do justice to the contributions of my editors. Helen Higbee's share in the present volume is the largest, my debt to her the greatest. Together with me, she went through draft after draft, eliminating verbiage and repetitions, helping to improve the flow of the argument, insisting on clarifications, pointing out contradictions and, all along, doing most of the checking and retyping. And although she joined the project only after I had written and revised a first, much briefer version, I am especially indebted to her for composing the index and helping to see the book through the press.

Following in the footsteps of my former student, my friend and collaborator David Hillman, William West continued to edit most of the chapters in what is now going to be the final, as yet unfinished volume in this series. Before Helen took over, it was he who first encouraged me to single out and helped revise, in its first draft, the present *offspring* from what then was the block of the larger project. In view of my long-standing cooperation with Will, I wish to express my appreciation and gratitude both to him and Helen. Their enthusiasm and intelligence, their patience and resourcefulness have been invaluable.

Next to my two editors, I wish to thank all those who, both practically and through their criticism, contributed to the completion of the present book. Over almost a decade's work on these volumes, I enjoyed and benefited from the research assistance of three of my students in the Drama Department at the University of California, Irvine. Michael Fox, Erin Johnson, and Bryan Doerries each in his own way gave dedicated support, working in libraries, on the computer, and asking good questions. In the concluding phase of the work I was fortunate (and grateful to Ingeborg Boltz) to have access to the Shakespeare-Bibliothek at Munich University just as, at earlier stages, I felt privileged to avail myself of the unique resources of the Huntington Library and again became indebted to the hospitality of the Stratford Shakespeare Institute Library and its friendly staff. Finally, when all seemed (but was not nearly) said and done, I found wonderfully adroit help from Silke Meyer (Bonn University) who, thanks to a grant by Deutsche Forschungsgemeinschaft, put finishing touches on the entire typescript, after she had already contributed to the as yet unpublished part of the project. Great thanks to Silke and my assistants at UCI.

At the same time, it was a pleasure and a source of inspiration for this project to teach graduate courses in my department, with welcome attendance by PhD students from the Theater and Literature departments of UC San Diego, among them, first and foremost, Helen Higbee and D. J. Hopkins, who provided a fantastic first design for this book's cover. What pleasure and profit accrued from my work at UCI would have been unthinkable outside the friendly and thoroughly congenial atmosphere that, together with the material support for research assistance, I owe to colleagues and, especially, two chairs of my Department, Stephen Barker and Cameron Harvey, along with the encouragement coming from the Dean of the School of the Arts, Jill Beck, and the head of our PhD program, David McDonald.

The present study in particular has been enriched by friends and colleagues who, at various stages of its composition, took time off from their own work to read draft versions of individual chapters or even the entire typescript. Altogether I cannot here do justice to what their criticism, encouragement, and stimulating readings have meant for me on top of the actual improvements they provided for this book (whose failings of course remain exclusively my own responsibility). Let me just record the extremely thoughtful responses that William Dodd, Bryan Reynolds, and James Siemon gave to an early version. At a later stage Laurie Elizabeth Maguire graciously read and commented on two chapters that touched on issues of textual scholarship. I owe a very special debt indeed to William Worthen who richly annotated the Introduction and had sagacious comments on several other chapters. I am equally indebted to Michael Bristol who shrewdly helped to sharpen the book's 'topical hook' and stimulated its historical perspective. Stephen Greenblatt and David Scott Kastan generously agreed to read the entire final draft version; the help and the support they gave was much greater than they perhaps would believe. Last not least, it was Stephen Orgel who, as series editor, gave thoroughly helpful criticism and unfailing encouragement to a project that he had generously accepted when far from being finished. Finally, the greatest debt of all is, as ever, nearer home: it is impossible here to express my gratitude to Maja for her sustained help, patience, and forbearance.

Acknowledgements: I wish to thank both the editors and publishers of *New Literary History*, *Representations*, and *Shakespeare Quarterly* for permission to use and reproduce material previously published on their pages. This material is taken from essays – with one exception listed in Works Cited – which are either heavily revised or reproduced after a largely selective fashion in the present study. The exception is the more recent essay, "Playing with a Difference: Revisiting 'Pen' and 'Voice' in Shakespeare's Theater," *Shakespeare Quarterly* 50 (1999). Additionally, a somewhat earlier version of Chapter 1 appeared in the collection, *Die Wunde der Geschichte: Aufsätze zur Literatur and Ästhetik* (Weimar: Böhlau, 1999), whose editors I thank for permission to use that material.

Introduction: conjunctures and concepts

> A division occurred, between writing and action, which has become more apparent in each successive phase of this culture. One of the sources of this division was print: the attachment of writing to this static form, away from the human voices and movements to which it stood in a merely abstract relation. Another source, of a deeper kind, was a revaluation of action within the society. Certain 'representative' modes of dramatic writing seem to have developed, hand in hand, with certain 'representative' institutions for political actions and decision. Near their most serious interests, most men learned to give up the idea of intervention, participation, direct action, even as a possibility, in favour of indirect, conventional and reacting forms.
>
> Raymond Williams, "Argument: Text and Performance," *Drama in Performance* (1968), p. 185

This study seeks to revisit relations of writing and performance in the Elizabethan theatre at a time when in our own cultural and critical discourses the authority of the printed text is undergoing far-reaching reassessments. While both the institution of authorship and the stability of the text have become controversial issues, 'performance' and 'performativity' are dominating critical discussion almost, as one provocative critic believes, "to the point of stupefaction" (Diamond, *Performance*, Introduction 2). 'Performance' has advanced to something like an ubiquitous concept which we use either to sound, or intercept our discontent with, the epistemology of representation. But even though 'performance' and the 'performative' have come close to constituting a new paradigm bridging several disciplines, the study of theatrical performance has, somehow, remained in the doldrums.

As Richard Schechner declared in a *Tulane Drama Review* editorial (1992): "The new paradigm is 'performance,' not theatre" (Schechner, "New Paradigm" 7). Philip Auslander, in his acutely informed recent study, *From Acting to Performance*, notes in reference to the work of distinguished contemporary theatre directors, performance artists and theoreticians, "that what they call 'performance' can be seen as deconstructing 'theatre.' They suggest that performance exists in an antagonistic

1

relationship with theatre," obstructing "theatre's essential features" (Auslander 54). In Europe as well as in America, there is by now a fairly wide-spread desire, on the part of avant-garde practitioners and theorists of performance, for "the emancipation from any necessary relationship with a 'text'" (Hilton, *New Directions* 6). In these circumstances, as a highly perceptive observer notes, drama in the theatre tends to be viewed as "an increasingly residual mode of performance," one that is bypassed in what is assumed to be the culturally and politically far more exciting search for "nondramatic, nontheatrical, nonscripted, ceremonial and everyday-life performance" (Worthen, "Drama" 1093–94). Small wonder, then, that "the burgeoning of performance studies has not really clarified the relation between dramatic text and performance" (1094).

To a good many readers, the current upheaval in the relationship of dramatic text and performance may perhaps appear to be quite remote from any of the major issues in today's Shakespeare criticism and production. But my point in calling attention to these revaluations is that, sooner or later, they will have a growing impact on the horizon of expectation against which Shakespeare's plays are produced, received, and critically re-examined in the twenty-first century. To say this is not necessarily a defensive or, for that matter, an opportunistic gesture. Rather, there is overwhelming evidence in the history of Shakespeare's reception that his cultural preeminence was closely linked, even in direct proportion, to what was most vitally alive, most absorbing, searching, or disturbing in the minds of his readers and spectators. This phenomenon is different from, and must not be reduced to, the time-serving assimilation of the bard to the latest fashion. What for Shakespeare critics, scholars, and theatre practitioners is perfectly legitimate, and in fact, a desideratum of some magnitude is to be wide awake to what is happening in our own contemporary theatre and culture.

The current trend in the non-academic reception of Shakespeare is a case in point. Today Shakespeare critics confront a cultural environment in which performance – including the highly varied forms of its technological reproduction – has overtaken text as the preferred medium of access to cultural experience and expression. For a significant, and significantly increasing, majority of people the encounter with Shakespeare is not through reading what he wrote but through watching certain electronically processed images of filmed performances. To acknowledge this major shift in the reception of the classic is to take cognizance not simply of deep-going changes in the media of access; no less important, the shifting mode of reception significantly affects the meaning of what is received. The parameters of what now authorizes and energizes the uses of his plays are themselves in flux. What we see emerging before our eyes is a new poetics of cultural response that has its own demands and gratifications different from those of a predominantly textual assimilation of the classic.

This new poetics of cultural response, while it has reached academia only marginally, points to untapped sources of reproducible pleasure and profit in recycling the culture of the past – effects largely unanticipated in Walter Benjamin's celebrated essay. In this process, the authority of Shakespeare's writings recedes behind the authority (or is it, bluntly, accessibility) of what images of performance the electronically reproduced version of the text can be made to yield. In "the wake of the present displacements of book and literary culture," a major trend is to invoke "the high status literary text only to dismiss it in favor of the actor's performance" (Boose and Burt, *Shakespeare, the Movie* 10). This state of affairs once again enhances what Michael Bristol in *Big-time Shakespeare* has called the "chronic tension between a more exclusive culture of the book and a more popular culture of performance" (x; cf. 30).

In the Elizabethan theatre, as I shall suggest, this recurring tension constituted a source of strength through concomitant theatrical practices marked by doubleness and contrariety. This alone should make us wary of any rash disparagement of either of these communicative modes and their socio-economic hinterland. In studying Elizabethan uses of word and show in their mediated mode of interaction, it is both unwise and unhelpful, I believe, to deplore these shifts in the channels of access to cultural goods and services. But in our time the shift in media access, even when it enables many more people to assimilate easily reproducible versions of Shakespeare performed, is different from Elizabethan practices both in its effect and direction. The contemporary cultural drift from word to image, from text to show, from production to reproduction, counterpoints the Elizabethan moment of differentiation *and* inclusion between them; this drift raises questions that, from the point of view of Shakespeare criticism and scholarship, are troublesome rather than simply encouraging. In Raymond Williams' phrase, "the attachment of writing" to the static form of print was a move away from "human voices and movements." But can the attachment of Shakespeare's work to the screen, whether video, TV, or cinema, in any way hope to implicate people's "most serious interests" more effectively? Rather, the (by no means unambiguous) evidence more often than not suggests that the appropriation of Shakespeare's playtext by these media (and their political economy) is in its turn bringing forth "representative modes" of reception that are even more remote from cultural "intervention, participation, direct action."

Here, I must content myself with these bare notes on the changing horizons of Shakespeare's contemporary reception. The suggestion is that the best way for Shakespeare criticism to view in perspective today's rapidly changing parameters in the reception of the classic is first of all to re-examine relations of language and show in their historical context, which is the Elizabethan theatre. If, as I shall suggest, these relations participate in the circulation of unfixed, largely untried and unsettled sources of appeal, the use and impact of a largely underestimated "scaenical authority" (Dekker's term) deserves to be considered more closely. Was the Elizabethan purpose of playing, perhaps, predicated upon far more fluid, direct, and less "representative" premises than mainstream twentieth-century criticism ever allowed for? For an answer, the present study seeks to explore the 'contrarious' element in the conditions and locations upon which a vulnerable alliance of early modern playing and writing unfolded. The element of contrariety was incompatible with, in fact it was the undoing of, the dominant Renaissance poetics of literacy. But once this element was absorbed by and adapted to the writing itself, it in its own turn helped for a certain time to keep viable more than one purpose of playing. In this context, "bifold authority" drew upon and reinvigorated a peculiar double-bind in Shakespeare's dramaturgy, even when the appeal of this doubleness was inseparable from the overall vulnerability and contingency of the cultural institution itself.

The precariously relative balance of word and action on the Elizabethan stage is probably unique. This is one more reason why this book rejects the notion of any analogy between early modern and late modern shifts in the accessibility and authorization of communicative media. Analogies between then and now carry perils; the facile establishment of similitude invites at best self-projection, at worst self-congratulation. It is an entirely different matter, however, to grapple with what elsewhere I have called the ineluctable conjuncture of "past significance and present meaning."[1] The idea is not simply to read and revitalize Shakespeare through our own haunting concerns, or use our sense of contemporaneity as a probe into previously underestimated or obliterated uses of his plays; rather, there is a simultaneous and equally urgent need to disclose the liabilities and uncertainties in our own cultural condition by exposing them to standards marked by the difference between what was possible then and what is (im)possible now.

In a project like this, my own limited critical awareness of, and unlimited indebtedness to, contemporary thought and scholarship should readily be indicated. As every student knows, in today's Shakespeare studies great attention is being paid to the staging of his plays in performance. For that alone, we all owe a heavy debt to those who broke the path, colleagues like Bernard Beckerman, Michael Goldman, and J. L. Styan, to name only these. But 'performance' in Shakespeare criticism by and large is viewed either as performance *of* the plays or as performance inscribed *in* dramatic speech – never or rarely as a formative force, as an institutionalized power in itself, as a cultural practice in its own right. No doubt there is good reason for the reluctance, among Shakespeare scholars and critics, to dissociate – if only momentarily – the act of performance from what verbal meaning it seeks to convey. For centuries, the involvement of the poet with the theatre was taken to be at best a necessary concession to a circumstantial world marked by an extreme degree of contingency, the very opposite of poetry's presumed autonomy. But even in our own day, when the Elizabethan theatre has come respectfully to be considered as a catalyst of Shakespeare's greatest achievement as a poet, it appears exceedingly difficult, in reference to his stage, to use 'perform' intransitively, that is, without an object, the writer's text. Although in our own world 'performance' is being practiced and studied in ways that do not necessarily presuppose a verbal text, let alone a pre-scribed meaning,[2] when it comes to Shakespeare, most of us have difficulty believing that, in the Elizabethan theatre, "performance was not seen to be sustained by its text, nor by a uniform relation to its author" (Worthen, *Shakespeare* 28).[3]

There is, then, a great need to reconsider relations of writing and playing in their early modern context and to attempt to answer the question of how and to what extent performance in Shakespeare's theatre actually *was* a formative element, a constituent force, and together with, or even without, the text a source of material and "imaginary puissance." Even to formulate this question seems difficult today without taking into account certain deep-going yet somehow inconclusive shifts of emphasis in current studies of literacy and orality. At a time when a new generation of literacy studies with a strong sense of historicity, context, and theory has come to the fore, a highly critical perspective has developed *vis-à-vis* those more traditional approaches that, in the words of Harvey Graff, "labored under the spectre and shadows of modernization theories with their strong assumptions of literacy's role, powers, and provenance."[4] While the post-Enlightenment synthesis of humanistic and social scientific studies has crumbled, concomitant expectations have been contradicted "that literacy's roles are [. . .] relatively unmediated, highly pervasive, and requisite and responsible for individual, societal, and national advancement" (134). Together with the technology-led theory of cultural change, the idea of a 'great divide' between orality and literacy, as advanced in studies inspired by Marshall McLuhan, W. J. Ong, E. A. Havelock, and partially at least by Jack Goody,[5] has increasingly been questioned. While some of the work of these eminent scholars – such as that of Havelock on Homer and classical theatre[6] – is of considerable significance to the present project, it seems unhelpful, especially in European Renaissance studies, to isolate these largely overlapping, interpenetrating oral and written media of communication from larger social and cultural formations, needs, and interests.

For very good reasons, then, scholarly attention has come to be focused on what is a crucial nexus in the present study – the process of interaction among written and oral forms of communication. As Ruth Finnegan, emphasizing the different ways oral and literate elements may be combined, has noted, "it is now accepted among serious students of verbal oral performance that the *text* alone is an insufficient guide to the art form" (*Literacy and Orality* 125). For one thing, as she adds in a more recent study, "the traditional Western model of 'text'," having "strong links with the concept of a verbal cognitive mode of representation," omits "the kinesic, dramatic, auditory, and visual elements so important in personal interaction" ("Literacy as Mythical Charter" 39–40). But while such preoccupation with written language may provide what is in some respects "a surprisingly misleading guide to what people are actually doing and experiencing" (40), the same question in our context needs to be formulated more cautiously. In regard to Renaissance theatrical transactions, the question is to what extent and to what purpose will "the once taken-for-granted model of the predominance of the 'text'" (40) have to be modified or supplemented? In the present essay (advisedly, I use the word for the book at large), this question must be an open one. It may well be that, when all is said and done, the recent revaluation of literacy needs to accommodate itself to a renewed awareness that "the riches to which reading and writing can lead [. . .] are part of the identity and experience of huge sections of humanity across the globe and can by no means just be wished away" (42).

However, to say this is not to minimize the degree to which dramatic writing and theatrical performing in the English Renaissance found themselves in a socially and culturally precarious state of both cooperation and confrontation, interaction and 'interface' (I use the word à la Webster, as "something that enables separate and sometimes incompatible elements to coordinate or communicate"). Without, then, in the least wishing to underrate, let alone downplay the power and the poetry that distinguish Elizabethan dramatic writing, I propose to view its forms and functions as participating, together with performance, in important shifts of social interests and cultural needs. The shifts in the circumstantial world were correlative to the very conditions in which relations of "author's pen" and "actor's voice" evolved. These relations, untried and unsettled,[7] could be viewed "not in confidence," as the Prologue to *Troilus and Cressida* puts it. In exploring the changeful relationship of "pen" and "voice," my question is, have we perhaps overlooked an important constellation of cultural practices and interests in the Elizabethan theatre that helped bring forth, in

Thomas Dekker's words, "such true scaenical authority" (Dekker, *Gull's Horn Book* 2:249)[8] as was irreducible to the dramatist's writings? And could it be that this little, brief and very vulnerable authority derived from certain types of production and performance practices that, in their relationship to the text, were not derivative, or in Michael Bristol's word, "ministerial" (*Shakespeare's America* 105)?

To answer these as yet highly conjectural questions would require that, as evidence, we recover and/or read afresh some of the traces that help us envision an alternative model of relations between "pen" and "voice." But even if we do have evidence that endows performance with a validity all its own, a new awareness of performance as a cultural practice in its own right does not by itself minimize the cultural authority of Shakespeare's text. Only, what would it mean to situate Shakespeare's text in the environment of a culture in which the new learning and writing had not fully supplanted the vitality in the oral communication of the unlettered, particularly when the transaction of that text on a stage – theatrical performance – was itself an oral-aural process?

Besides, the authority of Shakespeare's text has accrued over the centuries; it is not exclusively a product of the Elizabethan theatre. Nor is it like cultural merchandise that can be dumped when demand diminishes. This text, as Michael Bristol reminds us, must be seen not as a commodity or market value but as a "gift" that, as other "great literary works entail[s] particularly complex and onerous obligations." As I have hinted on a preceding page, such obligations require that we fully expose ourselves and our own liabilities to what this demanding text offers today; what a gift of this size requires is, in Bristol's words, "honest reflection not only about the aspirations of our civilization, but equally about its costs, its betrayals and its failures."[9]

The ways to meet these "obligations" are likely to change, though, when the uses of authorship and representation are being widely redefined. Here, for some of the most thoughtful observers, the question is how Shakespeare "can be uncoupled from the decline of the book in an increasingly post-literate society" (Lanier, "Drowning the Book" 191). As the same observer notes, there is a highly effective "tactic for exorcising the textual Shakespeare"; but if this tactic is "to forge an affiliation between performance criticism and textual criticism" (190), the present attempt to reassess Elizabethan performance practice does not pursue any such exorcism. To say that the cultural space for writing and reading in our own world at least partially is being absorbed by technologies of an audio-visual order is one thing; but it is quite another matter insouciantly to take for granted any, in a democratic sense of the word, purely beneficial results of this process. At any rate, I believe it is rash for those of us who continue to stand for, simply by practicing, writing and reading to subscribe to "the decline of the book," rather than stubbornly continue to weigh as *pro* and *contra* its place and function in an electronically dominated new culture of information. In other words (as William Worthen has annotated this passage), "the book may be for us what orality was for Shakespeare" – still in many spheres a dominant mode of transmission.

Perhaps there are other, and better, ways to deal with "the textual Shakespeare" in "an increasingly post-literate" world. An undoubtedly valuable alliance between textual scholarship and performance criticism might just as well serve ends that – to adapt Geoffrey Hartman's phrase (and book title) – amount to "saving the text" in the circumstantial midst of its own much-invoked instability. The seeming paradox is that only by thoroughly questioning the cultural uses of the dramatic text can we realistically hope to keep it viable.

It is upon premises such as these that I propose to study both writing and playing in the Elizabethan theatre as different modes of cultural production marked by intense mutual engagements, by both disparity and concurrence. Through their interplay, live agents on stage inflect and mediate a textually inscribed semantics of representation. In the Elizabethan theatre, such inflection can modulate but also disturb the high pitch of Renaissance pathos in the representation of honor, chastity, royalty, and so forth, thereby pointing to the limits of the world-picturing "glass" or "mirror" in the text of the dramatist. At the same time, performers can sustain and enhance, through sheer impersonation, what is verbally alive and vibrant in the "mirror." My suggestion is that Elizabethan performance practice cannot be subsumed under any one purpose of playing; it must be viewed as plural, as serving a number of diverse functions, as – far from being unified or unifying – a contested field in which early modern literary meanings can be constructed but also intercepted.

To view the cultural space between text and performance in early modern culture as marked by indelible difference, it must be historicized, resituated as part of a larger social constellation of both stratification and inclusiveness, one that in both trends crucially helped shape the formative period of the Elizabethan theatre. As William Ingram, John Astington, David Bradley and others have suggested, this period by no means begins in 1586/87. Although the present study is strongly focused on the turn of the century, we need to look further to understand the extent to which, in the second half of the sixteenth century, writing and playing entered into a remarkably open, rapidly changeful relationship. Despite its much-admired results, this relationship drew upon an alliance that harbored an unsuspected degree of vulnerability and unexplored areas of friction. To say that the engagement was between a culture of orality and a culture of literacy is, as Leah Marcus has shown in her *Unediting the Renaissance*, a crucial first step that can be especially helpful to the extent that both are perceived as mutually overlapping and interpenetrating. As we have learned from Terence Hawkes' *Shakespeare's Talking Animals*, even when a "great feast of languages" (5.1.37) is put on stage in *Love's Labour's Lost*, the celebration is not without "tension" when "the resonant world of speech is comically opposed to the silent world of writing," and "the language of books" is engaged by the oral "music of the rhyme" and the "fertile" language of love "beyond the grasp of reason" (Hawkes, *Shakespeare's Talking Animals* 53–54). Remarkably, the early Shakespeare, deeply aware of the difference between the two modes of communication, privileges the oral-aural and the practical-physical over the world of the book. The writer for performances precludes any facile bias in favor of writing; thereby, he hugely complicates relations between "author's pen" and "actor's voice." But then the cultural difference cannot exclusively be identified with that between writing and talking. In a long perspective, the difference in question was social as well as cultural, implicating divergent modes of communication as well as diverse perceptions of space and non-identical uses of dramaturgy and knowledge.

In Shakespeare's theatre, this difference was both suspended and re-vitalized; if the degree of interpenetration between words and bodies was unsurpassed, it was also marked by an interface more complex than can be conveyed by any notion of complementarity. In fact, the unsettled state of the ménage of "author's pen" and "actor's voice" was inseparable from both the unstable condition of the text itself and the dispersed modes of performance practice. At least two decades before the end of the century, the balance was definitely turning in favor of impersonating what figurations the increasingly predominant text was made to yield. Still, memories of a larger space filled with bodies and voices – a space that was neither abstract nor, in Raymond Williams' phrase, "representative" – continued to hold their own "in this distracted globe" (*Hamlet* 1.5.97).

One difficulty in coming to *terms* with the unfixed, changeful order of relations of "pen" and "voice" in the Elizabethan theatre is that the present study has to cope with the lack of a sustainedly helpful *terminology*. But rather than inventing one I have, wherever possible, attempted to adapt, rather than simply adopt, Elizabethan terms and concepts.

As the book's subtitle may suggest, the alternating appeal of (and to) "author's pen *or* actor's voice" was not unknown – how could it be? – to the author of *Troilus and Cressida*. From the quarto of the same play I have used "bifold authority" (the Folio has "By foule authoritie") in order to point at the difference in the courts of appeal and validity between writing and playing, on the understanding that this difference finds a correlative in the poetics, the dramaturgy, and epistemology of the plays themselves. As I have argued elsewhere,[10] the issue of authority in its early modern connotations provides us with an extraordinary complexity that cuts right through an exclusively textual or, for that matter, juridical or political understanding.

In the Elizabethan theatre, the imaginary play-world and the material world of Elizabethan playing constitute different, although of course partially overlapping registers of perception, enjoyment, and involvement. In order to address the sites of conjunction, interplay, and duplication where "in one line two crafts directly meet" (*Hamlet* 3.4.210), I shall use the concept of 'doubleness.' Wherever such 'doubleness' assumes contestatory forms, that is, a deliberate, performance-inspired use of the cultural disparity in question, I propose to adapt, from Philip Sidney's use, in his *Defence of Poesy*, the term 'contrariety.' There, the word refers either to the process or to the agents behind the process ("our Comedients") of "mingling Kinges and Clownes" but especially the mingling of "delight" and "laughter," which "in themselves [. . .] have as it were a kind of contrarietie" (3: 39–40).

Intriguingly, Sidney might have heard – directly from the lips of some of the "Comedients" here referred to – the same word elaborated in *The Tide Tarrieth No Man* (1576), a mid-Elizabethan moral play, where Courage the Vice repeatedly, and with variations, uses the adjective form in reference to his performance practice: "Corage contagious, / Or courage contrarious" presents himself as juggling with the "seems" of a fleeting identity: "Corage contagious, / When I am outragious, / In working of yll: / And Corage contrary, / When that I do vary, / To compass my will" (Wapull, *Tide Tarrieth* lines 93–94; 99–104). Similarly, and no less significantly, the adjective form is used in a stage direction in Thomas Lupton's *All for Money* (1577): "Here the vyce shal turne the proclamation to some contrarie sence at everie time all for money hath read it" (147).

In this instance, the "contrarie sence" must have come close to signifying a more specific effect, potentially a resistance to what was represented in the proclamation. We do not of course know anything about the actual drift of the "contrarie sence," except that the effect must have been one of 'disfigurement.' In my use of the latter term, I adapt Shakespeare's well-known phrase from *A Midsummer Night's Dream*, "to disfigure, or to present" (3.1.60–61), where the 'disfigurement' goes hand in hand with a presentational type of delivery.

In pleading for an understanding of Elizabethan 'performance' that is not closed to "a myriad of performance practices, ranging from stage to festival" (Parker and Sedgwick, *Performativity* 2), I am influenced by a contemporary perspective on performance as "an open-ended medium with endless variables" (Goldberg, *Performance Art* 9). Such openness is not, as Rose Lee Goldberg suggests, an avant-garde phenomenon but, as Marvin Carlson has shown, profoundly related to other and much older locations of performance, such as "the great medieval and Renaissance fairs" (*Performance* 81). In today's performance theory, the space for presentation and display is now beginning to receive considerable attention;[11] what, even in the admirably innovative *A New History of Early English Drama*, have been noticed much less are the forms, the functions, and effects of Elizabethan modes of presentational practice.[12] Small wonder, when in the Renaissance language of the 'judicious,' and for centuries after, these were culturally and, of course, socially marked – or even stamped – by pejorative terms.

In exploring these variegated uses of performance, I propose a distinction between 'presentation' and 'representation.' Each of these theatrical practices draws upon a different register of imaginary appeal and "puissance" and each serves a different purpose of playing. While the former derives its primary strength from the immediacy of the physical act of histrionic delivery, the latter is vitally connected with the imaginary product and effect of rendering absent meanings, ideas, and images of artificial persons' thoughts and actions. But the distinction is more than epistemological and not simply a matter of poetics; rather it relates to the issue of function.

In the present project, my interest in the question of the "purpose," or function, of playing, is not in pursuit of either the cultural politics or the psychology of Elizabethan dramatic performances. These have admirably been explored by Louis Montrose in his study of *The Purpose of Playing: Shakespeare and the Cultural Politics of the Elizabethan Theater* and by Meredith Anne Skura in *Shakespeare the Actor and the Purposes of Playing*, respectively. Although of course culture and politics (and what epistemology can be subsumed under psychology) are positively implicated in the present study, I have not traversed any of the grounds so well covered before. Rather, my present concern with the "purpose of playing" is focused on differing sets of communicative, socio-semiotic, and poetic functions and effects. These, I suggest, are vitally at stake as soon as the dramaturgy of the Shakespearean scene (in)dividable comes into the picture.

In this connection, the traditional preoccupation with style in the study of Elizabethan performance can no longer satisfy. In seeking to establish a new nexus for doubleness and diversity in the purpose of playing and the function of (re)presentation, I will suggest certain parameters of interaction in the Elizabethan theatre's uses of language and space. There is a

significant correlation between multiplicity in the purpose of playing and
fluidity in the employment of theatrical space. Just as there is no unified,
fixed language of representation, so there is no given, unified code in the
uses of space on the platform stage. Rather, verbally as well as spatially,
there is an endless variety in coming to terms with what (dis)continuity
there was between the imaginary world-in-the-play and the playing-in-the-
world of early modern London.

In particular, theatrical space in Shakespeare's theatre does not admit of
any binary set of oppositions when both types of space, the symbolic and
the apparently material, are vitally and contradictorily implicated in what
Henri Lefebvre calls "the production of space": together they bring about
on stage the "repetitiveness, the circularity, the simultaneity of that which
seems diverse in the temporal context and which arises at different times"
(*Production of Space* 22). Still, the distinction between these two types of
theatrical space remains important on the levels of both the dramaturgy
and the epistemology of performance. In pursuing the differences between
them, I propose to develop further my early differentiation between *locus*
and *platea*-like sites in Shakespeare's theatre towards a historicizing perspective. In a very rough approximation, the gaps and links between them
correspond to Lefebvre's distinction between "representations of space,"
such as the locale in the story, and what "spatial practice" (33; 38–39),
apart from its symbolic code inscribed in the story, dominates on the
neutral, non-symbolic site of the stage-as-stage.

Paradoxically, it is the localized site of self-contained representations
(the purely imaginary images of locations in the story) that establishes, as
Colin Counsell has shown, the "abstract and symbolic" quality of the
locus; whereas it is the *platea*-like space of the open stage, that is not
isolated from the audience, which constitutes an "immediate and concrete" place (19). It seems difficult to grasp the full significance of the
distinctions here made without viewing them in reference to the path-
breaking work on space and time that has gone into Edward Casey's
monumental volumes, *Getting Back into Place: Toward a Renewed Understanding of the Place-World* (1993) and *The Fate of Place: A Philosophical
History* (1997).[13]

Here, again, this fairly pragmatic discussion of terms and concepts resonates with questions of theory. "Author's pen" and "actor's voice," as used
in the Prologue to *Troilus and Cressida*, are embedded in culturally
saturated types of space and production; as such they constitute *agencies*
for writing and playing. In using terms like "pen" or "voice" or, at least as
often, 'writing' and 'playing,' I presuppose, somewhat along the lines of
Pierre Bourdieu's proto-Marxian concept of 'practice,' habitually recur-

ring institutionalized activities rather than an isolated act. My terminology here not only reflects the fragmentary state of our knowledge on these subjects when, with few exceptions, we know very little about the individual agents, let alone subjectivities, involved. What is more important, the use of 'agency' in writing or acting, not unlike 'agency' in audience response, addresses activities or practices that, in the early modern period (as hindsight teaches us), *begin* to constitute distinct, socially marked locations of cultural authority.

Although in the present project I can attend to issues of theory only in passing, the concept of 'agency,' especially when used in conjunction with 'difference,' does call for some theoretical positioning. As for the latter concept, I fully subscribe to the Saussurean maxim that difference is a condition of meaning; in other words, theatrical signs – verbal, corporeal, and props – signify only in relation to, and as distinct from, other signs. But since the theatre is a material site and constitutes a social occasion for the production and reception of meanings, neither a purely verbal nor an exclusively textual parameter for difference will do. Since the actual social function of meaning can be established only semantically, in a socio-semiotic context, we need to look beyond the post-structuralist paradigm. (For reasons that Peter Dews has, I believe, conclusively established, Jacques Derrida's *différance* presents us with too many problems; it is a new "absolute" [Dews, *Logics* 24][14] and one, as Emmanuel Levinas has noted, that "is far more speculative in many respects than metaphysics itself" [Kearney, "Dialogue" 69]). This is especially the case where the discontinuity of texts and institutions is an issue; it is even more vital where this issue is to be explored in terms of social and cultural habitude. While there certainly is, in Derrida's phrase, no "transcendental signified," no objectifiable meaning separate from language, institutions may submit to but do not invariably obey the regime of language. In their materiality, institutions like the early modern theatre are subject to discursive as well as nondiscursive circumstances; their workings are dominated by parameters of profit, desire, production, consumption, and power – practices that constitute, and are served by, agencies.

While cultural agencies implicate highly complex relations to political institutions, power *per se*, as Michel Foucault has acknowledged in his *History of Sexuality*, is not identical with knowledge and truth.[15] Rather than assuming an equivalence between *pouvoir* and *savoir*, we need to make distinctions as soon as early modern institutions, like Shakespeare's theatre, are conceived as sites of cultural authority, sources of pleasure and knowledge that derive from the interaction, even the intersubjectivity, of several agencies engaged in acts of communication.

In my approach to these theoretically loaded questions, I have looked for help from what, arguably, is the most vitally sustained critical energy of our time, feminist criticism. Catherine Belsey's *The Subject of Tragedy* is of particular value here because, in conjunction with dramaturgic "collisions between emblem and illusion" (31) she can trace irresolutions and uncertainties in the construction of a self-consistent subject in the theatrical space of both tragic character and spectator. The "knowing, speaking subject" on-stage, existing "only in the process of knowing, and *in contradistinction to the objects of its knowledge*" is confronted with "the absent legitimation of its actions" (78, my italics). At the same time, there are material practices off-stage that achieve a tangible authority precisely "in contradistinction to the objects" of "knowledge" on-stage. As Jean Howard has suggested, in the Elizabethan theatre there were social and gendered agencies of contestation and struggle, as when "the material practices attendant upon stage production and theatregoing" were "at odds with the ideological import of the dramatic fables that the theatre disseminated." Along these lines, the attendance of women and their representation on-stage revealed "differences within the sense-making machinery of culture" (Howard, *The Stage* 7).

At this point, the feminist project is theoretically close to the difference, crucial to the present study, between the imaginary world in "dramatic fables" and "material practices" involving playing inside cultural institutions for stage productions. Performance, as Peggy Phelan notes, "implicates the real through the presence of living bodies"; the visible, audible result of this implication "clogs the smooth machinery of reproductive representation," precisely because performance "approaches the Real through resisting the metaphorical reduction of the two into one" (Phelan, *Unmarked* 146). As far as certain sixteenth-century performance practices stubbornly resisted the reduction of the real and the representational into one, they, including Elizabethan performers' voices and bodies, continued to penetrate the boundary between the signs of life on-stage and those off-stage. In doing so, they pursued an order of mimesis that, in its otherness, was strikingly different from the one privileged in the neo-Aristotelian poetic. This other mimesis, as Elin Diamond puts it, was "impossibly double, simultaneously the stake and shifting sands: order and potential disorder, reason and madness." It was a mimesis that, on the one hand, "speaks to our desire for universality, coherence, unity, tradition, and, on the other hand, it unravels that unity through improvisations, embodied rhythm, power instantiations of subjectivity, and [. . .] outright imicry" (Diamond, *Unmaking Mimesis* v).[16]

This definition, which is addressed to our own theatre, may seem to blur certain Elizabethan issues; and yet in the present context it is extremely helpful in that it precludes polarity and exclusiveness in coming to terms with both what was represented and what and who was doing the representing. If the result of such performance practice was "impossibly double," it helped bring forth – together with, rather than against, the Renaissance text – several versions of doubleness. Sixteenth-century writing itself was, as we have learned, not at all homogeneous in its cultural form and purpose. As Jonathan Dollimore has shown, there were "two concepts of mimesis" dividing Renaissance definitions of 'poesy' from those of 'history.'[17] This distinction relates to what David Bevington has called an "irresolution in the English popular theatre" where the "realistic expression of factual occurrence and the traditional rendering of a moral pattern" continued to exist side by side (*From "Mankind" to Marlowe* 261). The difficulty (but also the challenge for this project) is that these different types of mimesis were implicated in, and partially at least mediated by, what cultural difference there was between the socio-cultural matrix of writing and the provenance of playing.

In other words, in the Elizabethan playhouse, the institution of agency is vital, even though it must not be conceived as a source of anything autonomous. Rather than confronting a "smooth machinery" of Renaissance representation, the performance practices (and histrionic agents) of doubleness were already in collusion with a significant "irresolution" in dramatic writing. At the same time, the search for clearly demarcated workings of culturally isolated or socially sovereign agencies is even more futile when the boundaries between theatrical and other types of performance practices are acknowledged as altogether fleeting. As Michael Bristol has noted, "for the first few decades of its existence, the public playhouse of Elizabethan England was not fully differentiated from more dispersed and anonymous forms of festive life, play and mimesis" ("The Festive Agon" 73).[18] Even so, the forces of differentiation and exclusion were already gathering strength under the surface of the Elizabethan cultural amalgam.

Here, again, feminist criticism and theory has pointed the way when Judith Butler has credited ritual, festive, ceremonial as well as gendered "acts, gestures, enactments" with a performance dimension that clearly transcends a purely linguistic or semiotic definition of performative action. For Butler, performance suggests "a dramatic and contingent construction of meaning," especially where signification and performance, by governing "the intelligible invocation of identity," can "enable and restrict the intelligible assertion of an I" and, thereby, open possibilities of an "agency" that is "neither fatally determined nor fully artificial and arbitrary" (Butler, *Gender Trouble* 136–47). This, as I shall suggest, is especially helpful for establishing Elizabethan performance as a formative force, a cultural practice and agency in its own right.

The question of agency and, with it, the uses of cultural authority, deserve particular consideration since they have become an issue in recent approaches to Elizabethan dramatic writing no less than in discussions of performance. If, in Philip Auslander's phrase, "the actor's self is not a grounding presence that precedes the performance" (Auslander, *Acting to Performance* 36), it seems equally questionable to conceive of the playwright's self and his personal intentions as grounding the performed play text. It should not come as a surprise, then, that "author's pen" finds itself at a critical conjuncture wherever, in the wake of the recent upheaval in editorial and textual theory and practice, a highly personalized conception of the individual creative consciousness is discarded as providing an authoritative source of textually inscribed intentions and meanings. At this point, Shakespearean textual scholarship is finally faced with some of the questions that have inspired the work of editorial practitioners and theoreticians like Jerome J. McGann, Hans Walter Gabler, Peter Shillingsburg, Hershel Parker, and others, who have stringently questioned any single version of the text as determining or embodying the 'work.'

Incontestably, the refusal to take for granted auctorial presence and desire as a *donnée* of editorial responsibility has helped pave the way for a cautious sense of alignment between textual scholarship and theatre history. Thanks to a veritable phalanx of editors, textual scholars and critics like David Scott Kastan, Scott McMillin, Laurie Maguire, Stephen Orgel, Gary Taylor, Paul Werstine, and others, the agenda of authority in the Elizabethan playtext has immeasurably been broadened as well as complicated. It surely has become difficult to discuss this agenda without taking into account our new awareness of theatrical activities prior to the advent of Kyd and Marlowe in the London theatre. Nor can we reassess the circulation of authority, the springs of appeal, pleasure, and cooperation in London playhouses without paying more attention to playing in the provinces. With these and other developments in mind, critics have tended to relegate the dramatist, even the one from Stratford-upon-Avon, to a new, though still very important position as, simply, one among other agencies in the theatre. And, surely, Shakespeare's contribution to what ultimately materialized on the boards of Elizabethan scaffolds cannot have been an exclusive one if, with Richard Dutton, we assume "an author of mixed authority," a "hybrid poet-playwright" who "wrote with some facility, plays too long and complex to be staged in the theatre of his day" (Dutton, "Birth of the Author" 172, 175). And yet, the question remains an open one: why did he write too much? Was textual abundance a sign of a poet's status or that of a text-supplier? Would at the time such abundance be a sign of self-realization?

Not unlike the recent paradigm shift that makes it possible "to end the mutual isolation of literary theory and textual criticism" (Philip Cohen, *Devils and Angels* xiv), these are questions that implicate both text and performance in the history of the theatre, its productions and receptions. Elizabethan performers, like spectators and yet different from them – are users of dramatic writings. Far from being exclusively dominated by the text's linguistic system of differences, they themselves use and appropriate the text in a way that is different from the very system of differences that writing has inscribed in it. Users of a text, as Michel de Certeau notes, are not its makers; usage itself establishes a secondary level of activity that, ultimately, is inseparable from the lived practice of actors working with and assimilating the writer's text.

Such assimilation is dominated by purposes that are not always already inscribed through and in the act of writing. It is this secondary level of difference which, in de Certeau's phrase, "effects an appropriation, or reappropriation, of language by its speakers," which "establishes a *present* relative to a time and place; and it posits a *contract with the other* [. . .] in a network of places and relations" (de Certeau, *Practice of Everyday Life* xiii). For performers to use a text, even in the service of its mediation, is always an act of adapting it to materially given circumstances; the assimilation, therefore, is to something that is neither fully contained nor anticipated in the written representation itself. Nor can the rules, the codes, the effects of this adaptation be reduced to those inherent in writing.

Finally, the difference between writing and playing is irreducible. Was it perhaps, one is left wondering, that one unique strength of Shakespeare's theatre derived from superbly acknowledging this difference, from hiding it and seeking it, from playing with it even in *displaying* it? Whatever the answer to this question, the theatrical thrust of "this unworthy scaffold" was inseparable from the dynamic in the sense of (dis)parity between what was represented in the text and what went into the toilsome, playsome practice of performing it.

1   Performance and authority in *Hamlet* (1603)

Although *Hamlet*, as Anthony Scoloker noted in 1604, was perceived as a play that "should please all,"[1] its textual history tells a different story. If, as Philip Edwards observed, the "study of the early texts of *Hamlet* is the study of a play in motion" (8), the element that is most in question (and in motion) is the circulation of cultural authority itself. At issue is the fluid, composite source of this authority, its unsettled and dispersed locations between the writing and the production of the play. The unstable linkage between the texts and the performances of *Hamlet* can perhaps best be explored at the point of its own intervention in the forms and functions of playing. At this crucial point – rare in the entire history of the Elizabethan theatre – the actual circulation of authority in the performed play appears revealingly at odds with what in Q2 and F is taken to authorize in no uncertain terms the "purpose of playing" (3.2.20).[2]

In the so-called 'bad' quarto *Hamlet*, relations of writing and playing find themselves in a state of entanglement and differentiation that has a more subdued echo in the difference between the authorial amplitude of the Second Quarto (1604) and the more theatrical qualities of the Folio text (1623). Between these texts, there resonates a cultural preference in response to either the literary needs of "goose-quills" or the practical requirements of "common players" (2.2.344; 349). This preference is not something statically given but connects with a play, even an entire theatre, "in motion." As Harold Jenkins has suggested, Rosencrantz's reference to writer-dominated children's stages that "are now the fashion" may reflect "the fickleness of a public favour which readily transfers itself from the old established to the upstart" (Jenkins [ed.] 472). But this "fickleness" attests to more than the ups and downs of "public favour"; rather, it participates in an emergent set of cultural changes at the turn of the century that, as I shall suggest in a later chapter, went hand in hand with a process of cultural differentiation and reform. While Hamlet's own preference in the Folio text appears to be in defense of those berattled "common stages" (342), the lines of socially divergent theatrical options appear far more confusing and potentially divisive as soon as we look more closely at the traditionally underestimated 'suspect' text of the First Quarto (1603).

In this version, the recasting of the most hallowed soliloquy in the play and its *mise-en-scène* is a case in point. Here, Polonius (in Q1 called Corambis) prepares for Hamlet's entrance and King Claudius provides the cue; but five lines after Hamlet has entered, the King's withdrawal is yet to come (the future tense is unmistakable).

> *Cor.* [. . .] Your selfe and I will stand close in the study,
>   There shall you heare the effect of all his hart,
>   And if it proue any otherwise then loue,
>   Then let my censure faile an other time.
> *King.* See where hee comes poring vppon a booke.
>   *Enter Hamlet.*
> *Cor.* Madame, will it please your grace
>   To leaue vs here?
> *Que.* With all my hart.   *exit.*
> *Cor.* And here *Ofelia*, reade you on this booke,
>   And walke aloofe, the King shal be vnseene.
> *Ham.* To be, or not to be, I there's the point,
>   To Die, to sleepe, is that all? I all:
>   No, to sleepe, to dreame, I mary there it goes,
>   For in that dreame of death, when wee awake,
>   And borne before an euerlasting Iudge,
>   From whence no passenger euer retur'nd,
>   The vndiscouered country, at whose sight
>   The happy smile, and the accursed damn'd.
>   But for this, the ioyfull hope of this,
>   Whol'd beare the scornes and flattery of the world,
>   Scorned by the right rich, the rich curssed of the poore?
>   The widow being oppressed, the orphan wrong'd,
>   The taste of hunger, or a tirants raigne,
>   And thousand more calamities besides,
>   To grunt and sweate vnder this weary life,
>   When that he may his full *Quietus* make
>   With a bare bodkin, who would this indure,
>   But for a hope of something after death?
>   Which pusles the braine, and doth confound the sence,
>   Which makes vs rather beare those euilles we haue,
>   Than flie to others that we know not of.
>   I that, O this conscience makes cowardes of vs all,
>   Lady in thy orizons, be all my sinnes remembred.
> *Ofel.* My Lord, I haue sought opportunitie, which now
>   I haue, to redeliuer to your worthy handes, a small remem-
>   brance, such tokens which I haue receiued of you.[3]

Although this version presents us with an unusual, indeed perfectly staggering degree of departure from what, according to Q2 and F, Shakespeare wrote in the longer versions, we should be wary of dismissing it, as generations of editors did, as 'corruption' *tout court.* Aside from any evaluative parameters, Hamlet's speech epitomizes in miniature more than anything a reduction in the authority of the author of Q2 in the playtext of Q1.[4] We are confronted with highly mobile and thoroughly contingent relations between the poetics of writing and, as can be shown, certain nonliterary preferences for another "purpose of playing." My reading of the passage, moving from what it says to how it is staged and, finally, received, will emphasize three points.

Semantically, in its uses of language, this version of Hamlet's "To be or not to be" speech foregrounds a perspective on the hardness of ordinary living that is markedly different from what we have in the received soliloquy. Eliding the question "Whether 'tis nobler in the *mind*" to "take arms" against hostile circumstances (3.1.56; 58), the utterance replaces the purely intellectual, stoical, and culturally elevated forms of resistance by an entirely plain, everyday horizon of harsh living, one that at least in part is inspired by an undisguised awareness of inequality in social relations.[5] "Scorned by the right rich, the rich curssed of the poore" moves in a semantic space that verbally as well as socially is far below "the proud man's contumely," the "law's delay," and the "insolence of office" (3.1.70–72). If the oppression of the "widow" and the wrong of the "orphan," not to speak of the "taste of hunger," is more predictable, it is for all that more physically concrete than the desperate metaphor of using weaponry against a "sea of troubles" (58). In the longer versions, the repeated imagery of battle ("shocks/ That flesh is heir to" [61–62])[6] is subsumed under a naturalized and socially elevated notion of inheritance. The First Quarto avoids this; rather than debating, in Edwards' phrase, "which of two courses is nobler" *vis-à-vis* the continuous punishing hostility of life itself, the early quarto has more brevity and directness, characteristically without letting go of the indiscrete language of the body, as in "To grunt and sweate vnder this weary life."

Dramaturgically, the differences in Q1 are even more significant. The *mise-en-scène* of the speech, inseparable from its uses of language, reveals an extraordinary, swift, even perhaps blunt directness, an acceleration of stage business that presupposes a sovereign command of and an extreme fluidity in the uses of theatrical space. There is none of the preparatory action motivating and anticipating the withdrawal of Gertrude, Claudius and Polonius *before* Hamlet's entrance ("*King.* Sweet Gertrude, leave us two [. . .] *Pol.* Withdraw, my lord" [3.1.28; 54]). Instead, his entrance *precedes* their withdrawal. There results a simultaneity in the staging of the scene that works in so far as, in view of the continuing presence of four major characters on stage, the appearance and stage representation of

Hamlet is not automatically integrated into the scene at large. If anything, Hamlet's entrance provides, as it were, a cue for the unhurried subsequent withdrawal of the others. It is as if there is no need for him, as yet, to honor an iconic frame of reference marked by represented characters such as Corambis or the Queen. It is only six lines later, through the act of speaking the speech, that a fully representational status accrues to his performance practice. Thus, Gertrude can take her leave, Corambis find his place in hiding, and Ofelia assume her pose, all *after* the player playing Hamlet, here the observed of all observers in the audience, has come onto the stage. Far from constituting the unified site of a dramatic scene that, in a fiction, would be dominated by psychologically compelling signs of symbolic action, Hamlet enters and lingers on the threshold between role-induced perception, seeing and hearing, and an actor's more neutral presence, for whom the unity of place and the logic of perception do not obtain. At the frontiers of his absorption by the symbolism of a fully integrated space of dramatic action, the player, as it were, can resist his being lost in a unified scene until the last moment. In other words, the physical presence of the leading actor on stage helps defer what closure we have in the opening of this scene. Literally, the visible player comes first, the fiction of 'invisible' concealment second, not vice versa. The demands of performing on an open stage go hand in hand with a dramaturgy that, after almost 400 years, appears far from inefficient, let alone despicable. Thus, a modern actor (Peter Guinness) playing the role of Q1 Hamlet can express his "joy to have that muscularity and directness," while another performer of the same role (Christopher McCullough) observes that "There are all sorts of clues in the play about how actors were working; [. . .] we're seeing the possibilities of theatrical energy, of the way space was used, of how actors related to audiences [. . .] the First Quarto is giving us clues about the much more open-ended nature of the Elizabethan theater" (Loughrey, "Q1 in Recent Performance" 125; 126).

Finally, in the entire cast of the "To be, or not to be" speech, we can observe how a peculiar type of *audience response* is invited by a specific and yet far from univocal mode of theatrical transaction. As far as it is at all possible to isolate this type of response, it appears to be more strongly in favor of a mode of presentation that is contiguous with, and yet different from, that representation which, in the strict sense of 'impersonation,' constitutes an inward self through soliloquy. (I shall elaborate the distinction between presentation – the performant function – and representation, the rendering of imaginary events and characters, at greater length in chapter 4.) As modern actors like Guinness and McCullough have suggested, for Hamlet to say, "I there's the point," is to address spectators rather than his own interior state of mind. His altogether abrupt turn to Ofelia (in his last line) indicates that little or no transition is required to return from a *platea*-like address to genuine dialogue. The presentation of this speech can be viewed as integral to an audience-oriented transaction whereby the action comes to fruition in a moment of display, which *is* the act of delivery.

The uses of such display on an open-ended stage, together with the relative prominence of a presentational mode of delivery, needs to be seen in a larger context. In the First Quarto, the lines of division between drama, show, and ceremony tend to be more easily blurred than, say, in Q2. This blurring of boundaries between dramatic action and theatrical display, representation and presentation, may well have been in response to, but also in aid of, circumstances characteristic of the itinerant stage. As the *Records of Early English Drama* and other archives (to which I shall return) indicate, Elizabethan traveling players continued to rub shoulders with all sorts of jugglers, dancers, singers, tumblers, and related showmen. Performers such as these were relatively unconcerned with the symbolic, let alone iconographic, dimensions of their actions. Their concern was to get the show across, that is, to privilege *vis-à-vis* the audience an *immediate* – literally: an iconographically and symbolically 'un-mediated' – space for delivery. Thereby, the responsiveness of spectators was implicated in the very transaction itself, in the sense that the skill and competence in the speaking of the speech were offered to them as worthy of public display.

It seems difficult to ignore this rather undifferentiated background of late sixteenth-century performance practice when the dispersed and "distracted" (4.3.4) circuit of authority in Shakespeare's *Hamlet* is to be accounted for. In the Elizabethan theatre, the diversity of cultural practices and interests must have been particularly pronounced wherever the imaginary world-in-the-play, that is, the dramatic representation, engaged and was engaged by the material and economic logistics of playing-in-the-world of early modern England. As the concluding chapter will argue, Shakespeare quite deliberately used the threshold between the stage-as-imaginary-world and the stage-as-stage; at least in part this threshold overlapped with the line of "cultural difference" that Leah Marcus has persuasively traced between "orality and writing as competing forms of communication within the Renaissance playhouse" (Marcus, *Unediting the Renaissance* 176).[7] Once the gap between these two types of communication is seen to participate in an unfolding spectrum of differences among all sorts of cultural practices, conventions, and expectations, new questions about the "distracted" circuit of authority arise. Could it be that there was a link between the instability of a Shakespearean text like *Hamlet* and its openness to altogether diverse standards in poetics, performance, and production?

As an entirely provisional answer, I propose not to complicate further what hypotheses or highly circumstantial evidence we have about the theatrical provenance of Q1 *Hamlet*; nor would I wish to link this text to the problematic assumption that, primarily, the play derived from an act of memorial reconstruction.[8] Instead, let me look more closely at the first printed version of *Hamlet* for what evidence we can glean about this 'open' circulation, in the production process, of diverse cultural discourses, interests, and functions. Here, Hamlet's advice to the players is perhaps the most tantalizing scene in Shakespeare's theatre – a scene in which the administering of cultural authority itself is staged and dramatized. In the First Quarto, this site is marked, uniquely, by an astonishing difference in what, in Q2 and the Folio text, is called "the purpose of playing" (3.2.20).

> And doe you heare? let not your clown speake
> More then is set downe, there be of them I can tell you
> That will laugh themselues, to set on some
> Quantitie of barren spectators to laugh with them,
> Albeit there is some necessary point in the Play
> Then to be obserued: O t'is vile, and shewes
> A pittifull ambition in the foole that vseth it.
> And then you haue some agen, that keeps one sute
> Of ieasts, as a man is knowne by one sute of
> Apparell, and Gentlemen quotes his ieasts downe
> In their tables, before they come to play, as thus:
> Cannot you stay till I eate my porrige? and, you owe me
> A quarters wages: and, my coate wants cullison:
> And, your beere is sowre: and, blabbering with his lips,
> And thus keeping in his cinkapase of ieasts,
> When, God knows, the warme Clowne cannot make a iest
> Vnlesse by chance, as the blinde man catcheth a hare:
> Maisters tell him of it. (F1-F2)

As Harold Jenkins pointedly observes in a note, Quarto 1 "provides, ironically enough, an instance of the thing complained of"[9] in Hamlet's advice. The Prince, "thus" performing a clown's "cinkapase of ieasts" and, with another "thus," so "blabbering with his lips," is telling the players what not to do, but he does so by doing it himself. Thereby, he can in one and the same speech collapse two different orders of authority in the purpose of playing. One follows humanistically sanctioned, mimetic precepts associated with Donatus and Cicero, the other – in the teeth of their rejection – the contemporary practices of Tarlton and company. By formally rejecting the latter while actually cashing in on them (even, as John Dover Wilson and George Ian Duthie have shown, drawing on jests that Tarlton is on record as having used[10]), the First Quarto exemplifies one important area of divergence in the genealogy of the Elizabethan theatre.

It is that divisive area which, taking a phrase from Sidney's poetics, I suggest serves as a catalyst for what "contrarietie" we have on Elizabethan stages.

The Prince of Denmark, in his rehearsal of the clown's stale jokes, proceeds to do what his humanist alter ego declares to be against "some necessary point in the Play." When Hamlet's advice culminates in the Prince dis-playing the clown, even the empathy-cherishing, Stanislavski-inspired critic will have difficulty accounting for this in terms of representational cogency. The least that can be said is that the quasi-performance of these jests indecorously exceeds the purpose of instructing the players; these "frivolous jestures" (Richard Jones' term) certainly do not serve the protagonist's disguise or any other strategy of concealment or revenge. If anything, this specimen of clowning is "far unmeet" for that matter of "worthiness"[11] that, in the longer texts, Hamlet's plea for a poetics of neoclassical discretion seeks to convey to the players. In fact, the Prince's demand, "mend it all together," is more than contradicted by Hamlet's "cinkapase of ieasts." Even if, as is likely, the Prince through overemphasis burlesques these jests, his travesty is in line with an ancient, almost ubiquitous practice of unscripted, unsanctioned performance. Prince Hamlet himself embodies a site on stage where – to anticipate Polonius' phrase – the "law of writ and the liberty" (2.2.401) of the performer clash. Rather than unambiguously disapproving (as the Q2 Hamlet does) of what in both the moral and the social sense of the word is "villainous" (3.2.44) in clownage, the 'suspect' Hamlet is double-dealing somewhat in the vein of Ambidexter in *King Cambises*, who says, "Now with both hands will you see me play my parte" (Adams [ed.], line 783).[12] As, handy-dandy, the princely agent and the "villainous" object of reform exchange places, there emerges a "bifold authority" in Hamlet's own purpose of playing. The ambidextrous capacity for both recommending and undermining the self-contained Renaissance play aids both the representation of character and the presentation of such conceits as befit the fond sport and frivolous game of jesting mother-wits. Although Hamlet's duplicity is not nearly as blatant as that of the old Vice Ambidexter, the cultural difference is within the configuration of the protagonist himself. Since this difference here clearly affects his own "purpose of playing," it goes significantly deeper than the distantly related contrast, in the language of Q2 and the Folio, between Hamlet the humanist courtier and Hamlet the "rogue and peasant slave," the "John-a-dreams" (2.2.550; 568).

Here, the First Quarto, if it is recasting a previously given text, does not invalidate its writer's authority from any ideological point of view. It is the social semantics, the cultural semiotics, and the dramaturgy, rather than the politics of the play that point to what Kathleen Irace in her recent edition of the play calls "the reasons behind the differences between Q1 and the longer texts."[13] Nor can the text be viewed as an aggressive counter-version indicating "actor's voice." What theatrical practices, agencies, and interests are here projected already participate in a moment of cultural 'reform' and differentiation. Even so, the culturally inclusive uses of language – unsettling at least momentarily the identities of prince and clown – collude with an instability in both the text and the purpose of playing; thereby they affect both the staging and, closely connected with it, the significations of the text. Here we have very much a "mixed" composition that, in Hamlet's advice to the players, slides easily between the representation of character – the character of a princely Maecenas – and the presentation, à la Tarlton, of "such conceits as clownage keeps in pay" (Cunningham [ed.], Prologue 2). Between them, there is no single, overriding, unified "purpose of playing." Again, I am deliberately using the phrase from Hamlet's advice to the players in Q2 and F1 in order to suggest that the singular form ("the purpose," as used by the Prince) is far from being an adequate description of late Elizabethan performance practice.

In order to study the coexistence, even interaction of diverse modes of playing, I propose to look at the Nunnery scene in the First Quarto. Here – to return to a distinction made earlier – the presentational purpose of playing throughout commingles with the representation of character. In this scene, where the protagonist is shown in his most eccentric moments, his eccentricity must have displayed something eminently worthy of show, an exceptional kind of exhibit. Accordingly, Ofelia is made to *present* the Prince of Denmark to the audience a few lines after his "To be, or not to be" speech, where, in Q2 and F, his "unmatch'd form" is said to be "Blasted with ecstasy" (3.1.159–60).

> *Ham.* To a Nunnery goe, we are arrant knaues all,
>   Beleeue none of vs, to a Nunnery goe.
> *Ofel.* O heauens secure him!
> *Ham.* Wher's thy father?
> *Ofel.* At home my lord.
> *Ham.* For Gods sake let the doores be shut on him,
>   He may play the foole no where but in his
>   Owne house: to a Nunnery goe.
> *Ofel*: Help him good God.
> *Ham.* If thou dost marry, Ile giue thee
>   This plague to thy dowry:
>   Be thou as chaste as yce, as pure as snowe,
>   Thou shalt not scape calumny, to a Nunnery goe.
> *Ofel.* Alas, what change is this?
> *Ham.* But if thou wilt needes marry, marry a foole,

> For wisemen know well enough,
> What monsters you make of them, to a Nunnery goe.
> *Ofel.* Pray God restore him.
> *Ham.* Nay, I haue heard of your paintings too,
> God hath giuen you one face,
> And you make your selues another,
> You fig, and you amble, and you nickname Gods creatures,
> Making your wantonnesse, your ignorance,
> A pox, t'is scuruy, Ile no more of it,
> It hath made me madde: Ile no more marriages,
> All that are married but one, shall liue.
> The rest shall keepe as they are, to a Nunnery goe,
> To a Nunnery goe.   *exit*
> *Ofe.* Great God of heauen, what a quicke change is this?
> The Courtier, Scholler, Souldier, all in him,
> All dasht and splinterd thence, O woe is me,
> To a seene what I haue seene, see what I see. *exit* (E-E2)

With the exception of one truly dialogic phrase ("At home my Lord"), Ofelia's utterances, being neither addressed to nor received by Hamlet, are dominated by a presentational mode throughout. Referring to Hamlet in the third person, she qualifies her distance from participation in the represented scene by an articulation of dismay about the eccentric actions of the Prince of Denmark. In her early interjection, "O heauens secure him," and, even, "Help him good God," the figures of Christian invocation and compassion that characterize her response (and involvement), may yet predominate. This is very much the case in Q2 and F1, where Ophelia's interjections are distinguished by even stronger signs of pity and piety ("O, help him, you sweet heavens!" [3.1.133]; "Heavenly powers, restore him!" [141]). However, it is only in the First Quarto that Ofelia, in her reference to Hamlet, twice proceeds to a purely demonstrative "this" as something pointed at rather than spoken to: "Alas, what change is this?" – "Great God of heauen, what a quicke change is this?" It is true, the rhetoric of interjection continues to draw on figures of piety and perplexity, but the iteration itself reduces the capacity for effectively subsuming the presentational *gestus* under a characterizing representation, on Ofelia's part, of pious concern and consternation.

All this while, Ofelia is made to point out, even perhaps point at, a virtuoso display of mad humor. With gender relations as his theme (always a favorite of audiences), Hamlet himself performs an outrageous piece of misogamy, richly dressed with misogyny. While the texts of the two quartos here are more or less identical, only the First Quarto Hamlet goes to the length of a seven-fold iteration of "To a Nunnery goe." In doing so, the Prince uses the phrase scandalously, like a refrain or a signature tune, not unlike Iago's "put money in thy purse," or the punning, ambidextrous Vice harping upon the titular theme of the play in *Like Will to Like* or *The Tide Tarrieth No Man*. And whereas Q2, not irretrievably crossing the frontiers of dialogic representation, has, "I say we will have no moe marriage" (3.1.147), Q1 is closer to F in that Hamlet's use of the plural form distinctly swerves from a dialogic stance. Almost certainly, the plural in his "Ile no more marriages" correlates to an open stage, *platea*-like position, as does the duplicity in the enhanced iteration of the refrain that juggles with two meanings ('nunnery' could also denote a brothel). From this spatial position, the protagonist in Q1 can more consistently ignore the conventions of represented dialogue and harangue not Ofelia, but a plurality of spectators, among them, men ("wisemen know [. . .] What monsters you make of them") but especially the women (the plural form in "your paintings" is unmistakable, as it is in "you make your selues another" [face], where F has "your selfe"). The resulting effect must have been an uncanny blending of alarm and laughter, extreme dismay and reckless merriment.

There is then, as the briefest comparison could establish, in the First Quarto more of a fluidity in relations between a Renaissance dramatist's "pen" and a sixteenth-century "actor's voice." Such a comparison is especially revealing if we assume, as I think we must, that Q1 *Hamlet*, "a version specially abridged for performance on tour,"[14] was adapted and reconstructed by traveling members of Shakespeare's own company. In these conjectured circumstances, the textually established area of divergence in the purpose of playing can be motivated rather nicely, even with some cogency. However that may be, the same writer's authority appears to be either partially absent or short-shrifted; the demands of performance practice are strongly asserted and inform at least some of the features of the play. Thanks to the work of scholars like Sally-Beth MacLean, Alan Somerset and contributors to the *Records of Early English Drama* series, we have for good reasons come to revise the anti-provincial bias of a previous generation of critics: provincial touring, we must assume, can no longer be viewed as "the enforced banishment to the bucolic backwaters that touring has often been taken to be" (Somerset, "How chances it" 50; 60).[15]

Still, in its remove from a stringently sustained authorial authority and in greater proximity to all sorts and conditions of performance, the First Quarto *Hamlet* would more strongly foreground the presentational voice and delivery of the performer. But the play, even as it was relatively open to such multiple purposes of playing as departed from the poetics of self-contained Renaissance representations, would remain deeply indebted to a unique "author's pen." What ultimately we have is, in Thomas

Clayton's acute observation, "a far from homogeneous, 'mixed' text, excellent in part but also divided against itself and apparently in 'authority'" (Clayton, *The 'Hamlet' First Published* Introduction 23). In other words, the First Quarto was marked by a hybrid source of authority, one that was as "divided against itself" as the double-dealing poetics that, simultaneously, informed Hamlet's antic clowning and his own advice against it.

2   A new agenda for authority

To view the present revaluation of Q1 *Hamlet* in perspective, I propose, as a first step, to ask why and under what circumstances the practice of performance, especially its impact on the shape and thrust of Shakespeare's plays, was radically obliterated, disputed or ignored for almost three centuries. It was under these circumstances that writing in the Elizabethan theatre came to occupy a position of unquestioned preeminence, constituting a source of unrivalled, more or less exclusive authority. In addressing these questions, I intend – in a first section – to focus on the early, eighteenth-century version of the traditional scenario of poetic authenticity and playhouse corruption in presenting the Shakespearean text.

However, in a critical review of the modern bias in favor of writing it is neither helpful nor necessary to idealize the First Quarto of *Hamlet* or, for that matter, to elevate Elizabethan performance practice to the status of any self-determined, originary alternative source of authority. On the contrary, it should freely be admitted that perfectly sound reservations about the First Quarto cannot easily be dismissed. For good reasons, editors like Harold Jenkins, Philip Edwards, and G. R. Hibbard, in spite of their preference for either Q2 or F respectively, take a conflated version of Q2 and F as their base text. Philologists and critics almost as a matter of course tend to prefer a text that in its poetic qualities and intellectual dimensions is greatly superior to what, to all intents and purposes, is a sizably reduced as well as reconstructed version of the play. Presumably even those critics who have begun to revise their appraisal of the First Quarto in light of its socio-cultural use and context would follow Leah Marcus' ironic evaluation of the playtext, that when "it comes to aesthetic judgement, the elite is unquestionably to be preferred over the popular, and the highly literate over the low and suspiciously oral" (Marcus, *Unediting the Renaissance* 176).

Still, there is a broad array of reasons why, in our own late Gutenberg culture, the standards of a purely literary aesthetics alone are no longer sufficient when it comes to a reappraisal of a highly complex conjuncture of writing and playing. In response to the ongoing debate about the issue of textual authority in Shakespeare's theatre, I therefore proceed to discuss – in a second section – some of the major options in reconstructing a new agenda for authority. In the Elizabethan theatre there is, I suggest, a circulation of authority from writing to playing and, simultaneously, from playing to writing, with both circuits connected to a crucial court of social appeal and cultural patronage – the responding, judging, applauding audience. But to trace writer's "pen" in player's "voice," and vice versa, cannot collapse the difference between them, cannot culminate in a reconciliation of what, in the first place, is *not* conceived as a pair of opposites. As soon as the relationship is framed in terms of varying social interests and cultural needs, the line of division is more than, simply, a textual or theatrical matter.

While talk about a new agenda of authority, then, implicates a call for understanding relations of pen and voice differently, it also has – as in my third and final section – a consequence that has rarely been confronted. The point is that not only do we need to understand the situation differently; the situation itself was changing. The workings of 'authority' as circulating between the production of texts and the production of plays through performance is one thing; while this needs to be explored further, such exploration can best succeed where early modern notions and institutions of authority themselves are redefined as in a state of vast and far-reaching changes. Thus, there are intriguing links between the circulation of authority in Shakespeare's theatre and certain incisive (re)locations of power and legitimacy in early modern culture and society – links that Shakespeare inflects in the themes and forms of several of his plays. As Robert S. Knapp has shown in his remarkable study of *Shakespeare: The Theater and the Book*, it was through "an uncertain intersection of word and deed, text and other, literature and excessive act" (184) that "his own unusual authority" was established and used to sound unprecedented meanings, as in *Richard II*, in the represented "conflict between two interdependent yet partly incompatible sorts of authority" – one "signified in names, forms, and ceremony," the other "an authority enacted, empowered, and embodied" (187–88) in action. But it was in conjunction with a groundswell of change in the channels of communication, literacy, and entertainment that a new order of partly incompatible modes of authority emerged in the first place. In particular, the dramatist wrote for the playhouse where, in Stephen Orgel's phrase, the "dependency" of playing "on the text was often in doubt" ("The Authentic Shakespeare" 7). The Elizabethan theatre offered a location where authority could not be of an exclusively literary provenance. In these circumstances, as W. B. Worthen suggests, "both text and performance [were] construed as vessels of authority."[1] They together

served as a new and newly effective form of cultural authority that henceforth could both jar with or complement the powerful regime of an
enforcable authority in politics, jurisdiction, and government.

The "low and ignorant" crust of corruption

The historical context in which the notion of the poet's sovereign presence
in his plays first emerged deserves to be recalled because, for one thing, the
near-absolute triumph of literate authority was inseparable from a corresponding depreciation, even invalidation, of the work of the performer. To
revisit this scenario among Shakespeare's eighteenth-century editors reveals the extraordinary extent to which a predominantly literary concern
with authorship would distance the dramatic text from the circumstances
of its production. Although the *raison d'être* behind the isolation of the
writer's authority may appear to be fairly obvious (the poet's Muse of lofty
inspiration had to be purified from the taints of common scaffolds, corporeal labor, and so forth), a facile response to this phenomenon will not do.
To be sure, the radical devaluation of performance in the eighteenth and
nineteenth centuries articulated itself in a tenaciously upheld concept of
textual purity and superiority, as if the dramatic text, after an immaculate
conception in the mind of its creator, was unfortunately exposed to a drab
world of impurity inhabited by the gross practicalities of production and
publication. As Margreta de Grazia poignantly notes, "corruption justified editorial intervention; in principle at least, the edition that had received
the most editorial attention, the most recent edition, was the purest because the most purified" (*Shakespeare Verbatim* 62). In this tradition,
performance was not of course the only source of corruption; it vied with
printing as a further, potentially no less aggravating, source of contamination. As David Scott Kastan observes, since even in our time the Elizabethan "playhouse and the printing house were seen as corrupters of the
texts entrusted to them," editors have by and large continued to understand "their task as the effort, in Fredson Bowers' loaded phrase, 'to strip
the veil of print from a text'" (Kastan, "The Mechanics of Culture" 32).

    However, even more consequential from the point of view of the present
project was the prolonged attempt to strip the vulgar traces of production
and performance from the text. We only need to look at recent editions of
Shakespeare to realize that what we have are distinct products of "editing
and criticism holding fast to a modern text that derives from an eighteenth-
century tradition" (de Grazia and Stallybrass, "The Materiality" 256). But
in the past, as Michael Dobson, de Grazia, and other critics have shown,
the supreme authorization of 'Shakespeare' as sole and sovereign source of
the plays contributed to a cultural project that thrived on aims and

interests that, as a matter of fact, had little to do with the assumed purity of textual access to the bard. It was not only that in the early eighteenth century "adaptation and canonization become ever more mutual processes"; the "more exalted Shakespeare's authority becomes, the more thoroughly it is diffused, and the less visibly it is connected with his actual achievements as a playwright" (Dobson, *Making of the National Poet* 14; 214). Such appropriation of the Bard brings us to the point of "the domestication of literature's last truly public sphere – the theatre – and with it the final salvation of Shakespeare from his own vulgar dramaturgy." As Dobson further puts it,

the stage, rid of these socially and aesthetically incoherent intrusions, has been successfully colonized as an appendix to the study. [. . .] The experiences of reading Shakespeare and of seeing his plays performed [. . .] are here reunited at last, but only because the private, self-contained activity of critical reading has completely subsumed the atavistic, communal, and socially miscegenating experience of play-going. (210)

Along these lines, *Bell's Edition of Shakespeare's Plays* (1773–74) – to give only one example – although designed as an acting edition, performs a thorough-going purge of the text from its association with low theatricality – the project that a contemporary reviewer in the *Monthly Review*, using Richard Jones' term for a similar undertaking nearly two hundred years earlier, celebrates as the expunging of "deformities."[2]

It is perhaps not too much of an exaggeration to say that it was against this sense of a contamination of the Shakespearean text in the Elizabethan playhouse that in the eighteenth century the editorial project in one of its major impulses first came to constitute and define itself. Editors at the time almost unanimously agreed on the need to guard Shakespeare's text from the ill customs of the age and especially from those of the players. Actors were believed to be singularly incapable of reproducing the lofty original text without garbling it or adulterating it with low matter. In an ironic and deeply revealing comparison, Pope, in his "Preface" to *The Works of Shakespeare* (1725), noted that "Players are just such judges of what is *right*, as Taylors are of what is *graceful*" (D. Smith, *Eighteenth Century Essays* 48). The crucial point that more than anything appeared to legitimate the editorial rescue operation was driven home by Sir Thomas Hanmer, in the Preface to his 1744 edition of Shakespeare.

There can be no doubt but a great deal more of that low stuff which disgraces the works of this great Author, was foisted in by the Players after his death, to please the vulgar audiences by which they subsisted: and though some of the poor witticisms and conceits must be supposed to have fallen from his pen, yet as he hath put them generally into the mouths of low and ignorant people, so it is to be remember'd that he wrote for the Stage, rude and unpolished as it then was; and the vicious taste of the age must stand condemned for them, since he hath left upon record a signal proof how much he despised them. (D. Smith, *Eighteenth Century Essays* 86–87)

In this view, Shakespeare, far from being a culprit, or at least an accessory to the fact, was actually a victim, his text "disgraced" by the usurped license of common players meddling with his authority. In Hanmer's reading, the inspiration of the poet stood opposed to the vulgarization and falsification of the players practiced on a "rude and unpolished" stage. On the one hand, the "works of this great author [. . .] hath left upon record a signal proof how much he despised" the "vicious taste of the age" and the stage for which he wrote; on the other, those disgraceful "players," more intent on pleasing "the vulgar audiences" than faithfully serving the works of a poetic genius, left marks of their own coarseness and ignorance when working with his texts.

Such a position paved the way for a strange but singularly persistent redefinition of the text/performance relationship. Although there were dissenting voices like Richard Flecknoe's and, of course, Samuel Johnson's, who knew better, one main thrust of eighteenth-century editorial criticism was to salvage the dramatic text by isolating it from the circumstances of performance. William Warburton's 1747 editorial project in fact linked the player to the printer as responsible for the unwelcome encrustations of a century of neglect:

Shakespeare's Works, when they escaped the Players, did not fall into much better Hands when they came amongst Printers and Booksellers: [. . .] The stubborn Nonsense, with which he was incrusted, occasioned his lying long neglected amongst the common Lumber of the Stage." (D. Smith, *Eighteenth Century Essays* 89)

The text, then, far from being intended for performance and transmission by the agents of the theatre, was thought to have been overlaid by them with something inferior and damaging.

Under these circumstances, it was apparently impossible even to think of Shakespeare's text as a circuit of diverse types of cultural interest, labor, competence, and authority. As a revered monument to his genius, the poet's works were by definition as immovable as his half-length effigy in the chancel of Holy Trinity Church, Stratford-upon-Avon. No matter how much adaptation, rewriting, reprinting, rereading had gone into them, the works of this genius could only be regained from underneath the "vicious" desolation wrought upon them by theatrical practitioners. The result was that these determined efforts to sift out the infringements of performers tended to petrify what must have been mutually responsive, fluctuating lines of demarcation between dramatic text and theatrical performance.

Nor was the ground-breaking work of Edmond Malone exempt from further fortifying the gulf between "pen" and "voice." His remarkable search for authenticity was achieved at the cost of renewing, with the credentials of a historical biography, the age-old antihistrionic bias. Invoking Spenser's "Tears of the Muses" against that "ugly Barbarisme And brutish Ignorance," which supposedly marked the "wretched state of the stage in 1589 and 1590" (2:172), Malone above all sought to vindicate Shakespeare's "higher character of a poet" ("Life of the Poet" 169). Even in granting the Bard some "histrionic merit" (279), the critic conceived of such merit against the foil (as well as through the lens) of Richard Jones' Preface to *Tamburlaine* (1587), which Malone – italicizing "frivolous gestures" and "graced deformities" – cited at some length (280). The supposed evidence derived from the latter was supplemented by reference to a letter from the privy council commissioning a "sufficient person, learned and of judgement," to contain the players' "scurrility and licentiousness" as a part of the cause of "the reforming of the plays" in the theatre (270).

As Margreta de Grazia has suggested, Malone's concept of 'authenticity' conferred upon Shakespeare a hitherto unprecedented degree of personal identity and autonomy.[3] This new approach, vindicating Shakespeare's qualification as proprietor of his works, encoded "a relation of ownership into editorial practices" (179). Although Malone labored under what de Grazia calls a new "strain of exclusivity" (224), this view of the "higher character" of the poet advanced and enhanced parameters of authority that derived from a singular notion of writing as inalienably sustained by a unique, self-consistent identity. The paradox, then, was that Malone's fresh, historicizing point of departure (and his legacy for modern editors) perpetuated an emphatically literary, antihistrionic perspective on the preeminence of dramatic composition in the Elizabethan theatre.[4]

Henceforth, the provocative gap between "author's pen" and "actor's voice," deepened by eighteenth-century criticism and editorial practice, grew into the chasm that reached its greatest depth in the Romantic period. In the words of Charles Lamb, there was, on the side of the genius, "that absolute mastery over the heart and the soul of man, which a great dramatic poet possesses"; there were, on the side of the actors, "those low tricks upon the eye and ear, which a player by observing a few general effects [. . .] usually has upon the gestures and the exterior" (Jones [ed.] 96).

Since the gulf between the "mastery over the heart" and the "tricks upon the eye and ear" turned out to be as deep and lasting as it was, we need to do better than dismiss it as merely an eighteenth-century invention. What we are dealing with is so much more than an antitheatrical "prejudice." A prejudice it certainly was; however, when examined in its specifically antihistrionic direction, the bias in question must be read as a discourse that participates in a complex and conflict-ridden constellation of socio-cultural practices and interests. What in this connection needs to be considered is the substantial underside to the prefix in this '*pre*judice'; in other words, what was it that actually and materially *preceded* or helped stimulate this particular judgment?

As a provisional answer, let me suggest that the prejudice-laden division between poet and performer was much aggravated but not invented by several generations of editors and critics between Pope and Lamb. Rather, the ingrained devaluation of the performer reflected submerged or unre-solved issues that "in their seeds and weak beginnings" lay unhatched and hidden in the Elizabethan and Jacobean theatre itself. As Barish has shown us, the eighteenth-century suspicion of the theatre is certainly anticipated in the seventeenth century, where there is more than one voice echoing positions close to those of Hanmer and Warburton. Take, for instance, Thomas Rymer's exasperation, in his reading of *Othello*, at that "long rabble of Jack-Pudden farce between *Iago* and *Desdemona*, that runs on with all the little plays, jingle, and trash below the patience of any Country Kitchen-maid with her Sweet-heart."

Never in the World had any Pagan Poet his Brains turn'd at this Monstrous rate. But the ground of all this Bedlam-Buffoonery we saw in the case of the French *Strolers*; the Company for Acting *Christs Passion* or the *Old Testament* were Carpenters, Coblers, and illiterate fellows, who found that the Drolls and Fooleries interlarded by them brought in the rabble and lengthened their tune, so they got Money by the bargain. (Zimansky, *Critical Works* 144)

The charge of illiteracy is significant. The actors, uneducated fellows, in their ignorance and greed had "interlarded" the plays with lots of playful, gamesome material. Pointedly interlacing the physical and the fictitious in a submerged metaphor ("interlarded"), the Restoration critic underlined a double affiliation in Shakespeare's dramatic texts, both to the sanctioned art of tragic representation, and to "all this Bedlam-Buffoonery" derived from strolling players in the market-place. The basic differentiation was between the truly meaningful representations of the literate and the "rabble"-rousing "little plays, jingle, and trash" of the "low and ignorant."

But then again, this Restoration disdain for performers was at least in part anticipated in the theatre of George Chapman, Ben Jonson, John Marston, and Francis Beaumont. Looking at these dramatists, we cannot seriously doubt that, beginning at the turn of the century, the circulation of authority among poets and players (as well as audiences) could be effectively contested. With a rare sense of good humor, such contestation is ironically rehearsed in Francis Beaumont's *The Knight of the Burning Pestle* (1607), where Rafe, a self-authorized performer if ever there was one, enters, if we may borrow Hamlet's indignation, as "a robustious" helmet-pated "fellow" only to tear the text of a regular city comedy "to totters, to very rags" (3.2.9–10). Rafe performs against the text, "with all his scarfs about him, and his feathers and his rings and his knacks"; as self-embodied Summer Lord, he comes not to represent but to "*present* the merry month of May" (4. Int. 10–11; 27; my emphasis). But as opposed to earlier Elizabethan drama, gentle Beaumont's representation of Rafe was, as publisher W. Burre noted, "no offspring of any vulgar brain"; "the privy mark of irony" witnessed the depth of the wedge between dramatic writing and the laughable uses of popular, including amateur, perform-ance practices. As the play uniquely shows, these could be both abetted and sanctioned by "rhyming mother-wits" like the play's naïve spectators, George the grocer and his wife Nell (Beaumont, *Knight of the Burning Pestle*, Dedicatory Epistle 6–7).

On a different, much less humorous level, on the title pages and in the prefatory material to Jonson's plays, the early seventeenth-century drama-tist ceases to validate his dramatic compositions as theatrical performan-ces. Now the printed play, far from brandishing the acclaim (and author-ity) of its performance, will contain a text that is exclusively authorized and partially rewritten by the author.[5] For Jonson, the actor's voice con-stituted, in Barish's cogent reading, "an unpredictable and untrustworthy element over which he had too little control; print offered an escape into a stabler medium." The end result was "to make the printed script rather than the live performance the final authority; the play moves formally into the domain of literature" (Barish, *Antitheatrical Prejudice* 139).[6] With-drawing "from the turbulence of the public arena," the culture of literacy and learning cancels whatever authorization there was for the performer independently to help mold dramatic representations. Refusing to be tainted by the actors' pleasure and the crowd's applause, these representa-tions more and more tended to resist the process of being ignorantly appropriated on unworthy scaffolds. From now on, performance was rarely sanctioned as having a validity and court of appeal of its own.

Towards a circulation of authority in the theatre

Recent critical discourse has traveled some length towards (re)exposing the products of literacy in the theatre to the realm of disorder and contin-gency that, on a certain cultural level, was denied them almost as a matter of course. As Stephen Orgel notes, "the basic instability of texts" in the

Elizabethan theatre is inseparable from "a fluidity that is built in" so as to accommodate changing circumstances of performance. In such cases, "the printed text is simply one stage in a continuous process, with no particular authority over any of the other stages in the process" (Orgel, "What is an Editor?" 23). Without taking such fluidity and such processing into account, it seems difficult to comprehend the 'distraction' itself in the locations of energy, interest, and authority in "this distracted globe" (*Hamlet* 1.5.97). Thus, to establish a new perspective on Elizabethan relations of writing and performing we need, as David Scott Kastan cogently suggests, "to uncover the full network of agency involved in the production of the text, restoring the literary work to the collaborative economies necessary for its realization" (Kastan, "The Mechanics of Culture" 34). Such "realization," it must be added, is no less than a transmutation that thrives on the 'surplus value,' the semantic and semiotic overcharge, that results when a verbally composed representation submits to material (voiced, corporeal, and other audible and visual) articulations.

It is of course true, as Orgel has conceded, that for editors there remains a considerable gulf between potentially historicizing and actually editing the Shakespearean text. It is surely a formidable task to uncover the full network of contrarious effort and agency in the theatre and, thereby, accommodate unsuspected areas of conflict as well as concurrence among diverse social and cultural investments that went into the formation of Shakespeare's theatre. To a considerable extent, the instability of the Elizabethan playtext participates in the precarious, unstable circumstances of theatrical production itself. And these, of course, tend to resist fixation by editorial inscription. The problem, then, as we have learned from the editors themselves, is how to wrest a textual end-product from an extremely fluid, largely unrecorded, partially oral process of working, writing, copying, rehearsing, and of course playing in the theatre.

But even before such an end-product (which is final only in terms of the aims and needs of an editorial assemblage) can be isolated in print, the entanglement of the text with diverse manifestations of theatrical authority needs to be further explored. Where, in the script of dramatic representations, do traces of performance retain an authority of their own? How much of the strength of such dramatic representations derives from the visual, playful, energizing 'overbid' associated with transactions in the midst of live audiences? How much of it is due to performed actions that are in excess of, even eccentric to, the strictly representational uses of dramatic language and yet able to conjoin the intellectual and the material springs of theatrical production? In Shakespeare's theatre, I shall suggest, some of the answers to these questions are likely to be found in a deeply ingrained (dis)continuity between the visible display of sensuous action and the imaginary, invisible play with represented meanings. Such (dis)continuity invokes unpredictable links and gaps between the game-some thrust of self-staged playing and the comic or "tragic glass" of verbally inscribed dialogue. The underlying potential of tension as well as the area of potential affinity between them can best be studied in their respective historical contingency, where the frontiers shift and are redrawn as, for instance, between game and knowledge, between the "self-resem-bled show" (Hall, *Virgidemiarum* 1.3.44) of the player's body and the strictly absent, fictional order of world-picturing representation and sub-ject-constructing characterization.[7]

Once, then, the 'distraction' of energies and authorities in the Eliza-bethan theatre has been established, the issue of authority in the playtext cannot be revisited on the assumption that it simply derives from the author, 'from what he actually wrote,' or from his presumed 'foul papers' or any surviving piece of authorial holograph. At this juncture, recent directions in textual scholarship appear to converge with a more widely felt critical discontent with the 'text itself.' As Stephen Greenblatt has poign-antly noted, "the whole notion of the text as the central, stable locus of theatrical meaning" is in question, when "it is impossible to take the 'text itself' as the perfect, unsubstitutable, freestanding container of all its meanings." If, therefore, the text by itself fails "to bind and fix the energies we prize, to identify a stable and permanent source of literary power" (Greenblatt, *Shakespearean Negotiations* 3), we are well advised, and especially so in the theatre, to look for a wider and different framework of reference in which to revitalize a workable conception of the links and gaps between "pen" and "voice."

In a situation like this, the new textual scholarship, with its sustained scepticism *vis-à-vis* the unity and stability of Shakespeare's theatrical texts, raises a number of troublesome and as yet unanswered questions. Since it is unhelpful to deny (or simply ignore) authorship in the Elizabethan theatre, any new approach to the issue of authority needs carefully to redefine what Susan Zimmerman has called "the social agency of the author" (Zimmerman, "Editing Early Modern Texts" 72). Let us not forget that the author "is a historical agent and no mere instrument or effect of a linguistic order," even while the same author "is not autono-mous and sovereign, neither the solitary source nor the sole proprietor of the meaning that circulates through the text" (Kastan, "Shakespeare after Theory" 366). Along these lines, historical scholarship, in Kastan's preg-nant formulation, "at once disperses and reconstitutes Shakespeare, re-vealing him to be something more than a product of the text and some-thing less than its exclusive producer" (366). The point is that, in their circumstantial constraints, the acts of both producing and composing can, in Judith Butler's words (above, p. 15), establish a point of agency that is not "fatally determined" by that culture and discourse within which Elizabethan dramatic writings and performances were situated. Thus, once the agency of playwriting is reconstructed as an important component of a larger nexus of socio-cultural and economic relations, this agency is neither totally determined nor altogether autonomous in collaborating with, or dissenting from a given set of institutional circumstances. Thereby, the playwright's contribution in its uniqueness remains as a matter of course subject to what contingency resides in the transactions, transformations, and interpretations to which his performed text is ineluctably exposed.

In order to specify these entirely generalized premises, let us for a moment retrace that significant stage in the nexus of authority which very likely marked the move of a good many dramatic compositions from page to stage. As a revealing entry in Henslowe's *Diary* suggests, he gave to the Lord Admiral's Men a sum of 5s. "for to spend at the Readinge of that boocke at the sonne [Sun] in new fyshstreate" (Foakes and Rickert, *Diary* 88). Provided of course that this entry, in the specification of its locality, did not record an exceptional type of procedure, the written text would be orally submitted to the players for approval and acceptance. It must have been at this point when the players, well entertained and perhaps heated by their hospitable impresario's contribution, first began at least tentatively to think about the order of casting and – almost inseparable from that – about possible uses of platform space. One may doubt if indeed they followed the text as passive listeners or as mere recipients, especially when, as Greg says about such readings of the text, "the more readily and vividly it could be followed [by the company] the better its chances would be" (Greg, *Shakespeare's First Folio* 124).

Beyond such early attention by the players, the writer's text was further intercepted on its way from page to stage by the work of a 'plotter.' The 'plotter,' as R. A. Foakes briefly defines his task, was to provide a play's "outlines for the prompter's use" (Foakes and Rickert, *Diary* 326). Six such 'plots' are extant (a seventh has survived in a nineteenth-century variorum edition) and their renewed reading has only recently helped retrace the treatment of the 'book' from author's text to theatre script. As David Bradley in his reconstruction of the 'plot' of George Peele's *The Battle of Alcazar* has suggested, such plots must have achieved a significance that was at least partially independent of what the author's text actually contained. While the 'book' was submitted to the Master of the Revels for licensing, "rehearsals would have to carry on in the absence of the Book for some time." In the circumstances, the 'plot' served as "the skeleton key by which the actors' parts [could] be fitted together in rehearsal" (Bradley, *Text to Performance* 91). Regardless of whether the 'book' was absent or otherwise, the "craft of plotting" was crucial when it involved "a process of mutual adjustment between the Book and the cast available" (175). At this stage, decisions about the required numbers of actors in casting would certainly not be made by an absent author. Such questions could not be answered without some fairly concrete notions of who was available for how many roles, which answer in turn might easily have implicated changes – contractions, deletions, and so forth – in the script.

We do not of course have any evidence about how (dis)similar the preparation of a script for the stage was in the case of Shakespeare's own company. But whichever procedure was chosen in the case of the Lord Chamberlain's Men, the emplotment of space must have been made in accordance with the actors' perception and sense of physical movement, behind which any purely self-sufficient, imaginative parameters of writing would take second place. In the theatre, what legal rights of authorship existed were surrendered to an appropriation of the text by the agents of theatrical production in the marketplace of early modern cultural goods. The trajectory of dramatic compositions from page to stage was a function of these unstable relations of production. And conversely: the chequered pattern of Elizabethan theatre history cannot be reconstructed without examining the extent to which the unstable texts of Elizabethan drama-tists, and especially the so-called 'bad' quartos, can be viewed, in Leah Marcus' words, "as registers of cultural difference" ("Shopping-Mall Shakespeare" 165).

However, these registers of difference were neither static nor socially immovable, nor were they shaped by purely linguistic parameters of the 'difference' in question. Perhaps this is one of the reasons why the present "revolution in Shakespeare studies," as Margreta de Grazia and Peter Stallybrass term it, has not provided us with satisfying answers yet; as a "revolution," it is not without its own problematic – one in which, admit-tedly, the present study participates. Thus, on its editorial side, the new textual scholarship is beset with a scarcely concealed danger: the reduction or, even, obliteration of the agency of dramatic writing goes hand in hand with what must be viewed as the unwelcome assertion of an all-too-articulate, deliberately inventive editorial agency. On the one side, the author is seen to be absorbed by an institutionalized 'network,' if indeed he is not made entirely to vanish in it; on the other side, such reduction of the author as an important referent of the dramatic text tends to enlarge the scope of choice and intervention (and of course subjectivity) for the editor. As in the case of the theatrically oriented Oxford edition of *The Complete Works* (1986), the text of *Pericles*, for instance, has been supple-mented by skillful but utterly conjectural insertions, by way of an adaptation of parts of George Wilkins' prose treatment of the story. The inventive editors in question presumably would not dispute the existence of an agency behind what on their title page is *William Shakespeare*; in a less eclectic undertaking this kind of editorial practice, once it is turned into a declared policy of systematic re-editing, might very well thrive upon disregard of, rather than respect for, the composition. The displacement of past agency and subjectivity is bought at the price of subjective intervention in the present – an intervention, as has been shown, marked by alien standards of order, unity, and harmony that are grafted upon the Elizabethan text.[8]

Some such problematic has been with us ever since recent editors and textual critics began to question the premises on which the New Bibliography sought to trace the dramatist's presumed intentions and meanings. But, again, it is one thing to acknowledge, as the remarkable work of Laurie E. Maguire does, that bibliographic standards often reflected "personal taste rather than textual corruption" (Maguire, *Shakespearean Suspect Texts* 187). It is quite another question to define and clarify the new premises, and to do so beyond the confines of unacknowledged "taste" and ideology, by renegotiating editorial standards in reference to a more inclusive circulation of authority in the Elizabethan theatre.

At this point, the new textual scholarship itself invokes the uses of cultural and theatrical history. Bibliographical scholarship, at least by implication, had tended to take for granted that the superior quality of authorship was incompatible with the artistic palates of actors and the quality of audiences in the provinces. Such parameters of judgement were potentially reductive at the point where carefully sifted historical evidence was wanting. Rather than exploring in depth the grounds on which the necessary difference between the palates of players and the preference of dramatists occurred, the new bibliographers *tout court* reduced this difference to the level of an aesthetics dominated by the emergent culture of literacy. It was a value judgement very much in the wake of eighteenth-century editors. And these in their own turn inflected the standards of certain early seventeenth-century learned dramatists like John Marston who in his *Histriomastix* actually anticipated the charge that it was the performance practice of ignorant, beggarly agents like Belch, Clout, Gulch, and Gutt – *nomen est omen* – who were liable for deviations from and, thereby, contamination of a true poet-scholar's text.

The new historicizing perspective on textual authority especially deserves our attention where, as in Scott McMillin's work on *The Book of Sir Thomas More*, the question of an authority residing purely in the author's intent is suspended in a theatrically alert recasting of priority and validity within relations of text and performance. Resisting any biographical and palaeographical concerns and "refusing to quail before Hand D's identity" (142), McMillin effectively divests the manuscript of the epithets of corruption that it has traditionally received. Far from lacking "decent continuity," from being "reduced to incoherence," to something "unfinished and chaotic," to a perfect "mess" (18; terms used by scholars of the stature of W. W. Greg, Harold Jenkins, and T. W. Baldwin), McMillin shows that the playtext occupies an entirely "regular" niche (52) in the Elizabethan theatre. *The Book of Sir Thomas More* was "brought to a particular stage of completion," in this case, not insignificantly, up "to the point where the actors' parts can be copied" (49). That this performance-related state of the text appears to traditional editors to be incoherent suggests how profound a distance there might be, under very unexceptional circumstances, between a twentieth-century editor's perspective and an Elizabethan performer's on the same (so to speak) play.

The amplification of the grounds from which to derive authority in the production of theatrical scripts is of immense consequence when the Elizabethan playtext now tends to be tied not to the isolated act of an "onlie begetter" but to a productive and reproductive process involving diverse cultural energies and institutions. Here, the path-breaking work of Jerome McGann has pointed the way with his early vision of a deep "crisis in editorial theory," his critique of "the rule of final intentions," and of the identification (and fixation) of authorship "through this process of individualization" (*Critique* 11). According to his contextual redefinition of "authoritative texts," the "location of authority necessarily becomes dispersed beyond the author" (84) and cannot be decided upon in isolation from historically given "productive relations" (93). Authority in this wider understanding connects with the *use* of literary productions and does not rest with an originator alone. It is in this sense that – to recall McGann's phrase – authority is "a social nexus, not a personal possession" (48).

Thus, the previously impenetrable barrier between the author's hand and nonauthorial interventions in the production process is in question, even before any compelling set of generally accepted editorial criteria for coming to terms with this new fluidity are available. Whatever in the past had inspired an unending fascination with the isolated author gives way to a broader view of the production (and the competence behind it) and the consumption of signs and meanings in the theatre. As a consequence, a so-called 'bad' quarto like the first printed *Hamlet* can no longer be viewed as "completely illegitimate and unreliable," or as marked, in E. K. Chambers' terms, by "gross corruption, constant mutilation, meaningless inversion and clumsy transposition."[9] But if, in Leah Marcus' phrase, this quarto betrays astonishingly comprehensive "registers of cultural difference,"[10] how can we positively attempt to supplement the literary court of appeal by one closer to the actual material relations of theatrical production?

One of the most obvious difficulties is that we cannot with any certainty recover the circumstances which allowed for the existence of what Kathleen Irace calls "skillful theatrical adaptations, fast-paced popular versions" (Irace, *Reforming the 'Bad' Quartos* 159). It is mainly by conjecture that we can explain the need, especially on the part of traveling companies, for abridging and adapting London stage plays. But since touring in the provinces has come to be recognized not as a purely make-shift but, rather, as a fairly widespread and reputable practice, the adaptation and reconstruction of playtexts can be understood as providing an entirely 'normal' or conventional procedure in response to impromptu cultural occasions and demands. This is not to say that a "competent (albeit pedestrian)" reconstruction like the First Quarto of *Hamlet* would entirely preclude certain actors from freely using their memory; but since, according to Laurie Maguire's criteria, a case for memorial reconstruction can be made for only a relatively small group of quartos,[11] the uses of such reconstruction may have been quite different from what traditional textual scholarship had assumed.

This is one more reason why the aims and effects of such reconstruction and adaptation deserve to be studied more closely. Ultimately, the 'bad' quarto may not have been so remote from a London-based practice of insertion where items, added in the course of performance, could potentially "become incorporated into the playbook" (189). Here as elsewhere, the Elizabethan theatre participated in a residually oral culture that affected certain variant playtexts such as *Doctor Faustus*, where orally transmitted commonplaces, stock phrases and expressions occur with particular frequency and significance.[12] Hence, as Albert Weiner in his edition of *Q1 Hamlet* had argued many years ago (anticipating some of the results of Paul Werstine's recent systematic scrutiny), all these omissions, repetitions and so-called contaminations are unlikely to derive from piracy or any other stealthy mode and purpose of memorial reconstruction.

Players, printers, preachers: distraction in authority

To draw attention to the transition, in Tudor England, not so much from an oral to a written culture but from what Brian Stock describes as a "predominantly oral to various combinations of oral *and* written" (*Implications of Literacy* 9) is one way of viewing in perspective the ever-recurring sites of mutual entanglements between dramatic scripts and oral performances. If Elizabethan and Jacobean playwrights held "mixed, if not conflicting, attitudes towards writing and printing" (Cole, "Dynamics of Printing" 97), they were also at the cutting edge of "a new 'cultural mix' that was essentially a new force in the sixteenth century" (Kiefer, *Writing on the Renaissance Stage* 271).[13] These mixed cultural forms themselves participated in a veritable revolution in educational facilities and communicative technologies. Together with a great expansion of the products of the printing press on the one hand and a considerable amount of uncontrolled preaching on the other, the oral uses of written language in large public amphitheatrical buildings in their own turn made possible a proliferation of verbal codes and meanings for thousands. Even while at this stage "literate expectations were slowly winning ground away from earlier modes of operation" (Marcus, *Unediting the Renaissance* 137),[14] the performed end product remained, as Andrew Gurr has recently noted, not primarily a text but a cultural event.[15]

Fortunately, there is sufficient (and sufficiently vivid) evidence to illustrate highly significant responses to the changing premises and locations of authority that ensued in the wake of a staggering proliferation of discursive practices in sixteenth-century England. Halfway through the century, in the spring of 1547 Stephen Gardiner, then bishop of Winchester, turned against "such errors as were . . . by ignorant preachers sparkled among the people." Objecting to "loose" uses of discourse, he coupled Protestant "preachers" with "printers" and "players" on the grounds that they all "make a wonderment, as though we knew not yet how to be justified, nor what sacraments we should have" (*The Actes* 6:31).[16] Gardiner's concern was the unsanctioned demand for a new type of religious legitimation ("how to be justified") that went hand in hand with an unsatisfied "wonderment." The latter in turn was contiguous with the cultural provocation of a desire, as Richard Bancroft put it in 1588, "to be alwaies seeking and searching," to "Search, examine, trie and seeke" (Bancroft, *A Sermon Preached* 39). With regard to such "wonderment," Gardiner took an exemplary position. He was determined "not to suffer [. . .] to slip the anchor-hold of authority, and come to a loose disputation" (*The Actes* 6:41).

This was written in response to certain blatant, particularly strident mouthings under the Protectorate. But half a century later a similar (and in view of its secular terms potentially even more pressing) concern is articulated in the language of jurisdiction. William Lambarde, indefatigable Justice of the Peace, author, and ever-faithful servant to the Crown in Kent, could warn his "good neighbors and friends" at the Quarter session at Maidstone, April 1, 1600 in these terms:

such is nowadays the bold sway of disobedience to law that it creepeth not in corners but marcheth in the open market. [. . .] yet how few are there found amongst us that will use the bridle of authority which they have in their own hand and cast it upon the head of this unruly monster. (Read [ed.], *William Lambarde* 143)

"Authority" in these religious and juridical discourses clearly served as an unquestioned instrument of rule; it was taken, Lambarde said elsewhere, as "already given" (Read [ed.], *William Lambarde* 80)[17] to the justices. In Lambarde's as well as Gardiner's discursive practice (as well as, surely, in the former's non-discursive actions) authority was asserted as something given prior to the act of representation and jurisdiction, prior even to the performance of violent punishment, through which "authority" – always already sanctioned – was merely applied or used like a "bridle" on the unruly and disobedient.

As against these distinctively political uses of "authority" through certain material and ideological tools of enforcement, the sixteenth-century theatre, not unlike unsanctioned modes of preaching and printing, pursued a distinct cultural agenda of appeal, empowerment, and legitimiz-ation. To underline what is perhaps the most crucial difference between Lambarde's and Shakespeare's uses of 'authority,' it may be said that, in juridical discourse, the same authority that was represented was also doing the representing. In Lambarde's text, the representation of authority pre-supposed an altogether fixed and closed relation between signifier and signified, a mode of signification that in its turn posits *and* supports a static view of society as an unchanging entity.

Here, the point that needs to be made is not simply that Gardiner and Lambarde in their language and violence are worlds apart from the repre-sentation of authority in Shakespearean drama. What is far more signifi-cant is that sanctioned uses of authority like Lambarde's, being widely prevalent at the time, tended to be readily inscribed in some of the dominant texts in the pre-Shakespearean theatre. A late morality play like *The Tide Tarrieth No Man* provides us with a particularly illuminating instance, in that here the representation of authority is, as it were, actually folded out upon itself through an allegorical figure bearing this very name: "Authority," in alliance with "Correction," enters the play to have its Vice, "Courage," arrested and punished. In this play, the allegorical representation of Authority provides several physical and imaginary cor-relatives to the political and judicial acts of representation in the discourse of Justice of the Peace William Lambarde. In the first place, the character Authority uses, and is supported by, theatrical images of physical force, as when he says to the figure of Correction,

> Draw neare Correction and thine office doe,
> Take here this caytife vnto the Jayle. (1813–14)

Quite unambiguously, Authority is *represented* as being in alliance with the "office" delegated to pursue justice and correction. Authority has the officially sanctioned power to enforce through his "commaundement."

Second, Authority is conceived of as *representing*, and addressing himself to, a previously established order existing prior to his own act of representing and defending that order through force. As the play draws to a conclusion, Authority feels empowered to pledge to Christianity:

> O Christianity vnto vs draw neare,
> That we thy abused estate may redresse.
> And as freely as this power vnto vs is lent,
> Here we now by force of the same:
> To thee faythfull few do here condiscent,
> That thou Christianities estate shalt frame. (1858–63)

Again, "this power" is "freely" and unquestioningly given; insofar as the "estate" of Christianity is abused, it needs only to be redressed "by force of the same" power which "vnto vs is lent." Authority, in other words, is viewed as preordained, indeed as always already there; in the moral play he needs only to be found and established in order to have his regime ensured.

This highly selective excursion into a pre-Shakespearean representation of authority must suffice to serve as a mere pointer to the altogether different uses of authority in Shakespeare's theatre. Here we can only recall in passing *2 Henry IV* where the issue of authority is debated between the Lord Chief Justice and Falstaff (1.2.96–213) or refer to the theme of a "little brief authority" in *Measure for Measure* (2.2.118) to suggest that in Shakespeare "authority" is not given but an issue in motion whose constituting elements are not simply office and enforceable power but wit, insight, and integrity. Even more significant, as against a universally applicable source and standard of validity, authority on the Shakespearean stage emerges as a "bifold" project, consonant with such self-reflexive divisions in discursive practice as emerge in that "madness of discourse / That cause sets up with and against itself!" (*Troilus and Cressida* 5.2.142–43). The "spacious breadth of this division" (150) could be foregrounded and turned into yet another, uncommon fabric of contrariety, here informed by the "fragments, scraps, the bits, and greasy relics" (159) of sensuality. Cutting through the binary order of things in allegorical representation, an even larger space for division was to be inscribed in the language of Lear when he in *his* "madness" projected contrariety into the most deeply fissured representation of authority that we have in Shakespeare. Here, division in authority resided in the very perception of it, when "the great image of authority" (4.6.158) was redefined socially and semiotically as, "handy-dandy," an inversion of justice itself. The perception is not from the point of view of those who (like Lambarde) wield authority but from the angle of those who suffer from it and (running from a farmer's "cur") have reason to fear it, as "a dog's obey'd in office" (160).

Such uses of authority in the Shakespearean theatre need to be seen historically, against the mid-sixteenth-century background of uncontrolled authorizations. As this context amply suggests, players, printers, and preachers among others had begun both orally and scripturally to expand the public circuit of signs and meanings, unleashing in their own distinct way a ground-swell of new, partially uncontrollable shifts in early modern locations of authority. What these and other emerging forms and media of communication foreshadowed was a gulf between traditional positions of a materially enforceable or always already posited authority and the advent of new and far-reaching ways of writing, acting, and preaching. These media – the ubiquitous pulpit of Protestantism, the potentially unsanctioned uses of the printing press, and the spread of platforms for secular dramatic entertainment – had, on top of their long-term, largely unpremeditated effects, one thing in common. They all established an unwonted density in the public exchange of news, information, and opinions. Colluding with an ever-expanding range and a new intensity of interpretations,[18] these new media provided grounds on which an unprecedented number of people were *de facto* justified, even prompted to respond to an increasing and ultimately uncontrollable range of discursive practices.

No less important, the conditions of "incontinent rule" in the Liberties of London – so well described by Steven Mullaney – made it difficult for any single source of authority to be considered unambiguously given. As distinct from both the orthodox representations of vice and virtue and the judicial differentiation between the justice and the thief, authority in Shakespeare's plays was not a topos clearly circumscribed or in itself conclusive. Nor was it possible to think of authority in terms of only one function or location. Between its cultural and its political uses, authority was no longer of a piece. Perhaps Coriolanus' words may be read in this wider context:

> my soul aches
> To know, when two authorities are up,
> Neither supreme, how soon confusion
> May enter 'twixt the gap of both, and take
> The one by th'other. (3.1.108–12)

Although here the denotation is strictly political, there was also, in Shakespeare's theatre, a "gap" between political and cultural articulation; between them "two authorities [were] up" and, in the resulting "confusion" continuity, let alone congruity, was not as a matter of course available. Concurrence between them was impossible to achieve when each in its making pursued a different mode of legitimation. While in Elizabethan politics authority was prescribed or simply given, in the theatre the dramatic representation of authority could often enough undermine any imaginary sanctions of its bulwark. In fact, the challenge of represented political authority was most formidable where cultural authority in its own specific business of representation carried a theatre ringing with applause all before it. But then such cultural authority in the theatre was strongest where it was least assumed to be given. Rather than being given, say, at the beginning of the play in performance, the theatre's authority, its sheer impact and resonance was implicated in a cultural process – in the effect of, in the response to, the dramatic production itself.

Thus, in the early modern period, England as well as Spain and other West and Central European countries saw the emergence of a new and powerful type of "cultural authority." As Marina Brownlee in her use of this concept suggests, this new cultural form of authority was inseparable from a "division" between fixed sources of traditional validity and more recent and mobile ones. Such new grounds of authority were marked by "a dynamic struggle in which the threat of difference had to be first perceived and then resolved into identity, into sameness" (Brownlee and Gumbrecht, *Cultural Authority* xi). This was the case in the virtually uncensored publication, during the German Reformation, of innumerable pamphlets or *Flugschriften*, often in dialogue form and graphically illustrated. There was a different but related opening in Spain's Siglo de Oro where the "legitimate and authoritative" could be challenged by "alternatives to the official discourse," which "themselves both require a cultural authority of their own and problematize that authority" (x). Like England, Spain had its own educational revolution, producing educated men in search of social mobility and cultural opportunity. Early Protestant preaching, pamphleteering, popular Renaissance fiction and drama in England were part of a broad European movement validating 'inofficial,' that is, purely cultural and partially unsanctioned locations of discursive authority.

Viewed in this wider context, the Elizabethan theatre appeared both to thrive on, and contribute to, a crisis in the "anchor-hold" function of one supreme location of authority. Not unlike the popular anti-Episcopalian pamphlet, the playhouse provided a site where authority, now that it was less securely given before an utterance began, came to constitute itself through the workmanship, the perceived cogency, and the actually experienced appeal of signifying practice itself. On common stages, as in no other institution of the time, two modes and sources of signification – writing and playing – came together to multiply, and make dynamic, the theatrical process itself. As the new signifying potential in the dramatist's use of language was mediated, intercepted or enhanced through voices and bodies, the unsanctioned double-bind in the authorization of performed meanings must have achieved an unprecedented density.

Once this emergent cultural authority accrued in the *process* and as a *result* of verbal and corporeal articulations, its appeal became largely incompatible with "base authority from others' books" (*Love's Labour's Lost* 1.1.87). In its own turn, the newness of dramatic representations, even their 'news value,' was inseparable from the way that common stages participated in a political economy where there was a commercial need to offer a certain amount of freshness to large and mixed audiences. The early London playhouses constituted, as Leeds Barroll has graphically shown, "a largely untried and new focus of public expression"; as an institution, they themselves were "so turbulently new to London that no comfortable conceptual models" (Barroll, *Politics, Plague and Theater* 8) were yet available. The task that must have been particularly untried was to sustain, on secular grounds, supply and demand in the new institution in relation to so many people; and, even more difficult, to do so by effectively coordinating the forces of theatrical production that, uniquely, constituted the double-bind in the workings of the theatre's cultural authority.

In these circumstances, authority as circulating in the Elizabethan playhouse was marked by distracting areas of nonidentity, such as those between the authorship and the ownership, but also between the composition and the censorship, and finally the reception, of playtexts. After the playwright had sold it, the 'book' was either in the hands of actors or, in Henslowe's case, of an accountant and banker who in all likelihood did little to stage-manage acting companies. But although business practices at the Rose could not have differed substantially from those at the Globe,[19] the shareholding and housekeeping arrangement in Burbage's company must have benefited the player-poet and given him a rare degree of integration, security, and influence. Even so, the question of equitable rights or claims between playwriting and performing was not thereby settled; this question may well have remained a sensitive one where authorship was subsumed under what was almost certainly a player-dominated arrangement of profit and ownership, as documented in the case of the complaint inscribed in *Greene's Groatsworth of Wit*.[20]

Thus, the element of distraction in the authorization of playtexts was intriguingly – though by no means directly – related to larger uncertainties and unpredictable developments associated with the emergence of a distinctively cultural authority in the period. In its earlier phase, the work of the Lord Chamberlain's Men, probably like Shakespeare's pre-1594 association, was – as far as we know – marked by the absence of radically divisive positions in the company. In the history of the Elizabethan theatre, this was a time preceding, in Timothy Murray's words, the transference of "intellectual authority from the communal structures of the

[. . .] theatre to the private domain of the author and subsequent possessor" of the dramatic text. In these circumstances, "the tension" remained undeveloped "between the desire for creative autonomy and the pressure of inherited or conventionally accepted authoritative systems or voices" (Timothy Murray, *Theatrical Legitimation* 96).[21] For instance, if in the early 1590s a university trained writer like Robert Greene quarreled with the players, it was because he felt personally betrayed and cheated, but not because he thought he was defrauded of any right to see his text performed according to the spirit and the letter emanating from the author's pen. Similarly Marlowe, in his eagerness to "lead" the theatre away from the clowning, jigging standards of the past, left no trace in his plays that bear witness to any concern about the adulteration of Renaissance endeavors of art; enough for him, it seems, when the grand design, the mighty line of humanist rhetoric had made a breach in the pre-1587 tradition on common stages.

Here to emphasize the element of cultural inclusiveness and the absence of the more glaring forms of stratification among the popular and the 'better sort' is not, even in this early phase, to underestimate the strength of the collision among conflicting claims on the aims and uses of the emergent cultural authority. For that, the alleged death-bed composition we have under the title *Greene's Groatsworth of Wit* is a revealing case in point. Shakespeare in 1592 was launched on a career whose distinguishing characteristic was its positioning between two different locations of theatrical production. Here was "an absolute *Johannes fac totum*" (line 942)[22] that, as a mere player, presumed to snatch the socially and academically privileged "rare wit," those "admired inventions" that were previously thought to be legitimized solely by an Oxford and Cambridge education. For Shakespeare to be called "an upstart Crow, beautified with our feathers," and to be scornfully hailed as *factotum* was significant enough. There were of course the natural metaphors of envy and distaste against "those Anticks," mere players from the country, and, even more, against that actor-dramatist serving the "pleasure of such rude groomes" – sentiments revealing an undertone of insecurity and threatened privilege.

Even more important in the present context, the shifting agents of dramatic writing were to be shielded by the authority of class and education; the prestige of the latter had to be summoned against the sheer capacity of a mere player for bombasting out a blank verse like "the best of you." What, it seems, was most resented was a mode of theatrical authorization whereby a versatile concurrence of hitherto separate activities, now usurped by an agent of performance, appeared sufficient to guarantee public success in the theatre. If we read "*Johannes fac totum*" as "a Jack of all trades, a would-be universal genius" and, even, as "one who meddles with everything" (*OED*), then the academically sanctioned authority of possessing "rare wit" and owning the fine arts ("*our* feathers") could be seen as being hijacked on behalf of the players, ungrateful and uncompromising villains, as anyway Greene must have perceived them – including Shakespeare, himself.[23] Thus, the gentle arts of eloquence and composition could be seen as contaminated by their sheer proximity to common pastime; in fact, they were perceived as at the mercy of such unliterary and indecorous institutions as next day would harbor bear-wards, bull-fights, and all sorts of juggling, somersaulting, piping vagabonds. As long as all kinds of shows, fights, and feats could be seen to jostle side by side with plays at untried cultural occasions, it must have appeared scandalous for some to make the composition of blank verse coextensive with its reproduction on the stage and, even worse, with its impersonation by plebeian actors. This undifferentiated absence, *factotum*-wise, of division in cultural labor appeared unacceptable to Greene, who, in articulating his personal disappointment, emphasized social distance between "author's pen" and "actor's voice."

Shakespeare's association with an inclusive circulation of theatrical authority continued, albeit in diminished form, well beyond the turn of the century, when a culturally effective differentiation was imminent between the rare wit in the writing and the dullness of "self-misformed" clowns and gaping multitudes. This state of affairs cannot of course be established on the solid ground of any biographical evidence. However, we do have at least some circumstantial indications that, almost certainly in line with his colleagues and former fellow players, his writing tended to retain, even finally recur to, an open, inclusive position on these matters. As Douglas Bruster has suggested in his intriguing rereading of the opening scene of *The Tempest*, the "confusion of authority and division of labor on the deck of the ship" draws on the contemporary trope – found in Thomas Dekker, Robert Daborne, and, of course, Prospero's epilogue – of the stage as ship. And indeed, both "are wooden structures packed with people [. . .] sites of labor where work is usually concentrated and frantic" and demands "intensive cooperation" (Bruster, "Local *Tempest*" 37). In our context, the point of this analogy in a play rich in allegorical subtext is that Shakespeare sides with, in fact identifies his own use of "authority" (1.1.23) with the work of the players in a demanding "tempestuous" scene with "thunder" (1.1. SD) and shipwreck. Faced with a precarious representation like this and, what is more, the language of "bawling, blasphemous, incharitable" (40–41) abuse from their represented betters, those who are in charge of doing the job of running the ship-stage answer back: "What cares these roarers for the name of the king?" (16-17). "You are a councilor; [. . .] Use your authority." (20–21; 23) "Out of our way, I say" (26–27). It is topically as well as tropically not at all out of the question that, as Bruster believes, this scene responds to the irksome usurpation of – in Dekker's words – "such true scaenical authority" by stage-sitting gallants on the boards of Blackfriars. As the Boatswain tells the aristocrats in no uncertain terms, "I pray now keep below" (11). In this opening scene, the thrill of liminality, especially viable at the play's beginning and ending, may well have inspired a playful way of dealing with the nuisance of a notorious privilege.

For the play to propose "our labor" (13) as an alternative to "your authority" (23) was a gesture all the more remarkable in that, in a later scene, Ferdinand says about "my labors,"

> some kinds of baseness
> Are nobly undergone; and most poor matters
> Point to rich ends (3.1.2–4)

Here, authority as derived from status as unquestionably given was made to collide with the emergent source of early modern validity – the authority that accrued from competence, knowledge, and experience, discourse and work. So to rehearse the politics of authority in the playhouse must have been gratifying to the players, irrespective of what degree of annoyance the stage-sitting gallants actually constituted.

Whatever authority "this unworthy" ship-stage could claim for itself had to be wrung from "some kinds of baseness" and humility; what was finally delivered (and delivering) had to be endorsed by mixed audiences. It was by conjuring the "spell" this ultimate court of appeal exerted, that the circulation of authority between writing and playing became not just possible but both functioning and functional. For Shakespeare and his colleagues, this stage business, as far as it did receive applause and filled the sails (and coffers) of their "project" towards success, was one of those "most poor matters" that "Point to rich ends" – "rich" in both the material and intellectual senses of the word.

Could it be that John Heminge and Henry Condell in 1623 echoed related sentiments that they shared with their author? I believe they did, both in the dedication to the earls of Pembroke and Montgomery and in their epistle "To the great Variety of Readers." In the former, they humbly introduce themselves as "Presenters" offering "these trifles" to their Lord-ships, even when these actor-managers in their written dedication "cannot go beyond our owne powers. Country hands reach foorth milke, creame, fruites, or what they haue." Still, the topos of rural modesty must by no means be taken at its face value; Heminge and Condell make it perfectly plain that their "owne powers" both as men of the theatre and literary executors are far from despicable. Not only do they determine that *The Tempest*, with of course its first scene coming first, was given pride of place in the opening of the Folio. Quite obviously, what they have to offer to "the great Variety of Readers" has been acknowledged, and thereby authorized as entertaining value, by a most reliable court of appeal.

> And though you be a Magistrate of wit, and sit
> on the Stage at *Black-Friers*, or the *Cock-pit,* to arraigne Playes dailie,
> know, these Playes haue had their triall alreadie, and stood out all Ap-
> peales; and do now come forth quitted rather by a Decree of Court,
> then any purchas'd Letters of commendation. (A3)

This "Court" fully exemplifies the strength of the new cultural authority. The latter is quite different from a mere pronouncement, or "commendation," that authoritatively precedes the actually experienced result, the felt value and achievement of the article in question. For good reason, Heminge and Condell use the language of civil jurisdiction: having been exposed to prolonged deliberations and "stood out" all appeals and judgements, these plays are acquitted, which is to say, they enjoy a standing (not to say authority) marked by freedom and success. In addressing an undifferentiated "great Variety" of readers, the editors apply a modern touchstone of civic authority *par excellence*; it is one that, residing in the work of the theatre, becomes available only through the *result* of a public examination, in the *wake of* multitudinous testing, by which the plays here offered "haue had their triall alreadie."

3   Pen and voice: versions of doubleness

As the Prologue to *Troilus and Cressida* begins to address the audience, his unabashed assurance of place ("In Troy, there lies the scene," 1.1) gives way to a strange kind of anxiety, a distinct lapse of assurance about both the text and the acting of the play.

> and hither am I come,
> A Prologue arm'd, but not in confidence
> Of author's pen or actor's voice, but suited
> In like conditions as our argument (22–25)

The question that I propose to ask is whether and to what extent this want of "confidence" can be read in conjunction with a late Elizabethan difficulty in coming to terms with the circulation of authority between writing and performing in the theatre. Clearly, the representation of textually inscribed meaning (deriving from "author's pen" and the matter of history, myth, or romance) and the practice of performance (requiring the physical, audible presence of "actor's voice" and body) are not the same. Rather than identifying with either of these, Shakespeare's Prologue is "suited / In like conditions as our argument." In other words, his appearance is warlike. While in opening the play he *presents* "the scene" to the audience, he also and simultaneously *represents*, is even costumed, or "suited," to stand for "our argument." Characteristically the Prologue belongs to, and thereby bridges, both worlds, the represented world of the play and the (re)presenting world of its production and performance. May we assume, then, that in his liminal position, he points to an element of uncertainty, even friction, in the circulation of authority between the two worlds? And, in particular, could he be concerned with a situation in theatrical production where it was difficult for reciprocity between writing and playing to be viewed "in confidence"?

If this question is too conjectural to be given an unambiguous answer, let us at least underline the significance of the phrase and recall that and how the conjuncture of "pen" and "voice" was crucial to the workings of the popular Renaissance theatre in early modern England. At its most elementary level, the rise of the Elizabethan theatre was unthinkable without this conjunction of largely oral, physical, spectacular, body-centered practices of performance and display *and* the availability, in the early modern marketplace, of literary 'endeavors of art' derived from a university or grammar school education in rhetoric and composition. It was the interaction of these socially, aesthetically, and educationally diverse practices that brought together radically different sources of cultural pleasure, validity, and function. In their (dis)continuity, writing and playing, pen and voice, allowed for both reciprocity and difference at the heart of their relations in theatrical production. While in the theatre these sources of cultural articulation could coalesce in one person's (Robert Wilson's, Heywood's, or Shakespeare's) activities, they did not and could not altogether conceal an element of difference in their provenances and alignments. Indirectly rather than directly, incidentally rather than causally, this difference informed diverse uses of language, space, and audience rapport in the Elizabethan theatre.

In particular, it is difficult to understand the depth of the gaps or the strength of the links between role and actor, between the world-in-the-play and playing-in-the-world, without taking into account this double-bind in the theatre's provenance and purpose. No doubt, some divided form of authority can be traced in any kind of theatre; as Julian Hilton notes, theatrical performance is never a purely imaginary phenomenon, but is "simultaneously representation and being" (*Performance* 152). In the language of today's performance theory, this is equivalent to and requires an attempt "to propose a 'drift' between presence and absence" (which certainly "is not to hitch performance to an old metaphysics of presence – the notion that an absent referent or an anterior authority precedes and grounds our representations" [Diamond, *Performance and Cultural Politics* 1]). The point is that in the Elizabethan theatre these two poles of theatrical performance, the imaginary and the existential, illusion and delivery, could potentially be mobilized in their 'drift,' in the moveable state of either their continuity or their discontinuity. The socially aggravating, though never static gap between them (and the 'gushing' temptation to bridge it) was a crucial impulse in Elizabethan playing, but also, and simultaneously, in dramatic writing.

However, to trace (in the plural) versions of this double-bind in *both* playing and writing is, right at the outset, to point beyond any binary opposition between performance and text. The gap between the imaginary, represented world-in-the-play and the visible, audible playing-in-the-world of the playhouse is such that it inflects theatrical performance *and* dramatic writing without obliterating important areas of difference between them. But, as we shall see, these areas are thereby heavily criss-crossed, mutually mediated on the levels of dramaturgy, epistemology, and semiotics. To view in conjunction the imaginary and the material constituents of Elizabethan theatrical productions and receptions is one way to "present a more capacious, confusing, and complex picture of early drama" (Greenblatt, *A New History of Early English Drama,* Foreword xiii).

It is for purely pragmatic (and genealogical) reasons, then, when I propose first of all to look at the gap *between* "pen" and "voice" in what is a truly epiphanous moment in the history of the Renaissance popular stage in England, Christopher Marlowe's *Tamburlaine*, Part I (1587). In Marlowe's play, as well as in Thomas Kyd's *The Spanish Tragedy* (1587), we first find acknowledged the fully fledged difference between the "high astounding terms" of humanist rhetoric and what the players in their own right contributed to making these verbal "exercises" (John Lyly's term) eventful and, as a presumable eye-witness wrote, "greatly gaped at." The question that perhaps most poignantly addresses the hidden genealogy of Marlowe's stage is, how was it possible, on the strength of a humanistic education in composition and rhetoric, to "lead" common players, jesters, and jugglers to new horizons of textual fidelity and histrionic excellence?

"Frivolous jestures" vs. matter of "worthiness" (*Tamburlaine*)

Christopher Marlowe's prologue to the first part of *Tamburlaine the Great* is arguably the most forceful articulation of the early Elizabethan dramatist's sense of his own authority and entitlement to transform the common stage into a Renaissance cultural institution. This project was to create a more or less self-contained verbal picture of an imaginary world, containing a protagonist capable of "Threat'ning the world with high astounding terms." The move was from partially pre-symbolic locations of entertainment to a highly eloquent mode of representation by which signs, the worldly cogency of the icon itself, served to make present captivating events and stories. The claim to emerging leadership in the theatre was in glorious blank verse, celebrating itself in the act of ousting the cultural commerce of unlearned hacks and wayward players:

> From jigging veins of rhyming mother wits
> And such conceits as clownage keeps in pay,
> We'll lead you to the stately tent of War,
> Where you shall hear the Scythian Tamburlaine
> Threat'ning the world with high astounding terms
> And scourging kingdoms with his conquering sword.
> View but his picture in this tragic glass
> And then applaud his fortunes as you please. (Prologue 1–8)[1]

This, as a recent editor notes, was "clearly a challenge, almost a manifesto: away with the old, here comes the new (and considerably better)" (Dawson xi). Such difference between the old and the new was, as another critic contends, posited on the premise that the "jigging veins" were "at once recognizable as the jog-trot fourteeners of the popular drama in the years preceding Marlowe" (Leech, *Christopher Marlowe* 42). Although there is some truth in so drawing the line between the old and the new forms of meter and composition, this truth is partial to a degree in that its parameters are exclusively textual and literary. Actually, the jig and related "jestures," resonant with memories of tales without the "glass" of *imitatio vitae*, pursued a purpose of playing that was and is far from being accessible in terms of the meter, rhythm, and matter of literary endeavors of art.

It is precisely at this point that Marlowe's challenge, and what it implied for a new purpose of playing, deserves to be reconsidered. To do so is not at all to deny the refreshing contrast between the loping regularity of the old meter and the stirring, varied cadence of his iambic verse. But what is equally significant, and in fact, goes hand in hand with Marlowe's "mighty line," is the aggressive fashioning of a new writerly authority. This authority is posited and thrives on a considerably biased and sharply contestatory devaluation of performative practices involving "jigging veins" and clownish entertainment. Marlowe leaps for the difference between "the old" and "the new" so as to better foreground what new 'meaning' there is in his own departure. The "stately" matter of literary, world-picturing representations is authorized through this gesture of exclusion. The inscribed sense of superiority in the shoemaker's son's condescension to the players is perhaps best spelled out in the words of Robert Greene, one of his 'shifting companions,' when the latter, in his polemic against a certain player-playwright, presumes to view the players as "those Antics," "such rude groomes," and "such peasants."[2]

Marlowe's Cambridge education endows him with the literary language and the symbolizing capacity for circumscribing the power of a new, Renaissance type of mimesis on common stages. This mimesis is strictly harnessed to a textually determined purpose of playing. Here was a learned pen on a popular site, holding up a "glass" in which to view the "picture" of a "world" that, for all the lofty terms of its maker, was devised for common players to render and vulgar spectators to applaud. Among the promised feats, the most noteworthy were those of language use itself, surpassing even those of the "conquering sword." Remarkably, the socially and culturally "high" terms of rhetoric are referred to as "astounding" – not least, one would assume, because in such a place they must have caused astonishment and surprise. There is a homology between the ardent impetus of Marlowe's presumed leadership in this short prologue and the iambic rhythm of his language. Eloquence itself is turned into a presumed tool for both a grand new kind of appropriation and an expulsion. "This tragic glass" defines both the "picture" and the picture-making project; the *histoire* and the *discours* of the representation, its object and its agency, entertain a lively interrelationship. This interrelationship establishes a radically new cultural poetics, an absorbing, masterful world-view, an entire *episteme*. By implication, this new poetics has henceforth to be co-opted by all performers who, to use Hamlet's words, seek to "imitate humanity," not – if I may play upon false etymology – ab(h)ominably, but humanistically.

What here emerges is a new epistemology empowering writing as the dominant agency of knowledge, inspiration, and meaning, a source of restless energies and such unfathomable authority as "Doth teach us all to have aspiring minds" (2.7.20). In the last resort, such aspiration is inseparable from an early modern desire for appropriation, both in terms of intellectual assimilation and material and juridical acquisition. The irony is that by the time of its performance, ownership of the text will have passed from the author to the actors or – if the earlier venue (1587) anticipated the textual property relations of the 1594/96 revival – to an enterprising businessman like Philip Henslowe, whose diary records fifteen performances of Part I for the later date.[3] Surely, such great success was unthinkable without this picture-making pen, this masterful writing in a "tragic glass" that, by "climbing after knowledge infinite," could hope to reveal "The wondrous architecture of the world" (*Tamburlaine* 2.7.24; 22) in high astounding words and images.

If Marlowe's eloquent blank verse can, as I suggest, serve as a new medium of both appropriation and expropriation, a brief comparison with Shakespeare's no less stirring Prologue to *Henry V* gives food for thought. Although there, a comparable "Muse of fire" is invoked, the invocation is far more inclusive. The play's imaginative extension in the use of signs, symbols and *loci* confronts the players with an exacting agenda whose demands differ considerably from Marlowe's lofty literature-derived poetics of the "tragic glass." This is so at least in part because the newly demanding authority that inspires the "swelling scene" in Shakespeare's play is prepared to share an *ensemble* commitment to "this great accompt." Such writerly authority constitutes itself as part of a collective effort that carries the production; behind it there is also, humbly, "Our bending author" (Epilogue 2), one who – unblinded by his own supreme literacy – is patient enough to attend to the needs of "those that have not read the story" (5.0.1).

Although Marlowe, as I have argued elsewhere, will proceed remarkably to readjust his rating of the players' practice in *The Jew of Malta*, in the earlier play he may well have been content with what Richard Jones, the printer,[4] assumed in his Preface to the Octavo edition of *Tamburlaine the Great*. There we find ample acknowledgement that these fruits of a literary imagination would have appealed "To the Gentlemen Readers and others that take pleasure in reading Histories."[5] Moving easily from stage to page (and cashing in on an unusually successful playhouse production), the play in its two parts may not have disappointed the printer's hope that "the two tragical discourses" would be "no less acceptable unto you to read after your serious affairs and studies." These eminently readable representations recommended themselves in terms of what "worthiness" the "eloquence of the author" promised to deliver. The printer, in alliance with "author's pen," sought to rub it in: the flow of authority was to be from author to text to a textually prescribed performance, or – an even closer circuit – from writing, via printing, to the studies of those familiar with "reading Histories."

Or so at least Jones, a not entirely unbiased observer, would have it. London theatre audiences appeared to take a different view. Although hugely thrilled by Edward Alleyn's portrayal of Tamburlaine, they also "greatly gaped at" an altogether different type of show, a performance practice that, ignoring or resisting, even perhaps parodying the violent rhetoric of appropriation, was associated with what Jones called "fond and frivolous jestures." But these did not find their way into the text; to judge by Jones' Preface, the printed version of the play was curtailed in a drastic manner:

I have purposely omitted and left out some fond and frivolous jestures, digressing and, in my poor opinion, far unmeet for the matter, which I thought might seem more tedious unto the wise than any way else to be regarded – though, haply, they have been of some vain, conceited fondlings greatly gaped at, what times they were showed upon the stage in their graced deformities. Nevertheless, now to be mixtured in print with such matter of worth, it would prove a great disgrace to so honorable and stately a history. Great folly were it in me to commend unto your wisdoms either the eloquence of the author that writ them or the worthiness of the matter itself; I therefore leave unto your learned censures both the one and the other, and myself the poor printer of them unto your most courteous and favourable protection.[6]

The "worthiness of the matter itself" (which he continued to emphasize) appeared to Jones quite incompatible with the "graced deformities" that performances on public stages entailed. Participating in the countermanding flow of authority, even snatching part of it for himself, the printer, seeking to acknowledge himself as a discriminating reader, bowdlerized the performance text. In particular, he eliminated traces of a performance practice that to him must have appeared ill suited to the new purpose in representation. The tragical discourse of world history was not to be contaminated by some entirely unnecessary "fond and frivolous" blabberings of mere players; the traces of these poor vulgar antics had to be ignored or refined out of existence, as befitted "so honourable and stately a history." Note how from his position Jones anticipates, shares, and qualifies the sense of "distance," deliberately foregrounded by Shakespeare, between "this unworthy scaffold" and "So great an object" (as we have it in *Henry V*). Whatever the "distance" was between material stage and imaginary representation in the production of *Tamburlaine*, this distance provided a liminal site on which certain practices had a way of metamorphosing certain discrete forms of worthiness into, precisely, "graced deformities." Although we are told that these were "far unmeet for the matter" of worthiness, was there perhaps a performance practice that, deliberately, went much further towards what Shakespeare's chorus called 'Minding true things by what their mock'ries be" (4.0.53)?

As far as we can infer, the greatly gaped-at production must have carried an overcharge of theatrical "jestures," a strong performative not contained by what was represented in the text. The question is, whether, and if so, to what degree, this digressive, extravagant element of performance had disturbed, resisted, or otherwise molested the textually inscribed matter of "worthiness" itself. Or was it that the textual treatment of this matter itself was somehow contaminated, possibly in anticipation of what, from the Cambridge graduate's point of view, was the antic quality of its theatrical venue? As critics have suggested, there may in fact have been a laughably oversized pathos, an element of unsettling burlesque that either was part of the Marlovian design or, more likely, coaxed out of the text when it was presented on platform stages to gaping audiences. At any rate, the text may well have induced "varied provocations to laughter," deriving from "the mirth of exhilarated partnership, or the defensive laughter of shocked conventionality," as Cunningham suggests in his edition of the play (28). But if indeed there was some elective affinity between the rebellious writing and the unsanctioned playing, this does not put in question the social and educational gulf between them.

True enough, the printer's humbly remonstrated position is not necessarily identical with Marlowe's, even when, to judge from Marlowe's own disdainful reference to common performers, not much sympathy with the tradition of "rhyming mother-wits" can be assumed. But then the 1590 edition of the play, as Fredson Bowers has argued, bears no sign of the playhouse; it must have been based on "a fair copy, whether holograph or scribal," predating playhouse adaptation. Still, Jones in his Preface "may have a pertinence" in that, possibly, his intervention was dictated by "an attempt to anticipate that they [the 'frivolous jestures'] were not present, though acted" (Bowers [ed.], *Complete Works* 1:75).[7]

If this was so, then the performed version of the play bore the impress of players' practices which were unauthorized on literary, but authorized on extra-literary grounds. Again, Hamlet's performance of the thing complained of in the First Quarto's advice to the players may provide us with a certain analogy. There is a considerable body of evidence that such inclusive circulation of authority in the playhouse must have been more common than our own culture of literacy has led us to believe in the past. As Eric Rasmussen, rereading *The Book of Sir Thomas More* in manuscript, has recently argued, the volatility of the Clown's part can best be explained if we assume "that hand B was not creating the role of the Clown, but simply writing down in the promptbook lines that an actor had improvised on stage" (Rasmussen, "Setting Down what the Clown spoke" 130).[8] Significantly, the traditional proposition that the source of the Clown is the writing of hand B, may have to be turned upside down. Applying Rasmussen's searching reassessment of dramatic composition to the lost playhouse script of *Tamburlaine*, we may well have to consider the possibility that the authority for those "frivolous jestures" was not a writer's, but the performers'.

Still, the line of distinction here drawn between a performer-dominated site of entertainment on the one hand and the authorially sanctioned, homogeneous space in representation on the other can be misleading when conceived as being mutually exclusive. The threshold between them, as we shall see, was a site of doubleness itself that inspired contrariety in mutually overlapping, different types of space, such as those that went with "frivolous" and those that went with "worthy" uses. In Marlowe's early play, complicity between these different types of staging remains fairly minimal when compared with Shakespeare's uses of contrariety. Even so, it is clearly not helpful, in any exclusively dichotomous manner, to pit the strong performative of those frivolous jesters against the worthy text of the play as we know it. For one thing, there is in the Cambridge graduate's writing an author-function that by itself is enthralled by performative uses of rhetorical language. More specifically, the peculiar drive and energy of Marlowe's text are not, even when it was composed in absence from the London theatre, unaffected by what to all intents and purposes was its prospective venue. Thus, his eloquence is both publicly displayed *and* related to a consistently upheld design for world-picturing representation and characterization. As Jill Levenson, in a closely argued rhetorical study of the verbal dynamic of the play, put it, "Marlowe confronts us with a presentational – instead of a representational work of art" (Levenson, "Working Words" 112). If, as I assume, the alternative in question here is not offered as an absolute one, the "presentational" mode in the play must have agreed well with what current conditions of pre-1587 theatrical transaction allowed for.

No matter then how arrogant the early Prologue was in his claim to have taken over, so as to "lead" the stage to new horizons of representation, the verbal armory of the protagonist turned the "worthiness of the matter itself" into an article of spectacular resonance in the playhouse. The much vaunted eloquence of the dramatist, in satisfying latent expectations of large and mixed audiences, thereby achieved a considerable amount of ambivalence. Once the new art of rhetoric and composition was assured of its appeal to multitudes, the authority of signs, and dramatic form itself, as opposed to fond "*de*formities," became a dynamic article in the theatrical circulation of cultural capital and energy. Sharing in the triumph of a huge success, the poet's pen and the leading actor's voice together attempted an endeavor of the "highest sort." Conquest, art, and "knowledge infinite" came together in an overreaching representation of and for "aspiring minds."

> For he is gross and like the massy earth
> That moves not upwards, nor by princely deeds
> Doth mean to soar above the highest sort. (2.7.31–33)

Blurring the boundaries between the furious pride of the protagonist, the 'soaring' ambition of the playwright, and the desire in the audience for upward mobility, the popular Renaissance theatre achieved a "thund'ring" display of signifying sound and fury. Marlowe here must be seen in his own right; so far, he had deliberately avoided the step that Shakespeare was to undertake on a much larger scale. But at this juncture, the common stage had a way of further absorbing, alluring, or simply challenging the literary craft; for the products of the pen fully to goad the voice and body of the actor, required a reverse movement whereby the strength of the author's pen in actor's voice had to be supplemented by, simultaneously, the actor's voice infusing the writing of the dramatist.

Bifold authority in *Troilus and Cressida*

Marlowe's play provides us with an early version of the gap between "author's pen" and "actor's voice" that can serve as both a foil to and a perspective for the very different Prologue to *Troilus and Cressida*. In Shakespeare's problem play, relations of pen and voice are no longer discussed so as to make room for the "high astounding terms" of the writer's eloquence; rather, these relations intriguingly inflect the absence of confidence in the play's nexus of word and action. It is an issue that in the play itself will assume great significance for both the warring parties: duplicity and contingency in relations of textual meaning and performed practice grow rampant in both Troy and the Grecian camp. Here we can only recall the most glaring disjuncture between word and deed, Hector's persuasively sustained speech in the Trojan council scene advocating peace and his subsequent *and* preceding action, "I have a roisting challenge sent amongst / The dull and factious nobles of the Greeks" (2.2.208–09). Throughout the represented world in the play, the rupture between what is said and what is done must be seen by indirection to connect with a divided authority in the dramatic representation rendered by words and bodies.

This reading may appear less speculative when, even before further pursuing this argument, we link the unconfident Prologue in *Troilus and Cressida* with comparable articulations of uncertainty in plays of this period. There is, first of all, the undoubted anxiety in *Hamlet* over what the Folio labels a "controversy" in which – in Rosencrantz's words – "the poet and the player went to cuffs in the question" (2.2.355–56). The "prologue arm'd" of *Troilus and Cressida* and the "controversy" (354) in the Folio *Hamlet* are divided by, arguably, not much more than a year.[9] Both may be read as allusions to the so-called War of the Theatres when, under the impact of the children's stages, cultural relations of writing in the private, and playing in the public, theatres came to constitute an emerging scene of uncertainty and friction. But what has scarcely been acknowledged was that part of the friction derived from a new and entirely unprecedented acrimony by which writers like Marston and Jonson now went out of their way to attack players – in what must be seen as antihistrionic rather than antitheatrical deprecations. This element of acerbity must have struck contemporary observers as an outburst of something new when, for instance, it made for a stark contrast with as recent a play as *Henry V*, where the Prologue served as a mouthpiece of collective confidence, with "author" (Epilogue 2) and each and every performer, figured forth as "ciphers to this great accompt" (Prologue 17).

However, in Shakespeare's theatre the area of difference in relations between "author's pen" and "actor's voice" finds a far more intriguing space, one that profoundly affects, and is absorbed by, theme and *mise-en-scène*. In problem plays like *All's Well that Ends Well* (1602) and *Measure for Measure* (1604) there is at work, albeit on an entirely different level, a divided mode of authorization which results in the grafting of a new element of literary buffoonery, satire or novelistic complication on traditional practices such as clowning and disguise. Following close upon the departure of Will Kempe, the problem plays, including *Troilus and Cressida*, reach towards a restructuring of theatrical thresholds between the two worlds – one represented, the other representing – in Shakespeare's playhouse. In this connection, there obtains a recomposition of traditional links between the world-in-the-play and the stage-as-stage; these links are experimented with so as to reconstitute the uses of open space according to socially indifferent and symbolically ambivalent parameters.

Along these lines, "confidence" in the nexus of word and action is further, even more insidiously disrupted in these plays. In *Measure for Measure*, where the Duke is instrumental in installing a *platea* convention, both Angelo in his office and Duke Vincentio in his disguise reveal an almost unfathomable abyss between the representation of what verbally they claim to be and do and what, in their action, they actually perform. Even more explicitly than in *Hamlet*, the fissure implicates the issue of authority, in particular the "little brief" (2.2.118) moment of authority's embodiment on stage. Through his own duplicitous strategy, the figuration of the Duke exceeds and at least partially contradicts what "noble and most sovereign reason" (*Hamlet* 3.1.157) a Renaissance ruler verbally stands for. After the "mad fantastical trick of him to steal from the state," Duke Vincentio "would have dark deeds darkly answer'd" (3.2.92–93; 177). Lucio here scarcely overstates the case but prepares the audience for a stratagem where "Craft against vice" (277) is applied and where the craftiness of deception itself is to deceive the deceiver.

In the words of the Duke, "Making practice on the times" (274) is to be answered by "Making practice" on what its agents do as these times go. Since the underlying notion, as Brian Gibbons comments, is that of a "puppeteer manipulating the characters [. . .] making them play his game" (147), including the game of the bed-trick, the split between words and deeds goes deep; the humanist "confidence" in an equivalence of language and delivery is profoundly disturbed by a bifold scheme, even and especially in the emplotment of justice and jurisdiction. There is no way for a magistrate or ruler ("He who the sword of heaven will bear" [261]) to "be himself a pattern, of knowledge, of grace and virtuous action, for others to follow" (146) – as Gibbons paraphrases the Duke's "Pattern in himself to know" (263). Rather, "disguise shall by th' disguised [. . .] perform an old contracting" (3.2.280–82).

Remarkably, the invoked "pattern," another virtuous "mould of form" (*Hamlet* 3.1.153), is "blasted" (160) through the use of the word "perform." There is, in the doubleness of the Duke's own role-playing, a surplus of performative energy shining through the scriptural assimilation and adaptation of the masquerade. It is as if the actor, in performing a character in disguise, *presents* a playful version of his *métier*. The result, spoken in the form and meter of a chorus, even an epilogue, is a gamesome performance of his own competence in pulling the strings of his puppets. In doing so, the Duke, in this liminal moment, displays his own version of counterfeiting doubleness in images of identity and transformation.

As in several other plays of this period, from *Henry V* to the two masterful comedies, the figure of disguise serves as a major vehicle of such doubleness in the authorization of both words and deeds. There is, on the one hand, a carefully calculated stratagem in the writing, artfully adapted from literary sources; on the other hand, the performer's skill shines through the representation as if it were a somewhat threadbare garment for the display of a bifold dimension in histrionic skill. What carries the role – be it the Duke's or Helena's in *All's Well* – is a performative zest that alone can sustain the masking of the mask, the counterfeiting of counterfeiting. In other words, the duplication (and, in female roles, triplication) of disguise foregrounds its ultimate agency in the work of the actor.

Thus, in *As You Like It* and *Twelfth Night*, Rosalind's and Viola's masquerade has come full circle. The boy actor returns to and thrives on a dramatized image of what, through his primary performance, actually obtains onstage – a boy playing a girl playing a boy; that is, a young body counterfeiting doubleness in his/her gendered identity. At this juncture, the symbolism of role-playing is at least partially lost in the act of its bifold representation. Coming almost as a relief from a twofold, threefold strain on symbolic form, histrionic being leaks through the several dovetailed images of counterfeit gender and status. What re-emerges in these cases, but also in Portia's role-playing, is histrionic agency, the performing mind and body of a young male actor. The disguise is full of duplicity in that it actually seeks to expose and allude to its existential underside, the life and blood of the gendered bodies behind the cross-dressed heroines. The disguise of disguise points back, over and beyond its textualized representation, to the work and body of the performer, his own "self-resembled show."

Here, as in other plays of this period, the gulf between word and action is deeper than (and must not be reduced to) a lapse of confidence in relations between "author's pen" and "actor's voice." As the gap in question is deliberately inscribed in the represented image of character, it thereby helps to suggest what, in the composition itself, is a new, almost unfathomable dimension in characterization. Even so, the depth of the resulting ambivalence, the vibrant display of a doubleness betwixt word and show, can best be conceived on the threshold of, and through the interplay between, "textual authority and performative agency."[10]

While the masterful comedies with unsurpassed felicity thrive upon gendered versions of doubleness between imaginary text and material body, the problem plays are, in the full sense of the word, 'dark' comedies in that the artful transparency in socio-gendered confusion gives way to something that is less perspicuous and far more troublesome. *Troilus and Cressida* in particular projects the doubleness in penning and voicing meanings onto a falsely shared or divided plane of authority. Upon closer inspection, this divided plane draws on and derives from a rift in the purpose of playing. Leaving aside for a moment the question of authority in poetics (to which I shall return in the chapter on *Hamlet*), *Troilus and Cressida*, in its linkage of war and love, presents us with a particularly full spectrum of moral, political, and epistemological parameters of (in)validity between word and action. It is here that Troilus' phrase, "Bi-fold authority" (Q 5.2.144; is it altogether fortuitous that F has "By foule"?) adumbrates a doubleness in division itself. There is division not only in the search for knowledge and the grounds of perception, but also in the uses of performance space and function. The link between philosophy and dramaturgy in the play being particularly close, we can say that divisions in represented knowledge and perception are sustained by, and partially conveyed through, cultural difference in theatrical practice.

> This she? no, this is Diomed's Cressida. [. . .]
> If there be rule in unity itself,
> This was not she. O madness of discourse,
> That cause sets up with and against itself!
> Bi-fold authority, where reason can revolt
> Without perdition, and loss assume all reason
> Without revolt. This is, and is not, Cressid!
> Within my soul there doth conduce a fight
> Of this strange nature, that a thing inseparate
> Divides more wider than the sky and earth,
> And yet the spacious breadth of this division
> Admits no orifex for a point as subtle
> As Ariachne's broken woof to enter. [. . .]
> Instance, O instance, strong as heaven itself,
> The bonds of heaven are slipp'd, dissolv'd, and loos'd,
> And with another knot, [five]-finger-tied,
> The fractions of her faith, orts of her love,
> The fragments, scraps, the bits, and greasy relics
> Of her o'er-eaten faith, are given to Diomed. (5.2.137; 141–52; 155–60)

As soon as we read the speech in the context of the scene at large, it becomes clear that whatever 'meaning' the textually designed representation contains is processed by and projected through divided uses of performance. As a consequence, the phrase "Bi-fold authority" is pregnant with more than one level of meaning. On the one hand, and primarily, the reference is to a discourse, "That cause sets up with and against itself," whereby "authority" surrenders its traditional connotations of a fixed location of validity. The crisis in moral and epistemological authority here takes the form of a rupture between godlike reason and sensory perception. Placing "madness of discourse" against "rule in unity" involves a juxtaposition that circumscribes a maddeningly contradictory position between the "bonds of heaven" and the "fragments, scraps, the bits, and greasy relics" of sensuous as well as sensual experience. Authority disturbingly surrenders the parameters of an unquestioned givenness. For Troilus, such "madness of discourse" serves as a vehicle of discontinuity, upsetting the cultural and semiotic order of representations through a bewildering separation of visible signs from transcendental meanings. A deep gulf divides the authority of cosmological order from the discourse of individual experience as ratified by "th'attest of eyes and ears" (5. 2.122).

But this philosophical and moral gulf has a correlative in the discontinuous quality of space and purpose in the playing of the play. In the performed event, certain characters, such as Cressida and Diomed, *represent* a fairly self-contained action, presumably in front of the *locus* provided by Calchas' tent. At the same time, there is at least one performer who, not being 'lost' in the representation, *presents* it and, through the "abuse of distance" (*Henry V* 2.0.32), views it in perspective. In doing so, the player playing Thersites remains unobserved and is not overheard by these characters or, for that matter, those intermediate personages, Troilus and Ulysses, who hide and watch.[11]

The entire scene is marked by a doubleness in the parameters of its staging. The presentational *gestus* associated with Thersites is particularly intriguing; in his open, presumably downstage position, he can address the audience directly and, from an almost extra-dramatic perspective, comment in the language of the professional performer: "A juggling trick – to be secretly open" (24). From his *platea*-like position, he communicates an awareness of the needs and figurations of performance, invoking Morality vices like "the devil Luxury, with his fat rump and potato finger" and, of course, "lechery" (55–57). He views the representation as, almost, a show of performative achievement. Spurring and sarcastically cheering histrionic delivery at a point where the boundary line between the performer and the performed gets blurred ("Now the pledge, now, now, now!" [65]), he can, as it were, coax performance out of the players, accompany and praise their accomplishment ("Now she sharpens. Well said, whetstone!" [75]), or simply pursue age-old gestures of inversion ("that that likes not you pleases me best" [102]).[12]

Such interplay of presentation and representation, game and fiction, theatrical craftsmanship and classical story, draws on firmly entrenched, but flexibly handled conventions associated with such diverse purposes of playing as we have noted in our reading of Q1 *Hamlet*. Remarkably, the physical/metaphysical division in the authorization of knowledge unfolds on and through the divided stage itself, with Troilus and Ulysses spatially and emotionally caught between upstage illusion and downstage disillusionment. But then the link between "division" in thought and divisions on the stage implies neither homology nor continuity. Rather, relations between these two modes of division remain entirely pragmatic and largely indeterminate. Fluidity in diverse uses of theatrical space predominates throughout. The breach between knowing and doing is enacted on a stage marked by the simultaneous availability, even the interaction, of localized and unlocalized areas. These, in their turn, interlock with multiple cultural functions of performance on the Elizabethan stage, where a performer (like the boy-actor playing Cressida) is, and is not, lost in a character.

This version of doubleness is inseparable from a peculiar use of theatrical discourses that, acknowledging an "unworthy scaffold," yet sustain the representation of classical "matter of worth." Richard Jones' phrase (cited in full above, p. 59) can here be used only ironically, when the treatment of such worthy matter itself reveals how "bonds" are "slipp'd" and love itself is smirched in "the spacious breadth of this division." "Bi-fold authority," which goes with this "division" in discourse and on stage, attest to a troublesome bifurcation between divine reason and "greasy" experience, between transcendental meanings and iconic signs and signifiers in *mise-en-scène*. Nor can spectators in their reception escape from some bewilderment when, as Anne Barton notes, the play "demands a dazzling variety of response from its audience, a combination of detachment and involvement, sympathy and criticism, more exacting than is usual with Shakespeare" (Introduction to Riverside text 479).

Such torn response between detachment and empathy is especially appropriate in coming to terms with Troilus' speech. As Malcolm Evans has brilliantly shown, this speech on "the divided subject and sign," rehearsing a dual stagecraft, gropes towards "a recovery from the trance of mimesis in a simple statement of fact about acting" (*Signifying Nothing* 139–40). The gulf between the expectation of a reasonably represented world of characters and the shock of a different kind of theatrical experience crystallizes in the duplicity of the line, "This is, and is not, Cressid." Here, the imaginary product of representation (the role and female identity of Cressida) "is, and is not" continuous with the actual theatrical process (the work and the body of the boy actor who plays the part). At one remove from both the *platea*-like space inhabited by Thersites and the *locus* marked by tent and torch, Troilus is perfectly positioned to stimulate the audience simultaneously to view the performed and the performer. As spectators face the depth of the division on several levels of authority and representation, they (in Thersites' language) are not allowed to swagger themselves out of their own eyes (cf. 5.2.136).

As in the case of *Hamlet*, the extant textual versions of *Troilus and Cressida* are marked by an element of difference in the cultural register of their authorization. Taken together, these texts themselves illustrate the impact of a bifold authority that provides a potent nexus for diverse social, spatial, and semantic/semiotic figurations in the Elizabethan theatre. The quarto text of 1609, uniquely, occurs with two significantly different statements on the title pages. Midway through the printing of the original title version (QA), the title page was replaced by another one (QB), with substantial changes in its cultural and communicative alignments. While the much debated reasons for this change cannot even be summarized here, the former (QA) had underlined the theatrical association of the text: "As it was acted by the Kings Maiesties servants at the Globe." This was supplanted in QB by a reference to the matter of the plot: "Excellently expressing the beginning of their loves, with the conceited wooing of *Pandarus* Prince of Licia." QB also includes an epistle from a "never writer" addressing an "ever reader." In this remarkable Preface, the play-text is radically reauthorized, even isolated as precisely a *text*, "never stal'd with the Stage, never clapper-clawd with the palmes of the vulger." Even more revealing,

such dull and heavy-witted worldlings, as were never capable of the witte of a Commedie, comming by report of them to his representations, have found that witte there, that they never found in them-selves, and have parted better wittied then they came. (cit. Riverside 526)

The audience, apparently, that could not by themselves muster "the witte of a Commedie" could get that same wit from "representations," leaving open the question of whether these were in the form of a performed comedy or one that was consumed by an "ever reader." Plainly, the case is one of bifold authorization. Whatever the play's audience(s) were, its apparently problematic history on the public stage is, through appeal to the superior wit in writing, turned into a recommendation for the quarto to please judicious readers. Offering them a text free from "the smoaky breath of the multitude," the epistle as a matter of course appeals to their gentle "Iudgements." The "Famous" matter of worthiness that now is advertised on the title page appeals to the classical education of those that are styled "Eternall reader[s]." An ordinary theatre audience, dominated by "the palmes of the vulger" seems to have been unable to appreciate the "grace" of such "gravities." Cultural differentiation and social separation from "the multitude" lurk beneath the pronouncements of this Preface.

As the remarkable textual history of *Troilus and Cressida* suggests, bifold authority does not simply derive from the difference or dissociation *between* writing/reading and performing. Rather than positing any facile opposition or dichotomy between the two, we need to conceive of this cultural difference as affecting both "author's pen" and "actor's voice" respectively, as informing important textual as well as important performance practices from within. As for the latter, it is helpful to recall the different forms and functions of performance shared out between, say, Diomed and Thersites. Obviously, there were diverse types of histrionic delivery, and their interaction certainly helped to revitalize the fluidity of a stage that could house both localized and unlocalized types of theatrical space. Again, the one mode of performance conjoins with a represented locality (the "tent" in Diomed's case); the other with a more or less open, unlocalized place (in which Thersites could speak and watch without being heard or seen by the more strictly represented characters). This doubleness in the uses and the attributes of theatrical space presupposed and allowed for a contrariety in performance practice, wherewith it was possible for the material and the imaginary, body and representation, profoundly to interlock and engage one another. As Sir Philip Sidney had noted, such "contrarietie" derived from some staged incompatibility among "thinges moste disproportioned" (Sidney, *Prose Works* 3:40). In our text, the discrepancy was not primarily the one between true "delight" and "loud laughter" but, rather, the contrariety between the courtly, mellifluous voice of Diomed and the raucous, scabby body and organ of Thersites.

"Unworthy scaffold" for "so great an object" (*Henry V*)

In Shakespeare's prologue to the staging of *Henry V*, the gulf itself between the (written) story and the (performed) transaction is spelled out so as to be used quite deliberately. The gap between imaginary representation and the imperfect site of its staging constitutes the crucial space in which all the collaborative "ciphers to this great accompt" (1.0.17) meet a supreme challenge, and where spectators, too, are most in need of making their "imaginary forces work" (18). There is probably no other text in Shakespeare's *œuvre* that, in setting out the doubleness of the theatrical frame of reference, shows how deeply the business of *mise-en-scène* is implicated in it. The staging of *Henry V* is actually made to thrive on the use (and "abuse") of the threshold between the imaginary, represented product (the shown play) and the material process of bringing it about (that is, the playing of the play, the showing of the show).

Again, in *Henry V* the doubleness of an action, which is also a transaction, goes hand in hand with rendering a duplicity in meaning – here, a duplicity between what the play is about and what the Chorus says the play is about (Walch, "Tudor-Legende" 46). At this point, I must content myself with tracing the material as well as the poetic and ideological elements in the double order of Elizabethan staging. In his sustained concern with the gap between the world-in-the-play and playing-in-the-world of the Elizabethan theatre, the Prologue and Chorus to the play is obviously struck by a sense of disparity.

The Prologue begins in a tone of excessive modesty that, when looked at more closely, serves directly to underline both the depth and the use of this disparity. An apology is offered for

> The flat unraised spirits that hath dar'd
> On this unworthy scaffold to bring forth
> So great an object. Can this cockpit hold
> The vasty fields of France? Or may we cram
> Within this wooden O the very casques
> That did affright the air at Agincourt? (9–14)

Since the "imperfections" (23) of this "unworthy scaffold" are being emphasized in terms of their physical limitations right into the epilogue ("In little room confining mighty men" [3]), there is more to be said about the pronounced disparity than is usually assumed. What, ultimately, was at stake was a heightened awareness of the gaps and a concomitant need to forge links, between the narrative of history and the stage-as-stage. The Prologue's response to these issues comes close to offering a reassessment of the doubleness within this twofold frame of reference, and it does so from a point of view that realigns the difficult job of the actors with a positive appeal to cooperation on the part of the spectators.

At the same time, there is a sense of urgency in authorizing a purpose of playing that, in its doubleness, was confronted with a growing disparity among the constituent parts and affiliations of its traditional frame of reference. As the Chorus sets out, he asserts the greatness of his royal "object" and the authority of the playwright, fortified by recourse to a "Muse of fire" (1), to reach out from a mere platform and "ascend / The brightest heaven of invention" (1–2). Still, the theatre-poet's authority is inseparable from that of his institution: the "unworthy" stage itself is authorized to reject the learned unities so as to "digest / Th' abuse of distance; force a play" (2.0.31–32). The neo-Aristotelian unity of place in particular is broken up; the distance between "this cockpit" and "the vasty fields of France" is acknowledged. But for the "swelling scene" the same distance is both a challenge and a source of strength – provided it can stimulate a larger representation involving hitherto unknown and untried symbolizing, signifying, and "imaginary forces" (1.0.18). On the platform stage, these forces were at the heart of the representational process, as this stage, with the help of the spectators, localized or neutralized the space between the imagined *loci* of Southampton and France on the one hand, and, on the other, the awareness of a mere stage-as-stage inside "this wooden O."

Along these lines, the traditional complementarity of voice and pen is redefined in terms of a relationship that is made to bridge the gap, without forgetting the difference involved, between "this unworthy scaffold" and, to recall the printer's Preface to *Tamburlaine* (p. 59), the "worthiness of the matter itself." Somewhere in between these two, the Chorus, as Prologue and throughout the play, attempts to strike a continuing balance against what must have been a sense of increasing odds. Mediating between the representational needs and strains of a "great" historiographical subject matter and the spatially limited (and socially unsanctioned) institution of the common stage, the Chorus embraces both these disparate grounds of representation at the point where their conflicting claims are being negotiated. The Chorus as presenter is of course well suited to come to terms with this doubleness – especially after there was no Falstaff to do the job from within the story space. But in coming to terms with the gap between text and institution, the presentational stance of the Chorus is authorized as well as authorizing with an entirely new emphasis. There is the ravishing, even, in Andrew Gurr's phrase, "coercive" (*King Henry V*, Introduction 6) use of iambic language: the golden throatings of a "Muse of fire" seeking to captivate, entrance, and carry away the spectator. But then the eloquent presenter also achieves a fair degree of liberty to counterbalance the play in action. There is great partiality in the business of his (re)presentation; the Chorus is made to select from, re-emphasize, misread, even partially obliterate the text of the play.

The resulting discrepancy between what the play does and what the Chorus says it does is, as Günter Walch has shown ("Tudor-Legende," 40–42) blatant enough. The Prologue projects a war-like image of "sword and fire" (7) but the play does not contain one battle scene; the second Chorus invokes a stirring altruistic patriotism but a few lines later Pistol and Nym expect that "profits will accrue" (2.1.112) from the war; most irresistibly, the fourth Chorus forecasts the "praise and glory" (31) of Agincourt while the following scene presents us with conscientious objections to the price of "all those legs, and arms, and heads, chopp'd off" (4.1.135–36). Such discrepancies, to name only these, raise questions that vitally concern the relationship between textual "matter of worth" and "unworthy scaffold." It is clearly not sufficient to reduce these contradictions to the question of whether the Chorus faithfully reflects or indeed reinvents the play itself. But if, as an expositor, the Chorus is extremely unreliable, we need to confront the question of how and why the exposition itself is plagued by redundancies, irrelevancies, and a heavy dose of ideology. Nor can we at this late date account for the obvious gap between presentational efficacy and presentational 'untruthfulness' by renewed recourse to the doubt "that the choruses and the play were written by the same hand" (Warren Smith, "The *Henry V* Choruses" 57). The discrepancy remains and its perception has become more and more significant since recent criticism has convincingly rejected traditional premises on which "the actual purpose" of Prologue, choruses, and epilogue were believed, purely and simply, "to sound a patriotic note in exaltation of the heroic king," so as to "link the five acts together" (Law, "The Choruses in *Henry the Fifth*" 15).

Without wishing to minimize the sheer volume of patriotism in the Prologue's voice, I suggest there is a duality in the function of the Chorus himself. This function finds an equivalent in the play, especially in what Annabel Patterson has called "the play's unstable representational field" (56). Such instability begins with the playtext, especially when we take into consideration the large area of difference between the Folio and the Quarto versions of the play. By omitting the Prologue, chorus, and epi-logue, the Quarto eliminates the play's vulnerable self-(re)presentation of its thresholds as well as the idealizing voice of epic stylization – without, however, obliterating the humble, earthy language, including those parts of the play in which figures like Pistol or ordinary soldiers like Bates and Williams figure prominently. At the same time, the published text of the Quarto (between August 4 and 14, 1600), coming well after Essex had returned from Ireland in the autumn of 1599, must have been under some quite formidable pressure to pre-empt, at least as prophecy, the ambiva-lently anachronistic claim of the Chorus that "the general of our gracious Empress" was "from Ireland coming, / Bringing rebellion broached on his sword" (5.0.30; 31–32). Since, in these months, merely to praise Essex could result in imprisonment, it was, as Patterson has shown, "hardly surprising that the published quarto text of the play makes this interpreta-tion unreadable by erasing it" (53).

If, then, the textual history of the Prologue seems to indicate hidden tensions in the act of authorization itself, such tensions re-emerge between the art of the playwright and the presenter's all-too modest claims about it. In fact, the entire theatre's competence seems palpably impaired by an excessively humble, even apologetic, tone. But here again, we need to recall the element of unreliability in the Prologue's discourse, reflecting as it does a showmaster's staginess in address. There is a note of excessive modesty when the Chorus asks for "pardon" (1.0.8) on behalf of "The flat unraised spirits" (9), and continues to do so through the five acts. Although the task of writing and performing the intractable matter of pre-Tudor history must have been formidable, the apologetic note somehow rings false. But then, almost unnoticeably, the *topos* of humility gives way to a masterful account that confidently, in a revealing phrase, assures us of the unworthy scaffold's ability to "force a play." On platform stages where presentation has not entirely been absorbed by representation, forcefulness and veracity are liable to be at loggerheads. The need for getting the play across is what really matters. The job implicates the uses of physical space, in particular the spatial assimilation, in the performed play, of "distance." Again, the question is not how to truthfully or at least adequately represent a movement across the political geography of England and France; rather, what needs to be tackled and 'digested' is, I suggest, a forceful relationship between the representation of the (wide open) imaginary space in the story, the worthiness of a particular discourse, and the (severely limited) material space on a vulgar, culturally underestimated and quite vulnerable platform stage.

Here, then, was a challenging element of doubleness in the staging of the play, culminating in the difference between the demands and limits of the cultural occasion in "this cockpit" and what weightiness there is in the representation of "the vasty fields of France." Just as the play at large seeks to cope with this difference, so the task of the Chorus is to face it, to expound it and, thereby, exploit it, make the most of it. In order to do so, the presenter of the play as a matter of course is not himself 'lost' in the representation. In the stirring rhythm of his blank verse, the gap is addressed as a source of energy, as a site on which "imaginary forces" in the audience but also, I assume, among the performers, are unleashed beyond the discursive scope of Renaissance worthiness in a story of royal exploits and imperial projects.

Thus, the Prologue's treatment of the "distance" between, topographically and culturally, two different types of space serves as more than an apology for the all too obvious "imperfections" (23) of a bare stage. Between the two sites of representation (which, once more, accentuate (dis)continuity between the world-in-the-play and playing-in-the-world of late Elizabethan London) the "distance" is positively used but it is also, as the Prologue has it, 'abused.' The theatre's project is to "digest / Th' abuse of distance; force a play." For the second chorus to use a culinary metaphor and, no less telling, to refer to the production as a 'force'-ful process is to acknowledge the pragmatic, even the pleasurable freedom to reject Sidney's neoclassical postulate that "the Stage should alway represent but one place" (*Prose Works* 3:38). More important still, the authority associated with the dominant Renaissance poetics is toppled in favor of a forceful acknowledgement of a gap between what is represented and what is doing the representing. If anything, this new, pragmatic authority draws (un)common strength from what abusive contrariety can be found or elicited in the Liberties of London. This, then, is the powerful connotation of "force a play": it is to turn the "distance" into an extension of energy, a site where "imaginary *forces*" can be stimulated, where – onstage as well as off-stage – "imaginary puissance" (1.0.25) reigns supreme.

Once the authority of neoclassical poetics was dislodged (or 'abused'), a "swelling" proliferation of forceful signs and potent meanings could hold sway. Hence, the Chorus appealed to a sense of "motion of no less celerity / Than that of thought" (3.0.2–3): "Imaginary puissance" was to come "with winged heels" from "here and there, jumping o'er times" (1.0.29). Such expansive thrust of signification conjoined the written text with the exigencies of performance itself, bridging the cultural and physical gap between the eloquent representation of distant places and a mere scaffold. And yet "this unworthy scaffold" was one on which a matter of past "worthiness" now had to be performed in the presence of socially mixed audiences. What better way to map out the difference between stately matter and common occasion than on a plane marked by both "distance" in regard to space and velocity in regard to time. To "force a play," then, was to make compatible the twofold momentum of "distance" and "motion"; it was, on the platform stage to mobilize the kinetic energies of performers and the swift vision of spectators through what "puissance" was to come "with winged heels."

To appropriate the stately matter via the "imperfections" of the scaffold stage was not to homogenize the two or reduce them to one level. Far from erasing the difference in question, the use of "digest" echoed with its root, Latin *digerere* (to carry asunder, separate, divide, distribute, dissolve), while even the culinary metaphor ("digest" in the sense of "To prepare [. . .] for assimilation by the system" – *OED*, under 1 and 4) emphasized the notion that something had to be absorbed by converting matter (or *food* for thought) into a different sort of (nourishing) substance. To understand the full thrust of "digest" here, in conjunction with the uses of "distance," required an awareness of disparity; what was presupposed was the absence of identity between two locations or positions, and the need for assimilating the one to the other. It was of course paramount to have "the scene . . . transported" (2.0.34–35) from the Globe in London to distant places in the story; but, parallel to that, it was equally important, "with no less celerity," for players and spectators to traverse the intricate field between present actors and their absent dramatic identities. Such agility would have been impossible without a deliberate doubleness in *mise-en-scène*, the bifold capacity of Shakespeare's theatre to bring together and "to carry asunder," to project and "dissolve" the scene, to associate and to "separate" theatrical signs and their meanings, in a word, to digest both the use and "abuse" of distance.

The suggestion is that the "unworthy scaffold" harbored a highly complex scene that did not provide a unified space for representation. Accordingly, the Prologue must be seen as a singular and quite extraordinary attempt to redefine and master the element of doubleness in the location of time, place, and authority in the Shakespearean theatre. To grapple with "so great a project" on an "unworthy scaffold," to relate both sides through their difference and still to coordinate them, required an unprecedented density of symbolizing and signifying practices. To abuse the neoclassical postulate, and digest the unsanctioned space for difference that marked diverse types of "distance" was not an easy matter, when an underlying disparity had to be 'swallowed' and absorbed between here and there, between now and then, between players and their roles. The attempt to meet this task demanded what in a different context Bernard Beckerman called "a new theatrical endeavor" (*Shakespeare at the Globe* xi).[13] Whatever else the Prologue stood for, he articulated a new awareness of the needs and constraints of representation on a 'scene (in)dividable.'

What, finally, is most noteworthy in the Prologue's articulation is that, in view of an unprecedented acknowledgement of the Elizabethan theatre's own, unique authority, the discourse of imperial historiography appears so devastatingly triumphant. Kempe has left the company; Falstaff's version of "honour" is absent from the fields of France, and the self-resembled uses of theatrical place are substantially reduced. Residual functions of the *platea*-dimension are either minimized or reappropriated with a view to stimulating the celebration of national unity and popular royalty. There is a fanfare note in the trumpet of the Chorus, as in the iambic language that opens Act 2: "Now all the youth of England are on fire, / [. . .] and honor's thought / Reigns solely in the breast of every man" (2.0.1–4). And yet, in the most stirring speech of them all, when the Chorus in Act 4 articulates the patriotic fervor of "brothers, friends, and countrymen" (34), the tensions between the "true" story of Agincourt and "this unworthy scaffold" remain quite unresolved and unexpectedly culminate in these lines:

> And so our scene must to the battle fly;
> Where – O for pity! – we shall much disgrace
> With four or five most vile and ragged foils
> (Right ill-dispos'd, in brawl ridiculous)
> The name of Agincourt. Yet sit and see,
> Minding true things by what their mock'ries be. (4.0.48–53)

At this crucial moment, the reiterated, seemingly uncalled-for reference to theatrical circumstances serves as a welcome vehicle of *platea* awareness, counterpointing the jubilant memories of "Agincourt" with an unambiguous sense of self-resembled place and property in the Elizabethan public playhouse. The Chorus, at the height of his powers, serves as a down-to-earth reminder of a make-shift mode of theatrical representation. The ferocious weapons of victory are transcribed into "four or five most vile and ragged foils"; the glorious battle itself becomes a "brawl ridiculous."

This, indeed, is a peculiar way to "digest / Th'abuse of distance." Signifying the signs of the signs of glory can indeed "disgrace" the discourse of history through the "incontinent rule" (Mullaney, *Place of the Stage* 49) of unsanctioned interpretation, especially when a socially mixed and somewhat licentious audience is, in no uncertain terms, urged to assist. At this point, the "imaginary forces" of "mean and gentle all" become an unpredictable element in the production of theatrical meaning. To tell such a varied audience, "'tis your thoughts that now must deck our kings" (1.0.28) is, to say the least, to expand the margin of indeterminacy in interpretation and to express considerable confidence in, even to bestow authority on, the signifying capacities of ordinary people. Rarely on the Elizabethan stage, with the possible exception of the ending of *King Lear*, do we have the audience acknowledged as 'so great' an authority. Here, spectators, in alliance with the actors' playing of "our kings," are authorized in no uncertain terms as agents in the production of meaning.

As we read again, then, the opening lines of the Prologue, the humble apology for "this unworthy scaffold" seems strangely at odds with the stirring confidence in the dramatic powers of "invention" to serve and inspire the play's opening:

> O for a Muse of fire, that would ascend
> The brightest heaven of invention!
> A kingdom for a stage, princes to act,
> And monarchs to behold the swelling scene!
> Then should the warlike Harry, like himself,
> Assume the port of Mars, and at his heels
> (Leash'd in, like hounds) should famine, sword, and fire
> Crouch for employment. (1–8)

To appropriate "A kingdom for a stage" with the help of imaginative "invention" seems a task competently handled by the Prologue. Such a stage, assimilating, absorbing, authorizing "princes to act" can, without much fuss, locate a "kingdom" in the strictly delimited, unassuming space of a scaffold stage. Rather than reinforcing the traditional interrelation between *locus* and *platea*, the positioning of royalty on common stages collapses, to a degree, the difference between elevated, self-contained locality and open platform space. It is one way of securing the expansive force of localizing and visualizing the stage in the interaction of its differing sites and effects. Such force informs "the swelling scene," that is, the enlargement from within, borne out by the unfixed, performative thrust of drama in production. It is a "scene" with the capacity for both 'crescendo' and 'decrescendo' of locale, involving constant motion, growth in force and volume from within a motion that resembles waves, in ebb and flow, bringing forth and dissolving a local habitation and a name. Again, such expansive use of theatrical space is inseparable from a cultural semiotics marked by a new kind of "trafficke" and contingency, an exorbitant kinetic energy in relations of signifiers and signifieds – in short, the movable, audible, visible extension in the use of signs, symbols, and localities in rapid succession and interaction.

Thus, the space of kingdoms and the title of a prince can freely be appropriated on the scaffold stage. All this while the self-representation of the theatre in the language of the chorus cannot itself be dissociated from an unfixing, swelling quality in the very relations of text and institution. In mediating between the two, the Chorus fulfills a dramatic role which is not that of either "author's pen" or "actor's voice." Rather, there is duplicity in his own treatment of doubleness. His thickly performed account of interactions between the "rough and all-unable pen" and the uses of "the swelling scene" is strangely untrustworthy. It is one thing modestly to avow the difficulties of absorbing, in writing, the vastness of the canvas represented. But it is an entirely different matter, especially in view of "those that have not read the story," to so use the topos of humility. For one thing, the Prologue's double-dealing language was perfectly appropriate to authorize, even to apologize for, the alleged "imperfections" of historical representations on the scaffold stage. But then the question needs to be asked, was it because these "imperfections" are established so emphatically, that the audience should feel compelled to supply those "thoughts that now must deck our kings"?

4   Playing with a difference

Elizabethan *mise-en-scène*, inflecting the interface of "author's pen" and "actor's voice," could freely draw on an element of doubleness in the wide frame of its reference and function. Both written text and performance practice provided certain pre-established patterns for staging that, on a "scene individable," involved not simply an assimilation of the disparity among these agencies of cultural production; in the process, this disparity could be turned to good account in a hybrid practice of staging that, for its reference and function, encompassed both standards of Renaissance rhetoric and poetics *and* a continuously viable tradition of common playing, jesting, and display.

In order to explore the theatrical uses of this doubleness further, I propose to introduce two Elizabethan terms, 'contrariety' and 'disfigurement' with which to specify the resulting purposes and effects of playing. The former, as suggested in the Introduction, is taken to connote not simply the existence on sixteenth-century stages of cultural disparity, but the ways and means by which this disparity could stimulate some "contrary" impulse to playing, a "contrarious" impetus in the production and reception of stage plays. While such 'contrariety' derives from a dramatically assimilated clash of two cultural patterns in staging and performing the play, 'disfigurement' more specifically points to certain sites of parody or resistance to Renaissance rhetoric, form, and proportion. On these sites, the high Renaissance poetics of representation, the entire postulate of 'modesty,' 'discretion,' and 'nature' in the neo-Aristotelian mirror of what 'should be,' is challenged, burlesqued, or reduced to something disproportionate and formless.

Both contrariety and disfigurement drew on age-old, disenchanting forms of a mimesis that either preceded or at least partially precluded representation. They contained residual elements of a "deformed discourse" that negated "the ontological status of 'copy'" while allowing for "contrarieties and opposites" to be "joined and mixed" (D. Williams, *Deformed Discourse* 79, 85).[1] In the Elizabethan context, the impelling force was performative; it was inspired by common practices of playing that were quite remote from humanist doctrine or learning. As Sidney noted, on these public stages "we have nothing but scurrillitie unworthie of anie chaste eares, or some extreame showe of doltishness"; "our Comedients" conflate discrete "delight" with indiscrete "laughter" to an effect such as "almost ever commeth of thinges moste disproportionate to our selves, and nature" (3:40). For Sidney, the resulting "contrarietie" clearly was inseparable from a "disproportionate" relation of the mirror to "nature." These "Comedients" played havoc with the laws of just proportion; not heeding what should be, they flatly rejected the standards of Renaissance decorum and worthiness in representation. Such absence of proportion, form, and modesty could, if the "contrarietie" between worthy matter and performed image was willfully used, inspire all sorts and conditions of disfigurement.

However, in studying the absence of important postulates of humanistic doctrine in the Elizabethan theatre, we need to confront a complication that Sidney's learned pen either could not fully anticipate or deigned to acknowledge only in passing. The difference between the worthy discourse of Renaissance form and figuration and its execrable treatment on common stages was, although vitally indebted to certain types of performance practice, not reducible to archaic or purely histrionic propensities of common players. Rather, what was historically and epistemologically[2] a performance impulse was absorbed, perhaps one may say *indecorously refined*, by dramatic compositions for public stages. Here Sidney briefly hints at "our Tragedie writers" and their complicity in "observing rules neither of honest civilitie, nor skilfull *Poetrie*" (*Prose Works* 3:38–39). In other words, in the teeth of humanistic disapproval, part of the cultural difference between high Renaissance form and matter and the frivolous disregard for what should be was inscribed in dramatic texts themselves. In the 1590s, contrariety, far from being obliterated, advanced to an important article in the unformulated poetics[3] and, of course, dramaturgy of the popular Renaissance theatre. Thus, elements of cultural difference between Renaissance writing and common playing could positively be absorbed in major play texts. For more than two decades, it was possible to 'play out' this difference or, as I suggest in the present chapter's heading, to play *with* it in both writing and performing in the Elizabethan playhouse.

To "disfigure, or to present" (*A Midsummer Night's Dream*)

Let us begin to study performance-inspired uses of disfigurement by recalling the presentational impetus in Elizabethan playing as it almost certainly informed the "fond and frivolous jestures" in *Tamburlaine.* These "jestures" – to use the printer's phrase – were considered "digressing" and "far unmeet for the matter"; they appealed to spectators not exclusively from within but also from without the play's inscribed representational frame of reference. Besides, the products of "rhyming mother-wits" were more and more considered inappropriate wherever, in Richard Helgerson's phrase, a barbarous "taint of inferiority" was not entirely "removed from rhyme in the face of its undoubted medieval origin" ("Barbarous Tongues" 284).[4]

Even more important, deformity in Elizabethan culture contradicted dominant notions of form and decorum; disfigurement jarred on the concern in high Renaissance art with self-contained, well-balanced, and, in Heinrich Wölfflin's phrase, symmetrical form. If we understand Renaissance form, in Thomas McAlindon's words, as the search for "the apt relationship of substance and shape, of thought and expression" and add to this understanding an assumed "connection between form and duty" (*Shakespeare and Decorum* 45), then any radically unrelenting deformation must have inflicted smarting wounds on the moral as well as the aesthetic idea of the proper and the fitting. Deformity, rather than form, *dis*figurement rather than pure figuration was what these practices excelled at.

While in Shakespeare's plays the "fond and frivolous jestures" are confined to no more than a residual element (as the First Quarto Hamlet "blabbering with his lips"), the assimilation of "graced deformities" is an entirely different matter. *A Midsummer Night's Dream* in particular presents us with a burlesque version of presentational performance, one that, in resistance to its good-humored ridicule, does not submit to either the use of rhetoric and decorum or to any modest, discreet, natural, let alone illusionistic, uses of impersonation.

> *Quin.* [. . .] But there is two hard things: that is, to bring the moonlight into a chamber; for you know, Pyramus and Thisby meet by moonlight.
> *Snout.* Doth the moon shine that night we play our play?
> *Bot.* A calendar, a calendar! Look in the almanac. Find out moonshine, find out moonshine.
> *Quin.* Yes; it doth shine that night.
> [*Bot.*] Why then may you leave a casement of the great chamber window (where we play) open; and the moon may shine in at the casement.
> *Quin.* Ay; or else one must come in with a bush of thorns and a lantern, and say he comes to disfigure, or to present, the person of Moonshine. (3.1.47–61)

The phrase that is most revealing is Quince's notion of "one" who must "come in" and "say he comes to disfigure, or to present, the person of Moonshine." What this richly loaded parody conveys in one sentence is so much more than a correspondence, let alone an equation, between disfigurement and presentation. Revealingly, it is not "Moonshine" that is (re)presented but "the person of Moonshine"; it is, then, not 'moonshine' that is to be 'disfigured,' but "the person," the player's image that brings 'moonshine' on stage with the help of "a bush of thorns and a lantern." What is at issue is the depth of the gap that, unquestioningly, is taken for granted between what is to be represented and what and who is doing the (re)presenting.

The same unformulated poetics is at work when Snug the joiner is to do the lion. Note how Bottom, condescendingly but also encouragingly, provides directorial instruction.

> *Bot.* [. . .] If you think I come hither as a lion, it were pity of my life. No! I am
> no such thing; I am a man as other men are"; and there indeed let him
> name his name, and tell them plainly he is Snug the joiner. (42–46)

Rather than figuring forth the lion or the moonshine, the player presents the gulf between the imagined form of the lion or the moon and its visible figuration. In other words, the representation itself (and, incidentally, he who presents it) is disfigured. It is a perfect case of 'deformity' or deformation, when what we have between the form of the moon and its presentation is a fond gap inhabited by a player presenting himself in the act of disfiguring the object of representation.

At this point, Bottom is unrelenting when it comes to preventing the presenter from being lost in the representation. Clearly, these humble folk have pride in their identity when their craft – be it acting, joining or weaving – is at stake: "indeed let him name his name, and tell them plainly he is Snug the joiner." Although of course the rationale provided is just laughable, there is more than just ignorance and humility at play when the sturdiest of the players in no uncertain terms answers back from within the dramatic representation itself:

> *Pyr.* [. . .] O wicked wall, through whom I see no bliss!
>   Curs'd be thy stones for thus deceiving me!
> *The.* The wall methinks, being sensible, should curse again.
> *Pyr.* No, in truth, sir, he should not. "Deceiving me" is Thisby's cue. She is to
>   enter now, and I am to spy her through the wall. You shall see it will fall
>   pat as I told you. Yonder she comes. (5.1.180–87)

While the irony is of course lost on Bottom, he does – on the level of dramaturgy – provide us with a perfect example of what contrariety such playing with a difference may altogether bring forth. If, on this level, we may twist the meaning of Demetrius' interjection somewhat ("It is the wittiest partition that ever I heard discourse" [166–67]), the same 'partition' makes Bottom's response 'contrarious': the shape of Pyramus, the imaginary representation of a character, is easily sloughed off when the leading player, in his concern with the staging of the play, feels called upon to assert the needs and rights of the show. In the teeth of the ironic treatment of the partition between the form of a representation and what 'deformation' (and loss of decorum) his sturdy intervention amounts to, Bottom asserts an authority of his own – one that is of the craft of the player and the maker.

Again, what Bottom and the players blithely ignore is the most hallowed demand in the Renaissance poetics of representation, to narrow, if possible to eliminate, the gap between the object and the agency of representation, between the imaginary world in the representation and the material tools and means of rendering it. In their understanding, there is no Marlovian "glass," no "mirror" in which the image absorbs the image-maker. The rupture between the presented and the presenter is fundamental – or so it seems – to what purpose the disfigurement serves. As Bottom says, neatly underlining this peculiar type of doubleness in his role-playing, "I Pyramus am not Pyramus, but Bottom the weaver" (20–21). Theatre and what it represents, the unworthy scaffold stage and its "matter of worth," are categorically as well as culturally different. And yet, that is perhaps less than the entire story in this play.

In the burlesque assimilation of 'home-spun' playing to a grander occasion in *A Midsummer Night's Dream*, it is not an easy matter to establish the full range and tenor of the parody (and the unformulated poetics on either side of the parody) involved. The parody no doubt hints at a recurring connection between non-humanist uses of disfigurement and a presentational mode of performance that indeed (and necessarily) is "digressing" from the matter in foregrounding the presenter in his social, cultural, and corporeal identity. Even when hidden deep down in the conscience and body of the player, some such existential bearings go as alien, refractory energy into the presentation. What the playing within the play vividly suggests is that the act, the effort, the result of presentation is vindicated in and through its difference from what image, picture, or *re*presentation is to result. Partially at least, the difference in question is, ineluctably, that between the worthiness of the product and the unworthy process of bringing it about. Elizabethan performance was potentially inseparable from playing with this ineffable difference – ineffable, at least before Shakespeare addressed it in the form of the gap between "this unworthy scaffold" and "So great an object" (*Henry V* 1.0.10–11) of representation.

However, it is one thing to say that 'disfigurement' as a calculated effect of doubleness thrived on the deformation of certain forms and images of representation. It is an entirely different matter to put forward the claim (which, I suggest, is questionable) that the resulting "partition" between, say, the image of the "wall" and the practice of performing it, is absolute, like a rupture. For one thing, *A Midsummer Night's Dream* makes it perfectly plain that the craftsmen, even as they fail to cope with the rules of a Renaissance version of mimesis, do not seek to dispense with the mimetic impulse altogether. On the contrary, the desire to render through perform-ance is their strongest impulse and heaviest burden, especially where the object (say, a lion or a wall) defies representation on stage or where (alternatively) the image of character and action tends to obscure the act of presentation, or the actor behind it, and what work, what skill, what spell went with it. Nor are they content to accept the real thing when it comes to rendering moonshine or, no less impossibly, a wall ("You can never bring in a wall" [3.1.65]).

If these players do accept a version of mimesis that figures and, necessar-ily, disfigures things through the agents of their performance, they also and quite willingly submit to the need of performing through and with a text. As they are interacting with a written text, the relationship to this text approximates the way they, stumblingly, appropriate the imaginary world of the play.

> *Flu.* "Most radiant Pyramus, most lily-white of hue, [. . .]
> As true as truest horse, that yet would never tire,
> I'll meet thee, Pyramus, at Ninny's tomb."
> *Quin.* "Ninus' tomb," man. Why, you must not speak that yet. That you answer to Pyramus. You speak all your part at once, cues and all. Pyramus, enter. Your cue is past; it is "never tire." (3.1.93; 96–101)

What Flute naively misconceives is the most fundamental convention of dramatic representation, the dialogic form of verbal action on stage. For him, to "speak all your part at once, cues and all" is to use language narratively, perhaps on the implied strength of his assumed ties to an oral story-telling culture.

In Shakespeare's theatre, such uses of deformity must not be reduced to a good-humored recollection of sixteenth-century amateur acting, even when Bottom's company does of course invoke certain attributes of, precisely, the dim-witted work of laymen. But as soon as we glance at some of the mid or late Tudor professional plays, Hamlet's warning to avoid a performance practice that "out-Herods Herod" (3.2.14) may well be seen to address more than, simply, the theatrically most overcharged figuration in the cycle plays. Was it perhaps that next to the sheer delivery of a performative overbid, the 'strutting' and 'bellowing,' even the tearing of "a passion to totters, to very rags" (3.2.9–10) aimed at something more complex than the effusive manner of uneducated amateurs? As medieval performances of Herod and Pilate suggest, there was a repeated and quite deliberate attempt to overdo the horror and the fury ("My wytt away rafys [. . .] My guttys will outt thryng" or "all for wrath see how I sweat"[5]). Not unlikely, memories of ritual ranting were used to turn a terrifying threat into a grotesque, perhaps burlesque, medley of terror and laughter. We do not know, of course, whether in Hamlet's advice not to 'out-herod Herod,' there continued to resonate some misgivings about Elizabethan echoes of the horrific-comic effect; however, in a mid-Elizabethan comic context distinct traces of such deformation survived. As Ambidexter in *King Cambises* (published 1569) has it, "Some weepes, some wailes – and some make great sport" (733). The early stage direction then reads "*Weep.*"

> O my hart! how my pulses doo beate,
> With sorrowfull lamentations I am in such a heate!
> Ah, my hart, how for him it doth sorrow! [*He begins to laugh.*]
> Nay, I have done, in faith, now. And God give ye good morrow!
> Ha, ha! Weep? Nay, laugh, with both hands to play! (740–44)[6]

Here we have, between the representation of overcharged sorrow and the presentation of its laughable delivery, contrariety in action. Such playing with a difference culminates in a duplicity that effects a deforming purpose of playing clearly marked by bathos. This grotesque mode of presenting *and* deforming "sorrowfull lamentations" ensues after Smirdis, brother of the king, lies murdered in his blood ("A little bladder of vineger prickt" [S.D. 729/30]). The bathos is that of the leading player, double-dealer *par excellence*, whose oversized "lamentations" characterize what exuberance elsewhere in the same play emanates from a "deformed slave" (182) – who is of course the company's leading actor. As such he is the agent of a 'surplus' or overbid of performative action.

Despite Hamlet's remonstrances to the contrary, such duplicitous uses of contrariety must have continued well into the seventeenth century. As far as we can judge the effect of disfigurement by the polemical foil that later Puritans like William Prynne or Commonwealth academic writers like John Webster present, there must have been plenty of "ridiculous, and vicious" deformity in certain "historical personations," whereby "stage-players" continued to indulge in "scoffing and jeering, humming and hissing" (Webster, *Academiarum Examen*, 92).[7] Or, to take William Prynne in his *Histrio-Mastix*, that late ferocious *summa* of Puritan attacks on the stage, "filthy speeches, unaturall and unseemely gestures" remained an object of attack. Relating the "unnaturall" overcharge in the player's "gesture" to the latter's histrionic self, Prynne asks the question, "may we not say, by how much the more he exceedes in his gesture, he delights himselfe in his part?" (138–39). It is the *excessive*, the eccentric thrust in corporeal movement that most contrariously and, of course, visibly plays with what is different from the Renaissance regime of holding the mirror up to nature.

Although very much unlike anything we have in *King Cambises*, Shake-speare's treatment of the mechanicals in *A Midsummer Night's Dream* is such that they only marginally seek to reproduce, as in a "glass," imaginary places, events, and objects. Although their positive lack of interest in any self-sufficient representation is, in Shakespeare's text, rationalized by the unproven apprehension that "the ladies cannot abide" (11–12) or will "be afeard" (27) if anything frightening is shown in life-like fashion, the theatrical treatment of disfigurement tells a much more complex story which, in the play, is not delimited by the peculiar dramaturgy of *Pyramus and Thisbe*.

Even in Shakespeare's comedy, the element of "fond and frivolous" deformity is, on a wider plane, linked to a doubleness in the purpose of playing that – rich in *double entendre* – has a disfiguring effect on both words and bodies. On a verbal level, deformation is at work, most importantly perhaps, in the Prologue to the play within the play.

> *Pro.* If we offend, it is with our good will.
>   That you should think, we come not to offend,
>   But with good will. To show our simple skill,
>   That is the true beginning of our end.
>   Consider then, we come but in despite.
>   We do not come, as minding to content you,
>   Our true intent is. All for your delight
>   We are not here. That you should here repent you,
>   The actors are at hand; and, by their show,
>   You shall know all, that you are like to know. (5.1.108–17)

The Prologue – a feast of "graced deformities" – serves the liminal occasion of a welcoming audience address. Speaking on the threshold of the play within the play, Quince mutilates both the syntax of what he has to say and, with it, his meaning. To characterize the structure and effect of Quince's offering, it is not sufficient to recall Theseus' witty quibble, "This fellow doth not stand upon points" (118). Although of course the strategic purpose of the Prologue is to convey a bewildering degree of ignorance and innocence behind these homespun exercises, the more revealing focus is on displaying – as in the case of Flute's indiscriminate role-reading – a broken mirror of dramatic texts. But then the achieved level of disfigurement is such that Quince's speech sounds "like a tangled chain; nothing impair'd, but all disorder'd" (125–26). If we read Elizabethan 'tangle' (*OED*, under 3 and 4) in its present meaning, as I believe we may, the verb denotes the act of bringing together into a mass of "confusedly interlaced or intertwisted strands"; to entrap or involve in something that "hampers, obstructs, or overgrows" (Webster, *Univ. Dictionary*). To bring together something strangely unimpaired and yet disordered seems to recall the confusedly intertwisted use of "order" in Jack Cade's battle-cry, "then are we in order when we are most out of order" (2 *Henry VI* 4.2.189–90). For Quince to say, "All for your delight / We are not here" is the more harmless version of a hidden, topsy-turvying truth: The craftsmen readily offering "concord of this discord" (5.1.60), *present themselves*, and unmistakably so, rather than submitting to what, in their representation, might have been more representative of the courtly occasion.

Disfiguring the language, in particular the difficult, outlandish word, is a recurring feature among Shakespeare's clownish speakers. Dogberry excels himself when, significantly, his verbal deformations coincide with a pagan figure of inversion, as in his "O villain! thou wilt be condemn'd into everlasting redemption for this" (*Much Ado about Nothing* 4.2.56–57). David Wiles reminds us that Dogberry even in his stage denotations is not a stable character at all: denoted as 'Kemp,' but also as 'Keeper,' as 'Andrew' and of course as 'Constable' (Wiles, *Shakespeare's Clown* 75). Not unlike Dogberry, Quince so tortures the language of his Prologue that not fortuitously (but apparently despite himself) a rare truth about at least one major purpose of presentation is positively conveyed. "To show our simple skill" is, indeed, one of the ends of all kinds of performance, especially of those forms which, like dancing, singing, tumbling, fencing, and so forth, culminate in a display of the performer's competence.

For good reason, there is scarcely any other Shakespearean play whose "imaginary puissance" so thrives on a mode of disfigurement as the comedy that celebrates "anticke fables" (to cite the spelling of Q2 and F), "fairy toys" and "such shaping fantasies" (5.1.3; 5) as are contiguous with the deformation of actors' bodies in their role-playing. In particular, it is Bottom himself, the inspiring genius in the presentation of the amateurs' "skill," that embodies the power of disfigurement. Having verbally tangled "the flowers of odious savors sweet" (3.1.82), he is himself disfigured; his head is grotesquely transformed into that of an ass. Kempe, presumably the agile, strong performer behind the role, is 'translated' into something "monstrous" and "strange" (104). Such metamorphosis, allowing for "a most rare vision" (4.1.204–05), clearly exceeds the poetic parameters of 'imitating humanity.' In his speech concluding Act 4, scene 1, when his fellows have "stol'n hence" (204), he, alone on stage, tells the audience of his dream and how this dream surpasses "the wit of man to say what dream it was. Man is but an ass, if he go about [t'] expound this dream" (205–07). The dream transcends the poetics of "glass" or "mirror"; it is not primarily in aid of the representation or identification of Bottom's character as far as that, in Cicero's phrase, serves *imitatio vitae*.

Bottom's dream-like transformation into a "graced" deformity is of course part of a larger context in which Shakespeare's "most nearly ritualistic play" (Cope, *The Theater and The Dream* 219) both indiscreetly unfolds, and discreetly precludes, disfigurement. Bottom, even as he abominably inverts the perception of the senses ("eye," "ear," "hand," "tongue" [211–13]), is not the only begetter of his dream. His disfigured body implicates Oberon's intervention and the practical magic of one who by definition is strangely shaped. Says Puck,

> Sometime a horse I'll be, sometime a hound,
> A hog, a headless bear, sometime a fire,
> And neigh, and bark, and grunt, and roar, and burn,
> Like horse, hound, hog, bear, fire, at every turn. (3.1.108–11)

While Shakespeare here poetically transmutes a kind of disfigurement, arguably deriving from a late ritual capacity for theriomorphic transformations, he does not elsewhere in the play go as far as the mainstream of folklore had gone. In contrast to the latter, the dramatist decidedly refuses to treat "the fairy changeling as a threatening deformity in human society" (Latham 183).[8]

To "descant" on difference and deformity (*Richard III*)

As we look beyond *A Midsummer Night's Dream* to various uses of theatrical presentation and disfigurement, there is little doubt that the Globe playwright, unlike Marlowe, deliberately and with sustained effect assimilates in his plays what the printer of *Tamburlaine* dismissed as "graced deformities." Even in delimiting and further integrating the range and frequency of these modes of performance, Shakespeare continues to inscribe them in major scenes in his plays. Such adaptation usually results in some spectacular effect, where the distancing, or setting apart, of represented roles is conjoined with foregrounding the theatre's own sense of its presentational strength and vitality. Rather than exploiting the display effect *per se*, the Shakespearean theatre makes it intensely interactive with newly absorbing modes of impersonation. In most of these cases, where performance continues to excel at playing with a difference, that difference itself is also and simultaneously transmuted into characterization, that is, into the character's apartness, isolation, or simply an uncommon degree of social, moral, physical, spatial or ethnic difference (as in Richard Gloucester, Iago, Edmund, the Witches, Autolycus, Caliban, and Aaron) from the rest of the *dramatis personae*.

To explore this conjuncture of doubleness in the purpose of playing, I propose to look at several plays, but especially at *Richard III*. In this history play, the "graced deformities" in a Renaissance figure of nobility are particularly striking when they are conveyed presentationally and, at the same time, as a "misshapen" (1.2.250) character's sense of isolation. Gloucester, Duke of York, is different from other noble protagonists that fight, murder, die or simply live through the Wars of the Roses. In 3 *Henry VI* he appears, in King Henry's words, as "an indigested and deformed lump" (5.6.51) who, as Clifford says, is "As crooked in thy manners as thy shape" (*2 Henry VI* 5.1.158). What in Lady Anne's eyes will appear as a "lump of foul deformity" (*Richard III* 1.2.57) is, as he presents himself, a "Deform'd, unfinish'd" body that was "sent" into the world "before my time" (1.1.20). Even more significant in our context, Gloucester's disfigurement in shape and "manners" achieves its prominence against the foil of a Renaissance court, a world marked by "delightful measures," the harmony of "merry meetings" and the "lute." Being "Curtail'd of this fair proportion" (1.1.18), the protagonist knows how untimely, how inappropriate, how indecorous his deformity is *vis-à-vis* the "glorious summer" of victory and peaceful celebration of the house of York. This "foul deformity" (1.2.57) jars with, and profoundly disturbs the "fair proportion" of Renaissance form.

This is a villain-hero with a theatrical difference, one whose strength on stage, strangely, is inseparable from a performer's competence to "disfigure, or to present" the image of a noble Duke on common stages. At the same time, the deformity is one of character; it is used to motivate his apartness. On both levels, the disfigured body is conceived not so much as a hideous exception to well-proportioned nature but, rather, as an article, or even artifact, that on its way towards human perfection was left "unfinished" by its maker. The figure is "indigested," "misshap'd" or simply *not shaped* according to the rules of neo-Aristotelian mimesis, "scarce half made up" by the standards of high Renaissance form, perfection, and "proportion." There is a sense that Gloucester, in falling short of what a noble protagonist *should be*, is "rudely stamp'd" (1.1.16), and deliberately so, in the poetics of his dramatic composition and the dramaturgy of his theatrical transaction.

To a remarkable extent, Gloucester's sense of being "curtail'd," "cheated" (1.1.19) and deprived of a proper shape anticipates the recurring attributes of dispossession, bastardy, and apartness as shared by Faulconbridge, Iago, and Edmund. Although perfectly exempt from any signs of physical disfigurement, the dramatic representation of these artificial persons reveals how the unsanctioned world of the underprivileged and indecorous, always already "unmeet for the matter" of worthiness, can actually be made integral to it. The question was how to traverse the distance, proscribed by neoclassical authority, between form and deformation, between worthy "matter" and "graced deformities." In the Earl of Gloucester's words, contained in both versions of *King Lear*, there obtained a strange contrariety, a discourse marked by "Matter and impertinency mix'd" (4.6.174). For the more inclusive design of the Globe playwright, no preordained opposition between "reason" and "madness," seriousness and frivolity, form and deformity, was acceptable. If we comprehend the use of 'madness' as a specific mode of mental 'deformity,' we have for some of Shakespeare's greatest characters a demanding type of performance practice that excels at playing with the difference between the closure of representation and the aperture of its transaction.

It is largely in rebellion against this binary scheme of things that Shakespeare evokes the memory of a traditional figuration of deformity that, in pre-Elizabethan drama, was apt to moralize two meanings in one word, one gesture, one action. The figure called Vice in the moral play had, to a certain extent, defied the binary opposition of good and evil by deeply tingeing the latter with frolicsome fare and boisterous *bonhomie*. Such doubleness was inscribed in Courage who, in *The Tide Tarrieth No Man*, himself defines what identity he has as "contrarious" (Wapull, *Tide Tarrieth* 94). These were dramatic personae who, in their startlingly deliberate use of doubleness, could turn the latter into a sustained form of contrariety, one teeming with the kinetic energies of performance – the scheming, cunning, inversionary *élan* of theatricality, the unbound spirit of moral indifference and ideological negation.

In adapting these supreme creatures of doubleness, Shakespeare in *Richard III* unfolds an ambidextrous design from within the text of the representation itself. For such discursive practice there is no precedent to be found in the sources, either in the chronicles or in Thomas More's portrayal of the ferocious, "ill fetured," "crok backed" witty tyrant (More, *History of King Richard III* 7). But in Shakespeare's Duke of Gloucester, the ordinary idiom of tradesmen ("But yet I run before my horse to market" [1.1.160]) is followed by the poignant wit and stichomythic rhetoric of courtship and persuasion. In this scene, Gloucester makes good his "secret close intent" and *displays* "the readiest way" to win the "wench" (1.1.155–58). After Lady Anne's fierce hatred has melted in the heat of his violent play of wooing, Gloucester, again alone on stage, congratulates himself, not so much upon the represented outcome of an imaginary action as upon the skill of its performance:

> Was ever woman in this humor woo'd?
> Was ever woman in this humor won? [. . .]
> Having God, her conscience, and these bars against me,
> And I no friends to back my suit [at all]
> But the plain devil and dissembling looks?
> And yet to win her! All the world to nothing!
> Hah!   (1.2.227–38)

Appealing to an authority that resides in the unparalleled quality of the performance, the actor/character stands back as it were and looks at his own delivery in the preceding scene. Instead of replaying the aggressive strategy of his impudent courtship, he relishes the virtuoso quality of his "dissembling looks." The opening question is "frivolous" enough; its almost literal repetition urges the audience (and grants them time) to respond. The outgoing bravura is that of a self-congratulating entertainer who rejoices over an uncommon feat, success against formidable odds. What the performer (rather than the character) reviews is the high degree of his professional competence.

Gloucester here *post festum* presents, and thereby disfigures, both what solemn mourning and what gallant courtship the scene might otherwise have represented. This presentational stance, providing an epilogue-like ending, is of course part of, and subservient to, a brilliant representation. Even so, there is in Richard Gloucester a subtly wrought conjuncture, a strangely motivated complicity, between what Quince calls "to disfigure" and "to present the person." As Gloucester expounds the dazzling result of his delivery, he exclaims, "And will she yet abase her eyes on me, [. . .] / On me, that halts and am misshapen thus?" (246; 250). What the gesticulating actor through this "thus" displays is his "deformities"; Gloucester's presentation of histrionic triumph goes hand in hand with parading his disfigurement. Again, while the body that is foregrounded is a deformed one, Richard's hunched back remains an important article in the representation; according to this representational purpose of playing, Richard's deformity must be read as a (motivating) symbol of a need for rapacious compensation. Still, the order of his disfigurement is theatrically "graced"; it is part of and inspires the fascinating overcharge in the "tangled chain" of getting across the difference between the past world of a murderous history and the performer's *élan* in reproducing it on common stages.

Compared to the presentational *gestus* of his self-introduction in the opening scene of the play, the wooing scene provides an important new dimension in the uses of disfigurement. In the former occasion, Richard displays his own self and body as a habitation for deformity. Looking back upon his desperate success in eccentric courtship, the protagonist projects a disfiguring plot upon others. Deformity, his own signature, is writ large upon the canvas of the story – informing actions that devastate life and limb in the fair proportion of others. Thus, from being a vulgar attribute of the noble protagonist, disfigurement is turned into an agency that 'rudely stamps' the Prince of Wales' widow as a "wench" and, even more, affects the scenario of the play at large. As Marjorie Garber astutely observes, Gloucester's "twisted and misshapen body encodes the whole strategy of history as a necessary deforming and *un*forming" ("Descanting on

Deformity" 86). Thereby, deformity is turned into "a self-augmenting textual effect, contaminating the telling of Richard's story as well as Richard's story itself" (90). If we translate these terms of narrative and textuality into the language of the theatre, then deformity in both the plot and the plotting – the "foul indigested lump" in the representation of Richard's murderous rise to the throne (the "story") – is positively provoked and interactively sustained by the socio-cultural mode of its transaction on common stages.

There, the boundary between the world-of-the-play and playing-in-the-world can be crossed either way. Gloucester, in "the idle pleasures of these days," (31) has

> no delight to pass away the time,
> Unless to see my shadow in the sun
> And descant on mine own deformity. (1.1.25–27)

To "descant," as the Arden editor notes, is to "enlarge upon a theme" or, by figurative extension from this meaning, "to sing a melody against a fixed harmony" (Hammond [ed.] 127). If "fixed harmony" can be identified with the given idealizing moment in the high Renaissance poetics of 'what should be,' then the presentational *gestus* of the performer is strong enough to jar against it, even as he serves as the perfect Prologue to the play (Clemen, *Commentary* 11). The resulting (dis)figuration informs both the stark display of his own "deformity" and its potent use against the grain of "a fixed harmony." Along these lines, Gloucester figuratively *descants*, that is, enlarges upon the absence "of this fair proportion"; the player's profit is that he can exempt his role from having to hold up the mirror to an ideal image of a Renaissance prince. Through the frivolous sporting of a "rudely stamp'd" body, Gloucester contradicts – one is tempted to say, disfigures – "th'expectation and rose of the fair state" of nobility. "Deform'd, unfinish'd, sent before my time" (1.1.20), the ignoble hunchback plays in *and* against the Renaissance "glass of fashion"; on the performative strength of his disfigurement, he refuses to submit to "the mould of form" (*Hamlet* 3.1.153), including any unitary purpose of playing – empathy or otherwise – in signifying the hump on his own performing shoulder.

In contrast to the clownish disfigurement, à la Dogberry, of a certain type of literary meaning (but not at all averse to vicious wordplay), Gloucester's hunchback is not so remote from what equivocation marks the "imperfect speakers" in *Macbeth* (1.3.70), whose double-dealing use of language is close to its own version of "dissembling Nature." The weird sisters match their own deformity with a series of opaque utterances that cunningly disfigure meaning by disrupting conventionally assumed continuities between signifier and signified. Compare Richard's words as his brother Clarence departs for the Tower: "Well, your imprisonment shall not be long, / I will deliver you, or else lie for you. / Meantime, have patience" (1.1.114–16). Words like "deliver" and "lie for you" are twisted into a sinister contrariety of meaning where hope and support (in Clarence's understanding) are, handy-dandy, exchanged for threats and deceit. Thriving on all sorts of doubleness, Gloucester plays a perfect game of *double entendre*, where the dark irony in his forecast ("your imprisonment shall not be long") constitutes a nonrepresentable play with duplicitous meaning. The promise of imminent release and liberty is transfigured into a prophecy of doom.

As I have suggested, Richard Gloucester shares these uses of duplicity with several other Shakespearean figurations, but especially with adaptations of the Vice, in which the image of a character in isolation is either suspended in, or complemented by, *platea*-like uses of a presentational rather than representational type of performance space. For Faulconbridge in the opening scenes of *King John*, for Iago, Edmund, even the early Aaron, as well as Hamlet in his "antic disposition," the boundary line between self-presentational display and the representation of character becomes as porous as it is for Richard Gloucester. Whatever degree of moral or mannered "deformity" these strong figurations have, is (re)presented on the site of an invisible threshold between the imaginary world of the play and the common world of its production and consumption. Again and again, the doubleness of this position is transmuted into the semiotics of duplicity, into the *double entendre* of a design that profoundly disturbs, even partially negates, the world-picturing pathos in the discourse of high Renaissance representations. In all these figurations, not unlike the comic figures of Falstaff, the clowns and fools, the disturbing effect cannot be contained when – as in many uses of disguise – this effect is indissolubly tied to a performative thrust of great force and resilience. These enormous energies thrive on the difference between imaginary product and transactive process, between the swelling scene's "imaginary puissance" and the real endeavor to bring it about. Rather than seeking to displace or obliterate the threshold under their own feet, they turn it into a matter of play.

Here, the emphasis on doubleness in the uses of theatrical space (to which I shall return) is vital. As far as I can see, there is no other *tertium quid* in reference to which these three or four widely different groups of artificial persons can be said to have common sources of performative strength. While this is not the place adequately to differentiate these groups (Vice descendents, clowns, fools, and related comic figures, persons in disguise, and those marked by madness), we at least need to keep in mind the extraordinary extent to which a shared element of theatrical doubleness and liminality can be turned into diverse uses of contrariety, or more specifically, disfigurement.

Here there is just room to look at one or two figurations that suggest how permeable (and provisional) the boundaries among these groups are when it comes to playing with a difference in Shakespeare's theatre. (Nor is this grouping – to which Thersites, Apemantus, even Prospero and a good many others need to be added – by any means exhaustive.) Let us take a major, uncomfortably duplicitous character like Vincentio in *Measure for Measure*. Here results, with the help of a disguise, a transfiguration of a character's identity that does not so much disfigure as conceal and "descant on" the noble shape of a Renaissance prince. Although Duke Vincentio does not parade his own skill like Richard Gloucester, and although he certainly never assumes Pompey's purely presentational stance in delivering a mimicry of Jacobean men-about-town like Master Rash, Master Caper, and so forth (4.3.1–19), his position on stage is marked by both a presentational, even directorial stance and the representation of a character. Between the two there is a fundamental contrariety in the purpose of his playing but one that is not turned to any one consistently maintained effect. Alone on stage, Vincentio can display his own complicity with some kind of "false exacting" and the performing of an "old contracting." Note in his speech the use of a rhymed verse that, with its sententious irregular seven-syllabled meter, usually serves for Prologue, epilogue, or chorus-like speeches:

> So disguise shall by th' disguised
> Pay with falsehood false exacting,
> And perform an old contracting. (3.2.280–82)

When the Duke/Friar says, "Craft against vice I must apply" (277), craftiness in representational design and craftsmanship in presentational strategy coalesce. Again, the resulting mingle-mangle in performance practices culminates in a tangled medley whereby the Duke in his turn descants on his assumed shape as ordinary friar. The achieved counterpoint is as baffling as it is experimental; but what performative strength obtains is indebted to the degree that this playing with a difference goes beyond Renaissance parameters of decorum, discretion, and consistency.

As I shall presently suggest, these practices cannot be disentangled in terms of the traditional distinction between 'formal' and 'naturalistic' styles of acting. Rather, there is a much more pertinent (and subtle) interaction between the presented and the represented, between "disguise" and "th' disguised" (280). This distinction, which the text offers, provides a cue for that which is pregnant with social difference. But here as elsewhere, the different cultural uses of the figure tend to be blurred, not resolved, played with but not collapsed or integrated into anything unified. As far as there is, at least in sumptuary standards, an element of disfigurement (the Duke turned Friar), it is – although socially, not physically pronounced – scarcely strong enough to significantly inform the transformation. The "to-and-fro movement" in playing with two distinct roles, with two dramaturgies, two purposes of playing, permanently draws on and keeps alive doubleness on the Elizabethan stage. As Paul Armstrong notes in an important essay on "Play and Cultural Difference," such

'doubling' does not overcome differences but can make them meet productively. 'Doubling' perspectives will not necessarily unify them [. . .] although it can disclose potential alliances or common ground between opposing cultures which neither side had previously suspected. (164)

In this particular context the Duke/Friar, playing with these differences, constitutes a hybrid triangle marked by the partially disfigured Duke, the disguising 'Friar' and, somewhat incongruous with these figurations, the player who plays with the difference between them as well as with the difference between them and himself.

There is then very little that, in the semantics of his representation, Richard Gloucester has in common with Duke Vincentio or, for that matter, a late comic character like Autolycus, except that all these quite different characters, inhabiting a hybrid type of space in performance, can socially, verbally, and dramatically draw on standards of doubleness without obliterating a common pattern of underlying difference. In Autolycus' case, there obtains a staggering level of duplicity that, in its comic effect, combines disguise with an inversionary use of disfigurement. Collapsing the object and subject of representation, Autolycus can counterfeit the alleged victim of a thievery whose agent he is about to become (4.3.50–76). This is, in Thersites' phrase, another "juggling trick – to be secretly open." Throughout, the player plays with, and exhibits the "abuse" of or the "distance" from the imaginary site of his own represented action. In his appearance as peddler and entertainer at the sheep-shearing ceremony, his chosen disguise is almost taken for granted, so much so that his only prop ("my pedlar's excrement" [4.4.713–14] – his false hair or beard) is only casually referred to at a much later stage, when about to be abandoned.

However, before he returns to a state 'prior' to this disguise, a new attire and a new "juggling trick" is called for. Snatching the show of "us soldiers" (724) and that of a "courtier cap-a-pe" (736), Autolycus delivers such strutting and role-playing that the innocent rustics accept his "great authority" (800) and let him have their gold. The performed practice of disguise is displayed "secretly open," in a way that foregrounds the agency of role-playing and, with it, the act of delivery itself. As an article on display, such delivery becomes perfectly scandalous when turned into a mimicry of courtly manners.

I am a courtier. Seest thou not the air of the court in these enfoldings?
Hath not my gait in it the measure of the court? Receives not thy nose
court-odor from me? Reflect I not on thy baseness court-contempt?
Think'st thou, for that I insinuate, [that] toze from thee thy business, I am
therefore no courtier? (730–36)

Here, Autolycus is not so much represented *through the image of* a courtier
and gentleman; more accurately, he is a player who is presenting himself as
a performer of these roles. The mask is donned not because it serves the
representation of character but because the duplicity behind it is superb
entertainment. There may well have been a show of gloating in the mouth-
ing of words like "insinuate" or "toze," when the player himself advertised
how skillful he was in teasing out the rustics' resistance, imperceptibly
worming himself into their favor and their pockets by furtive, cunning
contrivance. Here, again, we have a performance practice of a third kind,
one that is neither formal nor naturalistic but which scandalously foregrounds, in the act of performance, the disenchanting zest, the potential
for travesty, in the profession of playing itself.

The gaps and links between the juggler's craft and the craftiness of the
character are such that no closure and little coherence obtains; the indexi-
cal relationship between who performs and what is represented is slight.
The poetics of verisimilitude and closure is dispelled by a "secretly open"
gloating on the player's lips and in his voice. Note the histrionic gusto
which informs the swaggering transition to blank verse (745) through
which the performer, celebrating his own delivery, self-embodies a certain
type of player ("How blessed are we that are not simple men!"). As the
Arden and Riverside editors, reproducing the Folio layout as verse, suggest, this metrical use of language must be entirely functional. In this scene,
Autolycus, not entirely unlike Falstaff, is not so much a laughable object of
satire as a self-conscious source of wit – one "of them that will themselves
laugh" (*Hamlet* 3.2.40–41) in order to provide a counterfeiting kind of
sport.

The dialectic of 'disfigurement' and 'transfigurement' is even more compelling on the entirely different plane of disguise. As I have briefly suggested in the preceding chapter, there are certain strategies of concealment in
Shakespeare's theatre in which a playful interface of two types of identity –
one symbolic, the other existential – tends to contaminate the imaginary
representation of character. The 'speakers' behind the mask of disguise are
in their own way 'imperfect' in that, through doubleness in their role-
playing, the gendered, physical agency of the player can shine through.
The game becomes theatrically irresistible when such playing with a difference turns out to be a play with contrariety itself. This at least is the case in
1 *Henry IV*, when Falstaff, shifting into blank verse, begins to play the king

(2.4.391–94). At least by indirection, but probably by deliberation, the imperfect degree of disguise in his and in Hal's roles foregrounds the imperfections that representation is heir to, especially when the king is played in the old-fashioned manner of "King Cambyses' vein" (387). Here, too, the poetics of *imitatio vitae*, with its learned, purely literary authority, comes to naught when the scene is secretly open, almost a play within a play or, to be more exact, a play with playing. In no time, the element of game is acknowledged by the onstage audience, as when the Hostess exclaims, "O Jesu, this is excellent sport, i'faith!" (390). Superficially at least, the donning of imperfect masks in this scene is almost entirely stripped of its representational purpose; disguise serves as a 'secret' gear through which openly to display (and enjoy) the "sport" of exuberant role-playing.

More often than not disguise in Shakespeare either exceeds the boundary of any unitary image of subjectivity or resists what verisimilar role construction, emplotment of desire, and passion in relationships we have. There remains an irreducible margin, even perhaps a surplus of performative energy shining through the scriptural assimilation and adaptation of variegated forms of masquerade. Hence, in the disguise of figures such as Duke Vincentio, Edgar, even Hamlet, there is a performative energy exceeding representational parameters of consistency, logic, verisimilitude, reason, and compassion.

In Shakespeare's cross-dressed boy heroines, a comparable type of performative energy results in a remarkable zest for role playing, counterfeiting, and self-disclosure. In *The Two Gentlemen of Verona*, the cross-dressed 'trimming' of Sebastian (disguised as Julia's alter ego) is a case in point. Sebastian recalls how in Julia's own "gown" he played "the woman's part" (4.4.160–61). When Silvia asks the "gentle youth" (173), how "tall" the absent Julia is, Sebastian's/Julia's answer offers a particularly revealing register (dis)closing the gap between the imaginary female character and the young male's performance of bringing it to life. The answer invokes the signs of gendered fashion, the 'seems' of representation, "As if the garment had been made for me" (163). In this account, as in Rosalind's but also Viola's and Portia's cross-dressing, the rigidly maintained difference in Elizabethan gender relations is fabulously played with. The representation of socially and sexually fixed roles is subjected to a bewildering volatility. Female/male identities are juggled artfully; the young actor's voice shuffles their images like playing cards, displaying in secret close intent the utmost skill in doing the job. Still, this supreme play with gendered difference does not quite surrender the representational design of character. Julia, as in the mirror of her primary role of betrayed lover, projects a dual but not indifferent image of fluid variations on playfully processed gendered identities. It is in the midst of these that the young male performer, precisely in having "to play the woman's part," can fall back upon, and invoke from within the representation, the "self-resembled show" of his own sex and body.

Thus, more often than not, disguise, in Shakespeare's theatre, like any play-acting or deliberate counterfeiting, constitutes the rehearsal of what the actor's work is all about: the performer's assimilation of the alien text of otherness itself is turned into a play; it is playfully delivered as an almost self-contained dramatic action itself. In other words, the actor in *performing* a character in disguise, *presents* a playful version of his own *métier*, a gamesome performance of his own competence in counterfeiting images of both identity and transformation. Obviously, the histrionic delivery of disguise is more than imitation; here, mimesis becomes indistinguishable from what Michael Goldman calls "a play element in which mastery is self-delighting as well as self-disciplining" (*The Actor's Freedom* 89). Performance in disguise requires this mastery *par excellence*.

As these illustrations suggest, playing with a difference pursues a double purpose of playing that, in Shakespeare's theatre, is shared among entirely dissimilar conventions, from the Vice descendents, clowns, and fools to the most prominent figuration of madness and disguise. As far as all these continued to participate in and profit from the legacy of an open, unenclosed space for cultural practices, they thrived on a mode of performance that served a presentational, rather than exclusively representational purpose of playing. But again, the coexisting modes of representational and presentational performance were propelled by varying degrees of mutual engagement, interpellation, and interpenetration. Under these circumstances, we can perhaps best characterize the respective give and take between writing and playing by saying that, while Shakespeare's pen strongly sustains and helps articulate the existential and professional needs of the "actor's voice," that voice itself is absorbed and adapted to Shakespeare's plays with a resonance and variety that is unmatched in the rich history of the early modern stage.

The "self-resembled show"

In modern Shakespeare criticism, the presentational moment on Elizabethan stages has largely been ignored or marginalized. And yet, to study this moment in its own right is not an easy matter. As the evidence that we have about its genealogy and cultural functions is largely derivative, we are more often than is helpful thrown back on mere traces in a context where the purpose of presentation is not yet made integral to a Renaissance poetics of the mirror. Still, to reconsider early modern performance practice beyond its ministerial function *vis-à-vis* the completed form of an extant text, demands that we relate the presentational mode to a concept of "performance as itself a contested space where meanings and desires are generated, occluded, and of course multiply interpreted" (Diamond, *Performance and Cultural Politics* 4).

Let me begin at a point, close enough to Shakespeare's own stage, with that unrivalled master of presentational strategies, the Elizabethan clown. Dick Tarlton's rise to fame in the 1570's was owed to a huge talent and a widespread interest in a performance practice in which jigging, dancing, drum-beating, jest-telling continued to exist side by side with theatrical acting. If, as was likely, it was Tarlton who transformed the late ritual, rural jig into a balladesque performance combining dance and song, his theatrical career as dramatic actor may well have been more incidental to his total achievement than we might think. Professionalizing the jig as an "offshoot of the folk art of song and dance" (Baskerville, *The Elizabethan Jig* 28), Tarlton left behind a legacy on which John Singer, Robert Wilson, and Kempe continued to thrive. At the heart of this legacy was not an ensemble acting, but rather, to use David Wiles' phrase, the clown as a "solo entertainer" (*Shakespeare's Clown* 21).

To an extent this was true of Kempe even as he advanced to become sharer and householder in the Lord Chamberlain's Company. Almost certainly it was Kempe who performed a jig or "ballet" as Bottom in *A Midsummer Night's Dream*. A revealing alternative to any representational endeavor to "expound," or to say "what my dream was" was to "get Peter Quince to write a ballet of this dream" (4.1.207; 213–15). Such dance with song and music was to be preferred, "because it hath no bottom" (216) – which, if read as a pun, is also to say, it was Bottom-less. In other words, there was no longer any imaginary character called Bottom in the "ballet" when this song and dance was Kempe's job and designed to celebrate the liminal occasion of the play's conclusion rather than to be in aid of any further characterization of a dramatic role. Stubbornly resisting any self-contained mode of representation, the jig could not be co-opted to signifying anything in the play proper. It continued to be performed as an appendix to the play proper – at least up to the point, at about the end of the century, when, as Wiles suggests, "the clown convention as a whole had become destabilized" (*Shakespeare's Clown* 75). We do not of course know whether the "ballet" at the end of *A Midsummer Night's Dream* was in any way traditional in that, as C. R. Baskerville suggested, it provided a parody especially "of legal and religious forms" (*The Elizabethan Jig* 101), as was a favorite of this genre. If this continued to be the case, the parody may well have served a purpose of playing that sought "to disfigure, or to present" what was to be held forth.

Remarkably, Kempe – as when playing Launce in *The Two Gentlemen of Verona* (2.3.1–32) – must have served as both the agent and the object of disfigurement – not unlike Quince who is to "come in" simultaneously to personate and to disfigure "the person of Moonshine." While not so much playing *for* as playing *with* the audience, the comic presenter was probably well prepared to join spectators in laughing at the presentation itself and what "doltishnesse" it involved. Again, I use Sidney's phrase in order to underline the cultural difference between "loude laughter" and what "delight" comic representations should convey to us. Such laughter, together with all the "unwoorthie" comedy on scaffolds was unacceptable wherever players "contrarily" felt free to embody and yet make scurrilous what in serious discourses was not so. Using a word that Hamlet was to pronounce as vehicle for his own mad contrariety, Sidney as an illustration invoked those "twentie madde Antiques," where we "shall contrarily laugh sometimes to finde a matter quite mistaken" (3:40). To mistake the "matter" was one way – a not at all innocuous one – to disfigure dramatic signs and meanings, as when Launce was told, "your old vice still: mistake the word" (3.1.284). It was a strategy that, in a serious context, lived on in Hamlet's speech when – the "matter quite mistaken" (3:40) – Guildenstern rebukes him, "Good my lord, put your discourse into some frame, and [start] not so wildly from my affair" (3.2.308–09).

While, in Sidney's view, those who make us "contrarily laugh" "stirre laughter in sinful things" or "at deformed creatures" (40), the true "ende of the Comicall part" is "that delightfull teaching whiche is the ende of *Poesie*" (41). And to illustrate the important difference between common "contrarietie" and "right Comedie," Sidney provides a series of suggestions that deserve to be quoted because they exemplify what by and large common players prior to 1586/87 were either not prepared or quite reluctant to do.

For what is it to make folkes gape at a wretched begger, and a beggerly Clowne [. . .] But rather a busie loving Courtier, and a hartlesse threatning *Thraso*; a selfe-wise seeming Schoolemaister, a wry transformed Traveller: these if we saw walke in Stage names, which we plaie naturally, therein were delightfull laughter, and teaching delightfulnesse. (3:41)

Note how Sidney, in using phrases that will recur in printer Jones' Epistle to the Gentlemen Readers, proceeds to link "gape" with the presentation of "doltishnesse," "deformed creatures," and related things "disproportioned to [. . .] nature." As opposed to these contrarious presentations of disfigurement, the gentle poet and humanist prefers that "we plaie naturally," so as to pleasurably "learne" from truly comic representations. But all the examples that he gives (the "Courtier," "Schoolemaister,"

"Traveller"), while duly holding "the mirror up to nature" (*Hamlet* 3.2.22) are not, in Hegel's distinction, "comic to themselves" (Hegel, *Ästhetik* 1091). Rather, they are representations, roles generalizing social types, images symbolizing a given set of attributes that, in the enclosed world of the play, can be laughed at but never laughed with – let alone be reason that spectators "shall contrarily laugh."

Sidney's account, at least in what it rejects, shows us what in the 1590s could at best be adapted to a rapidly changing situation in the theatre. Here was a dated and increasingly notorious heritage ever since a university-trained playwright like Marlowe had led audiences to a stately tent of war where a Renaissance hero "Himself in presence" could "unfold at large" (Prologue to *Tamburlaine*, Part II) the action of the play. With the resulting great impact on audiences, the climate of reception began significantly to change until, at the turn of the century, the "graced deformities" could be unambiguously derided by Joseph Hall in his *Virgidemiarum* (1597) and John Marston in *Histriomastix, or The Player Whip't* (1598/99). Hall's satiric sketch is among the most revealing depictions we have of players who, refusing to "plaie naturally," must have had enough voice and physicality to exceed any purely textualized, word-oriented acting.

> ·Midst the silent rout,
> Comes leaping in a self-misformed lout,
> And laughs, and grins, and frames his mimic face,
> And justles straight into the prince's place;
> Then doth the theatre echo all aloud
> With gladsome noise of that applauding crowd.
> A Goodly hotch-potch! when vile russetings
> Are matched with monarchs and with mighty kings.
> A goodly grace to sober Tragic Muse,
> When each base clown his clumsy fist doth bruise,
> And show his teeth in double rotten row,
> For laughter at his self-resembled show. (Hall, *Virgidemiarum* 1.3.33–44)

Again, the absence of modesty and discretion results in something that is "greatly gaped at," even heartily applauded. The acts of "leaping" and laughing, 'framing' faces, using arms and "fist," even 'justling' (with its combative semantic underside of aggressive pushing, shoving, nudging) all foreground 'doltish' uses of a body free from the need to submit to the regime of textually prescribed fictional roles. The indiscreet features of this "beggerly Clowne" are doubly degraded by signs of social inferiority (his "vile russetings") and the "rotten" teeth that complement the performer's "self-misformed" show. In other words, this "lout" is not the role performed but designates a performer who is comic for himself. As with Trygaios or Dikaiopolis in Aristophanes' Old Comedy, the clown defies social distance and humiliation. Not unlike Richard Tarlton's Derick in *The Famous Victories of Henry V* or William Kempe's Launce in *The Two Gentlemen of Verona*, his "self-misformed" appearance, not altogether unlike Falstaff's, is turned into the clowning object and the laughing subject, or self, of his own mirth. Hall's comedian is surely one of those "that will themselves laugh to set on some quantity of barren spectators to laugh too" (*Hamlet* 3.2.40–42). In that sense the performer himself, in distancing the role, even in extricating himself from it, can be his own laughing subject-matter, an agency that, unbound by representation, is more than anything concerned to present and to disfigure (and to laugh with the audience at) "his self-resembled show."

Throughout Hall's text, there is at work a strong sense of friction, or even irreconcilability, between the literary culture of the "sober Tragic Muse" and the presentational mode that emphasizes the performing body of the actor rather than the symbolic performance of the role. Again, this presentational mode was identical with neither the formal, declamatory, rhetorically-pointed style of Elizabethan acting nor with any 'natural,' life-like impersonation of character. Together with those "that will themselves laugh," this type of "self-resembled show" came under increasing pressure even before the end of the century. Wherever a trace, or even the countenance, of the performer leaked through the prescribed text of representation, the necessary question in the world of the story was taken to be subjected to something "far unmeet for the matter." At that moment, the player's hand and gesture turned into a "clumsy fist," the "actor's voice" into a "rotten-throated" organ of filthy articulation. But it was not simply the clown's solo performance, with its rural undertones (and obscene overtures) that fell into disrepute. By the 1620s and 1630s any larger space for the performer's "liberty," as opposed to the "Law of writ" (*Hamlet* 2.2.401), was considered a thoroughly dated relic of "the days of Tarlton and Kemp." That, the same source continues, was "Before the stage was purg'd from barbarism," when performers, challenging writerly authority, could fall back on "licence" still to extemporize:

> when you are
> To speak to your coactors in the scene,
> You hold interlocutions with the audients. (Brome, *Antipodes* 2.2.43–45)

Presentation, or the performant function

It seems difficult, then, to doubt that in the formative years of the Elizabethan theatre these "self-resembled" performance practices were an important part of a larger spectrum of purposes of playing. If this was so,

Elizabethan performance needs to be reconsidered, in Michael Bristol's phrase, beyond its "ministerial" function, as having an independent tradition, one that must be defined, in W. B. Worthen's phrase, as "not [. . .] sustained by its text, nor by a uniform relation to the author" (*Shakespeare and the Authority of Performance* 28). For such a reconsideration, the traditional approach to Elizabethan acting, unfortunately, is only of limited value. What has remained undeveloped is a sense of effect and function that interconnects theatrical performance with other important cultural practices; in particular, a sense of what diversity of expectations and interests was concealed under the not so innocent but enormously emphatic singular form in Hamlet's definition of "the purpose of playing" (3.2.20). Also, an awareness, in this connection, of the ways and means by which the much-studied style of performance is integral to what kind of poetics and epistemology inform the entire *mise-en-scène*. Further, a need for differentiation by which changing patterns of style, form and communicative effect of performance, such as those linked to the emerging strength of impersonation, can be seen in perspective, as part of the history of both the popular Renaissance theatre and changeful social relations and other cultural practices.

Some such awareness of change and contingency in the purposes of performance appears indispensable when, finally, the early modern conjunction of writing and playing is to be both specified and contextualized in a doubleness that, in Paul Armstrong's phrase, "does not overcome differences but can make them meet productively." In other words, to explore the interface between pen and voice in terms of a more inclusive circulation of authority in Shakespeare's theatre can help us not only to qualify the sovereignty of the text of representation, but also to expand and go beyond an exclusive concern with the performance *of* Shakespeare's plays and with one type of performance inscribed *in* the text of these plays.

Altogether there is, then, a significant desideratum. Over the last two decades, sites of difference and contestation in Elizabethan plays have received a remarkable, even perhaps overemphatic amount of attention. The same cannot be said about performance practices, although one would assume that their remarkable range and diversity cannot be altogether unrelated to those moments of division, change, and social empowerment that have been traced in Elizabethan dramatic texts. But even at this late date, the rare discussions of agency and social context in Elizabethan performance, such as those by M. C. Bradbrook, David Wiles, and David Mann, are still being overshadowed by two rather more dominant approaches to Elizabethan acting – one focusing on the style and the method, the other on the semiotics of performance.[9]

No doubt, the preoccupation with the style and method of Elizabethan acting has, by its own parameters, produced work of considerable value and distinction. As is well known, the principal line of divergence in the debate on Elizabethan acting was (or even is) between the standards of 'naturalism' and those of 'formal' delivery. Commentators from Alfred Harbage, B. L. Joseph, Marvin Rosenberg, Leonard Goldstein, R. A. Foakes, Bernard Beckerman, and Lise-Lone Marker to, more recently, Robert Cohen and John Russell Brown, have tended to document and interpret important forms and strategies of Elizabethan acting, while other scholars like Andrew Gurr and, more recently, Meredith Anne Skura and Peter Thomson have taken account of the psychological and cultural implications of the players' social status.[10] Historically informed changes in the work of Elizabethan performers were not ignored in what Goldstein years ago in the title of his essay suggested was a "transition from formal to naturalistic acting."[11] Such a "transition" could also be thought of or redefined in terms of a mixture, either as an actual blend or as an oscillation from the one mode to the other. But, as Bernard Beckerman noted, there resulted a good deal of confusion in that "the formalists describe the means at the actor's disposal [. . .], the naturalists the effect at which he aimed, the imitation of life" (111).[12] In proposing a "reconciliation of the contradictory demands of convention and reality," Beckerman acknowledged "the dual nature of the style" of Elizabethan acting by defining it "as at once, ceremonial, romantic, and epic" (216). This partially anticipated the definition in John Russell Brown's revised edition of *Shakespeare's Plays in Performance*, where 'a new Polonius' is invoked "to invent a definition," which is summed up in "the phrase 'Epic-romantic-virtuoso-formal'" (31).

In more recent years, scholars and critics have significantly broadened the agenda for the study of Elizabethan acting. Following G. E. Bentley's *The Profession of Player in Shakespeare's Time* (1984), along with Gurr's important work on the social status of players and changing cultural tastes of playgoers, as well as Bradbrook's and Mann's focus on the social matrix of Elizabethan acting,[13] some recent critics have begun to draw attention to what Meredith Anne Skura calls "the onstage tension between actor and character," between "mimesis or role-playing" and "performance, establishing a 'real' relation to the audience" (*Shakespeare the Actor* 29, 9).[14]

Similarly, yet on a different level, the structural-semiotic approach to the theatre has helped criticism to move beyond an exclusive concern with the dramatist's text and its purely literary realms of meaning. For instance, the attempt has been made to interconnect the dramatic text and the performer's practice through "a sense of intertextuality between the signifying systems of the written and the performed" (Aston and Savona, *Theatre as*

Sign-System 178). However, the hoped-for integration of textual and performance practices, which years ago Keir Elam set out to advance in *The Semiotics of Theatre and Drama*, has only very partially materialized. Approaching theatre as a multilayered entity (i.e., "materially heterogeneous and constructed of many different codes") semioticians like Marco de Marinis have attempted to transcend the structuralist framework which operates solely within the boundaries of the text (*Semiotics of Performance* 1). But although seeking to examine pragmatically "the performance text in relation to the conditions of its production and reception" (3), the semiological project remained fascinated by the ideal of textuality that it sought to escape: "Clearly, therefore, even the units of theatrical production known as performances can be considered as texts, and can thus become the object of textual analysis, provided that they possess the minimal prerequisites for consideration as texts" (47).

Here, precisely, is the rub: these "minimal prerequisites" make maximal demands when they presuppose "constitutive prerequisites of completeness and coherence" (47). In view of neoclassical parameters such as these, diversity and historicity vanish into the thin air of textualizing even "extratextual cultural codes," especially when these "ideological, epistemic, or axiological codes [. . .] are in fact part of the general text to which the performance text belongs" (121). As Keir Elam, now looking back on more than two decades of semiotic approaches to performance, sums up the situation: "The predicament of the semiotics of performance is that after years of preliminary theoretical ground-clearing and methodological weapon-honing with a view to a promised revolution in our cognitive dealings with theater arts, the awaited event, namely the actual encounter with the performance, seems never quite to have taken place" (Elam, "The Wars of the Texts" 87). To come to terms with this encounter, there is no way but to recognize, as Andrew Gurr put it, that "performance is an event, not a text"; but if this is so, "the exploration of Shakespeare's original staging has to be not a story of texts, even of lost texts, but of their frames, the contexts" ("The Bare Island" 30).

Still, theatre semiotics, as soon as it relinquishes a strictly textualized concept of the sign, can stimulate an awareness of important distinctions in Elizabethan performance practices, even enhance our sense of their "sheer dynamic, material, uncontainable, and unconfinable energy" (Elam, "The Wars of the Texts" 90). Once the need is acknowledged, as in Marvin Carlson's *Theatre Semiotics: Signs of Life* and Jean Alter's *A Sociosemiotic Theory of Theatre*, "for a more comprehensive grammar of the theatre's signs," there results a remarkable opening, with a revealing focus on "an inherent duality of theatrical activity" (Alter, *Sociosemiotic Theory* 29). Going beyond an understanding of signs as language and their "reference to a story that takes place in a mental space outside of the stage" (31), Alter – in part seconded by Carlson[15] – presupposes two basic functions of the theatre. On the one hand, there is the performer's "referential function" implicating a symbolic use of representational "signs that aim at imparting information." On the other hand, there is the "performant function" that the actor in the theatre shares with clowns, dancers, and athletes in the circus, the ballet, and the sports arena. As Alter notes in an essay on Mnouchkine's Shakespeare production,

> a theatre performance cannot, and must not, be reduced to its referential function alone. On the contrary, the very essence of theatre lies in a permanent tension between its referential function, which relies on signs to produce meaning, and what I have called the performant function, which involves no semiotic processes and satisfies the emotional need to witness special achievements: physical, aesthetic, technical, and so on. (32)[16]

In this sense, "theatre is also a public event, a spectacle or a show, attempting to please or amaze the audience by a display" of something extraordinary, "like sporting events or the circus" (31–32). Here one may quarrel with a somewhat narrow concept of "communication," as when "such performances" are said to be "not communicated with signs; they are experienced directly" (31–32). As Carlson has persuasively argued in his *Theatre Semiotics*, even if "the calculated rejection of mimetic elements [. . .] resulted in a nonsemiotic medium, there would remain semiotic implications still to be dealt with in the sender and receiver" (7). But once these reservations are made, Alter, by going beyond both the purely textual and the iconographic dimensions of performative action, provides an important conceptual framework for some of the enabling conditions of multiple sources of authority on Elizabethan stages.

Extending Alter's analysis from the theoretical to the historical, we may well say that theatre as "public event" involves performance practices that, being (ir)reducible to representation, can serve diverse purposes of playing. Formulated in the language of anthropology, the two major sets of these differing purposes – as developed by Alter – are implicitly functional and socializing. They relate first to the image of the human being as *Homo sapiens* and to the uses of representation in aid of information, knowledge, and meaning; and second to the image of *Homo ludens*, where what is foregrounded is not a mode of knowledge, meaning, or subjectivity but a relation to the world as play. In this second category, performative action pursues "the game principle," the play-element in playing, so that "the performant function would tend to override the referential function" in that "actors would primarily seek to display their acting talents and physical attributes, to astonish and delight the audience" (41). Here, the qualifications are of vital importance: there is no clash of binary opposites when, in *each* of these anthropological dimensions, one function can engage and "override" the other, and when, as a matter of course, "actors would *primarily* seek" to pursue one or the other purpose of playing.

The qualification is important not simply because it provides us with a larger perspective on performance in Shakespeare's theatre. This is particularly so in reference to the readings in this chapter, of such scenes as Falstaff's playing the king, Gloucester's wooing of Anne, Duke Vincentio's "Craft against vice" stratagem, Bottom's dream, and Autolycus' juggling with identities. Although in all these scenes and configurations, the actor's part, in Alter's phrase, does "draw attention from the story space to the stage space and break the spell of referentiality," their rousing effect (and effectiveness) derives from a "tension" between the different purposes of playing. Whether or not in each case this tension thrives on and feeds a dual need for knowledge/meaning *and* game/release, the choreography of these scenes comes closer to resembling a dance where the awareness of the difference in question is inseparable from playing with it. It is a 'dance' in that the holding up of the mirror itself is turned into a zestful movement away from all *prodesse*, into the "swelling scene" of a game of physical voices and bodies. As both words and bodies celebrate the encounter with, respectively, what is in each case its other, the voice in the text just as the pen in the voice swirl in a dazzling play of difference in identity.

Thus, even when Alter amply acknowledges certain types of theatrical and cultural performances that "draw the attention from the story space to the stage space, and break the spell of referentiality," his focus – helpfully, I submit – is on a "permanent" give and take between these different purposes of playing, as inclusively located in a dual need for knowledge/meaning and game/release. However, what Alter's semiotic distinctions quite neglect is that, in the circumstantial world of theatre culture and history, these nicely balanced, seemingly normative juxtapositions must be viewed as heavily marked by contingency. In view of highly changeful socio-cultural relations between writing and performing, the structure of their relationship, and thereby the uses of early modern performance itself, participate – as chapter 5 seeks to establish – in the world of social conflict and cultural change, both reacting to and producing change.

Shakespeare criticism, at least after the spell of the New Criticism, has been inspired by a growing interest in Shakespeare as poet in the theatre, even as 'man of the theatre.' As Inga-Stina Ewbank looked at "the relationship between the word and the other elements that go to make up the theatrical experience" (55), she underlined the absence of any "unbridgeable gap" between the two in Shakespeare's theatre. Weighing the dangers of "textual imperialism" against those of "the tyranny of 'the School of Performance,'" she arrived at a definition of language in the theatre as "the grammar of the dramatic situation," when words "all repeat in small what Shakespeare and the actors do at large" (712). Thus, while "it is impossible to say that one 'system of signs' has priority over all others" (72), "some of our keenest responses have to be literary" (58) as long as "language is the dramatic situation" (64).

Rereading this statement of about two decades ago, the question is, where have we – one trembles to use the word – *advanced* from here? Is it at all possible for Shakespearean critics to go beyond a position according to which, in Michael Goldman's phrase, "Shakespeare's text must be primary for us," precisely because that text *is* "a design for performance"? Viewing "Shakespeare's plays as compositions in the medium of acting," the same critic refused "to speak as if we have a choice between a literary and a theatrical Shakespeare" ("Acting Values and Shakespearean Meaning" 190).

There is no doubt that this finely balanced position has served us well in going beyond the purely verbal approaches dominant in the fifties and sixties. And yet, as in recent years more and more doubt is cast on the authority of the text as on anything absolute, can that text continue to serve as the one reliable "design for performance"? Since the decline in textual authority has come to affect important editorial, critical, and theoretical premises in Shakespeare studies, it may well be that the juxta-position, as in the Prologue to *Troilus and Cressida*, between "author's pen" and "actor's voice" needs to be reread as participating in a circula-tion of authorities in which the verbal "grammar" or "design" of textual meaning is as much exposed to the vicissitudes of live performance as that performance is in its own turn profoundly indebted to what even the most flitting, inconstant semantic positions in the text prescribe. While it would be rash to assume that the instability of the dramatic text can be off-set or in any way intercepted by the more material medium of performance, both can best be seen in an intensely interactive, mutual engagement where the language games in the text and the playfulness of performance relate in terms of a changeful and often undetermined space for both continuity and discontinuity.

5   Histories in Elizabethan performance

To account for both the strength and the decline of the performant function is difficult without viewing the larger spectrum of Elizabethan performance practices, and the actual diversity of cultural needs and interests behind them, in historical perspective. The performant function, which was one purpose of playing among others, was of necessity one that, in Polonius' terms, enjoyed more "liberty" than a mode of acting that followed "the law of writ." Hence, the presentational purpose of playing could assume a strong nonscriptural dimension that, however, found itself contested and largely intercepted by an increasingly dominant and ultimately more exclusive regime of literacy in dramatic representations. Any historical narrative of the genealogy of the Elizabethan theatre must come to terms with the modes, the results, and the space of this contestation. Theatre history is confronted with the need to account for the ways and means and of course the circumstances in which the language of dramatic characterization and the "mirror" of representational meaning came more and more to dominate performance practices.

At the present state of our knowledge, it seems premature to undertake anything like an exhaustive account of the complex field of socio-cultural forces, interests and circumstances implicated in this process. Rather than attempting an impossible task, I shall content myself with exploring some of the early signs of change and the incipient results of differentiation between the 'unworthy' stage practice of common players and the text-dominated theatre of the excellent actor and perfect impersonator. Far from constituting an always already given scheme of fixed differences, this process of differentiation was marked by fits and starts and a good deal of reciprocity on either side. For this reason alone, the process in question cannot be pigeonholed into a convenient time-frame; if anywhere, this process adumbrates new areas of social and cultural tension in the late 1580s and reaches its first full-blown stage at the turn of the century.

Elizabethan dramatists like Marlowe, Peele, and Shakespeare, who grew up in the 1560s and 1570s and began to write in the 1580s, set out to advance greatly the cause of poetry and rhetoric in the theatre, even while in their work they were increasingly prepared to draw on a remarkable degree of interplay between presentation and impersonation in performance. Thus, even in the early 1590s, there occurred a significant change of emphasis in their dramatic compositions. Whereas some of their earliest plays subscribed to strongly literate 'endeavors of art,' with distinct memories of a grammar school or university education, their later work fruitfully accommodated lively traces of presenting agencies. Such accommodation was most striking as Marlowe moved from *Dido* and *Tamburlaine* to *The Jew of Malta*, or Peele from *The Arraignment of Paris* to *The Battle of Alcazar*. Shakespeare, in his own turn, after his early Plautine adaptation, proceeded to *The Two Gentlemen of Verona*, a seminal comedy that strongly invited actor-centered, presentational practice like clownage and disguise.

In other words, the exclusion from Elizabethan stages of the clown, the jig, the self-resembled show, and all sorts of disfigurements was a long drawn-out affair, a by no means linear process in which acts of contestation between writing and playing could again and again be suspended. The question, then, that needs to be asked is not simply whether the theatre responded to larger differentiations in early modern culture and society, as studied by social historians like Peter Burke and Keith Wrightson. Rather, what is at issue is both the theatre's complicity with, and resistance to, the encroaching forces of division and stratification, reform and withdrawal. For instance, according to Patrick Collinson, the first wave of the withdrawal from widely shared cultural practices culminated in the 1580s. But the early modern theatre in England was slow to surrender the cultural space for a rather more inclusive "mingle-mangle" or "Gallimaufrey"[1] in the writing and performing of plays. It was precisely the Elizabethan cultural "Hodge-podge" (another term John Lyly used) that (re)vitalized, at least for a number of years, the always very vulnerable alliance of common players' voices and highly literate writers' pens.

Disparity in mid-Elizabethan theatre history

If anywhere, the matrix of disparity and diversity in sixteenth-century performance practices is hidden in the *terra incognita* of mid-Tudor theatre history. Despite valuable recent work of scholars like John H. Astington, David Bradley, William Ingram, Janet S. Loengard, Paul Whitfield White, and others,[2] the history of the Tudor stage, including that of the Elizabethan theatre before the advent of Kyd and Marlowe, leaves many questions unanswered. In particular, our knowledge about how early Elizabethan players subsisted, organized, and staged their shows in the face of a savage vagrancy legislation is painfully limited. No doubt these wandering groups in part hoped to join the ranks of those regular, licensed, provincial theatre troupes that can be traced in records and town archives as collected by J. T. Murray and, more recently, by the authors of the invaluable *Records of Early English Drama* volumes. Outside the circle of these groups there were, as Bradley notes, "amateur groups, as well as random collections of unemployed persons who might temporarily have found some kind of limited protection as players, and an apparent host of fencers, musicians, rope-dancers, acrobats, tumblers, mountebanks, puppeteers, and exhibitors of all kinds of marvels and grotesques" (*Text to Performance* 58). Compared with this ongoing wealth of diversion, the few London-based companies under the patronage of the Lords of the Privy Council and later the Crown came fairly late. Still, it was these privileged players who continued to travel to larger towns well after the great majority of their less fortunate colleagues must have found an itinerant subsistence more and more arduous.

If, in view of a suggestive mass of unconnected players' traces, the best that scholarly research can produce is "little more than a survey of our ignorance," there is at least one thing fairly clear in what may forever remain a bewilderingly hazy picture: "the disparity between theatrical activity and printed texts" (Astington, "The London Stage" 1). This disparity, particularly sharp before 1587, appears especially puzzling after we have learned that the setting up of the Theatre (1576) was preceded by the opening of the Red Lion playhouse (1567) near Stepney.[3] The enhanced distance between the beginning of a 'real' theatre in 1567 and the advent of 'real' drama with Kyd and Marlowe is, as Ingram observes, even more troublesome since it now must span nearly a generation: the "implicit sequencing in these dates – the notion that playhouses came first, then plays" is marked by the blatant absence of logic, as if "birdhouses engender birds, or doghouses dogs" (William Ingram, *The Business of Playing* 64).

Thus, more than ever we are here thrown back on writing a theatre history that is radically discontinuous with the history of dramatic literature. The obvious gap between them, however, can be taken to indicate more than, in Ingram's words "merely the old confusion" (64). Rather, the sequence of playhouses first, dramatic texts second, may not be quite so preposterous; once we dispense with the preconceived notion of textual composition as the primary impulse in affairs theatrical, we no longer need to derive continuity in theatre history from stability in the production and conservation of dramatic texts. Once theatre history has become conceivable in the absence of an authority in dramatic writing that allegedly leads to the setting up of playhouses, alternative locations of agency and authority can be envisioned. Such locations would then be closer to those who performed and, thereby, produced the need for the building of playhouses.

The highly revealing disparity between theatrical activity and dramatic writing appears even sharper if we take into account early venues for playing within the city's jurisdiction, such as the Bell, the Bull, the Cross Keys, and the Bel Savage. Together with "eighte ordinarie places" (John Stockwood's reference of 1578[4]) and the three theatre buildings of 1576, these may convey a notion about what one critic calls "the astonishing frequency of public playing" in the absence of a sizable body of dramatic texts. In view of the thirty-five identifiable playing companies that can be traced in the years immediately following 1576, William Ingram has calculated a potential need for a hundred or so different play scripts each year. Since their nonexistence cannot entirely be accounted for by loss, the inevitable conclusion must be Ingram's: "so long as our focus is on dramatic texts, we are likely to view this early period as a desert" (241). It is indeed a desert when compared to the feverish production of texts after 1587; in contrast, the preceding crucial decade, to judge by Harbage and Schoenbaum's *Annals of English Drama*, has scarcely a dozen commercial play texts that survive.

In response to this marked disparity, John Astington has submitted some remarkable suggestions. In view of the absence of or a reduced need for authorially fixed play texts, it seems likely "that one of the simplest and most portable elements of performance, that of the individual actor giving a taste of his quality" or "his skill in various 'veins'" ("The London Stage" 13) was an entirely customary, widely acceptable practice, one that constituted a crucial purpose of playing on these early stages. If we assume that the actor's display of his talents was versatile enough for improvised recital at short notice, like that of *Hamlet*'s First Player, then such "skill" must have amounted to a regular entertainment commodity. Indeed, as the example from *Hamlet* shows, "the actor's impressiveness in such a context" would result more from the performer's strength in delivery than from the brilliance of the delivered text. In the event, such delivery could be "quite removed from the context of the continuity of the dramatic fiction or the development of the character" ("The London Stage in the 1580s" 14). There was, as Astington continues to note,

the evident delight in the bravura with which such performances were carried off, the possibility of playing Jeronimo with a shoemaker for a wager, all these point to ways of enjoying the theatre quite different from our own. The actor almost seems to have been isolated from the play, within the fiction yet separate from it, both in the eyes of the audience, and perhaps, in his own. (14)

Such a serious, highly performative mode of delivery must have been complementary to what the comedian contributed with his capacity for repartee, singing, dancing, and mugging. It is certainly not fortuitous that the undisputed dominance of Tarlton in the late 1570s and early 1580s went hand in hand with an open episodic play structure and, at the same time, the absence of any significant writing for the public theatres.

Thus, rather than deploring the "clumsy, slovenly, incompetent, and contorted" uses of language in these plays and blaming these dramatists (including actor-playwrights like Tarlton and Wilson) for being "incapable of composing anything better than 'jigging' verse, lines that move jerkily and awkwardly" (Hibbard, "From 'iygging vaines'" 61), it is time for us to look elsewhere for the vital impulse, the resourcefulness, and resilience that must have inspired theatrical activities in the mid-sixteenth century and shortly after. Since the life-blood of these cultural practices did not pulsate in the aesthetic quality of the texts, at least not in those that survived, we should not off-handedly dismiss as altogether deplorable the "gross discrepancy between what is done and what is said" (65) on these stages. On the contrary, unless we are determined entirely to ignore theatrical experience in the twentieth century, the uses of this "disparity" or "discrepancy" may well have been part of what then made the theatre tick.

At this point, we are – ineluctably, it seems – driven to the question of whether the space for discontinuity between word and action was perhaps used quite significantly. In other words, could it be that the space for disparity between text and show participated in related patterns of cultural difference and divergence that informed early modern ways of living, thinking, and socializing? The gap between the arts of eloquent writing and those of corporeal display was not unbridgeable. Was there even a way to turn this gap into a usable site on which to present, explore, negotiate, release or displace smoldering tensions, serious discrepancies or comic incongruities?

It seems difficult to suggest an answer to this somewhat speculative set of questions without looking more closely at the context in which performative practices flourished in early Elizabethan England. Thanks to the *REED* volumes and related research in provincial archives, this context has become accessible on a scale that former historians of the Elizabethan theatre could only dream of. When seen together with the work of traveling players on the continent, who a few years later habitually and successfully sang, tumbled, and performed English plays without communicating through their language, playing in the provinces provides us with suggestive evidence that goes some way towards elucidating the circumstances in which, strangely, it was possible for players to participate in a performance and yet be "isolated from the play," in the sense, as Astington suggests, of being "within the fiction and yet separate from it."

Astington's phrase is helpful in that it further defines the doubleness of (re)presentational action as a hybrid type of performance practice that embraced both histrionic and nonhistrionic action, such as song, dance, sword-fighting, or acrobatic activities. Such hybridity in performance practice appeared to thrive under conditions where there prevailed a good deal of looseness in company formation. What gives us pause to think is that even in London there can be traced a good many transient, unaffiliated and unlicensed players, at least at mid-century and shortly after. For example, in 1550 the London Court of Aldermen drew attention to eighteen otherwise unaffiliated players whose unlicensed activities were cause of some concern (Chambers, *Elizabethan Stage* 4:261–62). Such loose and isolated existence of players was the more remarkable in that their repertoire was likely to contain more than purely dramatic offerings. Since, at the same time, the existence of unaffiliated players almost certainly went hand in hand with a good deal of looseness in their mode of association, there may well have been a connection between this looseness in company organization and the flexibility of their offerings, especially at a time when "the mode of playing at mid-century was still largely peripatetic rather than settled" (William Ingram, "The 'Evolution' of the Elizabethan Playing Company" 19).

Here, the later provincial history of the Queen's Men provides us with an extremely telling illustration. Their story pointedly underlines that the contiguity between mimetic and non-mimetic modes of performance practice was not limited to what William Ingram considered the "pivotal and significant" years in the formation of this Elizabethan playing company (19). In fact, the remarkable division of the company into one role-playing and one acrobatic troupe of performers speaks volumes. Henslowe's note about "the Quenes players when they brocke and went into the countrey to playe" (Foakes and Rickert, *Diary* 7) – dated May 8, 1593[5] – must be read in the light of this looseness *qua* flexibility of the company. Again it is their work in the provinces that is revealing in that it confirms a continued readiness for both regular acting and tumbling. One of the troupes (either the one led by Symons[6] or the one led by the Duttons[7]) was the principal acting company, while the other appeared to specialize in the display of all kinds of stunts and feats. Half a decade earlier, a company of Queen's players had performed at Bath on July 19, 1588 and received a reward "given by Mr. Mayor to the quenes men that were tumblers" (Chambers, *Elizabethan Stage* 2:98). That was a mere five years after the company had been formed. Not surprisingly, there appears in the papers relating to the Queen's Men "a Turkish rope dancer" who, as Bradley reads the records, was attached "to one or other of the [. . .] two companies and possibly at times to either" (65). As far as, in our context, the difficult history of the Queen's Men suggests anything, this history shows that the continuity of an important company and the crystallization of its identity as a role-playing ensemble did not necessarily go hand in hand. Nor can the growth and dominance, in the company's work, of symbolic and iconographic forms be automatically inferred from an otherwise unambiguous licensing regulation.

While in view of their patron her Majesty's players must have enjoyed particularly favorable conditions of hospitality, troupes playing in other provincial towns confirm but also qualify the picture of the Queen's Men at Bath. To take only Peter H. Greenfield's detailed analysis of playing at Gloucester, there is unquestionably a parallel in that professional entertainers other than players (that is, jesters, jugglers, and bearwards) were welcomed and rewarded by the city. According to the Lord Mayor's accounts in Gloucester for the years 1550 through to 1595–96 (no accounts have survived for the years 1596–97 to 1635–36), there was, however, clearly a falling off either of official expenses or recorded occasions for non-dramatic performers. While in the 1560s and 1570s these were listed side by side with the welcoming of actors, there are, with the exception of a late rope-dancer in 1636–37, no records for any such officially authorized occasions in the 1580s and 1590s – the period in which licensed troupes of actors visited most often.[8]

Although the distinction, involving plenty of contiguity, between dramatic and non-dramatic entertainers is in our context of great significance in that it documents long-standing grounds for interaction among diverse purposes of performance, a caveat is in order here. While bearwards, tumblers, fencers and perhaps dancers as a matter of course did not and could not very well pursue a purpose of playing that was marked by representational modes and aims, minstrels, jesters, and perhaps jugglers might well have constituted a border-line case. The latter found themselves at least partially on threshold occasions where the presentation of songs and jests would almost certainly have provided a certain amount of representational opportunities. In other words, even when in such cases the main emphasis was definitely not on the representation of dramatic action and character, the boundary-line between the two types of performance was likely to be on either side more permeable than the present account has so far been able to suggest.

Contemporary polemics against itinerant performers provide fairly reliable evidence that jesters and jugglers in particular may not in their use of language have been so remote from players. For example, it was possible for one William Alley in 1565 to rank "plaiers" among other licentious groups of entertainers who in their use of language were all proverbially loose and unbound by any textually administered control:

Alas, are not almost al places in these daies replenished with iuglers, scoffers, iesters, plaiers, which may say and do what they lust, be it never so fleshly and filthy? and yet suffred and heard with laughing and clapping handes. (Chambers, *Elizabethan Stage* 4:192)

Alley's lament distinguishes three offensive types of practice, all partially or potentially sustained by verbal (re)presentations, against which the joint forces of legislation and reform were about to target their energies. First, these practices were immoral and sinful, "fleshly and filthy"; second, they encouraged unregulated openings in which performers could "say and do what they lust" beyond any reach of a censorship which would have as its object a fixed text; and, finally, their licentiousness was publicly rewarded by the "clapping handes" of popular audiences.

For players, as well as "iuglers" and "iesters," to "say [. . .] what they lust" reflected a mid-century situation when discourses pro and contra the Reformation invited scurrility in polemics rather than pure doctrine in dramatic form. "Evil disposed persons," in the language of Mary Tudor's proclamation (1553) must have felt encouraged to

take upon them withoute sufficient auctoritie, to preache, and to interprete the worde of God, after theyr owne brayne, in churches and other places, both publique and pryvate. And also by playinge of Interludes and pryntynge false fonde books, ballettes, rymes, and other lewde treatises in the englishe tonge, concernynge doctryne in matters now in question and controversye. (Gildersleeve, *Government Regulation of Elizabethan Drama* 10)

The point that in reading these and similar proclamations has perhaps not sufficiently been pursued is that these players, together with irreverent "iuglers" and "iesters," performing "withoute sufficient auctoritie," interpreted Biblical or other textual matter "after theyr owne brayne." Once points of doctrine were "now in question and controversye," the "anchor-hold of authority" itself could be loosened, and unsanctioned discourses could be authorized. In a situation like this, many of these verbally inclined entertainers must have served as resilient vehicles for what David Bevington, in his eye-opening *Tudor Drama and Politics*, has called the mid-century "propaganda crisis." Since there was, as V. C. Gildersleeve noted decades ago, well into Elizabeth's reign "no definite system of licensing" (*Government Regulation* 15), local initiative for supervision and control was wayward and at best spontaneous; it is impossible to believe that the existing "system of censorship by local authorities [. . .] was ever rigorously carried out and that every play was carefully 'seen and allowed' before presentation" (13–14). The stage, in fact, provided an exceptionally large margin for players to "say and do what they lust." Such self-authorization may well have been rewarded by audiences, especially when, as Bevington notes, the "struggle for political control of drama as an organ of religious settlement had not yet ended" (*Tudor Drama and Politics* 126).

In these circumstances, the foregrounding of performance-as-performance, stage-as-stage, could lead to varied modes of self-presentation whereby the playing-in-the-world itself became a source providing, or at least enriching, the dramatic metaphor of topical meaning. For instance, in a mid-century play with Plautine borrowings, such as *Jack Juggler*, it was possible theatrically to assimilate the hotly debated issue of transubstantiation as an impious allegory of theatrical contrariety. The Protestant equation, as practiced by Cranmer and others, of 'transubstantiation' with 'juggling' (Paul White, *Theatre and Reformation* 126),[9] and the use of 'juggling' as interchangeable with 'gaming,' 'playing,' and 'conjuring' is seized upon by the Vice, Jack Juggler.[10] Usurping the looks, the habits, the identity of Jenkin Careaway, he turns his own play into a gleeful display of counterfeiting, masquerading, role-playing, and disguise. As the perplexed victim of this doubleness falls prey to this stark scheme of duplicity, he is displaced from both his dramatic text and identity: "whan I lost my selfe I knew verie well / I lost also that I should you tell" (736–37).[11] His staged confusion is that of a bewildered performer/believer who, in presenting himself, is lost in the identity of an other. Doctrinal conflict and wonderment are assimilated through the dual matter of self-made display versus the representation of roles. "Darest thou affirme to me / That [. . .] on man may have too bodies and two faces?" (784–86). The answer to this is anticipated by Careaway's Bottom-like remark, "And yet woll I stiell saye that I am I" (497). Or as he later has it,

> Good lorde of hevyne, wher dyd I my selfe leave?
> Or who dyd me of my name by the waye bereve?
> For I am sure of this in my mynde,
> That I dyd in no place leve my selfe byhynde. (602–05)

These lines, although spoken in a drama of the schools, rehearse the practice of players who "interprete the worde of God, after theyr owne brayne." For a sixteenth-century performer, 'to transubstantiate' could – in addition to either its theological meaning or its pejorative connotation of 'juggling' – also have the secular meaning recorded in the *OED*, of "to transform, transmute." To think of 'transubstantiation' as transforming one's self into a role and, vice versa, a role into one's own, presenting self, was to moralize more than two meanings in one word, and it was contrariously to foreground the craft and craftsmanship of playing *qua* juggling.

In *Jack Juggler*, there is another version of disparity between performance practice and textualized doctrine that is assimilated, as it were, to what the play actually communicates. To place topical meaning and controversial doctrine into the hands of itinerant players was a double-edged procedure that did not altogether result in a reconciliation of the differences between them. Unquestionably, such a procedure, at least to a certain extent, did call for an approximation of a sort between the presentation of church doctrine and the traditional ways and means of audience-related playing. But there always remained a gap; the players' expertise, their repertoire of juggling and ambidextrous strategies, could not ultimately be reduced to whatever purpose of instruction or edification was inscribed in the text. Since these unruly practices could at best be partially adopted or temporarily harnessed to conveying the message, the performed result was likely to contaminate the purity of any true doctrine or fervent belief.

As an illustration, the following *catalogue raisonné* of traditional uses of "holy," spoken by Hypocrisy, the Vice in *Lusty Juventus*, reveals the terrifying force of a presentation pure and simple.

> Under the name of holynes and religion,
> That deceyued almost all.
>   As holy Cardinals, holy Popes,
> Holy vestimentes, holy copes,
> Holy Harmettes and Friers,
> Holy priestes, holy bisshopes,
> Holy Monkes, holy abbottes,
> Yea, and al obstinate lyers.
>   Holy pardons, holy beades,
> Holy Saintes, holy Images,
> With holy, holy bloud
> Holy stockes, holy stones:
> Holy cloughtes, holy bones:
> Yea, and holy holy wood.
>   Holy skinnes, holy bulles,
> Holy Rochettes, and coules:
> Holy crouches and staues:
> Holy hoodes, holy cappes:
> Holy Miters, holy hattes:
> And good holy holy knaues.
>   Holy days, holy fastinges:
> Holy twitching, holy tastynges:
> Holy visions and sightes:
> Holy waxe, holy leade:
> Holy water, holy breade:
> To driue away spirites.
>   Holy fyre, holy palme:
> Holy oyle, holy creame
> And holy asshes also:

Holy brouches, holy ringes:
Holy knelinge, holy sensynges:
And a hundred trim trams mo.
  Holy crosses, holy belles:
Holy reliques, holy iewels:
Of mine own inuencion:
Holy candels, holy tapers:
Holy parchementes, holy papers:
Had not you a holy sonne? (Wever, *An Interlude* 406–43)

This monstrous piece of Saturnalian overbid was liable, even as it served a radical Protestant purpose, to get out of control. It deserves to be quoted despite its length because its doctrinal meaning is resolutely translated into a show-piece for the scoffing, juggling, jeering performer. The disparity between doctrine and display is such that, in their approximation, there remains a surplus, a performative overcharge that threatens to undo the presumed piety, the true inwardness, of the Protestant alternative. "Under the name of holynes," defined through a gloating, glaring burlesque, "religion" itself is said to have "deceyued almost all." In a manner totally different from Jack Juggler's metatheatrical play upon 'transubstantiation,' the performer radically relinquishes the convention of dramatic role-playing. The remorseless onslaught against a broad spectrum of religious practices is delivered not in the mirror of dialogic exchange or action but on the presentational strength and immediacy of its comic-horrific display value.

In the present context, the Tudor Reformation play is of particular interest in that the gap in parity between author's pen and actor's voice must have offered irresistible opportunities for players who, exploiting the anti-Catholic invective, filled this gap with mimetic forms of age-old parody, burlesque, and disenchantment. In such a situation, we may well assume a good deal of proximity, not to say complicity, between those players who performed ordinary roles, allegorical or otherwise, in moral interludes and those "iuglers, scoffers, iesters" that, only a decade or two later, came to be perceived as more and more objectionable in their complicity with dramatic performers.

To say this is neither to ignore nor to underestimate the range and persistence of noble patronage and clerical authorship that recent research has documented in the drama of the period.[12] On the contrary, if indeed there was "a nationwide system of Protestant patronage" and if, under these auspices, Protestant plays and playing continued virtually unhampered after their prohibition of May 16, 1559, in fact, "well into the 1570s" (Paul White, *Theatre and Reformation* 5, 164), the continuity of an actor-dominated dramaturgy on the itinerant stage appears all the more remark-

able. Whether or not the strength of the player's presence in these circumstances derived from the fact that "in all nonconformist acting, the player
is never totally subsumed by his persona" (Kendall, *Drama of Dissent* 127)
the continuing strength of this non-Aristotelian dramaturgy appears incontestable. And indeed, only the stubborn persistence of this strength can
bear out John Astington's answer to the problem of disparity between rare
texts and plentiful playing in the pre-Marlovian Elizabethan theatre.

When, in the course of the 1570s, the Protestant inspiration for drama
began to subside, many of the players as a matter of course would move
away from topical representations of verbally enshrined religious meanings. At a time when dramatic actors rubbed shoulders with all sorts of
jugglers, jesters, tumblers, and other performers, there must have been
plenty of alternatives to the preeminence in performance of anything as
abstract as an idea, as masterful as instruction, as controversial as truth in
the representation of belief. So when playing as a way of spreading the
Word had definitely become unacceptable, the scene was set for what, for
lack of a better term, Muriel Bradbrook called the "medley." As far as
descriptions of performances such as the spectacle given at Gloucester
about 1570 under the name of *The Cradle of Security* or that of Leicester's
Men at Kenilworth (1575) provide us with some rudimentary evidence,
these offerings could contain pageants, mummings, processions, and country shows such as the revived Hock-Tuesday "storial show," together with
merry-making sports, mixtures of show and song, and last but not least, a
celebration of the "triumph of players over preachers" (150).

In view of this extraordinary gallimaufrey, our modern concepts and
tools of analysis have obvious limitations; as Suzanne Westfall notes about
Elizabethan household theatre, we need to expand "our definitions of
theatre" in order "to examine these diverse and generally unscripted
constructs" ("'A commonty a Christmas gambold'" 39). At least we
cannot content ourselves with an exclusively modern point of view, according to which the underlying "transition from narrative" to drama was
said to have "engendered confusion, for the nature of drama was not
clear" (Bradbrook, *Rise of the Common Player* 123). If, indeed, the "degree
of confusion between 'show' and 'play,' antics and actors" (124) was
exorbitant, the question is whether common players or even, if they
existed, their popular writers did not know the difference between presenting and representing, or whether perhaps they knew full well what they
were doing, but simply did not care to observe, as the neoclassical poetics
prescribed it, "the difference betwixt reporting and representing" (Sidney,
Prose Works 3:19).

Reforming "a whole theatre of others" (*Hamlet*)

As the Elizabethan settlement in politics and religion was drawing to a close, the already existing "religious, social, and cultural lines of cleavage grew sharper than they had been" (Bush, *English Literature* 14). This is not to deny that, politically, a good deal of the Jacobean period continued to enjoy, in Christopher Hill's words, "years of a considerable degree of national unity" (*Collected Essays* 1:4). However, in the field of cultural practices the continuity of a nationally significant inclusiveness was being undermined by, among other things, newly articulate divisions and differentiations, in which the theatre, including relations of writing and playing, figured fairly conspicuously.

The climate of inclusive cultural expectations, in particular what more than a generation ago used to be called "the unity of taste" in the Elizabethan theatre (Harbage, *Shakespeare's Audience* 144),[13] was gradually giving way. In early modern England, the exceptional strength of the "mingle-mangle," that is, the hodge-podge force in what Cornelius Castoriadis defined as the "ensemblist-ensemblizing dimension" of both "social doing" and "social representing/saying" (238) was beginning to exhaust itself.[14] With the first immediate threat of Spanish invasion over, the execution of Essex must have made it difficult to find a consistently strong patriotic focus for an "Elizabethan writing of England" that, in Richard Helgerson's revealing phrase, could plausibly claim some viable core of interest and resolution among socially and educationally diverse positions.[15] The Elizabethan cultural "ensemble" had in its imaginary institution been witness (again, in Castoriadis' words) to important elements of a "self-identical unity of differences"; the days of the cultural alliance approaching an end, the entire "schemata of separation and union" (which mutually implied and presupposed one another) were nearing a state of "decomposition" (Castoriadis, *Imaginary Institution* 224). Now the alliance of court, city, and country, so crucial to the formative years of Elizabethan drama, was becoming a thing of the past; henceforth, this alliance could only be used to evoke nostalgic memories of the days of good queen Bess, as spelled out in the mingle-mangle title of Tarlton's posthumous collection of *His Court Witty Jests, His Sound City Jests, His Country Pretty Jests*, published in 1611. Even before Shakespeare returned to settle in Stratford, theatrical attendance in the London playhouses had reached its peak and was levelling off (Harbage, *Shakespeare's Audience* 38).

The emergence of a vociferous Protestantism in manners and morals coincided, by 1580 or thereabout, with a final and irretrievable rejection of the stage as a Protestant medium. Together, these trends pointed to the exclusion of the licentious and the withdrawal of the worthy from important cultural practices. As English Protestantism spread at the grass roots, as the channels of education broadened, the technology of print expanded, and reading and writing were more widely practiced, cultural and political articulation and discussion reached a level unprecedented in its dimensions.[16] Sir Robert Cecil in 1601 was perplexed that "parliament-matters are ordinarily talked of in streets."[17] It was in this context that, I suggest, the call for socio-cultural reform and refinement reflected an ambivalent set of both fervid hopes and deep anxieties. This was the time when, with hindsight one may perhaps say, it was high time that a sharper line was drawn between polite and popular pursuits, between "judicious" and vulgar standards in cultural production and consumption.

For the theatre, this moment was one of a particular dynamic. If my reading in the preceding section is not wide of the mark, the end of the alliance between drama and Protestantism or, as Paul White calls it, "the break-up of the pro-drama consensus among Protestants" (164), while it certainly reduced the range of patronage, was not of course the end of itinerant playing. On the contrary, as the *REED* records suggest, this period was preceded, in Bradbrook's phrase, by a "multiplication of troupes of poor players in the late sixties and early seventies" (*Rise of the Common Player* 125). Now the scene was set for a recrudescence of the most variegated secular performance practices. The end of Protestant inspiration and patronage coincided with the beginning of a withdrawal from the theatre of the better and, even, the middling sort, leading to the demand to "reform" the profession (the verb is used twice in *Hamlet* 3.2.36; 38). But these demands came at a time when, paradoxically, both playwrights and performers continued to straddle the emerging cultural divisions. Here I do not wish to anticipate a reading of the complex constellation in which *Hamlet* finds itself between a persistent element of inclusiveness and the assertion of a new authority of the "judicious." Let me content myself with the observation that, at the turn of the century, Shakespeare's plays thrived in a set of circumstances in which it appeared not only possible but, in view of continued audience appeal and attendance, desirable to confront and, even, playfully use elements of both "separation" and "union" in a multiple constellation of theatrical discourses and practices.

In order to illustrate the paradox involved in these circumstances, it must suffice here to note that, on the one hand, Shakespeare's plays continued to draw on a fairly inclusive frame of reference. The same Hamlet, who enjoins "modesty" and "discretion" upon the players (words that, as we shall presently see, are central concepts in the language of reform) is perfectly prepared to tolerate, even to exploit, the absence of such discretion in his encounter with the grave-digger.

> By the Lord, Horatio, this three years I have took note of it: the age is
> grown so pick'd that the toe of the peasant comes so near the heel of the
> courtier, he galls his kibe. (5.1.138–41)

At this point, there prevails some sort of balance between "union" and "separation," inclusiveness and stratification. It is an observation that neatly marks both the "mingle-mangle" of mobility and the awareness of social difference, with an implied need, or so it seems, for imminent differentiation of social status. The Prince of Denmark seizes on a new sense of both social collision *and* cultural proximity inside and outside the theatre. But then he does so without himself proceeding to any gesture of exclusion. Inspired as well as perhaps appalled by the mother-wit of a "peasant," the Prince resolves to "speak by the card," accepting the clownish mode of quibbling contrariety as a challenge ("or equivocation will undo us" 138) in his own freely initiated communication with the grave-digger.

However, Shakespeare's equivocal position – the demand for "reform" and the refusal to comply with it in one and the same play – is largely unparalleled. Elsewhere in the Elizabethan theatre, the forces of differentiation and exclusion were emphatically gaining in strength. At the turn of the century, even before *Hamlet*, as we know the play, was first produced, certain performance practices were increasingly singled out as a target for attack. This was the case in the emerging satire, as practiced by Joseph Hall (1597) and Everard Guilpin (1598), where the former, as we have seen, attacked the "self-resembled show" of the "self-misformed," self-disfigured player (Hall, *Virgidemiarum* 1.3.34), while the latter socially downgraded the jig and, with it, relegated Kempe the clown to the forbidding level of an exclusively vulgar type of cultural consumption:

> you rotten-throated slaues
> Engarlanded with coney-catching knaues,
> Whores, Bedles, bawdes, and Sergeants filthily
> Chaunt *Kemps* Iigge. (Guilpin, *Skialetheia* 83)[18]

This must have preceded by a year or two *The Return from Parnassus* (1599/1601), where, in Part II, a virtually illiterate or blissfully ignorant "Kemp" enters to say, "Few of the vniuersity [men] pen plaies well, they smell too much of that writer *Ovid*, and that writer *Metamorphoses*" (lines 1766–68). Here, the performed clown, good-humoredly, or so it seems, is made to attest to a distinct gap between learned pens and vulgar voices by 'disfiguring' classical author-ity at one of its most highly respected levels. Behind the laughable recreation of the clown, the tenor of a critical withdrawal from common playing is clearly, if somewhat ambivalently, foreshadowed.

Among the new generation of dramatists, this tenor became far more derisive and caustic. The new departures in the work of Ben Jonson, John Marston, George Chapman, Francis Beaumont, and even John Webster followed in what was, often enough, not so much an antitheatrical but, rather, an antihistrionic direction. In the work of these dramatists, the lapse of assurance and the growing gap in relations between "author's pen" and "actor's voice" was turned into a gulf. As an early but extreme example, the line of confrontation was quite unmistakably drawn in John Marston's *Histriomastix, Or The Player Whip't* (1598/99).[19] There, the "Ignorance" of the uneducated was ridiculed in the polemic of Chrisoganus, a writer's poet and scholar *par excellence*. Although the player-characters turn a deaf ear, Chrisoganus, a pure (but gravely misunderstood) figuration of Jonsonian literacy, rails against both common players and such despicable scripts as continue to "load the Stage with stuffe, / Rakt from the rotten imbers of stall iests" (D4*r*). What only a few years earlier was viewed as at least partially acceptable as a great audience attraction, now appeared as entirely contemptible, as a stale article, the hopelessly dated "stuffe" of poor mother-wits. Chrisoganus, for all his pedantic excess, may well have spoken on behalf of learned dramatists like Marston and Chapman when he exclaimed, referring to Roman precedent,

> Write on, crie on, yawle to the common sort
> Of thickskin'd auditours: such rotten stuffs,
> More fit to fill the paunch of Esquiline,
> Then feed the hearings of iudiciall ears (D4*r*)

Chrisoganus' conscience, being that of a humanist author, appears to be appalled at precisely those "jestures" and "deformities" that *corrupt* a dramatic text into interjections of vulgar voices and bodies. A "yawle" is a semantically deficient, animal-like use of voice that complements the image of filling "the paunch" of "the common sort." Animality, corporeality, and the "foggy Ignorance" of the illiterate serve as images of the reproof inflicted on the "player whip't."

As far as the subplot of *Histriomastix* may, in David Mann's words, be read as "a comprehensive indictment of the common player," as a "general summary of current prejudices against him" (148), it clearly marks a new virulence in the rapidly shifting relations between a learned author's pen and common players' bodies and voices. Indicted as almost illiterate ("Faith we can read nothing but riddles" [C2]), these common players are, even in the names they bear, represented as obtrusively concerned with bodily matters; there is a venomous focus on a gross and quite distasteful tenor of corporeality and sensuality throughout their dealings, as when "Gutt," "Belch," and "Gulch," to name only these, sing at the Lord's banquet, squabble with a playwright, and are finally banished, in fact, deported from the country.

Characteristically, the players are shown to perform not only as minstrels but to be in the denigrating, one assumes, neighborhood of morris dancers. Their own actor-playwright, Posthaste, presents a despicable alternative to the refined wit of Chrisoganus, for which he is ironically praised in these terms:

> Heer's no new luxurie or blandishment,
> But plenty of old Englands mothers words. (C2)

Again, the context recalls the one in which Marlowe, though without venom, had first rejected the tradition of "rhyming mother-wits." Could it be that the acrimonious, ungentle vein of the later author was in reference to the as yet unbroken strength of this same tradition – a strength that continued to rely on a matrix of "illiterate custome"? Chapman, another playwright of the 'better sort,' has a "Noble Man" in one of his plays declare, "how illiterate custome groslie erres/Almost in all traditions she preferres" (Holaday 771). As this reference to "custome" underlines, what was at issue was more than a lack of political correctness in the observation of certain rules in neo-Aristotelian poetics; the grossness of the error was part of a way of life, a "custome" from which the educated and the well-to-do now more and more saw fit to distance themselves.

The critique, predicated on a preeminent authorship, of performance practices, found its most virulent and sustained articulation in the work of Ben Jonson. In his plays, the common player (as well as the ignorant spectator) is taken to task in a fashion that deserves to be noted because the 'trussing' especially of the performer intriguingly implicates the issue of authority. Without being able here to pursue this question in its wider ramification, I wish to suggest that, in the first place, there are profoundly significant links between the socially complex need to discipline the popular performer and the rise of new, discursive and intellectual locations of cultural authority. While these new sources of authority, derived from universalizing uses of knowledge, form, and representation, first and foremost sought to accommodate, domesticate, even to challenge traditionally given, external or preordained locations of enforceable power, they could also be tapped to resist encroachments from 'below.' The need to do the latter emerged at a time when, as never before in European history, new forms and media of information, communication, and signification expanded beyond the "anchor-hold" of any privileged or controllable registers of articulation. That was a time when a modern sense of civil authority, premised on learning, rhetoric, and discretion, felt called upon to contain the outlets of hitherto unrecorded and nonrepresentable types of desire, interest and 'enthusiasm.'

Throughout the critique and reform of popular culture in the Elizabethan theatre, these larger issues remain deeply submerged, as some hidden political unconscious. But in Jonson's case, the issue of authority is made explicit at least on the level of this early and, at the time, unprecedentedly sustained assertion of a new type of authority in the popular Renaissance theatre.[20] Well before the Folio publication of his *Works* (1616), Jonson tells us on the title page of the Quarto edition of *Every Man Out of His Humour* (1600) that the printed text is one "as it was first composed by the Author B. I. Containing more then hath been Publickely Spoken or Acted" (3:419).[21] Similarly, we read in the quarto of *Sejanus His Fall* (1603) that the printed text "is not the same with that which was acted on the publike Stage" (4:351). As his letter "To the Readers" goes on to explain, "this Booke" (i.e. the Quarto) departs from the version acted by the King's Men because "a second Pen had good share" in the text of the latter: "in place of which I have rather chosen, to put weaker (and no doubt lesse pleasing) of mine own, then to defraud so happy a *Genius* of his right, by my lothed usurpation" (4:351). If, as is likely, the "second Pen" in the playtext was Chapman's, Jonson's refusal "to defraud so happy a *Genius* of his right" was one way of asserting a similar right for the different genius inspiring his own "Booke."

The crucial point here is that Jonson's appropriation of a newly privileged type of cultural authority as a matter of course entails the expropriation of other, hitherto freely accessible forms and means of cultural articulation. Actually, in the first version of *Every Man in His Humour* he had already begun to reject "the fat iudgements of the multitude" so as to drive home the all-important "difference 'twixt these empty spirits,/And a true poet" (5.3. 339; 341–42) – which "difference," deplorably, was ignored in "this barren and infected age" (340). But now the time had come for "Sacred inuention" and "maiestie of arte" (322, 325) to take over, so as to authorize the inviolable rights of the poet *qua* dramatist. The claim was on the purity of the text "composed," as the title page of *Poetaster* (1601) repeated (4:197), by what in the earlier play was called "a true poet." It must have been in these years, at the turn of the century or shortly after, that the mode of authorizing discourse in the theatre first emerged as an issue that anticipated a new, combined concept of authorship and ownership, somewhat of the type defined in *Leviathan,* where "he who owneth his words and actions is the AUTHOR: In which case the Actor acteth by Authority" (Hobbes, *Leviathan* 135).[22]

Here was a resolutely new, divisive pattern of empowerment, marked by the emergence of both masterful claims of writing and condescending, even contemptuous references to the paucity of standards among players and spectators. Although the private theatres and the Inns of Court offered the most conspicuous platforms, these authoritative uses of authorship cannot simply be derived from the impact of the boys' companies. Rather, at the turn of the century, a larger set of circumstances helped bring about a rift, or at least a need for dissociation and new clarification, when it came to define "the purpose of playing" (*Hamlet* 3.2.20) in terms of the degree to which writing and the poetics of literacy were to determine this "purpose."

Unfortunately, there is not the space to marshal here (plentiful) evidence that Jonson's position, while possibly anticipated by Marston, was generally shared among early seventeenth-century dramatists like Chapman, Fletcher, Beaumont, Webster, and others. In their polemical references to "foggy Ignorance" and "illiterate custome," the language of these dramatists clearly participated in the larger European process of increasing divergence between elite and popular forms of culture in the period. Now the full authority of privileged learning was marshaled against such arts of performance as continued to draw on simple "mother words" rather than on the arts of rhetoric and the rules of decorum. If indeed the persistent note of denunciation betrayed the continuing strength of the performative in its conjunction of public games, dance and 'sport,' the attack was leveled precisely at a compound ensemble of extremely checkered performance practices. These were the ones that well beyond the turn of the century continued to thrive, as when, as late as 1615, Thomas Greene, the clown, leader of Queen Anne's Men appeared in animal disguise, his body 'disfigured' as a baboon "with long tail and long tool."[23] This sort of thing, among other show-worthy items, may well have informed the work of those companies that played to continental audiences with no knowledge of English. These actors must have been able to draw on considerable resources of physical skill, corporeal dexterity, and remarkable uses of "voice" and face in song and presentation. Here we remember how Leicester's Men, when they visited the court of Denmark a generation earlier in 1586, were perceived and described as "singers and dancers" (Bradbrook, *Rise of the Common Player* 97).

The links between "illiterate custome" and a strong performative in playing were especially at issue wherever these performance practices (and the audiences who enjoyed them) were charged with "Ignorance" and even "barbarism." Since charges such as these would be leveled at a specific social class of people, the call for 'reform' in the theatre could drape itself in the threefold colors of morality, gentility, and literacy together. Against these, there was no countervailing, independent stance, let alone authority, among performers; in the long run, their position was too vulnerable to withstand the powerful process of differentiation between elite and popular forms of culture.

There is perhaps no text that recaptures the rapidly changing situation in performance practice quite like Thomas Heywood's *An Apology for Actors*. Here was an actor-playwright who addressed the need for a new conjunction between common players and their 'judicial' middle-class or gentrified critics in a remarkable manner. Very likely there was no one quite as qualified on social, moral, and dramaturgic grounds to cope with the pressure and at least partially to undo the damage to the profession done by Marston and the new satirists. Heywood, who in 1598 was a member of the Lord Admiral's Men, belonged to a younger generation of players and playwrights; his early, exuberant chronicle of *The Four Prentices of London*, produced *c.* 1600, is within a very few years succeeded by the more discrete, domestic pathos and gentle setting of *A Woman Killed with Kindness* (*c.* 1603). His *Apology* in itself attests to the further course of the actor-playwright's own reformation. It was dedicated, with generous praise, to "my good Friends and Fellowes the Citty-Actors." Published in 1612, the treatise was, according to Chambers, "probably written in 1607 and touched up in 1608" (*Elizabethan Stage* 4:250). Here Heywood, in his own words, attempted "to do some right to our English Actors, as *Knell, Bentley, Mils, Wilson, Grosse, Lanam*, and others"; but "these, since I neuer saw them, as being before my time, I cannot (as an eye-witnesse of their desert) giue them that applause, which no doubt, they worthily merit" (E3). His remarkable tribute, however, contained a cautious qualification that, in our context, speaks volumes:

I also could wish, that such as are condemned for their licentiousnesse, might by a generall consent bee quite excluded our society: for as we are men that stand in the broad eye of the world, so should our manners, gestures, and behauiours, sauour of such gouernment and modesty, to deserue the good thoughts and reports of all men, and to abide the sharpest censures euen of those that are the greatest opposites to the quality. Many amongst vs, I know, to be of substance, of gouernment, of sober liues, and temperate carriages, house-keepers, and contributary to all duties enioyned them, equally with them that are rank't with the most bountifull (E3*r*)

Here, the player and dramatist has so joined the ranks of the reformers that his own writing is instrumental in, literally, furthering an 'exclusion,' a crucial differentiation from within the profession of acting. As Heywood has it, his treatise is "not in the defence of any lasciuious shewes, scurrelous ieasts, or scandalous inuectiues: If there be any such I banish them quite from my patronage" (F4*r*). Thomas Greene and his like may not have felt too much concern about such banishment; but the strategy was to vindicate, even to celebrate the acting profession by identifying with what by now (1607/08) must have seemed a powerful call for restraint. What Heywood seeks to defend, even to fortify, is the privileged position of "the Citty-Actors" – his properly authorized colleagues whose cultural capital lay in the fact that "our most royall, and euer renoued soueraigne, hath licenced vs in London" (G3*r*). The epithets of respectability ("such gouernment and modesty," "sober," "temperate") come as easily to his pen as the writer's readiness to appropriate almost the full spectrum of the language of reform and the call for restraining the "degenerate" (E3*r*). At the same time, Heywood takes aim at the new, and for him, uncongenial, tenor of satire and disillusionment, "inveighing" against abuses, especially in the private theatres.

The liberty which some arrogate to themselues, committing their bitternesse, and liberall inuectives against all estates, to the mouthes of Children, supposing their iuniority to be a priuilege for any rayling, be it neuer so violent, I could aduise all such, to curbe and limit this presumed liberty within the bands of discretion and gouernment. (G4)

In finally deferring to the judgment of "wise and iuditial Censurers," Heywood is careful to lodge a request that they "wil not (I hope), impute these abuses to any transgression in vs" (G4). The notion of "transgression" derives not from challenging any external authority; rather, it is "in us." Its rejection is completely interiorized, as is the language of distaste derived from the "iuditial" court of reform.

The appeal to the authority of "iuditial" spectators seems significant. Heywood returned to the word in the epilogue to *The Golden Age* (1610), where "iudiciall spirits" (3:79) are summoned to assist in the proper appreciation of his version of classical lore. Although in the passage just quoted, the author of the *Apology* condemns "the liberall inuectives against all estates" that had issued from the private theatres, it is ironic that the new emphasis on learned judgement had actually begun among the children's companies. Leo Salingar in his own highly judicious British Academy lecture (1988) traces what is presumably the first theatrical use of the word "judge" as addressed to the "gentle gentlemen" in the audience of *The Wars of Cyrus*, acted by the boys of the Chapel Royal (*c.* 1588).[24] When Hamlet invokes the censure of "the judicious" (which must "o'erweigh a whole theatre of others" – 3.2.27–28), he echoes Jonson's appeal to "judicious friends" in the audience of *Every Man Out of His Humour*, produced by Shakespeare's company in 1599, about the time when, according to Jenkins, *Hamlet* was being written. But Shakespeare, making Hamlet turn the adjective "judicious" into a noun, gives the prince's language, as Salingar notes, "an extra touch of fastidiousness, even a hint of up-to-the-minute fashionable affectation" (231). In fact, there is only one earlier record of the word, used by John Florio in his Italian-English dictionary (1598) as an equivalent to *Giudicioso* (*OED*, 1.a).

Thus, Heywood leaps to what was a radically new notion of 'judgement' as an instance of reception in the theatre. While it was already a somewhat dashing gesture on the part of a public actor and playwright to censure the private stages for licentious "abuse," Heywood in his appeal to "wise" and learned judgement goes one step further still. In the exchange of the new word between Jonson and Shakespeare (to which Jonson recurred in *Poetaster*), "judicious" was "the keyword in a *dramatist's* approach to his public" (Salingar, "Jacobean Playwrights" 232; my emphasis). But now Heywood, author of *The Four Prentices of London*, a play ridiculed by Beaumont in 1607/08, in about the same year usurps the notion of "wise and juditiall censurers" in the audience to set it up as a new court of appeal for performance practice itself. It is difficult not to suspect the popular actor-dramatist, at least unwittingly, of some time-serving.

Heywood is anxious to catch up with a process of socio-cultural differentiation that his language goes out of its way to promote. While he uses an older form of the notion of discerning judgement, his adjective "juditiall" (recorded in the *OED* under the now obsolete meaning, something that "has or shows sound judgement" – under 5.) is in its cultural semantics quite close to what Sidney in his *Defence of Poesy* (1581) posits as the true quality of understanding and "comprehension," and which, significantly, is especially related to the "workes" of "poetrie" as far as they, among other things, accomplish a "purifying of wit" and an "enabling of judgement" (Sidney 3:11). Thus, with "juditiall," Heywood authorizes a specifically learned, literary criterion that, as parameter, is now grafted onto a discrete purpose of playing. Hence, his advice is "to curbe and limit" performances "within the bands of discretion and government." It is a humble pledge in support of the project of cultural reform through disavowal of former allegiances. Players now are urged to join the cause of "substance," showing, instead of those "frivolous jestures" that used to be "greatly gaped at," "that good demeanor, which is both requisite & expected" (E3*r*) at the hands of deserving and deservedly licensed actors.

Heywood's special pleading draws our attention to a significant shift in performance practices that must be looked at more closely. It is surely not fortuitous that the observed and/or recommended pattern of histrionic practice is altogether contiguous with the reform of "manners" – a reform that Heywood's text echoes in its implicit admonishment for actors to move from "liberty" and "licentiousnesse" to 'sobriety' and "substance." In fact, the political economy behind the changing position of 'many' of the performers is such that they joined the ranks of the 'middling sort' and, leading "sober lives," attained the status of such "house-keepers" as were "contributors to all duties enioyned them." Whether or not the author of *A Woman Killed with Kindness* had in mind the emergent middle-class status of some of the players of the period, including the success story of a certain colleague of his from Stratford-upon-Avon,[25] the undercurrent of political rhetoric is profoundly revealing. This rhetoric participates in the larger cultural context in which a new order of civility went together with a non-scandalous, non-licentious mode of fully authorized acting.

From common player to excellent actor

The move from "the liberty" of self-resembled, frivolous playing to textually-prescribed acting was of course not a linear development, let alone one determined by a one-dimensional set of economic or political pressures. It is far more helpful to view the changing patterns of late Elizabethan and early Jacobean performance practices as themselves participating in the political unconscious by which the reforming culture of modernity severed its ties from its pre-modern or early modern antecedents. We need to keep in mind this larger picture of currents and cross-currents, briefly set out in the beginning of this chapter, in order to understand the remarkable degree of variety and the near-complete absence of chronological sequence in the very uses of the terms "playing" and "acting."

Once the strong degree of their overlapping is appreciated, some of the connotations of these concepts deserve attention. As G. E. Bentley has shown in his study, *The Profession of Player in Shakespeare's Time, 1590–1642*, there was a distinct preference for the term 'actor' in the context of printed language, whereas manuscripts, including the entries in Henslowe's so-called Diary or in London parish registers almost exclusively used the word 'player' (x–xi). The latter usage appears to dominate especially in the provinces; to judge by local records in more than a dozen Kentish towns, the term 'player' is exclusively used among no less than some 700 to 800 entries. As distinct from these, 'actor,' in Bentley's reading, "seemed less tainted with the contemporary commercial theatre" (xii).

This distinction is taken further by Andrew Gurr, who refers the growing usage of the latter term not only to the well-established links between 'actor' and the 'action' of the orator but also to the need, especially after the turn of the century, for "a whole new term to describe [. . .] a relatively new art of individual characterization" (*Shakespearean Stage* 149). As opposed to the 'playing' traditionally associated with the common stage, this new term, 'personation,' first coined by Marston, was semantically and chronologically much closer to 'acting.' Hence, its validation on the title-page of Jonson's *The New Inn* (1629), where the complaint was that the play was "never acted, but most negligently play'd, by some, the Kings Servants" (6:395). To play "negligently" was, almost three decades after *Hamlet*, to relapse into the style of those comedians who, as the Prince of Denmark noted, felt free to wreak havoc on the "necessary question of the play" (3.2.43) or, rather, on the play's text. In C. H. Herford's and Percy Simpson's view, those that performed *The New Inn* "had grossly neglected, or openly even derided, their somewhat thankless parts" (*Ben Jonson* 2:189). In not attending to their textually prescribed roles, the players, in their own way, may have followed the lead of the audience who either walked out on the performance, or followed the players when they sought, as Jonson's "Dedication to the Reader" has it, to "possesse the Stage, against the Play" (6:397). Jonson almost certainly endorsed 'acting' as distinct from 'playing' for its closer proximity, not to say submission, to the authority of the dramatist's text.

As far as the underlying differentiation of these terms can be trusted, the increasing preponderance of 'acting' and the loss in cultural capital of 'playing' may serve as pointers to a long drawn-out cultural landslide towards new bearings in seventeenth-century performance practices. For the actors of *The New Inn* to "possesse the Stage, against the Play" was for them to reassert the authority of playing over and against the play text. But when we recall how Beaumont in *The Knight of the Burning Pestle* was able to burlesque the stage-crashing, stage-possessing practice of amateur player Rafe, the extraordinary take-over of Jonson's players in 1629 must have been a Pyrrhic victory – always provided that the sensitive Jonson was not exaggerating out of pique. This is not to say that henceforth the social occasion and the actors' deliberate display of their skills were almost entirely lost in their roles (they never are), only that the dramatists tended to control them more firmly through their inscription into the play text. Thus, actors were expected to do both – to impersonate characters 'to the Life,' *and* to persist in presenting characters, stories, and histrionic skills rather than creating any life-like illusion for the play at large. As Alexander Leggatt notes in his *Jacobean Public Theatre*, in the latter case the player continued to stand "as it were beside the character, showing it off, commenting on it, explaining it" (81), as when in *Edward IV* "the performer describes the happiness of his character as though from the outside" or when, in *A Woman Killed with Kindness*, it is as though Wendoll (and behind this represented figure, its performer) "is watching, helplessly, another man's ruin" (85–86).

Despite significant inroads in the performer's liberty, there was then, under the circumstances, an element of continuity in what Jean Alter calls the "performant function" in playing – a continuity that should not be concealed by the different connotations of 'playing' and 'acting.' Besides, the uses of these words continued to overlap at least up to 1642. But if the long-term change, quite irreversible after 1660, can be summed up in a deceptively simple formula, the general trend was from body-oriented playing to text-oriented acting, without the latter, of course, ever quite engulfing the former. But in the period that I am most immediately concerned with, a perception of a difference between such 'playing' and such 'acting' was in the air by 1600. This, indeed, was a perception of nothing less than the shifting space for cultural difference in performative practice itself.

Once we take this overlap into account, it is clearly wrong to view the alliance of impersonation and writing as an immediate or entirely direct one. It is true that earlier sixteenth-century uses of 'acting' could already be heavily overlaid with the learned language of academic rhetoric, as used by Thomas Elyot, Thomas Wilson, George Puttenham, and Thomas Wright. In his *Apology*, actor and playwright Thomas Heywood followed in their footsteps when he sought to defend 'acting' on the grounds that it was good for oratory. But, as Gurr notes, the connotation of such acting "unjustifiably suggests a prime concern in the players with the delivery of their words" (*Shakespearean Stage* 149). Since there is little evidence that many of the common players had any training in rhetoric, the text-oriented, literacy-inspired notion of "action," once in alliance with the postulate of histrionic moderation and "temperance," may well be assumed to have gradually been used as an article of reform. As in *Hamlet* – a play that here, again, articulates "on the top of question" – the use of "action" was at least partially stimulated by learned advice and thus, as I shall argue, grafted upon the traditional canon of Elizabethan performance practices.

It seems safe to suggest, then, that the gradual and entirely contradictory transition from game-inspired playing to role-oriented acting went hand-in-hand with the reform of what Heywood called "the presumed liberty" of the performer. Clearly, the days of the performer who was free to play upon the word, or with the text, were numbered. The bustling, jostling, self-assertive player at the frontiers of (re)presentation was succeeded by Heywood's actor who would "qualifie euery thing according to the nature of the person personated" (C4r). Since the stage-possessing thrust of self-resembled playing was disrespectful or, as Jonson charged, 'negligent' of the authority of the text, the reputation of authorship and the fruits of a literate education were better served by text-oriented acting. This, at least, is what is taken for granted in the writings of Webster, Marston, and Chapman. The resulting loss in the authority of the "actor's voice" and body was inevitable. As in the case of "discretion," another postulate in Heywood's *Apology*, the changing emphasis on the purpose of playing is again anticipated by Hamlet's use of "modesty" and "discretion" in his advice to the players. Both terms, freely shared between the two texts, addressing players/actors, turn out to be synonymous with key words and demands in the reform of, or move away from, the traditional neighborhood of popular and elite.

To illustrate the complex play of cultural difference in the use of 'actor' and 'player,' we need to glance at two well-known contemporary character sketches outlining the character of a "Common Player" and an "Excellent Actor" respectively. The former, written by "I. Cocke," appeared in the first edition of John Stephens' collection, *Satyrical Essayes Characters and Others*, in 1615. But before the second impression was published in the same year, there appeared, in the sixth edition of Sir Thomas Overbury's collection of characters (1615), the character "Of an Excellent Actor," evidently written as a reply to Cocke's essay. Cocke, in turn, was quick to provide a rejoinder reinforced by two epistles in the second edition of Stephens' *Satyrical Essayes*. Taken together, the opposing portraits with their radically different emphases bear witness to an ongoing debate about differentiations in the acting profession, whereby diverse cultural perspectives could be brought to bear on modes and functions of performance practice that were socially and dramaturgically next to incompatible.

In one of the epistles, the need for this differentiation is freely admitted by the author, charging the anonymous writer of an "Excellent Actor" with an "ignorant mistaking of approved and authorized Actors for counterfeit Runagates, or country Players" (Stephens, *Satyrical Essayes* A4). The difference made between "approved and authorized actors" and those freewheeling "country Players" helps constitute a cultural topography mapping out the advancing boundary line of reform, restraint, and "substance" between the unforgotten stigma of vagabondage and the newly accessible and desirable attributes of sobriety and housekeeping. The common player, unsure of his place in both the world of society and the world of the theatre, is said to be without conviction, pride, and identity. As a "Rogue errant," "beeing not sutable, hee proues a *Motley*: his mind obseruing the same fashion of his body: both consist of parcells and remnants" (Stephens, *Satyrical Essayes* 295–96). His insecurity and nonexistent education are apparent even in the playhouse, where he

dares not commend a playes goodness, till he hath either spoken, or heard the *Epilogue*: neither dares he entitle good things *Good* vnlesse hee be heartned on by the multitude: till then hee saith faintly what hee thinkes, with a willing purpose to recant or persist: So howsoeuer hee pretends to haue a royall Master or Mistresse, his wages and dependance proue him to be the seruant of the people. (296–97)

The vulnerability and self-consciousness of the player, so scathingly noted here by Cocke, attest to the "miseries which persecute" the unauthorized performer and to which "he is most incident."

There is, then, a deep gulf between these uneducated, unknowledgeable, forlorn survivors of the itinerant tradition and the self-assured, discerning stance of the judicious among both gentle spectators and respectable actors. It seems as if the pressures of withdrawal and reform have painfully castigated the latter-day colleagues of honest Tarlton and sturdy Kempe. Not that the capacity for the display of histrionic skills and jests is viewed to be quite *passé*, but the "cautions of his iudging humor (if hee dares vndertake it)" are such now (in 1615) that his extemporal repertoire is reduced to "a certaine number of sawsie rude iests against the common lawyer" or "the fine Courtiers" or "some honest Iustice, who hath imprisoned him" (297). In other words, although greatly subdued by formidable odds, the unauthorized, that is, the quasi-independent player retained a modicum of his former craft and impertinence. At least two of his traditional practices may be inferred to have survived. First, "he hath bin so accustomed to the scorne and laughter of his audience, that hee cannot bee ashamed of himselfe: for hee dares laugh in the middest of a serious conference, without blushing" (299). Here may well be a remaining link with those "that will themselves laugh to set on some quantity of barren spectators to laugh too" (*Hamlet* 3.2.40–42), even when such laughter, to use printer Jones' phrase, was "far unmeet for the matter."

While it is difficult to decide whether the comedian's laughter unashamedly, "without blushing," was actually one *with* the audience at his *own* self-disfigurement, the second type of practice certainly appears to confirm the viability of a qualified performant function and the continuity of a certain degree of audience rapport.

When he doth hold conference vpon the stage; and should looke directly in his fellows face; hee turnes about his voice into the assembly for applause-sake, like a Trumpeter in the fields, that shifts places to get an eccho. (Stephens, *Satyrical Essayes* 297)

The comparison with "a Trumpeter" who displays his skill "in the fields" seems suggestive enough to characterize a player who refuses to be lost in the representation of a purely verbal exchange. With the kinetic energy of one who "shifts places to get an eccho," the common player does not so much reply to his partner in dialogue ("looke directly in his fellows face") as he speaks "into the assembly." In other words, this performer, standing, in Leggatt's phrase, "as it were beside the character," continues to present rather than represent a dramatic occasion. In his refusal to be absorbed by the norms of verisimilitude in dramatic speech and matter, our player is not altogether remote from Hamlet, who in his antic disposition, is told by Guildenstern to put his "discourse into some frame, and [start] not so wildly from" (3.2.308–09) what the matter is. On an entirely different level, Cocke's common player feels unbound by the "frame" provided by "the necessary question" of the text. He "stare[s]" (the reading that Q2 *Hamlet* has for "start") at what to him, as presenter, is more important than "his fellows face" and meaning: the audience.

This is a far cry from what "approved and authorized actors" were expected to do by 1615 and what in their new art of impersonation they, not without justification, were praised for. Thus, as opposed to such "base and artless appendants of our citty companies, which often start away into rusticall wanderers," the "Excellent Actor" is "most exquisitly perfect" in the art of "the graue Orator" (*New and Choise Characters* M6). As the author, conjectured to be John Webster, notes, this actor, far from striving "to make nature monstrous," imitates it to perfection, so that "what we see him personate, we thinke truely done before vs." It is, again in Heywood's phrase, an imitation by which the personator is artfully lost in "the nature of the person personated" (C4r). And rather than seeking to play free with the dramatist's language and "to possess the stage" against the playtext, "Hee addes grace to the Poets labours" (M6).

Whether or not, as E. K. Chambers suggests, the model for this mode of characterization was Richard Burbage, there is no need, in vindicating a centuries-old, lost tradition of playing, to minimize the achievements of the 'personating' method that, forcefully or otherwise, prevailed. In tracing the different forms of performance practice, the task is to recover, to make visible again on our stages and in our studies, the mode of presentation, not to privilege it over any successful rival tradition. The present project seeks to establish the diversity as well as the contingency of early modern performances; in order finally in this chapter to relate and correlate these diverse practices to different types of discursive and non-discursive activities in the early modern period, we need to invoke the help of social historians in raising a somewhat neglected set of questions about cultural difference and differentiation both inside and outside the Elizabethan theatre.

Differentiation, exclusion, withdrawal

The lapse of confidence between writing and playing was hardly an ephemeral episode, nor one confined to the period of the theatre quarrel. There is more than a little evidence that, in the early years of the seventeenth century, a sense of friction, even conflict in relations of textual meaning and performed action continued to smolder. Perhaps the most notoriously amusing example of this hostility is, as I have suggested (p. 36), Francis Beaumont's *The Knight of the Burning Pestle* where the good-humored image of an amateur actor, spurred on by (fictitious) members of the audience, manages, in Jonson's phrase, to "Possesse the stage, against the Play."[26] Similarly, but much less amusingly, in the work of Jonson, Chapman, and Marston, relations between "pen" and "voice" are marked by a new element of discontent and disdain that implicates common players together with common audiences in some sort of vulgar complicity.

Significantly, the attack on the grounded capacities of plebeian spectators was leveled at a crucial court of cultural appeal that, in Shakespeare's and most of the earlier plays, went largely unchallenged. As Jonson's phrase implied and as Beaumont's play appeared to rehearse, these spectators claimed to 'possess the stage'; they continued to wield their authority, if need be in violent terms, thereby revealing their own ignorance of the finer demands of poesy. The most vivid evidence that we have is probably dramatized through the enhancing vision of hindsight, but even so remarkably explicit. As Edmund Gayton recollects,

I have known upon one of these *Festivals*, but especially at *Shrove-tide*, where the Players have been appointed, notwithstanding their bils to the contrary, to act what the major part of the company had a mind to; sometimes *Tamerlane*, sometimes *Jugurth*, sometimes the Jew of *Malta*, and sometimes parts of all these, and at last, none of the three taking, they were forc'd to undresse and put off their Tragick habits, and conclude the day with the merry milk-maides. And unless this were done, and the popular humor satisfied, as sometimes it so fortun'd, that the Players were refractory; the Benches, the tiles, the laths, the stones, Oranges, Apples, Nuts, flew about most liberally. (Gayton, *Pleasant Notes* 271)

While this testimony may be colored through many-layered recollections, there is some altogether reliable evidence that spectators, at this critical juncture, could wield a sovereign claim on authority – one not necessarily in alliance with that of boy players. As John Fletcher wrote in the prefatory verse (1608) to *The Faithful Shepherdess* in allusion to the public debacle of its performance, "for, of late"

> First the infection, then the common prate
> Of common people, have such customes got,
> Either to silence plaies or like them not. (3:493)[27]

As the contributions of Fletcher's literary friends and judicious sympathizers abundantly confirmed, the well-attested clash, the lapse "in confidence," among important sources of authority in the late Elizabethan and early Jacobean playhouse was accompanied, or even provoked, by a virulent assertion of a new authority and dignity in writing. What is more, the emerging new sense of proud authorship sought to define, even perhaps shelter, its privileged status and its socio-cultural identity through distancing, dismissing, and finally silencing "the common prate / Of common people" among both audiences and certain ranks of players.

The question is, whether and on what grounds these larger discontents attest to the diminution of a mutually supportive arrangement between writing and performance. Such arrangements, it seems, could no longer quite be taken for granted; an increasing awareness of friction between, on the one side, poets and, on the other, players and common audiences made it possible, at least on the children's stage, formally to stylize these problematic relations as either the rivalry or the reconciliation of contentious claims. As such these claims could be playfully negotiated and dramatized in Marston's *Jack Drum's Entertainment* (1600), where the "Tyer-man" – serving as a mouth-piece for "actor's voice" – enters with the embarrassing announcement that

> hee that composde the Booke, we should present, hath done us very vehement wrong, he hath snatched it from us, upon the very instance of entrance, and with violence keepes the boyes from comming on the Stage. So God helpe me, if we wrong your delights, 'tis infinitly against our endeuours, unles we should make a tumult in the Tyring-house. (A2)

The threatening "tumult" is prevented when "one of the Children" enters to explain that the dramatist, "Wanting a Prologue, & our selues not perfect," was loath "To rush vpon your eyes without respect," but now having been reassured,

> vowes not to torment your listning eares
> With mouldy fopperies of stale Poetry,
> Vnpossible drie mustie Fictions. (A3)

Tensions such as these could not have been entirely unknown on public stages, even though adult actors might scarcely have tolerated the outrageous attack on common players that, a year or two earlier, Marston, as collaborator or sole author,[28] had launched in his *Histriomastix* (1598/99). In both types of theatres these tensions must have continued, and Prologues or inductions could be used formally to 'contain' them (in both senses of the word) as, for instance, was the case on Jonson's stage. There, in a sterner fashion than *Jack Drum's Entertainment* suggests, the needs and standards of representing "the Booke" could be negotiated against traditional exigencies of theatre practice, especially when that practice was considered to be far from "perfect." The sophisticated writer in the Prologue to *Jack Drum's Entertainment* is content therefore to forestall the "tumult in the Tyring-house," and to let the boys enter as soon as a presenter is ready to apologize, in the language of the actors, for "his defects and ours" (A2). Thus, in Marston's early play, the space for mutual responsibility is comically – affectively rather than effectively – recovered, and "respect" toward the audience is reaffirmed as the actors promise "to gratifie your favour" and to "studie till our cheekes looke wan with care" (A2).

Between Marlowe's curt dismissal of "rhyming mother-wits" and the venomous rejection of "old Englands mothers words" in *Histriomastix*, there is in late Elizabethan England a groundswell of cultural change that begins to affect the purpose of playing on London stages. No doubt there is also a good deal of continuity in the work of common players in this period as when, in the latter play, the itinerant performers' mode of association is taken to be quite as unstable as we have seen it at mid-century. (Take only their pathetic song, "That once in a weeke, new maisters wee seeke / And neuer can hold together" [C4]). But at the turn of the century and after there is an altogether unmistakable increase in the sheer volume, emanating from more than one practicing "author's pen," of caustic condemnations. As distinct from these later attacks, those of the early 1580s (Gosson, Munday, Stubbes) were primarily moral, theological, and utilitarian; they were leveled at the entire institution of the theatre as, on the one hand, it parted company with the Protestant cause and, on the other, it had come to occupy, or so John Stockwood claimed in 1578, eight "ordinairie" places in and about London. But as against these practical and religious forays, the later antihistrionic bias is secular, social, and aesthetic, advocating a poetics of refinement that by and large inflects the culture of literacy, humanism, and a Renaissance sense of the poet as sovereign maker. Its primary target, as with Hall and Guilpin, but also Marston, Chapman, and Jonson, is ignorance and grossness, the vulgar and the antic, and all traditions that are incompatible with Renaissance models of classical antiquity. This learned invective becomes particularly corrosive when it takes aim at players who "wrest, peruert" the author's text or invent their own, as in Marston's reference to "this extempore song" – dismissed as "this base trash" (D1). Take only the near contemporary *Poetaster*, especially where Envy lets fly in the Induction at "players":

> Are there no players here?
>   [. . .] they could wrest,
> Peruert, and poyson all they heare, or see,
> With senselesse glosses, and allusions. (4:204; Induction 35; 38–40)

As soon as we stand back and view this drastic deterioration in relations of "author's pen" and "actor's voice" in perspective, it seems impossible – as many critics have thought – to account for it in terms of an antitheatrical prejudice. Although this bias may have played an aggravating role in deepening the gulf between common players and educated audiences, it cannot explain the unashamed sense of superiority that socially ambitious or elevated *writers for the theatre* articulate vis-à-vis the work of performers. Rather, I suggest we need to take a larger view of these changes, a long perspective that helps connect relations of writing and playing with an unfolding process of social stratification and cultural realignment in the period. Although the phrase can be misleading, this process culminated in what Peter Burke and other historians have come to call a European "reform of popular culture." Starting in the sixteenth century, the reform movement can be viewed as a sustained and quite powerful intervention promoting the causes of education and civil, moral, and devotional disciplining. It was, in the words of Burke, "the systematic attempt by some of the educated [. . .] to change the attitudes or values of the rest of the population, or as the Victorians used to say, to 'improve' them" (*Popular Culture* 208).

There was, beginning in Western Europe and followed by similar developments in central, Northern, and somewhat later in Eastern Europe, a fairly systematic, though not of course monolithic "withdrawal of the upper classes" (270) from what used to be a common store of sociocultural practices and assumptions. The "growing split between learned and popular culture" (274) was not limited to the world of pastime, dance, music, and theatre, although there is strong evidence that the withdrawal from participation in popular festivals was especially marked. As shown by Burke, "the reform movement" took different forms from region to region and from generation to generation, but "it was popular recreations which bore the brunt of the attack" (208).

The unfolding process of these interventions was anything but linear. The first phase in what Keith Wrightson calls "the growing cultural differentiation" (*English Society* 184) was nearly contemporaneous with the construction and use of public playhouses and the new fashion of private theatres in Elizabethan London. At the end of the sixteenth century and shortly after, the renewed and much increased interest in indoor stages was an important sign-post of an emerging exclusiveness in which, almost fatally, Shakespeare's own company was involved. Since by 1596 the twenty-one-year lease of the ground on which James Burbage had built his original Theatre was about to expire, he decided to purchase an imposing hall and the site on which it stood in the liberty of Blackfriars. Converting the building into a new indoor theatre, the Lord Chamberlain's Men aimed not simply at a suitable venue for the winter months, but at what Andrew Gurr has called "an emphatic shift up-market, from the ampitheatre serving primarily the penny-paying standers in the yard to the 'private' or 'select' kind of audience which expected seats and a roof over their heads"

(*Playgoing in Shakespeare's London* 24). Having spent £600 on this venture, Burbage and his company must have been shocked to hear that the Privy Council, upon petitioning by influential residents of this area, had issued a ban on adult actors performing there. It was only after the Burbages and company had failed to penetrate a superior residential area, that in 1599 they decided on what, again in Gurr's words, was "a rather desperate, second-best expedient," namely, to tear down the Theatre, transport the heavy timber over the river Thames and attempt on Bankside "a reluctant renewal of the old style of playhouse" (*Playgoing in Shakespeare's London* 26).

Although the Blackfriars venture turned out to be a somewhat premature gamble, the company in its own divided locations sought either to cope with or cash in on an incipient stratification among theatre-going audiences – a move that turned out to be entirely justified when, in 1608, the King's Men were finally able to secure Blackfriars as their venue for a 'private' clientele. This does not mean that gentry, foreign ambassadors, even the Duke of Buckingham stayed away from the Globe, even when, as Ann Jennalie Cook has shown, this amphitheatrical building "featured target fighting, rope dancing, juggling and fencing displays in the winter months" (*The Privileged Playgoers* 134).[29] The same privileged and/or educated clientele continued to visit the Fortune, occasionally even the Red Bull. But the question is whether the presence of the privileged in some of the less fashionable public theatres was not a residual lingering practice from an earlier period, a time when it was possible still for John Florio in his *First Fruites* (1578) to take for granted the invitation to a lady to see a play at the Bull innyard theatre, or when, more than a decade later, Gabriel Harvey could tease Edmund Spenser, then secretary to Leicester, to send "some other freshe starteupp comedanties unto me for sum newe devised interlude" (Harvey, *Letter Book* 67–68).[30]

When Shakespeare's company, under the signs of their royal patronage, finally moved into Blackfriars in 1608, relations between common players and humanistically educated writers had undergone a remarkable change. At this date, the company to a certain extent helped intercept the withdrawal of polite society from unregenerate public places of popular entertainment, even while, by retaining the Globe, they themselves continued to bridge the emerging gap between popular and privileged audiences. The least that can be said is that the King's Men, having one foot in the private world of Blackfriars, were well prepared for, even in fact helped bring about, the changing social climate of the 1620s and 1630s.

In this context, it is perhaps not too far-fetched to view the move to Blackfriars in the larger perspective of early modern social and cultural history.

In 1580 illiteracy was characteristic of the vast majority of the common people of England. By 1680 it was a special characteristic of the poor. At the time of the Armada, rural England possessed a vigorous popular culture of communal recreations and rituals. By the time of the Exclusion Crisis this traditional culture had been greatly impoverished, while its surviving manifestations were discountenanced by respectable society and participation in them was largely confined to the vulgar. In the middle of the reign of Elizabeth, English villagers had largely shared a common fund of traditional beliefs, values and standards of behaviour. By the last years of Charles II's reign that common heritage had become the property of those 'rustical', 'rude', 'silly ignorants' who remained wedded to their superstitions and their disorders. (Wrightson, *English Society* 220)

These of course are vast generalizations spanning an entire century. But since the direction of these changes is, I submit, beyond doubt, it is suggestive to view the disparagement of popular 'sport' and common places of entertainment in relation to this larger panorama. Insignificant in the perception of the early John Florio or Gabriel Harvey, the process gathers momentum at the turn of the century. The point is that this process of differentiation both between "pen" and "voice" and among performance practices themselves participates in changes affecting basic ways of living, working, and spending in society at large. At this juncture, as Wrightson suggests, "a deep social change of a new kind had opened up in English society," which linked an already divisive political economy of profit and acquisition to the impact of "educational, religious and administrative innovation" (*English Society* 226–27).

In connection with the aftermath of the Reformation, the growth of literacy, and easily accessible new media of communication, 'the middling sort' in important regions of the country were culturally authorized and technologically enabled to play an increasing role. To a certain extent, this role was crucial in hastening the divide between 'the better sort' and the plebeian majority. Impelled by the strength of newly emerging sources of authority – those residing in the uses of education, personalized faith, and fairly broad access to all sorts of discourses – this group tended to withdraw from the laboring poor. Provided they themselves were not reduced to poverty, they were quick to identify themselves, as Richard Baxter's family history abundantly shows (Collinson, *Elizabethan Puritan Movement* 375), with the call for sobriety, self-discipline, knowledge, and upward mobility. Their eagerness to place themselves in the forefront of sober behavior and practical learning accorded well with an ambition to join the more prominent ranks of house-keepers, rate payers, masters, and employers in their upward move towards a new disciplined order of civil society – one in which the authority of blood, descent, honor, and physical prowess or force gradually surrendered to the power, or at least the claim of it, of wealth, virtue, and knowledge.

Thus, the cultural upshot of this differentiation must not be seen in isolation. It was not only inseparable from the social impact of literacy, the emergence of Protestant sobriety and 'inwardness,' and the new ethic of workday versus holiday, but it complemented, as Wrightson notes, "the existing trend towards social polarization, enhanced social conflict and the realignment of social groups" (*English Society* 226). As the one trend suffused, or was superimposed upon, the other, material practices such as the acquisition of land and wealth were sanctioned, or could the better be maintained, through previously unknown levels of cultural norms, proficiencies, and moral postulates. As Mervyn James has shown, the educated, literate gentry pointed the way towards assimilating an individually acquired system of cultural, legal, and theological standards that helped them "to express their grievances, conflicts of interest, and convictions in generalized constitutional, religious or philosophical terms" (*Family, Lineage* 98).[31] This, precisely, was such stuff as world-picturing representations (and politically effective ideologies) thrived on.

At the same time, the advent of new, materially imbued, individually assimilated, and religiously sanctioned standards lent fervor and dedication to those agents and agencies that redefined the boundaries of recreation and put in question the permissibility of "fond and frivolous" uses of both pastime and knowledge. As part of a larger process of reform, the scornful rejection of "such rotten stuffs" as (now) offended judicious ears was part of an educational project fraught with powerful ideology. Its "political unconscious," again to use Fredric Jameson's term, was finally inseparable from what Burke calls "the establishment of tighter patterns of social discipline" (*Popular Culture* 227).

In this rough summary, the forces of cultural change are marshaled in a fashion that is much too schematic to do justice to the dialectic by which, on a European scale, the social patterns of exclusion could often enough overlap with countervailing moves for new integration and inclusion. As, for instance, Roger Chartier has shown for France, the cultural uses of print were socially marked by an increase in "relative uniformity," at least as long as "differences in book productions attenuated"; but at the same time, the greater availability of the printed word responded to "a desire for an increased differentiation in the modes of appropriation of typographic materials" (Chartier, *The Cultural Uses of Print* 182). Here as elsewhere, there was – in Cornelius Castoriadis' terms – a paradoxical conjuncture of "separation" and "union," differentiation and integration, in which these seeming opposites mutually implicated and presupposed one another.

At the same time, we must be wary of imposing any straightforward chronological order on this process. Instead, we need to take into account that *The Rise and Fall of Merry England* (to use Ronald Hutton's somewhat precarious book title) was a process covering centuries, only to be ultimately concluded "in the years between 1740–1850" (Hutton, *Rise and Fall* 246). In England, the moral and ideological imperatives of Protestantism, which had helped destroy much of the festive culture with which the old church had been linked, were no fixed or unchanging factor; in their later stages they were "reinforced" by "a growing fear of popular disorder among local élites" (261). Without, then, seeking to reduce the long drawn-out process to any one causal, temporal, and functional order, we must recognize – as the most cautious and skeptical observer notes – that the study of this process "undoubtedly offers a valuable approach to some aspects of the social history of early modern Europe," even when, as Martin Ingram continues to note, "there is scope for debating just how profound and far-reaching the postulated changes were" ("Ridings" 79).

It is no doubt also true that the process of socio-cultural differentiation offers no easy clue to an understanding of each and every cultural form. The charivari, as Ingram has studied it, is only one custom that bears witness less to social division than to a shared set of cultural practices. The same of course must be said of, arguably, some of the most important and absolutely basic forms and functions of dramatic performance, such as those associated with the representation of imaginary roles. Since the early years of the seventeenth century at least, these practices are in their *form*, partially even in their function, socially and politically indifferent; as such they have become more or less impervious to any cultural split.

However, the same can definitely not be said about certain other types of performance practice that are inclusively implicated in the watershed dividing the theatre from the unruly neighborhood of various types of show, display, and performance practice. Those who, in Patrick Collinson's phrase, "were cleaning up the shows" were first and foremost instrumental in eliminating any practice that transgressed or challenged the bounds of a purely dramatic form of role-playing. In this enterprise, the cultural cleansing was eventually so successful that the triumph of "civility" amounted to what Collinson calls "a cultural revolution" (*Birthpangs of Protestant England* 101).

It seems difficult to convey the varied texture but also the sweeping force of this "cultural revolution" except by reference to highly particularized results of local studies. Take, for instance, the village community of Terling in the years 1525 to 1700. Here the representatives of reform in religion and manners "inserted a cultural wedge" in the life of the village that, significantly, was not necessarily in consonance with social and economic standing. Rather, some of the most divisive parameters were specifically cultural in that "distinctions of religious outlook, education, and manners" tended to be "superimposed on the existing distinctions of wealth, status and power" (Levine and Wrightson, *Poverty and Piety* 162). The reform and/or resistance of popular culture had gained a momentum of its own that was not directly or in any tangible fashion determined economically. As a result, the lines of social and economic division could be blurred whenever "a popular culture of communal dancings, alehouse sociability and the like" began to retreat "before a more sober ideal of family prayer, neighborly fellowship, and introspective piety" (171).

Since these culturally marked differentiations, as Jim Sharpe underlines, "were far from complete by 1603 and were very localized" ("Social Strain" 208), it is of course difficult to generalize about the country at large, except in terms of the complex, nonlinear character of these culturally enhanced or mediated divisions. But even in an altogether uncharacteristic, strangely precocious Essex community like Havering, where the middling sort were declining in status and wealth and the leading gentry moved into offices in local government, the parishes, and charity as a controlling force, the appropriation of culture and learning served as a major catalyst of differentiation. As Marjorie Keniston McIntosh notes in her life-long study of this community, "access to education and attitudes towards the arts contributed to the breakdown of the community's common values and experience, separating the gentry from the middling families and cutting both off from the largely illiterate poor" (*A Community Transformed* 295).[32] Again, elsewhere, as Martin Ingram notes in another strictly focused analysis, these impulses could indeed be "as much vertical as horizontal" (*Church Courts* 118). Even as lineage patterns of collective determination receded, it was possible for "unspectacular orthodoxy" (Ingram's term, *Church Courts* 94) to persist and provide important space for viable areas of cross-class religious and cultural consensus that appeared impervious to the forces of social division well into the early years of the industrial revolution. For example – another illustration – the absence of firmly drawn boundaries between a ballad-buying public and the recipients of a vast literature of popular piety shows that, for several decades at least, the contradiction between godly and ungodly spheres of activity was of little consequence; the reformers, as Tessa Watt has shown, were helpless *vis-à-vis* the demand for such pious ballads and chapbooks as were engaged in "a dialogue between Protestant norms and traditional practices" (*Cheap Print* 327) and they could not preach away the "unwillingness to give up a merry tune" (73).

In the theatre, the process of differentiation and withdrawal was marked by a similar complexity that, despite social differentiation among audiences, defied any clear-cut division between private and public theatres at least as far as the purpose of playing and important modes of staging were concerned.[33] Even so, the process of withdrawal of important sections of the population from stage plays, especially in the provinces, can be traced fairly early. After about 1580, more and more provincial towns began to close their gates to strolling players. In this connection, a glance at the evidence of provincial playing, diffusely assembled by John Tucker Murray and, more systematically, in the *REED* volumes, is revealing. Although records of prohibited performances are rare, the account books and Lord Mayor's court books in several important provincial towns speak a language of increasing reserve and impatience towards performers. Not surprisingly, early news of a "gratuitie to desist" from playing comes from East Anglia, where on June 7, 1583 the Lord Mayor of Norwich gave the Earl of Worcester's players "in reward XXVI s viii[d] where uppo*n* they pro*m*ysed to dep*a*rt [and] not to play" (John Tucker Murray 2:216). Similar payments were made in Bristol 1585/6, but also much later in Plymouth 1599/60, Canterbury 1602/3, York 1607, and other towns (2:384;230;413). While a good many similar entries are ambiguous ("rewards" are recorded as given for both playing and not playing), there is in several areas a general tightening of control: patronage statutes are checked, the players' license more and more strictly circumscribed, and the trespassing of prohibitions more severely threatened with punishment.[34] Spurious patronage claims are uncovered (2:337), and there is occasional evidence of hostile "misdemeanoure," involving citizens' "misusage of wagon of coache of the Lord Bartlettes players" (Faversham, 1596/7; 2:274).

These traces of resentment of course need to be seen against the vast backdrop of earlier and continuing receptions of players and plays. On the basis of the material collected by Ian Lancashire in his *Dramatic Texts and Records of Britain*, there have survived about 1500 references to performers in the century and a half before 1558; a surely quite incomplete "Index of Playing Companies" assembles about three hundred in the same period (Lancashire 349–408). Similarly, the *Records of Early English Drama* cannot hope to provide a reliable survey of itinerant playing in this and the following half-century. But in many ways, the emerging picture helps confirm, even when it partially corrects, the material presented by older research. For instance, the substantial two *REED* volumes on Cambridge, that Protestant-inspired breeding ground for Elizabethan dramatists and musicians, clearly show that although frequently visited by traveling companies under the early Tudors, "beginning about 1570 [. . .] the University grew increasingly hostile to professional entertainment. From 1579–80 onward visiting troupes were often sent away, with or without payment from the University" (Nelson, *Records: Cambridge* 2:704).

Although there was more latitude for actors' companies in Coventry, we have what, prior to David Scott Kastan's discovery, was taken to be Robert Laneham's letter of 1574 about "the zeal of certain theyr preacherz: men very commendabl for their behaviour and learning, and sweet in their sermons, but sumwhat too sour in preaching awey theyr pastime" (R. W. Ingram, *Records: Coventry* lviii). Even though Coventry's remarkable Hock Tuesday play was first suppressed in 1561 ("Hox tuesday put down" (215)), it was to be warmly received by the Queen one more time in Kenilworth in 1575 (274–75). In other provincial towns, such as Chester, "an adverse stand against plays" did not predominate "until late in the sixteenth century" (Clopper, *Records: Chester* lviii), but the generally increasing resistance to performance, including dramatic performances, was unmistakable.

For that, there is probably no better evidence available than that which Peter H. Greenfield has assembled in his study of "Professional Players at Gloucester." The number of professional playing companies visiting Gloucester grew steadily during Elizabeth's early reign (six from 1550–59; nineteen from 1560–69; twenty-seven from 1570–79), reached its peak in the 1580s (forty), and then rapidly shrank to twenty-six in the 1590s and – with a gap in the records after 1596 – to none in the mid-1630s. As far back as 1580, even before the peak of the 1580s, the Town Council had issued an ordinance placing several major restrictions on playing in the city. In 1591 the same council passed another ordinance that regulated playing even further, to the effect that the recorded number of rewards given to itinerant players dropped from five and six to three, one, two, and three in the following four years (75, 81).

Intriguingly, these local restrictions on Elizabethan theatrical practice in the provinces overlap with a countervailing process of cultural synthesis and national integration. There was in the sixteenth century, as a phalanx of social historians, such as Peter Clark, G. R. Elton, Christopher Hill, Joel Hurstfield, Wallace MacCaffrey, A. Hassell Smith, Mervyn James, Patrick Collinson and Keith Wrightson have suggested, an increasing integration of the national and the local, "which both drew together provincial communities into a more closely integrated national society and at the same time introduced a new depth and complexity to their local patterns of social stratification" (Wrightson, *English Society* 222–23).[35] The emerging "stratification" was inseparable from what Lyly called "trafficke and travell"; but at the same time, this growth of trade and manufacture led to an unprecedented social mobility, a veritable "minglemangle" (Lyly, *Complete Works* 3:115) of social and cultural practices. The new commingling "gallimaufrey" in its own turn further extended the locally significant markets of material and cultural exchange, binding together diverse and formerly rather self-sufficient regional areas of provincial England in a new interdependence.

Trends towards integration were even stronger on the political level. The early Tudor regime – whether or not it engendered, in Elton's phrase, a "Tudor revolution in government" – had promoted a more centrally administered network of control that continued, in Elizabeth's day, to bring closer together, through conflict more than cooperation, county-based and court-oriented gentry.[36] But among the dominant classes themselves there occurred a change from a locally effective, more strictly feudal, lineage-oriented network of dependencies to one based on vastly expansive and more abstract patterns of wealth, property, and contract. A new type of empowerment and allegiance emerged that tended to follow ideas rather than persons, that thrived on loosening the ties with family and lineage background. Ideas, principles, generalities thrived to the extent that the signifying powers of language displaced the symbolism of hierarchy with its visual images, making it possible to authorize interests and desires in representative form, with new claims on universal validity. And even though these culturally authorized uses of discourse could be used as a battle-cry of great force, that same force could also become a spearhead of integration on the strength of a new sense of national mission and resistance against Spanish expansion, Roman religion, and papal church government.[37]

It is in reference to such integrative, nationally (rather than regionally) inspired patterns of socialization and acculturation that a new spirit of patriotism developed in conjunction with those discourses that Richard Helgerson subsumes under the concept of *The Elizabethan Writing of England*. But in the theatre the process of socio-cultural "mingle-mangle" and integration had reached its highest point at the turn of the century. At that time, the attendance of socially mixed audiences was about to decline.[38] The Elizabethan history play had seen its day, and the playhouse, as a highly sensitive seismograph of cultural shifts, began – in Helgerson's phrase – to be "riven by internal animosities" (*Forms of Nationhood* 202). The scene was set for a "widening split"; as far as this split, as David Bevington has suggested, suffused Shakespeare's mature comedies (1599–1601), "the very continuance of a truly national theatre" (*Tudor Drama and Politics* 297) was at stake.

Such intersection of division and integration appears particularly intriguing when the public theatre's relative degree of resistance to cultural differentiation needs to be accounted for. Although in the sphere of manners and politics the process of withdrawal by the gentry and middling groups was marked by "inexorability and dynamism" (Fletcher and Stevenson, *Order and Disorder* 10), [39] there were significant cultural areas where either reform by or the withdrawal of, the educated temporarily seemed to flag or even to falter. The public theatre in particular provided a limited respite for those who refused to take a "censoriously negative view of sports and pastimes" (Collinson, *Birthpangs of Protestant England* 108). There was, as Collinson further notes, a "moral and cultural watershed" between the earlier "protestant alliance of pulpit and stage" and the rise of "iconophobia" (*From Iconoclasm to Iconophobia* 8). As far as this "watershed" between the end of the alliance and the rejection of unacceptable images can be dated "in 1580, or thereabouts" (12), the popular Renaissance stage at least for a certain period seemed to be able to shelve the moment of dissension. Even after a good many towns in the provinces, as we have seen, had closed their gates against strolling players or fobbed them off with a gratuity, there were unnumbered other places where actors, especially those attached to noble or royal households, continued to be welcome well into the seventeenth century.

Although, then, plays and players were affected by the polite withdrawal from those popular practices that wanted refinement and 'discretion,' there was still no such thing that marked the early bifurcation, persuasively shown by Collinson, between balladry and psalmody. Having both evolved as adaptations of the music of the Tudor court, ballads and psalms continued to share the same tunes and the same meter. But as soon as, in the late seventies and the early eighties, "religious publicists" withdrew from "any attempt to compete in the popular market of broadside balladry" (*Elizabethan Puritan Movement* 18), the culturally significant division of the two genres was inevitable, and war was declared against ungodly minstrels.

Whereas in England the polemic against such phenomena was largely inspired by Protestant cultural policy, on the continent the basic divisions in question were not confined to (post-)Reformation culture. Rather, the process of differentiation was sustained by a deeper groundswell of social change that can be traced in Catholic as well as Protestant countries of Europe. For instance, the archdukes of Artois in 1601 issued an edict forbidding "jeux de moralité, farches, sonnetz, dictiers, refrains, ballades," which, characteristically, aimed at the oral, extemporal moment in poetizing and talespinning (Muchembled, *Popular Culture* 137). As Robert Muchembled notes in his magisterial study, "a movement for the constraint of bodies and submission of souls had begun [. . .] As the sixteenth century came to a close, all French cities followed the model of cities of the North" (164). Although the picture that emerges in different European countries is highly complex, partially regressive, and entirely nonlinear in the quality and timing of the changes involved, it does point to a cultural landscape of increasing reform and transformation.

In Germany, more than a century later, this process culminated in the highly explicit critique, from early Enlightenment positions, of the *Hanswurst* and those itinerant performers that continued to be led and enlivened by harlequin types of players. In her path-breaking mission, Friederike Caroline Neuber published *The Art of Acting Sheltered by Wisdom Against Ignorance* (1736), with a Prelude containing the banishment of *Harlekin* a year later. Together with Johann Christoph Gottsched, the enlightened, neoclassical critic and author of *The Dying Cato*, both advocated and emblematically put on stage the expulsion of the *Hanswurst*, thereby seeking to oust the combined legacy, well-remembered in early eighteenth-century Germany, of the Italian Arlecchino and the English Picklhering. Even though in Vienna the indigenous German counterpart, Kasperle, retained some of the improvisational clownishness of the figure, the trends towards exclusion and reform – traditionally termed *Literarisierung des Theaters* – as a matter of course had won the day.[40] In central Europe, as in most other European countries, the authority of literacy and, with it, the dramatist's resistance to the culture of the self-resembled, undisciplined, headstrong performer had finally triumphed.

Over the centuries, *Hamlet* has offered a poetics of representation, a recommendation to actors (as well as to critics) "to hold as 'twere the mirror up to nature" (3.2.21–22). The concept of the "mirror" in this postulate was made to sustain a "purpose of playing" that was designed to fortify areas of continuity and congruity between the poetics of writing and the practice of performance, its cultural function, and its unique object, the imaginary representation on stages. Along these lines, the Shakespearean "mirror" was thought to be all of a piece; "virtue" and "scorn," the "form and pressure" of things within and without the world of the play were believed to be given, even perhaps before the performance began. There was scarcely any difference made, and no split was allowed, between the *discours* of the play and the *histoire* in the play or, to phrase it differently, between the discursive practice within the play at large (the *enonciation*) and the *enoncé*, as the sum of what individual characters were made to speak and represent. Often enough, the poet's poetics, the protagonist's thought, the meaning of the story, and its performance in the theatre were all taken to serve one culturally significant purpose.

However, once we revisit "the purpose of playing" in the way it relates to both the poetics of "author's pen" and the practice of "actor's voice," we come up against the kind of paradox that we first noticed in our reading of the First Quarto *Hamlet*. As I shall attempt to show in the so-called standard versions of the play – Q2 and F1 – performance, in defiance of Hamlet's precept, is devoid of any one fixed purpose. Even more important, the grounds of representation are neither as unitary nor as incontestable as generations of critics and theatre directors have made it appear. This conclusion is noteworthy in that it does so much more than simply confirm our findings in the 'suspect' text of the play. In fact, the conclusion is startling to the degree that the element of instability in relations of "pen" and "voice" re-emerges as part of a larger scenario of difference in dramatic language, theatrical space, and cultural provenance in the play. On its most obvious level, the unstable, unsettled element in relations of writing and playing derives from, or is correlative with, the ways and means by which, in *Hamlet*, the culture of Renaissance humanism and the practice of antic performance engage one another. The resulting "scene individable" (2.2.399) is also an attempt to cope and work with a scene divided.

The degree of division and the quality of difference being anything but static, *Hamlet*, coming at the turn of the century, registers a high-water-mark, possibly the highest pitch of strength in the elements contending in the differentiation process. Thus, Shakespeare's theatre can celebrate the pinnacle of its inclusiveness at the very moment when the impact of socio-cultural differentiation began to seriously challenge the integration of the Globe's components. At this juncture, the unfolding process of extrinsic separation provides an intrinsic potential, in the play itself, of conflict and tension between elite and popular forms of culture. In this situation, "the purpose of playing" was crucial in that the question of exclusion vs. inclusion was posed inside the play's plot and meaning, as an issue *in* representation, but also and at the same time externally, as a material, not simply imaginary mode *of* representation, informing and engaging diverse forms of production as well as divergent forms and effects of performance.

Once both the internal and external uses of the "purpose of playing" are viewed in conjunction, they can be seen mutually to illuminate one another. As Louis Montrose has shown in his penetrating study of *The Purpose of Playing: Shakespeare and the Cultural Politics of the Eliza-bethan Theatre*, political positions in the play can best be understood as at "cross-purposes": the "princely patron of the city's professional players will employ a courtly command performance as an ethical instrument for the determination of political action" (100; 101). Thus, the element of internal inclusiveness (with its huge potential of socio-cultural conflict) in the handling of the play within the play has a distinct correlative in the circumstantial history of *Hamlet* in late Elizabethan society. The play's cultural politics, precluding "an either/or choice between subversion and containment, between resistance and complicity" (104), is both directly and indirectly related to the conflict-ridden area between the common purpose of playing and the Renaissance poetics of literacy.

With no "either/or choice" before us, the absence of certitude in the frontiers of alliance and the (in)validity of Hamlet's advice for the play at large does not permit the traditional conflation of what "the mirror" holds and what, before the holding of the mirror, is already there. If I may emphasize what the Folio text appears to suggest, the "mirror," in pursuit of a Renaissance poetics, always is held "to show virtue her *own* feature, scorn her *own* image." But then in the play's Denmark, which is "out of joint," Hamlet's mirror does not *hold* what it postulates, at least not in the way of an "anchor-hold of authority" (Stephen Gardiner's term, see above p. 44).

Thus, between "resistance and complicity," just as between inclusion and exclusion, the play keeps a good many questions open. In view of this open-endedness, it may after all be rash, simply on the grounds of its historical determinations, to reject Hamlet's advice to the players without confronting the full extent to which this text raises a number of uncomfortable questions for its questioner. It is not good enough to deconstruct the poetics buried in this text without simultaneously permitting it to interrogate our own poetics or what substitute we have for it. Since *Hamlet* for better or worse implicates so much of our own cultural provenance, the engagement is two-way, or even between where we come from and where we are heading. In other words, our own purpose of playing and reading the play is not helpful unless this purpose is conceived as one that is both indebted to and compromised by what Hamlet recommended.

Renaissance writing and common playing

The most effective way of reopening all these questions about the function of playing is to study the circumstances in which they were first posed. In Hamlet's utterance, the phrase was articulated in an early modern public institution, on a common stage, a mere "unworthy scaffold," on which a (neo)classical explication of mimesis must have appeared something of a *novum*, to say the least. Hamlet's demand for a well-tempered, disciplined, self-contained mode of playing occurs in a socially significant context whose dramatic potential, astonishingly, has usually been ignored or underestimated.

When, in lecturing the players, the courtly Maecenas appeals to the precept of "the judicious" (3.2.26) – a rare word, with profoundly divisive connotations (above, p. 129) – the First Player shows an extraordinary degree of reserve. Could it be that his laconic, almost curt response is designed to indicate certain scruples against following Hamlet's expostulations? According to the learned precept, the standards of the judicious are authoritative; "the censure" of only "one" of the judicious "must in your allowance o'erweigh a whole theatre of others" (3.2.26–28). Even when, in his response, the Player himself uses the language of reform ("I hope we have reform'd that indifferently with us"), it is difficult to dispel a note of reserve in the words he uses. The Folio text here adds a minimum of deference in the form of an appended "sir." But such a blank response, with its half-hearted qualifications, is not exactly convincing. In other words, the First Player just says, "I hope" that the problem has been taken care of, if only "indifferently" so. When compared to the much more polite, truly respectful address, "What speech, my good lord?" in the earlier scene (2.2.433; to be followed by a repeated "Ay, my lord" 539; 544), the Player here becomes strangely taciturn, if not perhaps evasive.

Whatever (limited) weight one would attach to the Player's one curt phrase, the Prince does receive the actors with a vocabulary of reform that traveling players in Elizabethan England must have been hard put to swallow wholesale. How, one wonders, could they stomach a vademecum of performance that urged them to follow the minority taste of an intellectual elite and, on its behalf, to disparage the appreciation of a "whole theatre of others" – the vast majority of their clientele? Having in the welcoming scene chosen a speech from "an excellent play" that was "caviary to the general" (2.2.439; 437), Hamlet's own preference can best be identified in reference to what Henry Peacham in *The Complete Gentleman* will call "learning and judgement" as conveyed by "that discrete apt-suiting, and disposing as well of actions as words." Peacham's classical model is Virgil, when, "worthy the knowledge of a divine wit," Dido's "All-trembling" desperation is held up as exemplary in terms of the "most judicious observations of the learned Scaliger" (*The Complete Gentleman* 95–96).

Avoiding the condescending, ironic or polemical thrust that was to become characteristic of Ben Jonson, John Marston, and Francis Beaumont, Shakespeare in the players' scenes addresses a recently debated sense of incompatibility between Renaissance poetics and certain traditional forms of performance practice. Against the gulf between poetic eloquence and performance willfulness, Hamlet articulates the need for a new continuity between word and gesture. The links, with their sense of balance and mutuality, between the "word" and the "action" are strongly emphasized. The proposed strategy for overcoming the state of discontinuity between them is to eliminate difference through representation. It is a representational poetics that offers, not to say prescribes, a culturally refined, socially selective, decorous understanding of "nature."

> Be not too tame neither, but let your own discretion be your tutor. Suit the action to the word, the word to the action, with this special observance, that you o'erstep not the modesty of nature (3.2.16–19)

The player, Hamlet suggests, should have a "tutor" whose name is "discretion." The same word, as we have seen, is used by Peacham but also in Heywood's *Apology* (above, p. 128), where players deficient in "modesty," in "sober" living and "temperate carriages," are advised "to curbe and limit this presumed liberty within the bands of discretion and government" (E3r). For Hamlet to introduce "discretion" as an interiorized, but for all that supreme court of appeal, is of great significance. As David Hillman has shown in his eye-opening study of the concept, "discretion" is "one of the 'key-words' of the English Renaissance" whose "varied usages point to profound epistemological changes in the realm of discourse and representation," among them those that "implicate the stunning social division and mobility of sixteenth- and seventeenth-century England" ("Puttenham, Shakespeare" 74). What in the present context is of particular importance is that "discretion," together with "judgement," "temperance," and "modesty," tended to be used as tools of "social classification (the separation of those who possess these attributes – the 'discreet' – from those who did not)" (74). Thus, at the end of the sixteenth century, the Latin root of "discretion" – *cernere*, to sift out – reinspired connotations of that process of differentiation which Peter Burke and other historians have brought to our attention. The paradox is that Hamlet, by grafting "discretion" upon the players' performance practice, aimed at a reintegration of "word" and "action" at the price of cultural separation or social stratification; the unity of text and performance was postulated under the sign of exclusion. Paradoxically, the difference of word and body was to be eliminated in the service of a larger differentiation implemented according to the standards of the discrete and the "judicious."

When, therefore, Hamlet enjoins the players to observe "discretion" at the very point where "word" and "action," text, voice, and body come together, relations of "author's pen" and "actor's voice" are very much at issue. At this point, it should be clear that the foregrounding of "discretion" as a touchstone of judicious competence in playing on stages is not confined to *Hamlet*. The use of 'discretion' in *A Midsummer Night's Dream* (5.1.232–38) but also in *King Lear* (2.4.149; 196) provides us with a pointer to Hamlet's connotation of the word in that in these plays the term implicates the need for judgement. There, the word, serving as a "lever of difference," is used "in explicit contrast to madness, impertinence, and rashness" (Hillman, "Puttenham, Shakespeare" 74).

Thus, once the player is induced to think of his own "modesty" and "discretion" as a guide, his own standards of "temperance" and "smoothness" are already made to subscribe to a culture of discrimination and education that used to be quite remote from the bustling world of unworthy scaffolds. This at least is what Heywood, not Hamlet, sought to impose upon undisciplined players as an obligation: "so should our manners, gestures, and behauiours, sauour of such gouernment and modesty" as made their rise on the social ladder a tempting possibility. Those actors who had made it already were men "of substance, of government, of sober liues, and temperate carriages" (*Apology* E3), provided they left behind the "liberty which some arrogate to themselves." This arrogant "liberty," one assumes, must have gone hand in hand with a stubborn resolve to continue to suit "the word to the action," not the action – comprising the use of voice and body – to "the law of writ."

Although of course important distinctions need to be made between the "excellent actor" in Webster's portrait (or in Heywood's *Apology*, for that matter) and the First Player in *Hamlet*, the latter is ennobled as one of "the tragedians" even when he remains "of the city" (2.2.328). Still, in *Hamlet* the language of social elevation is more of an adjunct to a new cultural poetics distinctly associated with the artful inclinations of a noble courtier and scholar; this is different from Heywood, who very much in the spirit of reform, expects "to plant humanity and manners in the hearts of the multitude" (C3).

At this point, a further, crucial distinction needs to be made. While for Heywood the purpose of playing is finally conceived to be as "sober" and as "temperate" as the actors' rise to respectability would demand, in Shakespeare's theatre the related call for "discretion" (17) and "modesty" (19) is not the last word. As the play itself shows, the theoretical dimension of Hamlet's advice cannot control and does not discipline the practical side of what the staging of *Hamlet* actually involves. If anything, Hamlet's precept, his entire notion of how poetic theory and histrionic practice connect, is not binding; rather, his recommended poetics is lodged against the foil of what the play has to say about (and is able to do with) relations of language and action, knowing and doing.

Much as Hamlet's theory cannot constrain performance practice, so knowledge in the play at large does not by itself instigate action. The *Mousetrap*, which follows hard upon Hamlet's lecture to the actor(s), becomes a self-conscious vehicle with which to probe into the dramatic constellation of uncertain knowledge and unsanctioned action – a problematic that suffuses Hamlet's revenge on almost every level. Along these lines, the theoretical, humanist-inspired conjuncture of text ("word") and performance ("action") is overlaid by, but also enlarges upon, a similar, but more questionable, relationship of knowing and doing in the play at large. The gap between them, and the attempt to bridge it, mark both Hamlet's politics and his poetics. Thus, the Renaissance idea of artful balance in the containment of unruly bodies (that "tear a passion," "spleet the ears," that "strut" and "bellow") provides a foil to, even while it achieves unforeseen resonance in, Hamlet's own tragic failure to accommodate knowledge and action, conscience and revenge in one encompassing design.

In order to unravel these complexities, let us look at the *locus classicus* in almost its entirety.

> Speak the speech, I pray you, as I pronounc'd it to you, trippingly on the tongue, but if you mouth it, as many of our players do, I had as live the town-crier spoke my lines. Nor do not saw the air too much with your hand, thus, but use all gently, for in the very torrent, tempest, and, as I may say, whirlwind of your passion, you must acquire and beget a temperance that may give it smoothness. O, it offends me to the soul to hear a robustious periwig-pated fellow tear a passion to totters, to very rags, to spleet the ears of the groundlings, who for the most part are capable of nothing but inexplicable dumb shows and noise. [. . .] Be not too tame neither, but let your own discretion be your tutor. Suit the action to the word, the word to the action, with this special observance, that you o'erstep not the modesty of nature: for any thing so o'erdone is from the purpose of playing, whose end, both at the first and now, was and is, to hold as 'twere the mirror up to nature: to show virtue her feature, scorn her own image, and the very age and body of the time his form and pressure. (3.2.1–24)

The trajectory of the speech, meandering between recommendation and disapproval, moves from a critical discussion of the actor's rhetoric and delivery to some far more general aesthetic informing the "purpose of playing." Although the former is discussed at greater length, the latter turns out to provide the essential parameters, even the final authority according to which the key elements in the proposed "purpose of playing" ("temperance," "discretion," and so forth) are established as a norm.

As in Heywood's *Apology*, there is a strong infiltration of the discourse of rhetoric, courtesy, and civil conversation. We only need to glance at Stefano Guazzo's widely-read *La Civil Conversatione* (translated by George Pettie and Bartholomew Young, 1581/86) to notice its cultural proximity to Hamlet's exhortation. Guazzo, in *The Civile Conversation* referring to "The Authours of Rethorike" (sic), makes a distinction – essential in what the players are told – between "the woordes" and the "jesture," advocating temperance and "moderation" between them (Guazzo, *The Civile Conversation* 1:128–32).

> The voyce must be neither fainte like one that is sicke, or like a begger: neither shrill nor loud like a crier, or like a schoolemaister [. . .] yet herein is required such a moderation [. . .] to see the woordes agree to the jesture, as the daunce doeth to the sowne of the instrument [. . .]. That is, wee must imitate those which neither Saintlike are too ceremonious, neither Jugglerlike are too quicke and too full of action. [. . .] So great agreement is there betweene the words and the countenance, and the countenance and the wordes. (1:130–32)

Calling for "discretion" and rejecting "a playerlike kind of lightnesse" (129–130), this discourse is inspired, even authorized by its remoteness from the stage. Guazzo "will propose unto you a kinde of conversation, not to stand us chiefly in steede in markets, Comedies, and other outwarde things subject to fortune, but to the ende wee may thereby learne good manners and conditions, behaviour, wherein are likewise comprysed our woordes and speech" (118–19). But although the concern is with "speech" as informing the conduct of gentlemen, the concept of language is profoundly marked by writing. In the entire literature of courtesy, the new predominance of "author's pen" is perhaps nowhere as explicit as in the most masterful of treatises on courtly conduct, Baldassare Castiglione's *The Book of the Courtier*. As Sir Thomas Hoby translates it, "whatsoever is allowed in wryting, is also allowed in speaking: and that speach is most beautifull, that is like unto beautifull wrytings" (50).

The paradox in this literary emphasis on the rhetoric of conduct is at least partially shared by Sidney and Puttenham in their concern with the uses of *prodesse* in poetics. In order to contextualize the uses of "glass" and "mirror" in *Hamlet*, we need to be aware of the permeability of the boundaries among manuals on rhetoric, books of courtesy and those on aesthetics, especially as far as Renaissance concepts of imitation are concerned. Sidney, for instance, defines "poesy" as "an art of imitation" that is conceived in the absence of any performative medium whatever. Thus, he calls upon "right Poets" in their imitation to be "onely reined with learned discretion" (*Prose Works* 3:9; 10) A similar lofty impulse is taken by Puttenham to heighten "poesie," which "ought not to be abased and imployed upon any unworthy matter." In particular, poesy demands

A metrical speach corrected and reformed by discreet iudgements, and with no lesse cunning and curiositie then the Greeke and Latine poesie, and by Art bewtified and adorned, and brought far from the primitive rudenesse of the first inventors. (Puttenham, *Arte of English Poesie* 38–39)

Thus, Hamlet's desire artfully to interconnect "word" and "action" and Heywood's related advice to the player, "to fit his phrases to his action, and his action to his phrase" (C3), together with the actually advanced "purpose of playing," are all crucially indebted to the literature of courtesy, rhetoric, and decorum. While Polonius, as we shall see, extols the arriving players for the doubleness in their capacity to play according to "the law of writ and the liberty" (2.2.401), Hamlet on the same occasion invokes the parameters of "learned discretion" (Sidney's phrase), in pursuit of which the play that he remembers was "set down with as much modesty as cunning" (440). Indeed, it is "the law of writ" that in his advice is inserted into performance practice. A similar Renaissance pattern of representational form is upheld when certain players, whose work is deficient in "accent" and "gait," are said to have "imitated humanity so abominably" (3.2.31; 35).

What Hamlet's advice targets, then, is the players' voices and bodies that do not submit to the precept of rhetoric and the discipline of the world-picturing Renaissance text. At the same time, the proposed "end" of performance is singularly remote from both the players' and spectators' own concerns (such as success or pleasure). All the "graced deformities," the grotesque arts of disfigurement, in a word, the elastic springs and unruly uses of performance are suspended in an attempt to (re)assert the matter of "worthiness" itself in representation – a matter far superior to what "the unskillful" tend to enjoy when, defying "the law of writ," players "will themselves laugh" (40–41). The reforming impulse here links up with Puttenham's desire to have "Art bewtified and adorned" and to move it forward, far away "from the primitive rudeness" of the unlearned. This impulse is such that Hamlet, when finally coming to speak of theatrical production and reception, will disapprove of certain types of audience appeal ("though it makes the unskillful laugh, cannot but make the judicious grieve"). In this connection, unwelcome forms of actors/audience rapport are again rejected on the grounds of a particular aesthetic, that is, in the interests of the well-wrought, self-coherent drama of the Renaissance whose presumed unity of substance and shape, parts and whole does not allow that "in the mean time some necessary question of the play" be neglected (42–43).

As Hamlet with great facility moves from precept to practice and again from practical matters to aesthetic scruples, the trajectory of his speech reveals its own "end" as a highly complex one. Its focus is neither exclusively that of Renaissance rhetoric or neo-Aristotelian poetics, nor that of Elizabethan theatrical practice, but one in which the demands of the former are viewed as either relevant to, or in unfortunate collision with the latter. What we have at the center of the utterance is the tension (at least as strong as the attempt to achieve some balance) between the wholesome mirror of representation and the distracting requirements of performance practice, between drama as defined by the humanists (editors easily note echoes of Quintilian and Cicero, via Donatus), and theatre as practiced by common players.

Although the tension between Renaissance poetics and Elizabethan histrionic practice has traditionally been underestimated if not entirely ignored,[1] it deserves to be taken seriously as, potentially, the most distracting element in "this distracted globe." Nor is the difference in question irrelevant to our own contemporary productions of *Hamlet*. On the modern stage, the full text of the speech often evokes the tedium of a well-known lecture. But a fresh reading of this scene, which does not quite take the unifying tenor at face-value, may replace a normative and fairly static understanding of the scene with a dramatized relationship between prince and player. In the first Quarto, as we have seen, an exceptionally potent incongruity between neoclassical theory and Elizabethan performance practice explodes in what antic mode of contrariety is behind Hamlet's own display of the thing complained of (see chapter 1). But in Q2 and F, the uses of cultural difference implicate a frontier between a humanist Maecenas who assumes he knows all about acting and the actor who is told he needs to know more about the correct purpose of playing. Along these lines, the subtext of this scene becomes *dramatic*, and Hamlet's long speech achieves a self-motivated sense of exhortation, even as it leaves behind some uncomfortable questions about how authority divides between the superior demands of Renaissance rhetoric and poetics and the craftsmanship of the practitioner.[2]

In this scene, *Hamlet* can be seen to intervene in one basic constellation in the history of the Elizabethan theatre. With its abundant sense of things theatrical, the play renegotiates the precariously achieved alliance, maturing in Kyd and Marlowe, between humanist learning and eloquence and histrionic spectacle and practice. But rather than contenting himself with leading the audience away from the "jigging veins of rhyming mother-wits" (as the prologue to Marlowe's *Tamburlaine* does), Hamlet confronts the players with new and positive demands for 'personation' and verisimilitude dressed under the authority of classical verities. But, as we shall see, the poetics informing his advice is either counterpointed or intercepted by the play at large; the issue in question is so reopened that it profoundly complicates the business of reforming the Elizabethan theatre. Rather than unreservedly sanctioning the cultural politics of reform, the play at large negotiates important differences between the two sides. What makes this discussion so vital is that it is open enough to encompass not only relations of neoclassical poetics and Elizabethan staging, but also, and throughout the play, the confluence of Renaissance writings and common playing. The difference between these is so significant in *Hamlet* because it informs important strands in the theme and emplotment of the play.

To view this reading in a larger context, we need to be aware of the extraordinary newness in sixteenth-century Elizabethan drama, of an encounter between a Renaissance Maecenas and itinerant players, especially as far as this encounter gives rise to a debate about relations of text and theatre, language and action. As Harry Berger, Jr., has pointed out, there is reason to assume a "problematic relation of Shakespeare's text to the instituted theatre process in terms of which he wrote" (*Imaginary Audition* xli).[3] In fact, there is considerable evidence to suggest that the image of the poet in the Elizabethan theatre was not an untroubled one; as Alvin Kernan has shown, there was "a need to resolve the very real tensions created in a situation in which the writers' conception of the nature and value of their art did not square with the actual circumstances" in which their plays were produced and performed. While this might well be said of the early generation of academically educated playwrights and, much more strongly, of Ben Jonson, John Marston, and George Chapman, Shakespeare's position is far more complex. If, as Kernan postulates, he was not exempt from having to cope with these "tensions," he "was, the evidence suggests, *suspended* between a vision of his art as noble as the highest Renaissance views on the subject, and questions about that art as it had to be practiced in the actual conditions of playing in the public theatre" (*Playwright as Magician* 53, my italics).

Unworthy antics in the glass of fashion

However, to say that the playwright was suspended between two culturally significant positions may unduly belittle the active, dramatically and thematically consequential uses to which the cultural difference in question is put. To say this is not to underestimate the extent to which in the play these different positions remain separate pure and simple, contradicting without actually engaging one another. To illustrate such disconnectedness of unresolvable differences, we only need to think of the area of discontinuity between Hamlet's strong disapproval of the groundlings' preference for "inexplicable dumb shows" (3.2.12) and what in Q1 and F is "myching Mallico" and "Miching *Malicho*," respectively, in the pantomime. The latter is just as inexplicable when it results in Ophelia's puzzled responses. The question is, do we here have another "instance of the thing complained of"? The phrase, as used in Chapter 1, is Jenkins', addressing Hamlet's mother-witted specimen of clowning in the First Quarto's adaptation of the advice to the players. Elsewhere, the gap between Renaissance precept and performance practice is quite deliberately used, and especially so in the projection of the protagonist. It is no exaggeration to say that the element of contrariety pervasively informs what is most enigmatic, but for all that highly effective, in the characterization of Hamlet. As perhaps nowhere else in Shakespeare's plays, the difference between a high Renaissance figuration and an antic practice is infused, not only into the double image of a dramatic protagonist, but over and beyond that, into the tragic theme of an entire play. Note how Ophelia's words address the collision, which is one of character but also one of theatrical discourses:

> O, what a noble mind is here o'erthrown!
> The courtier's, soldier's, scholar's, eye, tongue, sword,
> Th' expectation and rose of the fair state,
> The glass of fashion and the mould of form,
> Th' observ'd of all observers, quite, quite down!
> And I, of ladies most deject and wretched,

That suck'd the honey of his [music] vows,
Now see [that] noble and most sovereign reason
Like sweet bells jangled out of time, and harsh;
That unmatch'd form and stature of blown youth
Blasted with ecstasy. (3.1.150–60)

Ophelia's utterance is so significant because it reveals the deep clash, within Hamlet, between two discourses, two poetics, two social moorings. On the surface of this utterance, we have a highly dramatic, agonistic image of the shattering impact of the "antic disposition" upon high Renaissance ideals. The speech presents in miniature what happens throughout the course of the play, whenever Hamlet under the guise of his "confusion" (3.1.2) and "crafty madness" (8) departs from courtly standards of "civil conversation" and "oration fairly spoke."

These last words are Bassanio's in *The Merchant of Venice* (3.2.178); in the non-tragic context of a wooing scene, they mark a similar clash of discourses which can throw into relief the larger contours of Ophelia's anguished portrait of character. As Bassanio's composure is overwhelmed by Portia's abandon, he is, if not "blasted with ecstasy," "bereft" of a civil type of high Renaissance expression:

Madam, you have bereft me of all words,
Only my blood speaks to you in my veins,
And there is such confusion in my powers,
As after some oration fairly spoke
By a beloved prince, there doth appear
Among the buzzing pleased multitude,
Where every something, being blent together,
Turns to a wild of nothing, save of joy
Express'd and not express'd. (3.2.175–83)

Here, too, is a con-fusion of diverse discourses. The speaker, in an exceptional situation, appeals to the less discreet but more elementary language of "blood" and "veins" that, socially, is identified with an unrestrained response of the "multitude." At this deliberate remove from the courtly idiom of the "prince," there is a larger, albeit indiscriminate space for almost "every something," a strange medley that turns to a licentious "wild of nothing," a contrarious "Express'd and not express'd." If we read "wild" as 'untamed' and 'uncultivated' or, as Alexander Schmidt has it, as 'licentious,' 'distracted,' 'eccentric,' 'mad' (*Shakespeare-Lexicon* under 6, 9/10), the phrase comes close to connoting certain antic, potentially indiscreet and indecorous articulations that signify "nothing" except a "joy" which is ineffable. What first appears as speechlessness turns out to be recourse to a different idiom and a different cultural poetics of "confusion," where "blood speaks," enjoyment matters, and "nothing" is that is representative in terms of "some oration fairly spoke."

Although in Ophelia's speech there is the reference to a comparable art of amorous oration associated with Hamlet's former self and "the honey of his [music] vows," graver, political issues are at stake. Over and beyond the brief echoes of Renaissance courtship, it is the education of a noble prince, the fashioning of "The courtier's, soldier's, scholar's, eye, tongue, sword," and the studied preeminence of princely conduct. As here mapped out, these standards follow the language of sixteenth-century humanism in the depiction of "virtuous noble men." Compare Sir Thomas North, Cambridge graduate, son of Edward, first baron North, writing in his translation of *Plutarch's Lives of the Noble Grecians and Romans* (1579):

When I first beganne to write these lines, my intent was to profit other: but since, continuing and going on, I have muche profited my self by looking into these histories, as if I looked into a glasse, to frame and facion my life, to the mowld and patterne of these vertuous noble men. [. . .] Or is there any thing of more force, to teach man civill manners, and a ruled life, or to reforme the vice in man? (North 2:196)

Verbal equivalents ("glasse," "facion," "mowld") and other echoes between the two texts abound. The parallels are especially significant in view of the fact that North, working from the French translation of Jacques Amyot, freely Englished his text, drawing on images and concepts that themselves were fashioning "noble men" in Elizabethan England. Note how in this discourse "glasse," i.e. 'mirror,' is used both mimetically, in terms of a narrative recapturing and representing of past lives, and as a kind of receptacle, out of which a "mowld" is shaped that imparts a "civill" form and helps "facion" virtuous conduct. This language irresistibly points to the Renaissance mirror of the Prince of Denmark, image of "the fair state," himself "the glass of fashion and the mould of form."

This type of discourse in North, in Sir Thomas Hoby's translation of Castiglione (1561), in George Pettie's and Bartholomew Young's renderings of Stefano Guazzo (1581/86), but also in English equivalents from Sir Thomas Elyot (1531) to Henry Peacham (1622), projected worthy patterns of noble eloquence and action. These patterns, as Frank Whigham has shown, pursued "an intricate social purpose combining poetry and politics, philosophical speculation and social combat," and they conveyed "a sophisticated rhetoric, indeed an epistemology, of personal social identity – a new understanding of *how people tell who they are*" (x–xi). What in Ophelia's salient portrait crucially emerges as a high Renaissance courtly postulate is, then, Hamlet's characteristic as a "glass of fashion." The protagonist himself is a mirror "of the fair state," a figure of the highest aspirations, of everything that, in North's phrase, is a "pattern," that is, socially and culturally representative. Hamlet as an ideal "glass" of Renaissance ambition and privilege was designed to spur *imitation* at the very point where, in the Renaissance poetics, the uses of the 'mirror' served to convey more than just an image of virtue or perfection, namely the desire to mould things and attributes "that should be." In a world marked no longer by a secure, fixed language of identity *qua* social rank and sumptuary order, such ideal "mould of form" was designed to incite the gentle and judicious to imitate a model or pattern and thereby, as we have seen, to differentiate those who have these attributes from those who do not.

Once we recognize, in Whigham's phrase, this "social purpose combining poetry and politics," the Renaissance figuration of the Prince of Denmark appears intricately linked to "the purpose of playing" that the same Hamlet recommends to the players. The link in question is well brought out by Henry Peacham, the friend of Ben Jonson and William Drayton, when, in reference to the "Prince of Learning," i.e. Scaliger, he defines some of the "prime virtues" of both poets and gentlemen:

prudence, efficacy, variety, and sweetness [. . .] Under prudence is comprehended out of general learning and judgement that discreet, apt-suiting, and disposing as well of actions as words in their due place, time and manner. (Peacham, *Complete Gentleman* 95)

Here, an entire vocabulary ("judgement," "discreet . . . as well of actions as words") points to a conjuncture, indispensable to Hamlet, of politics and poetry in the formation of "a noble mind" and character. The confluence of discreet judgement in "actions as words" extends even further; Peacham, as noted, uses Scaliger to celebrate in this passage the classical art of the *Aeneid*, while "Aeneas' [tale] to Dido" (2.2.446) is of course the source of the highly favored speech that Hamlet asks the First Player to deliver.

The humanistic slant in this "glass" of noble excellence was the ubiquitous concern with the uses and effects of language. In the sixteenth-century, as Timothy Reiss has shown, the verbal arts of the trivium had become unthinkable except as tools for communication and teaching.[4] In this tradition, to hold the mirror up to virtue implicated norms of rhetoric and a style of oration that were taken to be politically effective to the degree that they submitted to the "discreet, apt-suiting" standards of decorum. Such use of the arts of language – in the wide, not purely verbal sense of 'civil conversation' – were considered, in Peacham's phrase, as "props to uphold a State and the onely keyes to bring in tune a discordant Commonwealth."

Closely allied to these political purposes (and they relate of course to Hamlet's resolve "to bring in tune" the rotten state of Denmark) is, again, the Renaissance aesthetic in both Hamlet's advice to the actors and in Ophelia's lament. Both speeches foreground the uses of "mirror" and "glass" with, clearly, the potential of an idealizing application. The exhortation of the actor at least partially recalls Sir Philip Sidney's "universall consideration" of poesy where the mirror stands for a purpose of playing that follows the "Art of *Imitation*" and such of its agents as

> most properly do imitate to teach & delight: and to imitate, borrow nothing of what is, hath bin, or shall be, but range onely reined with learned discretion, into the divine consideration of what may be and should be. (Sidney, *Prose Works* 3:9–10)[5]

In the Renaissance Prince of Denmark, the mirror of imitation is marked by a universal consideration of its own; Hamlet himself, up to a point, poetically recommends and politically embodies this mirror as a representative figure. As Ophelia recalls, he *was* a mirror, and as such the source of enobling imitation; he was "a glass" that fashioned others when they, as it were, through their own ardor and delight in the imitation of Hamlet's noble conduct, sought to vie with the latter's excellence. As chiefest courtier in Elsinore, Hamlet does for a conduct book what, another fifty lines further, he tells the First Player to do for theatrical performance. If this living "mould of form" is not, in the strictest sense, a mirror of representation he is, undoubtedly, a mirror of representativity, that is, a socially and poetically ideal example for serving as the "rose of the fair state."

There is, then, a remarkable homology between the "glass" of the "courtier's, soldier's, scholar's" finest conduct and that other glass which in the theatre needs to be held up high "to show virtue her own feature" (F). In either case, a norm of perfection is given even before the performance, the imitation inside and outside the theatre, begins. But while the "glass" as a mirror of conduct is an ideal representation, it also serves, in its exemplarity, as an agency in fashioning the hopes and expectations of a Renaissance court. Like Percy Hotspur, Hamlet "was indeed the glass / Wherein the noble youth did dress themselves [. . .] He was the mark and glass, copy and book, / That fashion'd others" (2 *Henry IV* 2.3.21–22; 31–32). The recurring language of cultural patterning is saturated with symbolic forms that rehearse the symbolism of "glass" and "copy" in a build-up of the Renaissance prince and, simultaneously, secure his privileged elevation and distance from ordinary standards. As the "rose of the fair state," he is what Jenkins annotates as "a symbol of the perfection of young manhood"; as "Th'observ'd of all observers," he is, to use Philip Edwards' paraphrase, "looked up respectfully by all who turn to others" (*Hamlet:Prince of Denmark* 8); as the "unmatch'd form and stature," he is the unsurpassed, ideal image (of youth in full bloom).

However, in the midst of what Hamlet "may be and should be," a gripping force of contrariety comes to disfigure the symbol of perfection. The Renaissance discourse of noble excellence, unchallenged in contemporary writings on rhetoric and courtesy, is profoundly flawed in Shakespeare's *Hamlet*. The blemish is not in the manner of Ovidian *discors concordia*; nor is it contained by anything analogous to Spenser's "disorderly order."[6] In the play, the recommended purpose of the mirror, although both socially representative and poetically representational, is far from what "purpose of playing" is actually pursued. True enough, here is the grandeur and dignity that we admire in high Renaissance paintings, but in their claim upon a "universall consideration" these discourses can scarcely conceal a static and hortatory pedagogy that must have constrained the more visceral energies of performance in the early modern public theatre. It is precisely at this point that the ideal "mould of form" in Hamlet's humanism is gravely disturbed by alien energies and forces; for good reason, these are non-representable in the language of Renaissance poetics and courtly ambition. Hamlet's task "to bring in tune" what is discordant in the state of Denmark is put in question when his "noble and most sovereign reason" appears "jangled out of tune."

This, precisely, is the point where antic practice forcefully intrudes upon "the glass of fashion." As soon as Hamlet seeks refuge in an "antic disposition," the mirror of Renaissance excellence is blunted, the "mould of form" disfigured, his rhetoric no longer serviceable as a political instrument of civil order. Whether in disguise or true madness, the Wittenberg student tends to disturb the customary rules of courtesy. The antic article in the "glass of fashion" precludes such uses of "oration fairly spoke," as advocated by Peacham, where the educated gentleman, who should know his Cicero, is advised to use oratory as "a principal meanes of correcting ill manners, reforming laws, humbling aspiring minds, and upholding all virtue" (*The Complete Gentleman* 18).

Since the crisis in the courtly and humanistic world of the play cannot be adequately dealt with in the language of courtesy and rhetorical eloquence, the play reaches out and taps another repertoire of articulations – those that resemble Bassanio's "wild of nothing." In defiance of the high Renaissance world picture, the "antic disposition" helps *overthrow* the exclusive hold of a discourse marked by "temperance," "smoothness," "modesty," and "discretion." Henceforth, we have throughout the play two radically different purposes of playing that continue to engage one another. But this engagement involves more than simply a mutual give and take. What Ophelia's words indicate is a clash between two discourses, culminating in uncourtly deformations. There results, as it were, a visible disfigurement,[7] as when Hamlet is said to appear with "his stockins fouled, / Ungart'red, and down-gyved to his ankle" (2.1.76–77). Even worse, "that noble and most sovereign reason" is brought "quite, quite down." The "mirror" in which and through which nobility is fashioned is radically impaired. The "glass of fashion" is being "Blasted with ecstasy." If we read the word as connoting an 'ex-static' element of fury, madness, and mobility, the strong force behind the "quite, quite down" becomes easier to define in terms of a different, kinetic type of culture that was not primarily literary and rational.

To illustrate the strong performative behind this aggressive intrusion upon a generally upheld "mould of form," we need to look more closely at the uses of the "antic disposition" in *Hamlet*. How was it that the "sweet bells" of "sovereign reason" could be "jangled out of tune"? What was 'ecstatic' enough in it to bring "down" the high Renaissance "mark and glass, copy and book" of courtly conduct? An answer to these questions is adumbrated at the beginning of the scene, when we hear from Claudius the related question of why Hamlet

> puts on this confusion,
> Grating so harshly all his days of quiet
> With turbulent and dangerous lunacy? (3.1.2–4)

A "lunacy" that can be 'put on' is, indeed, "a crafty madness" (8), as Guildenstern further defines Hamlet's "distracted" (5) state. Excepting Polonius, the court party in using Hamlet's own verb ("To *put* an antic disposition *on*"; my italics) is scarcely to be deceived about what is "turbulent" and "dangerous" in the wildness of the prince. In fact, Claudius appears to be on the right track when he perceives the staged "confusion" of his chiefest courtier as "Grating." Here, Shakespeare's use of 'grate' (as in "a dry wheel grate on the axle-tree" [1 *Henry IV* 3.1.130]) is identical with its modern meaning, to produce friction, or to make harsh, discordant noise – as if two ill-fitting objects or ways of articulation are being rubbed against each other. Thus, Hamlet's "antic" posture so "harshly" grates against Renaissance standards of civil conversation because its provenance is wildly incompatible with any "mould of form" and "sovereign reason."

Even more important, "antic" is embedded in circumstances that tend to resist the most crucial agenda in the Renaissance poetics, the project of representation. According to the *OED*, the word recalls a fantastic gallimaufry of human, animal, and floral forms "found in exhuming some ancient remains [. . .] in Rome, whence extended to anything similarly incongruous or bizarre." While the word in this context closely relates to Italian *grottesco* ("a caverne or hole under ground"), the conflation of human and other forms points to an early background of ritual where, for instance, theriomorphic patterns prevail. As Jenkins notes, the "word is particularly used of an actor with a false head or grotesque mask" (226). In English Renaissance writings (Marlowe, Drayton, Milton), the word connotes cultural practices according to which men "like satyrs [. . .] with their goat-feet dance the antic hay" (*Edward II* 1.1.67), but also the "antic hobnaile at a morris" (Milton). In particular, these connotations of dance and late ritual, especially in their grotesque, uncouth and ludicrous manifestations, come together in diverse associations with carnival (Joseph Hall) and festivity. Hence, the noun 'antic' for a performer who plays a grotesque or ludicrous part, a clown, mountebank, or merry-andrew.

While the word's semantic field does not of course by itself contradict a perfectly strategic, deliberate use of an "antic disposition" with which to elude the suspicion of adversaries, its wild, untamed, non-strategic, and non-logocentric meanings cannot easily be contained. The strength of these meanings is confirmed when the word as late as 1671 is used as part of that socially undifferentiated confluence of popular performance practices in which

> sword-players, and every sort
> Of gymnic artists, wrestlers, riders, runners,
> Jugglers and dancers, antics, mummers, mimics [. . .]
> To make them sport (*Samson Agonistes* 1323–28)

This brief excursion into early modern uses of 'antic' can helpfully remind us that, over and beyond its inefficacious function as a device for coverage, the "antic disposition" in Shakespeare's tragedy associates a semantic space in which, to say the least, all sorts of performance practices, sport, play, and display lie dormant. In its latent meaning, the "antic disposition" in *Hamlet* contrariously expands the field of courtly and humanistic discourses; it resituates the protagonist's secret close intent in the open space of the performer's skill in delivering versions of disguise, disfigurement, and grotesquerie. Moving between the character and the performer, the Renaissance hero, who is of course firmly embedded in the story-text of a tragic representation, can for all that have recourse to mad sport and mimicry, game and role-playing. Easily crossing the threshold between these two different purposes of playing, the character/actor achieves a remarkable thrust, even draws a kind of authority from the antic strength of his performance legacy. In what Jenkins all too cautiously calls "this dual role" ("the prince has also the satyr in him" ["Arden" 146]), Hamlet achieves a poignant self-awareness of this con-fusion, as when he says, "'tis most sweet / When in one line two crafts directly meet" (3.4.209–10).

"When in one line two crafts directly meet"

The "mirror" of Renaissance representation and the "antic disposition" constitute the two most prominent purposes of playing in *Hamlet*, and they inhabit two culturally different types of space on the platform stage. Between them, there is plenty of social and cultural difference that first of all informs the language and the action of the protagonist. Hamlet himself is the vital medium and ubiquitous sponsor of the play's double-barrelled impact. As a figuration, Hamlet is cast into this doubleness, with a capacity for both rupturing and forging the link between his high role and his low craft. As we have seen, he can *present* his own feigning craft when playing either on an open stage or with a *gestus* derived from it, and he can *represent* his strictly localized, self-enclosed "within" which knows no feigning and no audience.

At this point, the "two crafts" that meet in Hamlet's use of language – far from constituting difference on a purely linguistic level – implicate different spatial functions of the platform stage. If I may anticipate a distinction that will be developed in the following chapter, these "two crafts" intriguingly interact with two different projections of theatrical space: one – the antic – with an open, *platea*-like use of the stage-as-stage; the other – the representational – with a more or less localized scene dominated by a symbolic use of theatrical space as, for example, a house, a court, a chamber, and so forth. A *platea*-like position helps to foreground the protagonist's madness or disguise, enables him to display or 'put on' any number of antic stances and responses; his open stage *gestus* serves a purpose of playing that to a certain extent recalls the craft of the juggler, trickster, and presenter, the exhibiting of the show, and the skill to do the show competently. But in the representation of a locale or *locus*, the mere "show" of delivery is no longer good enough; a localized site can provoke "what passes show." Substituting a represented "within" for a presentable show 'without' character helps convey an invisible, imaginary identity that allows for empathy. Like the convention of strictly localized space, the new "epistemology of inwardness," as Katharine Eisaman Maus suggests, is in its representational mode "radically synecdochic"; the "validity of what is displayed" now turns out to be utterly questionable, amounting to actions that a man can play (*Inwardness and Theater* 31–32).

However, since boundaries between these different uses of the platform stage are absolutely fleeting and since, more often than not, these spatial conventions can as swiftly be assimilated as discarded, it is not helpful to juxtapose, as in the figure of an opposition, the localized and unlocalized positioning of the protagonist. Hamlet is the product of a new, brilliant mode of characterization, but he is also deeply tinged by the theatrical process of both advancing and resisting the new self-contained mode of impersonation. Throughout the play we need to envision the concomitant uses of theatrical space not just as thoroughly overlapping but as disposed of momentarily, even as associated with a culturally specific type of *gestus* rather than necessarily bound up with any physical movement up-stage/downstage. It is in terms of such suppleness and pliancy that different spatial equivalents would accompany, even in one line, conventions of speech and action as marked by 'mirroring' and "antic" practice.

As an illustration of these differing verbal, gestural, and spatial purposes of playing, Hamlet's own preoccupation with theatre and theatricality is a case in point. As Denmark's "chiefest courtier," he is with his localized role involved in about half a dozen differing areas of play and playing. If a modern terminology may pass muster, these derive from Hamlet's roles (1) as actor, to be praised for his "good accent and good discretion" (2.2.466–67); (2) as theatre critic, in which he artfully reviews the production of that unpopular neoclassical play ("as wholesome as sweet, and by very much more handsome than fine" [2.2.444–45]); (3) as theoretician, in which he recommends the *imitatio vitae* topos to the players; (4) as dramatist who offers to contribute to the play within the play "some dozen or sixteen lines, which I would set down and insert in't" (2.2.541–42); (5) as a somewhat meddlesome director who proceeds to arrange for the production of *The Mousetrap* and also serves, in Ophelia's words, "as good as a chorus" (3.2.245); and (6) as, simply, an Elizabethan man of the theatre, a hybrid version of Maecenas and *Johannes factotum*, who believes he manages the players in such professional fashion that, almost triumphantly, he can ask Horatio, "Would not this, sir, . . . get me a fellowship in a cry of players?" (3.2.275–78).

With the exception of the last instance, these variegated levels of theatrical interest and engagement are all more or less firmly attached to the *locus* of Hamlet's position as "chiefest courtier" and "scholar" at the court of Denmark. But over and beyond his socially and topographically determined position in the imaginary world of the play, Hamlet is associated with an entirely different range of histrionic practices, allusions to, and preoccupations with, play and playing. To a surprising extent, these rather different associations with theatre and theatricality tend to contradict the precepts that the Renaissance Prince enjoined upon the players. Thus, his words and actions at Ophelia's funeral are thoroughly at odds with his earlier injunctions:

> Woo't weep, woo't fight, woo't fast, woo't tear thyself?
> Woo't drink up eisel, eat a crocadile?
> I'll do't. (5.1.275–77)

If this utterance does not quite recall the common player who was said to "tear a passion to totters, to very rags," it surely retracts the "temperance" and "smoothness" which, even in the "torrent, tempest" and "whirlwind" of a passion, was demanded by the Prince.

However, the difference between the poetics of the Renaissance Maecenas and the sheer performance zest in Hamlet's own words and actions more often than not is marked by mutual engagement and 'molestation,' when in one scene, one speech, one word two purposes of playing directly meet. Take, for instance, the protagonist's speech, "O, what a rogue and peasant slave am I," where a level of *sermo humilis* (as in this first line) can perfectly well be made to alternate with the self-questioning introspection ("Am I a coward?" – "Who does me this?") of an impersonating monologue, celebrating the immensity of the spectrum between a Virgilian "dream of passion" (2.2.552) and the antic figure of "John-a-Dreams" (568). Significantly, in the contrarious context of this speech, the speaker's awareness of play and the reference to the (First) Player looms large.

> What would he do
> Had he the motive and [the cue] for passion
> That I have? He would drown the stage with tears,
> And cleave the general ear with horrid speech (2.2.560–563)

As the traveling player's capacity for rousing, piercing speech and action is imaginatively transposed onto the requirements of Hamlet's situation, the Prince himself contrasts his own inactivity with the discursive practice of the common performer. What the comparison implies is an astonishing paradox: to tear a passion and "to spleet the ears of the groundlings" (3.2.10–11) is held up as a model of action. It is the very strategy proscribed by Hamlet the humanist and Maecenas who would not tolerate anything that departs from "temperance" and decorum, even in the whirlwind of passion. Again, the preference is for the other purpose of playing, one that pursues a truly terrific impact on the audience and, thereby, requires the player to do "the thing complained of," that is, positively to "cleave the general ear with horrid speech." When it comes to what counts for both the Elizabethan playhouse and the cause of his own revenge, the Renaissance Prince leaps to endorse as exemplary what a scene or two later "offends" him "to the soul" (3.2.8).

Again, Hamlet, and with him the play at large, pursues more than one purpose of playing. In terms of high Renaissance standards of conduct and rhetoric it is paramount to condemn, though in terms of common stage conditions it is vital to practice, a mode of performance that can "cleave" or "spleet" the ear of London's playgoers. The entire speech resonates with an uncommon degree of doubleness. In the utterance, both self-inspection

("About, my brains! Hum – I have heard" [2.2.588]) and the craft of the performer come into the picture. Representational functions (as in reference to a localized, self-contained, imaginary court of Denmark) are in collision with an awareness of an entirely different set of performance requirements that transgress both impersonation and the teachings of rhetoric and civil conduct.

However, it is the "antic disposition" itself that provokes the most thorough-going, and yet dazzling, engagements between Renaissance discourse and another type of "word" and "action." In his feigned madness Hamlet still represents a *role*, a motivated, time-serving response to his perilous position as, potentially, a generally perceived threat to Claudius. Such mad role-playing is anticipated in Shakespeare's oldest sources, where it serves as some means of self-preservation, in the sense that young Amleth, fearful for his own safety, proceeds "to feign dulness, and pretend an utter lack of wits."[8] But in *Hamlet*, the "antic disposition" ambivalently defeats its purely defensive, strictly representational functions. Although motivated from within the needs of the self-contained play, Hamlet's madness at least partially jars with the representational logic of his own role in the play; in a strictly representational context, Hamlet's "antic" pose arouses rather than allays suspicion. Madness and folly can (as in classical tragedy) serve as a fragile object of representation. But at the same time, tragic madness "upsets distinctions between human and animal, often violently": "madness-daemons," mainly in compound form, as "female-*cum*-animal figures," tend to "make music" and "make their victims dance" in the theatre of antiquity (Padel, *Whom Gods Destroy* 141; 242). In *Hamlet*, where ritual origins are far more remote, severing the links between cultural conduct and social station deeply disturbs the representation of social order. Madness unhinges images of personalized identity or subjectivity; as a "method" (Polonius' word) of mimesis, it helps destabilize 'meaning' in terms of a perceived blurring of important links between signs and what they signify.

What, then, this "disposition" positively implied was a dispensation from playing the worthy role of a courtly "mould of form." Such release from the postulated need "to imitate," in Sidney's phrase, nothing but "pictures, what should be" (*Prose Works* 3:29) effectively authorized a double-dealing purpose of playing. To "bring forth / So great an object" and yet retain some fond and frivolous "deformities" was absolutely vital for a theatre that, staging and yet defying social differentiation, "should please all, like Prince *Hamlet*," as Anthony Scoloker noted in 1604 (Chambers, *William Shakespeare* 2:215).

To illustrate the intricate ways in which divergent purposes of playing make it possible for one "craft" to infiltrate another, let us look at some of the strategies and figures through which in one scene, one line, even one

word contrariety ensues. Here is, first of all, an especially revealing encounter between Hamlet and his informers.

Guil. The King, sir –
Ham. Ay, sir, what of him?
Guil. Is in his retirement marvellous distemp'red.
Ham. With drink, sir?
Guil. No, my lord, with choler.
Ham. Your wisdom should show itself more richer to signify this to the doctor,
    for for me to put him to his purgation would perhaps plunge him into
    more choler.
Guil. Good my lord, put your discourse in some frame, and [start] not so wildly
    from my affair.
Ham. I am tame, sir. Pronounce. (3.2.299–310)

Again, Hamlet's antic uses of language only partially submit to what rules
of representation help secure the convention of dramatic dialogue *qua*
courtly conduct. His mode of response can perhaps best be characterized
as, at first sight, provocatively digressive; his words, not unlike those "fond
and frivolous jestures" in *Tamburlaine*, are "far unmeet for the matter"
(above, p. 59). But there is "method" is his mad replies that, radically
exceeding the "graced deformities" of only a decade ago, constitutes a
strange kind of 'im-pertinency.' I here use the word with a hyphen to
suggest how the represented piece of insolence is inseparable from the
liberty of deviating from what is *pertinent* in the mirror of civil conversation. The answer is both impertinent in the sense of 'impudent' and not
really pertinent to what Guildenstern's "affair" is all about.

Although throughout Hamlet's mad uses of language, the boundary line
between pertinence and impertinence remains tantalizingly fleeting,
Guildenstern's response ("put your discourse into some frame"), as perhaps no other utterance in the play, helps define the duplicity in the "antic"
purpose of playing. For Hamlet to start "wildly from" the "affair" in the
dialogue is, indeed, to use "discourse" outside the "frame" of the picture
of courtly exchange. Here as elsewhere, the figure of "impertinency"
explodes the mirror of civil conversation and quite eludes the prescribed
course of give and take in dramatically represented dialogue. The impertinent speaker provocatively pursues a double-course; without conceal-
ing the difference or bridging the gulf between Renaissance reason and
antic inversion, he uses it, exploits it, puts it on stage like a verbal exhibit of
wit and daring. As both versions of *King Lear* have it, "matter and
impertinency" is so "mix'd" (4.6.174) that, in this "mingle-mangle," each
works on the other. Hamlet in his antic mode, in one and the same line,
resists the represented "frame" of dramatic exchange and yet allows for
indiscreet variation on "necessary" themes and questions. Forsaking his
role in the imaginary world of the play, Hamlet momentarily associates a

platea-like space onstage that is open to the world beyond the world-in-the-play. In its openness to unrepresented, even nonrepresentable experience, impertinency can blast the "mould of form" and confound indeed a "noble and most sovereign reason." Through its "graced deformities," it can challenge, distract, jostle, and hustle what Richard Jones in his Preface to *Tamburlaine* called the matter of "worthiness" through a crafty rift in the space of dramatic representation.

(Word)play and the mirror of representation

Since, then, these antic uses of space and language transgress the "frame" of "modesty" and "discretion" in civil conversation, they can seriously disturb, even undo important elements in Hamlet's poetics and, beyond these, in popular Renaissance representations themselves. Positively speaking, in Shakespeare's theatre these representations will be open for infiltrations of alien issues and practices – practices that inflect latent needs and demands of playing in the world of common entertainment. As figures in aid of these infiltrations, wordplay, 'misunderstanding,' and 'impertinency' stand for a purpose of playing that does not submit to the grafting of a literary poetics on what Jean Alter has called "the performant function" (*A Sociosemiotic Theory*, chapter 4). In line with the "antic disposition," these figures help unleash a poetically unsanctioned zest for play, for sport, and for playing the game, thereby instigating a different cultural poetics that is blatantly unburdened by any desire to serve the cause of Renaissance knowledge or humanist doctrine. The resulting deformation of a worthy meaning, whether in the form of wordplay, 'misunderstanding,' malapropism, or other modes of verbal non-sequitur, is free from seeking to "imitate," let alone "imitate to teach & delight." Often enough these figures resist such elevated purpose behind the "universall consideration" that, according to Sidney, was inseparable even from the "ende of the Comicall part" – which "ende" or purpose was, *tout court*, "the ende of *Poesie*" (Sidney, *Prose Works* 3:41).

In *Hamlet*, the preoccupation with impertinent play was by and large constitutive not so much of delight but an untamed type of laughter. Outside the theatre, as Mikhail Bakhtin has pointed out, such laughter could be a medium of polyvalence and as such participate in the dissemination of "heteroglossia" (*Dialogic Imagination* 262–75, 426). In particular, it was disrespectful and did not observe the more refined standards of discreet conduct. But in late sixteenth-century Europe, many forms of carnival or their analogues were on the defensive; the emerging cultural reform, accompanied by the withdrawal of the better sort from the customs of the multitude, positively disapproved of laughter in public. As Keith Thomas noted in his essay on "The Place of Laughter in Tudor and

Stuart England," the "new cult of decorum thus meant that it was only
the vulgar who could go on laughing without restraint," while those
"'most apt to laughter' were 'children, women and the common people'"
(80). These uncontrolled and undisciplined uses of laughter, with their
strong visceral component, continued to be at odds with the mould of
modesty and discretion in representation. Antic or clownish playing and
laughing went together like sport and mirth; each was part of a type of
'merriment' that was ignored, ostracized or, at least before the end of the
century,[9] grudgingly admitted in part by the judicious guardians of civil
conversation.

There was then an element of play that could not be contained in the
mirror of Renaissance representation. Play, especially its bodily and laughable underside, could exceed or subvert the discursive and behavioral
constraints in the disciplining, unifying rules of humanist composition.
Thus, these play-ful figures of deformation were anything but mere comic
relief; in their contrarious function, they underlined, even helped unleash,
moments of crisis and revelation. Take, for instance, the brief scene in
which Hamlet is confronted by Rosencrantz, Guildenstern, and other
courtiers in search of Polonius' body.

> *Ros.* My lord, you must tell us where the body is, and go with us to the King.
> *Ham.* The body is with the King, but the King is not with the body. The King is
> a thing –
> *Guil.* A thing, my lord?
> *Ham.* Of nothing, bring me to him. [Hide fox, and all after.] *Exeunt* (4.2.25–31)

The words that here conclude the scene – put in brackets by Blakemore
Evans – are in F but not in Q2. Harold Jenkins, in his preference for the
Second Quarto as the text closest to the author and, therefore, most
authoritative, does not print the Folio's last five words because "they have
in the context a subtle incongruity" (526). But this incongruity is precisely
the point; it helps sustain the confusing, distracting area of grotesque
difference between Renaissance discourse and antic playing. No doubt
these words do collide with logic and consistency and what elsewhere is the
"sovereign reason" in Hamlet's utterances; as Jenkins notes, these words
"show a desire to confront and contend with his adversaries rather than
elude them" (526). What, then, the resulting contrariety harbors is a
playful element of *agon* or contest; these concluding words, as critics have
pointed out, echo the cry in a children's game, in which the player who is
the fox hides while the others hunt him.

Hence, the "incongruity" attests to a remarkable use of cultural difference in the play. Here we have a highly performative replay of a well-
known children's game in conjunction with an irreverent deformation of
Renaissance political concepts. Together, they are in response to a deadly

serious summons by the King. Significantly, a largely non-verbal game of hide-and-seek complements the verbal play on the King's two bodies. Hamlet's cryptically threatening hint that the (natural) body is "with the King" but that this particular king Claudius is not identical "with the body" politic, jars (and yet colludes) with the representation of a political philosophy. On the platform stage, the need to disturb and thereby animate the highly abstract distinctions of Renaissance philosophy must have been only too pressing.

For reasons that we shall presently examine more closely, the element of play – both in its corporeal and verbal forms – defies and partially eludes the representation of a serious crisis in the play. As Hamlet's own quibbling use of irreverent language is being matched by sudden physical movement, something unpredictable, in revolt against all discretion and decorum, happens: Hamlet darts forward to make an extraordinary exit, readily embracing the self-envisioned game, playfully adopting the role of the hidden, hunted animal, presumably with a sudden shout. As Philip Edwards annotates the phrase, "Hamlet runs out followed by the others." Such a frantic move deliberately departs from, and in fact seeks to counter, the reasonableness of his own preceding words, "Bring me to him." The point of course, inseparable from the "incongruity" and the non-sensical element in both word and action, is precisely that the antic Hamlet is more eager to "contend with his adversaries" than to "elude them." The paradox is that he runs because he does *not* seek to elude them in the first place. The game is to reduce the others, the solemnly serious court party, to an undignified act, heaping on them the ridicule of chasing, as if in a children's game, someone who at this point cannot and would not in any way escape.

Whether or not enacted under the assumed mantle of lunacy, this grim, unpredictable conjuncture of play and representation releases great kinetic energies; here is one performing body that makes the other players, whatever their roles, follow suit. Hamlet in this scene is not so much confused but positively *confusing* the others. Again, to play upon the etymology of the word, it might even be said that, from the point of view of performance craft and skill, the character's "confusion" is, for the actor, a con-fusion. Hide-and-seek and the King's two bodies is, really, an odd assortment of play and politics; but far from their juxtaposition, the "two crafts" are designed, threateningly as well as ludicrously, to clash. What the antic component excels at is a propensity to perform, to play the game, to have the sport. In a tragedy, the alien energies of antic performance, violating the proper relationship of subject-matter and style, constitute what in the play was the most intractable piece of indecorum – "a discordant combination of things unlike, an 'evil mixture'" (McAlindon, *Shakespeare and Decorum* 14). Even more important, these energies assault symbolic form itself: the resulting "crisis of representation" is, as John Drakakis has shown in a brilliant reading of *Julius Caesar*, in "constitutive alignment with the openness and instability of the theatre itself" ("Fashion it thus" 68).

While the grotesque game of hide-the-fox strongly implicates grotesque physical motion, the disposition to play much more strongly permeates the uses of language. As M. M. Mahood has documented, there is no character in Shakespeare's gallery of artificial persons that uses more wordplay than Hamlet (*Shakespeare's Wordplay* 112). With his nearly ninety puns, Hamlet's language is made to "start wildly" from "the necessary question" in the dialogue, obstructing again and again the representation of civil conversation. Punning at this rate does not hold the mirror up either to "modesty" or "nature" in the way of speaking. Here, one illustration must suffice to suggest the gulf, but also some of the complicity, between the quibble and the *logos*. The play within the play opens with some pomp and circumstance: "Enter Trumpets and Kettle-drums," then King, Queen and the courtiers. In line with the high formality of the occasion, Claudius' first move is to address his "chiefest courtier," here the self-appointed master of courtly ceremonies:

> *King.* How fares our cousin Hamlet?
> *Ham.* Excellent, i' faith, of the chameleon's dish:
>   I eat the air, promise-cramm'd – you cannot feed capons so.
> *King.* I have nothing with this answer, Hamlet, these words are not mine.
> *Ham.* No, nor mine now. [*To Polonius.*] My lord, you play'd once i' th' university, you say?
> *Pol.* That did I, my lord, and was accounted a good actor.
> *Ham.* What did you enact?
> *Pol.* I did enact Julius Caesar. I was kill'd i' th' Capitol; Brutus kill'd me.
> *Ham.* It was a brute part of him to kill so capital a calf there. Be the players ready? (3.2.92–106)

Hamlet's initial response to the king's question follows a pattern of contrariety that illuminates a startling purpose in these uses of wordplay. Obviously, Claudius uses 'fare' in its metaphorical and altogether conventional sense, 'how does our cousin prosper'; Hamlet intercepts the proposed meaning and supplements it by 'how does our cousin eat and drink.' The 'misunderstanding' substitutes a material, empirical denotation for the all too trivial generality, eluding a symbolic reading of Claudius' language in favor of what is much less of an abstraction. Hamlet thereby evades the necessary question in the dialogue in aid of something more tangible, which (in the probable pun on "air," for 'heir') suggests the emptiness of thwarted expectations and the uncertainty of his prospects. But then the invisible threat behind the incertitude is made starkly visible in the image of young fowl fattened for slaughter. On the surface, this antic paraphrase 'starts wildly' from the king's apparent affair in the dialogue, so much so that Claudius is quick to deny any complicity in the subtext of these rather cryptic verbal games. But the subtext is there and it presents the audience with a bewildering underside that, paradoxically, in its own turn serves a representational purpose of playing. Again, Hamlet's speech has a double bind, when, as here, it is both impertinent and pertinent. The quibble with its untamed indiscretion, even when it quite upsets the rules of courtly conversation, *playfully* serves the *necessary* question in the play.

It is this strange doubleness that makes it possible for one word to be a site on which "two crafts directly meet." Shakespearean wordplay in miniature exemplifies how the quibbling, juggling and corporeal uses of play jarred with a dramatic mode of representation which sought to render an imaginary picture, possibly a world-picture, informed by notions, doctrines, and abstractions quite remote from the traditional world of common players and nonverbal performers.

In conclusion, we have perhaps no better witness to testify to the depth of the gulf between Renaissance writing and Elizabethan playing than Dr. Johnson. As a critical observer who, as usual, is a difficult instance to disagree with, his testimony is so revealing precisely because he believed that "the praise of *Shakespeare*" was "that his drama is the mirror of life." If, for him, there was anything capable of blurring this mirror, it was the "malignant power" of the dramatist's "fatal Cleopatra." The quibble, he wrote, led the great poet to "the sacrifice of reason, propriety and truth" (Nichol Smith, *Eighteenth Century Essays* 108); since his addiction to wordplay was "sure to engulf him in the mire," it made him "stoop from his elevation" (116–17). These are strong words, but – once divested of their neoclassical implications – suggestive enough to alert us to an all-important point that finally needs to be re-emphasized. As Thomas Rymer felt, Shakespeare stooped to the players when the poet had "his Brains turn'd at this Monstrous rate" (see chapter 2, page 35). It was the player-playwright himself who was not content to follow what rules and precepts the learned culture of literacy prescribed. For Dr. Johnson indeed did have a point when noting that a certain type of wordplay does dispense with (or, 'sacrifice') parameters of "propriety and truth." The concept of "truth" here is crucial because as a matter of course it postulates representation as an equivalence between what the text says and how the world goes. In other words, the plays represent truthfully because they serve as a "mirror of life." Wherever and whenever this mirror is blurred, Shakespeare's dramatic representations can be engulfed in an unstable, muddy ground. They land in the "mire," where the force of the quibbling will muddle "the fair state," jangle the "sweet bells" of reason, fuddle the finest understanding. Here we have a contrarious, very much obnoxious discourse that runs counter, again in Johnson's terms, to "the dignity" of a "disquisition," and the "exalting affection" that the rhetoric of "elevation," central to Renaissance representation, was heir to. What Dr. Johnson must have felt in his reproof was that the lavish use of wordplay interfered with, even fatally impaired, what in his day had become the one and only "purpose of playing." The quibble, the jingle, the riddle, much like other types of playful practice that, marring the mirror of the world, "lost the world, and [were] content to lose it" (*Eighteenth Century Essays* 117).

The Prologue and Chorus to *Henry V* had confidently asserted the theatre's ability to "digest" the "distance" in space between the absent imaginary landscape represented in the written text and the material site of its performance by visible, audible actors in front of living audiences. But the two different modes of cultural production, writing and playing, implicated not only nonidentical premises of articulation and response; they were partially at least predicated on differing concepts and conventions of space and its uses in and for entertainment. In fact, the nonidentity between them was contiguous with the difference between the newly expanding space *in* (imaginary) representation and the recently institutionalized, material space *of* its performance.[1]

On the Elizabethan stage the difference between the imaginary landscape inscribed in the story and the physical, tangible site of its production was of particular, perhaps unique, consequence. Since there was both continuity and discontinuity between these two types of space, the drama in production, drawing on both the products of the pen and the articulation of voices and bodies, could through their interactions constitute at best an 'indifferent boundary'[2] between them. In fact, the boundary between the inscribed matter and the performing agency of theatrical representations appears altogether fleeting; no matter how deep (or how deeply submerged) the cultural difference between them was, it never constituted a rigid division, let alone a binary opposition in either the semiotics or the semantics of theatrical space. Once written language was articulated orally, in the form of dramatic speech, and once performers' voices and bodies were sustained by prescribed roles, neither pen nor voice remained an isolated, univocal source of authority in the projection of theatrical space. Since this space was larger and more complex than either the writing of characters or the delivery of performers could occupy, only the given conjuncture of pen and voice could in each case decide on what grounds the place and time 'which speaks' might be larger than or otherwise different from the place and time which 'is spoken.'

The differential use of the platform stage was not of course a

Shakespearean invention; it was inseparable from a division, deep in the formation and function of the Elizabethan theatre, between the cultural poetics of playing and the more distinctive literary poetics of writing. In the early modern period, bodies and texts found themselves in a new and challenging relationship involving tensions and mutually consequential engagements between two orders of socially encoded communication – the visible, audible immediacy in the articulation of speaking/hearing bodies on the one hand and, on the other, the writing, whether in manuscript or print, with its distance between production and reception, signification and interpretation. Despite vast areas of overlap between them, these two communicative paradigms informed, through their very coexistence, what Harry Berger, Jr., has called "the general rift between the order of the body and the order of texts that characterizes early modern culture" ("Bodies and Texts" 166).[3]

Although together with Lyly, Kyd, Peele, and Marlowe immeasurably expanded the space *in* representation, the material site of performance practice continued to inspire, as well as of course constrain, a chequered set of purposes of playing. If a highly complex picture can be put in a deceptively simple formula, it seems best to suggest that the uses of space on sixteenth-century English stages resonated with partially resolved, partially persisting tensions between a literature-oriented, humanistically inspired poetics of imitation and the presentational order of performance practices associated with displays of extemporal wit, "jestures," bodily dexterity, song, dance, and related forms of juggling, posturing, and exhibiting. Towards the end of the century, the process of differentiation between these two modes of cultural articulation and reception was, as we have seen in the preceding chapter, considerably advanced; still, if my reading of *Hamlet* has established anything, theatrical uses of space – being far from unified – allowed for, and were positively kept alive by, more than one purpose of performance.

These different purposes of playing can further be explored in terms of the distinction, on Elizabethan stages, between different forms of dramaturgy associated with thoroughly pragmatic, highly flexible and unfettered adaptations of *locus* and *platea* conventions.[4] In what follows I shall work with and develop further my earlier distinction between the *locus* as a fairly specific imaginary locale or self-contained space in the world of the play and the *platea* as an opening in *mise-en-scène* through which the place and time of the stage-as-stage and the cultural occasion itself are made either to assist or resist the socially and verbally elevated, spatially and temporally remote representation. In particular, I propose to revisit some of the adaptations of *locus* and *platea* in specific playtexts that reveal complex uses of contrariety between diverse types of theatrical semiotics and semantics. To view these spatial conventions in a long perspective, I propose to begin with a cursory glance at their social provenance and cultural premises.

Space as symbolic form: the *locus*

The dominant poetics inspiring Renaissance representations would posit the world as a secular space that, once it can be thought of and re-created as a picture, assumes an iconicity that in itself is self-contained and at least at one remove from the historical contingency of a "foolish world" (Sidney, *Prose Works* 3:18). This 'transcendental' function of early modern art forms is interactive with a symbolic use of bodies, objects, and spaces that to a certain extent takes over some of the functions of their sacred representations in medieval culture. The resulting "aura," as Walter Benjamin called it (221), is constitutive of a new autonomy of art forms whose theatrical correlative is the self-enclosed apartness of the picture from the beholder. Erwin Panofsky's classic essay, "Perspective as Symbolic Form," can perhaps best point the way to the extremely complex matrix in which early modern perceptions of space were indissolubly linked with rapidly changing patterns of pictorial construction. In fact, it seems impossible to understand the divergent uses of imaginary and material types of space in the Elizabethan theatre without taking into account the advent of new, spatially as well as temporally stringent modes of symbolization, among which the rise of linear perspective is only one highly significant factor.

Following Panofsky, we can understand perspective as a "systematic abstraction"(3) from the structure of ordinary empirical perceptions of space. Perspective, while distancing the viewer from the viewed, differentiates their locations. Even though perspectival space was virtually unknown in the Elizabethan public theatre, the poetic and epistemological principles behind linear perspective help us to understand the workings of a self-consistent symbolic *locus*. In the circumstances, the *locus* can be seen as a strategic approximation to the uses of perspectival form: it implicated the establishment of a topographically fixed locality. As in early modern cartography, the fixation itself, being in aid of knowledge and discovery, was instrumental in differentiating space and, thereby, separating the fixed place per abstraction from other localities. In the theatre, such fixation of different secular locations was conducive to an unprecedented specification and proliferation of symbolically encoded *loci*. At the same time, it insulated performers in their represented roles and helped separate them from what, in the medieval theatre, was a much more undifferentiated space inhabited by a universally believing community of actors and spectators.

Panofsky's path-breaking synthesis cannot of course provide an answer to all those questions, as yet scarcely raised by theatre historians, that need to be asked about early modern cultural uses of space. In particular, as W. J. T. Mitchell has pointed out in his trenchant critique of Panofsky's idealism, it seems difficult to address the fluctuating interplay of verbal and visual representation without having specified the agencies involved in both their production and reception (*Picture Theory* 18). No doubt spectatorship and the prevailing modes of vision and perception are important issues if the projection of space, symbolic or nonsymbolic, on theatrical stages is to be historicized. In early modern drama, the perspectival use of space, like the projection of 'perspective' as a temporal and structural technique, implicates, as Manfred Pfister has shown, historically shifting strategies with profound implications for the semantics of the transaction process (*Studien zum Wandel der Perspektivstruktur, passim.*). As Jonathan Crary's study *Techniques of the Observer* demonstrates, the difficulties in coming to terms even with the changing modes of vision, including the envisioning of spaces and places, are formidable enough. In view of our severely limited knowledge, the present study can do little more than alert us to the need for viewing the uses of theatrical space in a larger, cross-disciplinary context. Here, I content myself with pointing toward some of the more influential positions in humanist poetics and Renaissance literature against which the Shakespearean adaptation of the *locus* and *platea* conventions must be revisited.

On Shakespeare's stage, the localization of dramatic action must be viewed in conjunction with the endeavor to establish a firmly controlled, closely circumscribed mode of staging the text. In a good many comic scenes but especially in an early comedy like *The Two Gentlemen of Verona*, there was no specific imaginary locale; as the text of the play reveals, the playwright simply was uninterested whether the location, in accordance with the represented action, actually was "Milan" or, as the Folio has it, "Padua" (2.5.2); whether later it still was "Milano" or perhaps "Verona" (3.1.81); or whether the play's final scene was no longer set in "Milan" but yet again, "Verona" (5.4.129). However, as Shakespeare moved to the problem plays and tragedies, the "local habitation" and "name" of dramatic action became more visible. In these circumstances, the *locus* in representation provided an authorized specification of discursive space – one, for instance, that in our reading of *Troilus and Cressida* was marked by Calchas' tent as localized site in the Grecian camp. Whether stage property or imaginative projection, this tent, much like the banquet table, the throne, the bed, and the tomb, represents a fairly verisimilar topos removed from direct audience rapport. While, as we shall see, a *platea*-related position – like that of Thersites, Apemantus, not to mention that of the "self-resembled" Clowns – tends primarily to be associated with the authority of what and who was doing the (re)presenting, the *locus* invariably privileges the authority of what and who is represented in the world of the play. Accordingly, the *locus* convention foregrounds an apparently self-contained space serving the picture of the performed, not the process of the performer performing. Such self-containment must have helped insulate representations from the circumstantial world of theatrical production and reception; it safeguarded these imaginary configurations from the limitations of an "unworthy scaffold" and the hurly-burly inside a mere "cockpit."

More often than not the *locus* served as the privileged site on which matter of "worthiness," the discourse of epic and romance, historical and novelistic narrative, could be presented. Thus, the banquet table represented an elevated site of hospitality, the throne the sphere of privileged royalty, the household a *locus* of patriarchal power, the bed a place of gendered lust and struggle, the tomb a topos of family dignity and piety. As a site of such discourses, the symbolizing potential of theatrical space went hand in hand with the expansive capacity of the sixteenth-century English language for evoking, through representations, relations of gender, class, and ideology. [5] Here was a site for the dominant discourse of honor, chastity, magnanimity, and warlike resolution. Such representations could draw on a rich repertoire of verbal and visible signifiers to denote a gate, a palace, a balcony, a house, a household, and the related strength of political and parental authority. The representational quality of such *loci* was to a large extent already inscribed in Shakespeare's narrative and dramatic sources; these signs of authority were part of the dominant culture of the Renaissance that found its finest icon in the figure of the "courtier's, soldier's, scholar's, eye, tongue, sword" (*Hamlet* 3.1.151).

The gripping power of localized discourse and its growing predominance in the popular Renaissance theatre must be viewed against the larger context of related representational practices in sixteenth-century culture. As I have argued elsewhere, early modern representations were greatly propelled by a number of circumstances that accompanied the decline of institutionally or metaphysically given types of authority. In the wake of newly independent modes of authorization, the spread of print and literacy, as well as new public platforms of theatrical entertainment, "printers, players, and preachers, would set forth some of their own heads."[6] In other words, once the sources, the availability, and the purposes of representational practices multiplied, the matrix of representations proliferated, their ranges enlarged, their aims diversified, and their sense of time and place heightened "their form and pressure" greatly.

Not unlike early modern narrative, pamphleteering, conduct books, and other types of pragmatic discourse, the use of the vernacular in the theatre found itself in a deeply problematic though not entirely negative relationship to the humanistically inspired poetics of the time. It is of course true that, in Sir Philip Sidney's phrase, the pre-Shakespearean common stages were deemed "faultie both in place and time" in that they refused to project stability and unity in their representations of dramatic locale – despite humanist injunctions that "the Stage should alway represent but one place" (Sidney, *Prose Works* 3:38). But although popular dramatists and players turned a deaf ear to the demand for correct representations of time and place as "the necessarie Companions of all corporall actions" (38), they did respond, at least within the space of the *locus*, to a Renaissance poetics demanding the "poeticall imitation" of "courtesie, liberalitie, and especially courage" (20). The emphasis in Renaissance poetics on imitation as an ennobling "tragic glass," a "mirror" for virtue and vice, was certainly in alliance with a strictly demarcated theatrical space in which, as in a picture, passion, ambition, friendship, love, valor, virtue, and knowledge could be represented. Thus, the authority of eloquence, in fact all the arts of rhetoric and the call for verisimilitude were conducive to a mode of dramatic writing that privileged the strictly localized, consistently focused scene. Such a poetics of theatrical space must have appealed to Shakespeare's "vision of his art" as one that was to be "as noble as the highest Renaissance views on the subject" (Kernan, *Playwright as Magician* 53).[7]

The humanistic poetics found a consistently congenial correlative, even perhaps response in the spatial layout and architectural structure of the Italian Renaissance theatre, as Sebastiano Serlio, Andrea Palladio, Vincenzo Scamozzi, and Giambattista Aleotti had designed in northern Italy. In their adaptations of Vitruvius and the classical legacy, these Italian Renaissance architects put a far stronger emphasis on verisimilitude. In line with neo-Aristotelian critics like Scaliger and Castelvetro, they all privileged a self-consistent locale as a radical departure from medieval public uses of open space, such as had marked pageants, processions, entries, large-scale performances of mystery plays but also the ordinary booth stage in the marketplace. As Marvin Carlson has shown, the Italian aristocracy took the lead in the appropriation of public places for theatrical occasions and, often enough, in the assimilation of these occasions to the entertainment of a select audience.[8] In this process the space of the *cortile* was by and large replaced by the enclosed *Sala Grande*, where both performance and audience were more or less absorbed in the body of the palace. Now the stage, no longer in the square or accessible from the street, could be reached only by way of access through the doors of buildings controlled by powerful privilege.

Although there were important exceptions like the Teatro Olimpico in

Vincenza, the dominant impulse in design and construction identified the space for theatrical performances with the spatial domain of the Renaissance prince. His authority came to institute itself in and through the closing of a sharply demarcated space. Cut off from the busy, everyday world of the *piazza*, the new theatre, displacing the playing-in-the-world in favor of the world-within-the-play, could now minimize the cultural difference between the worthiness of what was performed and what and who was doing the performing. Hence, the pre-scribed locale in representation became incompatible with any attempt on the part of the performer to assert his/her own world and identity from behind or from within the performed role. Whatever authority could be retained in the act of performance, it was not sufficient for the performer from within his own world to call a stage a stage. On the contrary, once actors confronted an iconography that, in Carlson's phrase, served "indexically to refer to a whole system of interlocking spatial and ideological relationships" (*Places of Performance* 168), any strictly self-reflexive element in their own signifying practice was severely impaired. Their practice tended to be 'lost' in the spell of what was signified through a magnificent ensemble of sculpture, ornament, and design that honored classical precedent and the aristocratic platform of its learned recovery.

In other words, once the imaginary space in representation had absorbed and become near-identical with the site of performance, the resulting state of homology between the two left no room for any "self-resembled show." The internal unification and the external circumscription of theatrical space went hand in hand with closure in representation. Again, the closure, significantly underlined by an emergent proscenium arch, was spatial and social as well as formal; the arch accentuated the separation of the world of the play from the world of a watching, listening audience. Performing within the aura of the self-consistent play-world helped control, contain, and isolate the actor's voice in two ways: through an effectively binding, prescribed text *and* a resolute socio-spatial differentiation between performers and spectators. Needless to say, the degree of closure could only be enhanced by the presence of the prince who, in his elevated and central position, was privileged (and further distanced from performance) by the new convention of linear perspective.

At this juncture, the introduction of linear perspective served as a veritable catalyst for a newly coherent and controlled laying out of theatrical space. In the English translation, rendered from the Dutch, five books of Sebastiano Serlio's *Architettura* (1611), the first Book on geometry is followed by Book 2, "intreating of perspectiue" – which "speaking of Perspectiue things" (F26), as we shall see in a moment, serves as a clue for conceiving, designing, and building a new type of Renaissance stage. Such uses of perspective were inseparable from a process of abstracting and symbolizing a world 'out there' in order to represent it more infallibly. As W. J. T. Mitchell has argued, the effect of the invention of artificial perspective "was nothing less than to convince an entire civilization that it possessed an infallible method of representation" – the more infallible in that this invention "denies its own artificiality and lays claim to being a 'natural' representation of 'the way things look'" (*Iconology* 37). Since the proscenium arch in its own turn came to affirm this self-legitimating moment in the method of truthful representation, the theatre of linear perspective was predicated on the spell of a vision, a whole mode of unifying perception whose authority – as innocent as it seemed self-evident – was enhanced by the Renaissance architectural balance of proportion, symmetry and controlled form. The new focused mode of perspectival representation first and foremost helped sustain a stringent, self-contained pictorial dimension; there obtained a natural-seeming consistency in the representation of an imaginary locality, a *locus* defined by, and in terms of, the near-autonomous, self-coherent matter of worthy stories and places. Here was, pictorially, a new 'objectivity' that went hand in hand with what Christopher Braider has called the early modern "deep and pervasive commitment to forms of picturing" (*Refiguring the Real* 3). This *locus*-oriented mode of representation lodged the icon of character or action at the center of an order that was closely enough woven so as to appear unified.

Such unification of theatrical space, while it did affirm "pictorial form" in what Braider calls "its peculiar authority and scope" (3), dually served both the dawning new sense of objects out there and the emerging demands of the sovereign self. The theatrical use of this physical space was in its layout continuous, isotropic, and homogeneous; at the same time, it served to differentiate among spectators. The picturing of this space was organized in terms of the point of view of a particular individual who in his privileged, elevated position provided "a visual anchor for the stage perspective" (Carlson, *Places of Performance* 137). It was a space in which the privileged observer, especially the observed of all observers, might hope to be "himself the measure." As Martin Heidegger suggested, there was a powerful nexus in the new, world-picturing form of representation: to set the image as an object before oneself and to set it forth in relation to oneself amounted to the "conquest of the world as picture." Such appropriation through representation not only affirmed "unlimited power for the calculating, planning, and molding of all things" but, at the same time, celebrated a doctrine of man as subject. Thus, "the more extensively and the more effectually the world stands at man's disposal as conquered, and the more objectively the object appears, all the more subjectively, i.e. all the more impetuously, too, do observation and teaching about the world change into a doctrine of man" (Heidegger, "The Age of the World Picture" 134–35).

Here to point in passing to the early modern uses of representation *qua* privileged appropriation of the world helps define a purpose of playing that, increasingly, came to inform, and draw upon, the meaning-inspired uses of locations in dramatic compositions. In this context to invoke the Italian picture-frame stage is not of course to suggest that there was any direct, let alone any immediately resulting, influence on Shakespeare's theatre. Nor can we assume, as G. R. Kernodle did, that the impact of Renaissance visual arts led to the introduction of some linear type of space on either public or private stages in Elizabethan England.[9] Still, as John Orrell has recently underlined, the court theatres of Westminster and elsewhere "began to show signs of Serlian (and at some remove, Vitruvian) influence" as early as 1584 when at the Whitehall Banqueting House "a strongly built proscenium arch or border was introduced" ("The Theaters" 95). Inigo Jones' later impact on court staging is too well known to require documentation here. But what in this connection deserves to be further pursued is the question whether indirectly rather than directly these innovative uses of theatre space could stimulate or participate in the growing importance of verisimilitude and localization in the Elizabethan theatre at large. The point is that, over and beyond the question of influence, these innovations in theatrical space and dramaturgy participated in the emergence of a larger cultural poetics embracing early modern architecture, painting, epistemology, and a wider European political economy of "trafficke and travell" with its own differentiations in goods, manners, and ownership.

While these interconnections are too vast and formidable to be pursued here, the Shakespearean mode of localization, in particular the use in his plays of a self-centered, coherent *locus*, is deeply implicated in a modern projection of space as symbolic form. Even though the platform stage practically precluded the introduction of linear perspective, the pictorial form of a *locus* participated in a symbolic abstraction from the here and now. There is a need, I suggest, to view the growing strength of the imaginary abstraction of space from the place of its performance in this larger context of cultural change. As Edward S. Casey suggests in his recent magisterial study of the problem, the early modern period witnessed to a "more or less irenic cohabitation of place and space," until by 1600 "place" is "shorn of its prior primacy" and space, conceived as an *infinitum*, "is no longer situated in the physical world but in the subjectivity of the human mind that formally shapes this world" (*The Fate of Place* 135–36).

While it is of course unacceptable to identify the philosophical concept of 'place' with the late medieval theatrical concept so called, changing relations of *platea* and *locus*, and the growing importance of the latter, participate in major shifts of spatial perception in the early modern period. While the preeminence of strictly localized action is not quite in the offing, the imaginary abstraction from the place of the stage is well under way in Elizabethan dramatic representations. The relative status of self-contained locale can best be explored in comparison with the geometrical, pictorial, and perspectival redefinitions of space in the Italian Renaissance theatre. These provide us, as I have suggested, with an approximation or at least anticipation of what a distinctly localized, coherently laid out space in the theatre amounted to.

Sebastiano Serlio's *Architettura*,[10] incidentally, appeared in London only a few years after *Othello* in 1604 was performed at the Whitehall Banqueting House on a stage, in Orrell's words, "bordered by a prototype proscenium arch" ("The Theaters" 95). In these (and other) circumstances, it seems reasonable to conjecture that Serlio's folio volume, beautifully bound and lavishly illustrated, must have been a matter either known or of great potential interest to leading members of the King's Men. Here was a volume, laying out graphically a resolute separation between a carefully designed imaginary space in the world of the story and the place of playing in the playhouse. More than anything, this separation was enhanced by "the subtill and ingenious Arte of Perspectiue" (Book 2, A1). Accordingly, as a subheading in Book 2 has it, there was a sense of a "Treatise of Scenes [. . .] to play in" (F24). To talk of playing *in* a scene was, right at the outset, to recognize the absorbing quality, the integrating strength of the imaginary locale, and to differentiate the site of dramatic action from the world of the audience.

In its own turn, the auditorium was carefully stratified in terms of a hierarchy of seating, from "Noblemen and Knights," via "Gentlemen of quality," to "common Officers and other people" (Book 2, F23). And, vice versa, the ordering of the place *of* representation was complemented by a differentiation of the space *in* representation. Since certain actions "happen always in the house of great Lords, Dukes, Princes, and Kings" (F26), the theatre was designed so as to have "good Art and proportion in things therein represented" (F26r). Further still, the socially significant differentiation *in* representation was complemented by generic distinctions derived from neo-Aristotelian poetics (scenes are made of three sorts, that is "Comical, to play Comedies on, Tragicall for Tragedies, Satiricall for Satires" [Book 2, F25]). As a matter of course, this well-controlled and enclosed world in representation would exclude all performers who could not be subsumed under the visually refined, privileged order of its imaginary unity. The latter is sustained even "while that the Scene is emptie of personages"; in such intervals, the worthiness of the location at all costs continues to be represented by "certain figures or formes ready of such greatness as the place where they must stand, will afford them to be" (Book 2, F26). These are to be made of "paste board, cut out round and paynted"; while they were animated or moved ("the figures passe along"), certain "Musitions" accompanying "some like singers" – appearing incompatible with the "good Art [. . .] in things therein represented" – were relegated "behind the Scene."

In a comparative reading of the uses of theatrical space in sixteenth-century England and northern Italy, the degree of difference is as striking as a distinct element of concurrence remains intriguing. In both theatres, there is a concern with localized, that is, spatially self-coherent representations. In Shakespeare's playhouse, there are a good many scenes that have a distinct, unmistakable setting (such as Macbeth's castle, Portia's Belmont, Gertrude's closet, Desdemona's chamber, Timon's cave, and so forth). They designate either a particular locality or a given place, such as a garden, bridge, court, gateway, or prison. But as Bernard Beckerman has shown in his admirable examination of "Localization in Shakespeare's Globe Plays" (in his *Shakespeare at the Globe*), among the 345 scenes in these plays, the strictly localized scenes altogether do not amount to a majority in numbers. Even when "the localized, usually interior and more or less realistic" scene is taken together with its opposite, "the unlocalized, exterior, neutral, and somewhat less realistic" type of scene, there remain more than 200 scenes unaccounted for (Beckerman, *Shakespeare at the Globe* 65).

Thus, while Elizabethan theatrical space is not of a piece and allows for considerable heterogeneity in the purposes of playing, the Italian Renaissance stage is more nearly unified, representational, and localized. Even where the *commedia dell'arte* had a subterranean resonance (a fresco in the Teatro Olimpico shows masked dwarf clowns onstage with tragic personnel[11]), the difference in the projection of space remains undeniable. This difference reflects, in the two types of stage, various degrees of differentiation between playing and writing. For the Italian Renaissance theatre to integrate theatrical space through both a perspectival scenery and the localizing force of a preeminent representation is to privilege the imaginary world in the play as prescribed in a written text. In view of such self-consistent localization, performers, overwhelmed by the spatially fixed and fortified strength of their roles in the world of the play, must forget about articulating their own circumstantial world and their practice of playing on stages. In the circumstances, any self-resembled showing of the performer-as-performer is out of the question. The authorization of players and playing derives from cultural norms and expectations that are worlds apart from the actual social needs and practices of these performers. As Serlio reveals in *The Third Book*, "intreating of all kind of excellent Antiquities," the final source of authority in the laying out of theatrical space is radically discontinuous with these practices: "wee should observe Vitruvius rules as our guide and most certayne and infallible directions" (F21).

Still, the gulf between the Italian and English stages in the authorization of space and performance is, although deep, not entirely unbridgeable. If Serlio invokes classical precedent for the former, we have in Shakespeare (not even to mention Jonson) a distinct reference to the same authority for the latter. As Shakespeare at the turn of the century, in *Hamlet* and the problem plays, debates a shifting circuit of authority between writing and playing, we hear from the Prince of Denmark a classical validation, as binding for players, of an exclusively representational poetics, "whose end, both at the first and now, was and is" (3.2.21) to imitate nature. And yet, while the twofold emphasis on the link between "was" and "is" would have pleased Serlio, the same play, as we have seen, projects multiple uses of theatrical space that go hand in hand with more than one style and purpose of playing, and vice versa.

While classifications are of limited value in view of Shakespeare's "swelling scene," distinctions have been made, at least since the days of A. H. Thorndike, among different types of localization, such as "the definitely localized, the vaguely localized, and the unlocalized."[12] Beckerman in particular, rejecting any dichotomy between localized and unlocalized scenes, preferred "a gradation from the unlocalized through the generalized to the localized setting" (*Shakespeare at the Globe* 67).

In almost every scene that is not unlocalized, the characters do not actually act in a dislocated void but are known to be in some more or less specific region. Even when attention is directly called to the stage-as-stage, the stage-as-fictional-world still remains. In such moments the audience experiences a double image. (65–66)

While the emphasis on "gradation" is invaluable in that it underlines an infinite variety of transitions, combinations, and mutual assimilations between these two types of stage, the "double image" of theatrical space has referents and correlatives that precede the image in question. These theatrical referents are marked by the difference between the "stage-as-fictional-world" and the "stage-as-stage." In spatial and temporal, but also social terms, the distance between them, as we have seen, could be considerable; it could be used but also, as the prologue to *Henry V* has it, abused. To do so – to "digest / Th' abuse of distance" – was to "force a play" (0.2.31–32). For the audience, therefore, to experience a "double image" was not to suspend the difference between the space in representation and the space for representation, when each type of space called for a different kind of response. But to bring them together, to "force a play" required, precisely, that the audience worked with rather than without the "distance" between them. Awareness of the difference in question was taken for granted; it provided the clue to, and was an enabling condition of, unending variety in the interplay of *locus* and *platea*.

The open space: provenance and function

Although, up to a point, the *locus*-oriented art of representation in the Elizabethan public theatre went from strength to strength in its imaginary reach and density, the peculiar authority and scope of its own pictorial form could in varying degrees be intercepted by a contrarious type of space. This space – the Elizabethan equivalent of the *platea* – normally refused to submit to the pictorial mode of symbolizing, and thereby unifying, place; rather, by assimilating thresholds between the imaginary world-in-the-play and the stage-as-stage, it tended to preclude closure. Hence, any consistently upheld *locus*, as represented icon of a given imaginary place, time, and action, could again and again be suspended in a partially, gradually or completely open regime of *mise-en-scène*.

To illustrate, Launce's audience address in *The Two Gentlemen of Verona* (2.3.1–32) constitutes a *platea*-like opening in response to what, in the preceding scene, is the localized action in Julia's house in Verona. This action is focused on the representation of Proteus' leave-taking under the temporal constraint of the incoming tide ("The tide is now" [2.2.14]). But while this specification is superficial enough for a thoroughly inland location like Verona, Launce upon entering in the immediately following scene at once breaks up the imaginary frame of temporal urgency ("'twill be this hour ere I have done weeping" [2.3.1–2]) only to end up, after his lengthy address, by playing upon and reducing *ad absurdum* the represented notion of "tide": "It is no matter if the tied were lost; for it is the unkindest tied that ever any man tied" (37–38). The reference is to his dog, but when seen in conjunction with the shrewd stage awareness in his burlesque representation of leave-taking, the dog, the scene, the man himself are no longer Veronese. Instead, they intercept the symbolic form of iconic action and location through a juggling game with a handy-dandy type of a "double image." Again, as we have seen before, the doubleness has plenty of duplicity in it. Launce's homely version of it confounds the pictorial art of representation, first of all, by a parody of leave-taking and, finally, by showing both a stubborn perception of the material that resists representation *and* the arbitrariness in relations between signified and signifying ("This hat is Nan, our maid. I am the dog – no, the dog is himself, and I am the dog – O! the dog is me, and I am myself; ay, so, so" 21–23).

This scene, which needs to be read in conjunction with those other comic/uncomic disruptions of closure I will discuss presently, illustrates but also qualifies the "gradation" that Beckerman has outlined. What is characteristic of Launce's *platea* positioning is not so much a progress, a gradation or change through a series of stages from the definitely localized to the unlocalized, but a recurring, more immediate overlapping or oscillation of player's role and player's self. Here, this doubleness itself is subjected to an exuberant probing into the limits of dramatic representation in an open space. Its openness is such that it suspends the boundaries between the actual site for playing and the imaginary landscape of re-presented departures, romantic vows, and courtly separation. The burlesque version of this doubleness cries out for laughter when finally the dog itself is up against the frontiers of representation – juggled as it is between a symbolic mode of impersonation and its own nonrepresentable and nonrepresenting physicality in the form, defying all histrionics, of the animal's sheer existence.[13]

In any discussion of the residual and/or revitalized uses of the *platea* dimension in Shakespeare's theatre, it is important to underline that, as Harry Berger, Jr. has recently noted, "both modes [*locus* and *platea*] are equally conventional" and as such informed by a convention of "theatrical practices that defines each mode in terms of and over against the other" ("The Prince's Dog" 49). Such differential interplay results in "modal shifts" "between theatrical presentation and dramatic representation" across the full range of "actor" and "character." Thus, between these two extreme poles, the uses of *platea* space in Shakespeare's theatre are such that, as a matter of course, its openness engages (and is engaged by) the imaginary space of localized action.

While the "polar continuum" is more complex than I can recapitulate here, it offers an extremely helpful diagram of the variegated degrees of doubleness in projecting theatrical space. Clownish *platea* figures such as Launce inhabit a space that permits them to play out the interface between performing their own performing selves and the presentation, with a difference, of an "actor-playing-character," resisting the terms of his own characterization. Thus, even the imaginary convention of creating a role and/or locale can result in an effect that is intercepted by, and yet adds strength to, the "unworthy" materiality of the stage-as-stage.

Along these lines, the adaptation of a flexibly handled *platea* provided the Elizabethan theatre and, in particular, Shakespeare's "dramatic transactions" with what Michael Mooney in his well-focused study calls a "double vision" for Elizabethan spectators, culminating in "the knowledge that their own lives were as full of provisional identities and imaginary posturings as those of the actors" (2).[14] At the same time, this extension of the play's dimension beyond the "indifferent boundaries" of the imaginary world of the textual representation made possible a complex mode of staging. The actor-character's *Figurenposition*, his 'figural' and 'figured' positioning, combined social and verbal parameters of identifying the ways and degree of departure from the principle of the self-contained locality. That principle, with its element of closure, could be accommodated by a *Figurenposition* within a concept of "theater space" (Scolnicov, "Theatre Space" 11) or "stage space" (Pavis, "Performance Analysis" 13–15) as a space *for* representations; but it was also, and at the same time, established *in* representations as a "space symbolized in the text" of the story (Pavis, "Performance Analysis" 15).[15]

If, therefore, the *locus*-centered authority of what was pictorially represented could, from within itself, be powerfully affirmed, it could also be profoundly challenged on spatial premises that, in the same play, harbored the 'performant function.' This function, in Jean Alter's sense of the word, could infiltrate the very space in which the language of privilege and the mirror of representation were faithfully held up to a previously conceived idea of virtue or vice "showing her own feature." In Q1 *Hamlet*, as we have seen, the doctrine of the "mirror" itself could be deflected from its customary *locus* by the prince's readiness "thus," with "blabbering lips," to deliver the vulgar presentation complained of.

It seems difficult to account for the trenchant force of these socially and culturally inspired disruptions unless we view this open, much less focused and less differentiated type of space in its historical context. This context was marked by a purpose of playing for which the differentiation between the arts of dramatic performance and the pursuit of pastime was considerably less developed. To be sure, the Elizabethan platform stage was not an altogether "undifferentiated space," in the sense in which Greg Walker defines the theatre of the Tudor great hall, "into which the actors walked and brought their play" without having any "scenic or temporal fixed points beyond the here and now" (*Politics of Performance* 49–50). As opposed to a totally undemarcated 'place' or *platea*, the platform stage offered distinct spatial correlatives for different types of language and meaning. While the dominant forms of poetic and rhetorical discourse, the themes and languages of novella, romance, historiography, and myth, dominated the *locus* and tended to constitute detached, more or less aloof worlds of their own, the *platea* in its adapted mode was usually marked by an entirely different type of prose discourse. It was a language close to the ordinary word and the native language of the jesting, riddling, punning "mother-wits," serving the immediate give and take of unstilted, possibly 'unrefined' perceptions of status, conduct, and ideas, and deeply aware of ordinary, everyday objects and relations among people. Along these lines, this rather unfixed space was marked by its openness towards the world of the audience, its reluctance to be lost in the symbolism of socially remote privilege and the story of distant, elevated representations.

While this resistance to illusion and decorum could be entirely inconsistent and self-contradictory, the Elizabethan projection of a *platea* implicated a number of material functions that derived from its downstage physical proximity to the audience. Here was the world of the "unworthy scaffold," beleaguered by 'ignorant' spectators, capable of a threshold to what, in the discursive field of Renaissance representations, was nonrepresentable. As far as a bare summary can do it justice, this open stage could accommodate three discursive and nondiscursive areas, especially in its downstage portion. As my reading of the Porter's scene will suggest (a reading born out by the two murderers in *Richard III*, the gravediggers in *Hamlet*, the "rural fellow" in *Antony and Cleopatra*, and others), the *platea* was used to foreground the shadowy realm of death and perdition, drink and desire, sexuality and the body in its regenerative and decaying dimensions. Invariably using monosyllabic, Anglo-Saxon language and, by implication, drawing on the most basic experience of living, these figures would point beyond the discourse of "worthiness." In their downstage space, they provided an opening for, and a threshold to, what in the existence of the human animal itself was and is liminal and, to a certain degree, irreducible.

Evoking the visceral world of ordinary living, the *platea* on a second level helped incorporate what was a marginal region in contemporary London. As Steven Mullaney has shown, the place of the London stage was eccentric to the city in that it had dislocated itself "from the strict confines of the existing social order and [taken] up a place at the margins of society" (*Place of the Stage* 8). Here was, outside as well as inside the gates of the playhouse, a world identified with scandalous licentiousness, with 'incontinent' forms of pastime. The spatial semantics in this threshold function of the *platea* reverberated with a sense of this unsanctioned neighborhood, overlaid by more distant recollections of festive exuberance, misrule, the spirit of 'carnival,' mirth and all sorts of display and distraction. Rather than primarily providing a passage from holiday to everyday, this second threshold function served, as it were, to season this passage and to help filter the transition to work-a-day through its own sieve of skepticism *vis-à-vis* the emptiness of symbolic pomp and glitter. As the downstage position of Launce and his dog, but also Falstaff, Parolles, Thersites, Lucio, Autolycus, and others suggests, their threshold functions were profoundly informed by the adjacent cultural landscape of both license in the guise of everyday, and everyday in its cynical, commercial, and burlesque manifestations just beyond the gates of the playhouse.

While the Elizabethan version of the *platea* certainly was contiguous with the space, in the liberties of London, for "incontinence," the liminal uses of the open stage were informed by a third function – one that in our context may well be the most important one. True enough, as Mullaney notes, the playhouse "earned its living by a theatrical slight of hand, translating work into play" (*Place of the Stage* 47). But at the same time, performing on the platform stage translated play back into work. As a new form of labor for profit and sustenance, such playing with its two-way transactions was bound to be self-reflexive wherever the self-contained world-in-the-story did not reign supreme. Thus, the thresholds to both ordinary and licentious forms of existence were overlaid by yet another, third opening that associated the moment of nonidentity between role and actor with an element of (dis)continuity between playing and working. Since the threshold as a matter of course faced two ways, the transactive move from role to actor (or play to work) could be complemented, vice versa, by a transition back from actor to role (or, work to playing). It is a dialectic that, as I have suggested above (page 97), can best be studied in the theatrical uses of disguise, where the primary role, which does not consume the uses of its own concealment, can go hand in hand with the display of a gap between impersonator and impersonated.

In late sixteenth-century England, these attributes of an open, fairly undifferentiated place at the frontiers of verisimilitude, rhetoric, and decorum remained remarkably viable, at least as far as that space continued to be used for the marginal, the visceral, the liminal, the otherwise nonrepresentable. This space was taken up by players doing porters, vendors, grave diggers, but also cross-dressed women and other figures in disguise and madness. Performers, even when playing these roles, also presented their craft, their skills, their own performing selves. What prevailed was a disinterest in, a certain defiance of, even perhaps an element of resistance to, the regime of an elevated, purely imaginary, self-contained world out there. More often than not, these performers were not entirely prepared to sink themselves into their roles. The time, the place, the language, even their gendered identity remained in part that of the function and the agents of playing, not exclusively that of the textually authorized image of something absent. It was through this liminal functioning of the *platea* that doubleness, including its deliberate use as contrariety, directly resounded in performance practice itself. Players, representing something and someone else, also (re)presented themselves.

Locus and platea in *Macbeth*

In order to explore further the doubleness in Elizabethan projections of theatrical space, it seems helpful at this point to illustrate the

Shakespearean adaptation of *locus* and *platea* conventions in a specific playtext. Focusing on the way that these double projections of space are entangled in early modern relations of authority and representation, I first propose to examine two major dramatic scenes in *Macbeth*. One – the banquet scene – is marked by an unambiguously established *locus* that is only slightly exposed to the disturbance of a *platea*-like intersection; the second – the Porter's scene – is one in which a strong residue of the *platea* is made to engage a particularly vibrant and stringently localized moment of tragic action.

The "great feast" in *Macbeth* (3.4.1–120), reaching back to earlier scenes (particularly an early banquet in the play) is, in George Hunter's words, "a climactic scene" where "bloodshed and treachery" cannot be repressed any longer (Hunter [ed.] *Macbeth* 19). The scene is clearly marked by its stage properties: a table with, presumably, stools or chairs, serves to symbolize the place and occasion of a banquet in the Castle of Inverness. But the "good meeting" (3.4.108) is a vulnerable occasion, with many things at risk, in which signifying props and images are somewhat fleeting and unstable in their purpose. On this same platform stage, minutes ago, Banquo was invited to join the same festive meeting as "our chief guest" whose absence would cause "a gap in our great feast, / And all-thing unbecoming" (3.1.11–13). It was the same stage on which only two short scenes ago Macbeth, after having challenged "fate into the list" (70), i.e., into "that enclosed ground in which combats are fought" (Alexander Schmidt, *Shakespeare-Lexicon*), commissioned the murderers. Here, also, in another "swift scene" (the term is from *Henry V* [3.0.1]), but certainly applicable here), Banquo was just slain a mere four lines before the Folio's stage direction inserts "*Banquet prepar'd*," to be opened by Macbeth's "hearty welcome" (3.4.2). Even before this word of welcome is spoken, the focal point of the scene – underlined by the stage direction – is taken up by the host, who apportions the social space of privilege at the *locus* according to a given order of seating ("You know your own degrees, sit down" [3.4.1]).

The banquet scene comes at the end of this breathless sequence. The setting up of its *locus* must be assumed to have followed an established pattern, as when, in *Henry VIII*, 1.4, a similar scene was introduced by the bringing on stage of a "*table for the guests.*" The table was one on which, as early as *Cambises*, "the cloth shalbe laid" (969) and where, in *Titus Andronicus*, Titus "*like a cook*" was "placing the dishes" (5.3.25,26). But in *Macbeth*, the "*Banquet prepar'd*" is marked by a series of "flaws and starts" (62), culminating in a situation where the host himself has "displac'd the mirth, broke the good meeting, / With most admir'd disorder" (108–09). In the process of this displacement, Macbeth himself is disordered in fulfilling his household obligations. In his own words, "You make me strange / Even to the disposition that I owe" (111–12). Having sought to "play the humble host" (4), he himself is *estranged*, emotionally as well as spatially, from both his own role and duty and his seat "i' th' midst" (10) of the occasion. The estrangement is an inward disturbance, but it is also one marked by spatial conventions informing the place and purpose of the actor's performance at the table.

The disruption sets in when the First Murderer enters with the unpublishable news that Banquo is slain and Fleance has escaped. Macbeth, leaving a physical "gap" in the midst of the banquet table (as if to match the one felt by Banquo's absence), intercepts the murderer and his news on a site that, largely unfocused, is semiotically distinct as well as spatially separate from the *locus* of the banquet table. Macbeth's apartness from the feasters allows for a bifold purpose of playing in that it commingles the language of dramatic exchange and an awareness of stage direction. Together, both sustain his elliptic, even inversionary, responses to the blood-stained murderer:

> Macb. [*Goes to the door.*]
>   There's blood upon thy face.
>   Mur.   Tis Banquo's then.
> Macb. 'Tis better thee without than he within. (3.4.13–14)

The resulting breach in the layout of the scene is spatial as well as social. Since the protagonist himself is the agent of rupture, a playful duplicity in his language use, the punning, topsy-turvying figure of contrariety itself, must serve to distance or transgress the *locus* convention. For a brief, transitory moment, the self-enclosed, strictly symbolic representation of the feast is broken up when the spatial order of "within" and "without" is turned upside down. At this point, Macbeth – not unlike such leading characters as Hamlet or Prospero – uses language metadramatically, thereby underlining what Anne Righter calls the Shakespearean "equilibrium of involvement and distance" (*Shakespeare and the Idea of the Play* 205).[16] As far as Macbeth's "involvement" is at stake, the meaning is that it is better to have the blood outside, upon the murderer's face, than inside, in Banquo's veins. The chilling logic is that the blood is "without" the murderer, but it is Banquo who is without the blood.

At the same time, for Macbeth to play upon these bloody outsides and insides attests to his relative distance from the *locus*. Could it be that this distance allows for yet another, spatially informed play of stage business? Macbeth's preferred scenario is for the murderer to be "without" the banquet rather than Banquo "within" it as a guest. In a (meta)theatrical context, the order of "within" is without the audience; it is an order that connotes, if not the tiring house, at least an enclosed space, perhaps a localized interior. But whether or not this somewhat cryptic use of language is designed momentarily to play with and invert the strictly localized scene of the banquet party, the protagonist's exchange with the killer situates itself in a remarkably hybrid space, best described as one at the intersection between *locus* and *platea* conventions. Since the space between them was open either way, it may well have served as a site that was particularly conducive to more than one purpose of signification.

Nor was the verbal order of inversion "far unmeet for the matter" at hand. Upon the murderer's arrival, the norms of hospitality – which included "our chief guest" Banquo – are doubly violated. Having "displac'd the mirth" (107), the host of the feast also and irretrievably displaces both the *locus* and the meaning of hospitality. Confronted by Banquo's ghost, a "strange infirmity" (3.4.85) befalls him. Although the "fit," as Lady Macbeth says imploringly, "is momentary" (54), it must be read as an attack of mental disorder, that is to say, as "a fit of madness" (*Comedy of Errors* 5.1.76), not unlike the "fit or frenzy" that "possess[es]" Lavinia when she like "Hecuba of Troy / Ran mad for sorrow" (*Titus Andronicus* 4.1.17;20–21). On the Elizabethan stage, such madness tends to exceed the bounds of representational closure.

In *Macbeth*, such fitful "folly" (72) prevents the protagonist from resuming his seat at the banquet table, despite the combined attempt on the part of both Lennox and Ross to plead with their host, "May't please your Highness sit" (38) and, "Please't your Highness / To grace us with your royal company?" (43–44). Mental disorder here has a spatial correlative which, keeping him apart from the mid-stage *locus*, incapacitates the host from closing the "gap" at the banquet table. It is a twofold gap that, ironically, cannot be closed even when filled by Banquo's ghastly apparition. This gap becomes an embarrassing gulf between the time-honored rules and expectations of hospitality on the part of the guests and the scandalous "flaws and starts" (62) in their host's absence and absent-mindedness.

After the "strange infirmity" (85) in sustaining his place and office, Macbeth in later scenes continues to linger at the frontiers of closure and (dis)order. Consulting the weird sisters, he confronts the "unknown power" (4.1.69), a nonrepresentable force "high or low" (67) that drives him, "Even till destruction sicken" (60). And while the sisters "perform [their] antic round" (130), the limen between *locus* and *platea* ceases to function; equivocation reigns supreme and another mode of "admir'd disorder" reinstates the incipient confusion, where "Fair is foul, and foul is fair" (1.1.11). Once Macbeth's presence in the play is associated with unlocalized, to a certain extent even unrepresentable, agencies of "disorder" and "folly," his language cannot quite be contained by the dominant order of localized space. Rather, we have, as Malcolm Evans has convincingly argued, "A space of excess and, in a double sense, 'play'" (*Signifying Nothing* 132).

Macbeth, dwarfed by the 'borrowed Robes' of kingship – *is* the poor player whose mediations block any smooth passage to what is being represented and, like the mad language of the "Ideot," foregrounds the irreducible materials of signification in signifying nothing. [. . .] The material residue of actors, costumes, movements and characters is thrown into the cauldron of signifiers that will never be fully absorbed in symbolic meanings but remain the ground and negation of all ideological and metaphysical absolutes. (134)

However, Macbeth, the fretful "player" of ambition and treacherous "folly" only very partially adopts undetermined space. He assimilates space in excess of his *locus* position only as far as that associates and helps project both his "infirmity" and his complicity, in confusion and negation, with the witches and their "deed without a name" (4.1.49). Thus, Macbeth becomes an intractable figuration but one that still remains subsumed under the dramatic representation of character. It is a tragic figuration whose matter of "worthiness" is at times infiltrated by an alien energy derived from a contrarious purpose of playing.

Nor is Macbeth unique in this. There are in Shakespeare's plays several tragic or serious characters who are marked by an entirely eclectic, momentary capacity for revitalizing, from within the figured representation itself, a purpose of playing that tends to forestall spatial, verbal, temporal, and epistemological unity as associated with the *locus*. This is what happens in Richard Gloucester's sinister performance games, in Faulconbridge's impertinence, in Duke Vincentio's transformation through disguise, in Hamlet's "antic disposition," in Iago's scandalous conspiracy, in Lear's madness, in Prospero's directional regime, and in Enobarbus' awareness of his own "place i' th' story" (*Antony and Cleopatra* 3.13.46). In all these figurations, the dominant self-contained *locus* can be relayed by a thick performative that precludes any ultimate closure in representational terms. Although these figures invariably retain or return to their prescribed status as self-consistent characters, they emphatically conjure, through their language use and their gestures of conspiracy with the audience, late Elizabethan memories of the *platea*. In doing so, they generally tend to go beyond the limited, strictly momentary displacement of symbolic space that is characteristic of Macbeth as a tragic character in the represented world of the play.

However, while Macbeth falls short of definitively crossing the spatial boundaries of the *locus*, there is at least one figure in the play that strongly revitalizes on the Elizabethan stage an equivalent of the unenclosed *platea*. Serving as both foil and radical extension of the 'worthy matter' in the story space, the Porter in *Macbeth* appears to take for granted the dramatically inscribed authority of the performer to acknowledge the time and place of his physical presence and that of the audience. While the tragic protagonist moves within the absent world of the play as situated in a Scottish past, the Porter, as far as he is a representation at all, is contemporary, not of the time and world of the play but, rather, of the time of playing-in-the-world of early Jacobean England.

> *Enter* a Porter. *Knocking within.*
> Port. Here's a knocking indeed! If a man were porter of Hell Gate, he should
> have old turning the key. *(Knock.)* Knock, knock, knock! Who's there, i'
> th' name of Belzebub? Here's a farmer, that hang'd himself on th'
> expectation of plenty. Come in time! Have napkins enow about you, here
> you'll sweat for't. *(Knock.)* Knock, knock! Who's there, in th' other
> devil's name? Faith, here's an equivocator, that could swear in both the
> scales, against either scale, who committed treason enough for God's
> sake, yet could not equivocate to heaven. O, come in, equivocator.
> *(Knock.)* Knock, knock, knock! Who's there? Faith, here's an English
> tailor come hither for stealing out of a French hose. Come in, tailor, here
> you may roast your goose. *(Knock.)* Knock, knock! Never at quiet! What
> are you? (2.3.1–16)

Here, the Porter's time and space are not of those who are represented but of those who are doing the representing and the watching of the play as a performed event. Critics have conclusively established in the Porter's language a thick texture of anachronisms. There is an allusion to the "farmer that hanged himself on the expectation of plenty" (recalling the prosperous harvests in the years 1605/06); the reference to the "equivocator that could swear in both the scales against either scale" (alluding to the trial, on 28 March, 1606, and the hanging, on 3 May, of terrorist Father Garnet, the Gunpowder plotter); and there is the mentioning of the "English tailor [. . .] stealing out of a French hose" (recording current fashion changing from wide breaches to narrow 'French' fitting).

While this gallery of the damned at least in part recalls a medieval catalogue of sinful estates and professions, it has of course a representational underside supplementing the dramatic theme of equivocation between the sayings of the Witches and the doings of the protagonist. But allusions such as these constitute only a representational subtext that, subsumed under the grotesque game of devil-portering, is contained from within the *platea* occasion. I use the word 'game' in order to underline not only the openness (towards the audience) but also the playfulness, even the theatricality, of this mode of performance. Along these lines, the Porter deliberately *plays* with memories of the late medieval cycle theatre.

Here I underline the playful uses of a medieval scenario so as to fore-ground the discontinuity, together with the continuity, between traditional versions of the Harrowing of Hell and the devil-portering in *Macbeth*. No doubt there is substantial, including pictorial evidence (as in the case of the Passion Play at Valenciennes) that the representation of Hell was asso-ciated with images of a castle, guarded by devils and surrounded by walls with a fiendish gorge for the hell-mouth. But though in the English cycle plays devils are called for to "sette furthe watches on [the] wall" (York 37:140) and hell-castle is threatened to be "beseged" (Towneley 25:147), the actual correspondence is limited. The one vitally consequential link between Shakespeare's Porter and those noisy, frightfully busy medieval devils is the appearance in the Towneley Plays of a *Secundus* demon who serves as "Oure porter at hell yate" ("The Judgement" 30:373) and may well have had a considerable resemblance to the devilish officer Rybald in both the York and Towneley cycles and even, perhaps, the Wakefield Tutivillus, who sarcastically greets in doggerel rhyme "ffals Iurars and vsurars" (30:363) at what may be assumed to be either the gated walls or the yawning pit of hell-castle.[17]

Although, as I shall suggest in a moment, the entire medieval scenario of the devil's castle is turned upside-down in *Macbeth*, the process of its adaptation and radical transmutation is in our context of considerable relevance. If we look for the provenance of the scurrilous, noisily banging element of contrariety in Shakespeare's tragedy, the poetics of the late medieval theatre provides part of the answer. The answer remains incom-plete, however, as long as we can only speculate about the grotesque, irreverent quality of Rybald's appearance and his perception of "this ugly noyse" (Towneley 25:95), let alone his potential proximity to those "graced deformities" which will assume an undisguised frivolity in a secular context. So rather than stipulate a linear succession of Shake-speare's Porter from what, in their overall impact, were liturgically solemn, mostly uncomic, frightfully serious representations of hell in the medieval drama, we are thrown back on what at best were "fond and frivolous" mediations by secular performers.

Whatever the ways and means or the extent of such secular mediations, the major point is that in Shakespeare's play, the "fond and frivolous jestures," deleted in Marlowe's *Tamburlaine*, are advanced to a clownish disquisition on the visceral and spiritual bounds of existence. Accordingly, the space for its enactment is circumscribed not primarily by what can or cannot be represented of these boundary zones, but by a grotesque response to the limits and the ludicrousness of representing the near-unrepresentable. At the same time, this response is *not* "far unmeet for the matter" when it helps direct the audience's reaction to a densely inscribed tragic action. In fact, the Porter's persiflage provides a powerful subtext to what is a very necessary question in the play's world-picturing design. As Thomas de Quincey noted in his celebrated essay, "On the Knocking on the Gate in *Macbeth*" (1823), "when the deed is done [. . .]: the knocking at the gate is heard; [. . .] and the re-establishment of the goings-on of the world in which we live, first makes us profoundly sensible of the awful parenthesis that had suspended them" (de Quincey, "On the Knocking on the Gate 93). But this stupendous counterpoise, as the Romantic critic perhaps unwittingly implies, evokes "goings-on of the world in which *we* live" – "we," that is, those in the world of the audience, then and now.

As an outrageous piece of self-awareness in performance practice, the knocking on the gate inhabits thresholds on more than one level. The Porter, to begin with, serves as a fascinating but entirely unstable medium in the stage business of (un)localizing theatrical space. Not unlike his puns and anachronisms, the drumming, staccato tenor of the knocking is greatly in excess of what immediate 'meaning' its reiteration may be said to represent. Clearly, these reverberating signs and symbols have a bifold point of reference: they convey the demand for admission both on the part of Macduff and Lennox and on the part of the damned. (And in his gesturing, the Porter who "thought to have let in some of all professions" may well have made a show of recruiting those damned from among the audience.) The knocking, therefore, exemplifies in one signifier the manner in which localized and unlocalized space can coalesce in what Beckerman called one "double image." The difference between them – far from being obliterated – constitutes the terrific quality of the effect to which the overlapping of two orders of space and time contributes.

The knocking, then, has unsuspected levels of significance in the play. Since no rhetoric of *copia* could possibly account for the strangely pro-longed banging at the tiring house doors, the sheer volume and duration of these signals deliberately (and to great effect) underlined the protracted juggling with different points of interactive reference. While the Porter's strange delay in answering the call for admittance would be quite comic in itself (loitering in the face of urgency), his temporizing is significant on more than one level. At the same time, the knocking, together with the Porter's response to it, served emphatically to highlight the threshold between the *platea*-related space of the devil-portering and the 'necessary' office of the castle's south-gate custodian. In either space, the stubborn, unyielding demand for passing the gate could not but draw attention to this liminal action as a perfect site of contrariety. But rather than simply denoting, as in Sidney's sense of the word, the conflation of comic delight and loud laughter, "contrarietie" here constitutes an uncanny con-fusion between the gate of the castle and the gate of hell.

Such moralizing of two meanings in one locality – denoted by the tiring house doors – must have reverberated with distinct memories of a related use of theatrical space in the medieval theatre. There, hell was projected in the form of a castle usually marked by a monstrous mouth or infernal opening. But in *Macbeth*, this traditional representation of medieval hell in castle-form is grotesquely inverted. Here, the primary representation, the castle, is not so much used to convey the *locus* of hell but, rather, the image of "Hell Gate" is grafted upon, and made to connote, an opening to the castle. In other words, in the mystery plays the figure of the castle served as a signifier for a notion of hell; in *Macbeth*, a hellish gate to damnation is, as signifier, used to connote the complex signified of a murderous stronghold. But while the representations in both cases retained a good deal of fluid give and take between signs and meanings, this act of performance in *Macbeth* actually must have thrived on the interface of these duplicitous significations. The devil-portering clown, ambidextrous to the extreme, juggled with several meanings in these unstable uses of platform space.

In the midst of this spatial and verbal juggling, the knocking can best be viewed as part of a hybrid purpose of playing where two different localizations mutually engage and at least partially suspend one another. In fifteen lines, the word "Knock(ing)" recurs, stage directions included, seventeen times – an indisputable cue to what, at least in its volume, may have involved a terrific dramatization of "this ugly noyse." Since the stage directions themselves no less than four times are followed by the Porter's double and triple reiteration of the word, both textually inscribed directions and physically performed actions appear almost to coalesce in function: the player's language physically orchestrates the rhythm, and re-hearses the materiality, of an (un)localizing stage business. The actor's voice, resonating with the nonverbal signifiers of physical knocking, is turned into a medium of *mise-en-scène*. Through his performance on an open stage, the player himself stage-directs the sound scenery[18] 'within.' Being authorized as a forceful agent of production, the player is not at all lost in his roles as either hell-porter or castle porter. Playing at the frontiers of representation, he both highlights and, through travesty, subverts representational business. Thus, the ostensible response to the knocking thrives on a burlesque, outrageous logistics of admission. The Porter, in staging a hilarious show of im-pertinence, can celebrate an orgy of deferral. The gap could not be wider between the represented sound scenery in the world of the play (the knocking on the castle's south gate) and what, in refusing to play a *locus*-determined role, the clown 'after his own braine' actually makes of it. What results is an unparalleled misreading of a precisely localized, perfectly unambiguous nonverbal signifier demanding entrance. Such misreading celebrates 'disfigurement' of a high order.

"That knocking" is first perceived by Macbeth, after the deed is done, "when every noise appals me" (2.2.55). Only a few lines later, Lady Macbeth's "I hear a knocking / At the south entry" (62–63) in no uncertain terms localizes the source of the noise and subjects it to the represented time and place at Inverness castle. The initial knocking is entirely continuous with the stark horror of the immediately preceding scene of murder; so far, the audience would seek to associate the knocking with the firmly localized site of climactic action. Thus, when the rapping on the gate is first heard by Lady Macbeth, her response is to retire to "our chamber" and put on a "night-gown" (63; 67). Again, such response is stringently tied to a *locus*: her action conforms with the time, the place, the circumstances in the castle. Here, relations of signifier (nonverbal/verbal "knocking") and signified (unexpected arrival, threat of discovery) tend to be marked not by instability and indeterminacy but closure.

However, this cultural semiotics of (dis)order is completely upset when a mere seven lines later the Porter enters. On the spur of the moment, he is free to redefine not only the place and time but also the 'meaning' of the knocking. It seems as if such signifiers in the theatre's stage business can without much fuss be harnessed to radically different sites and purposes of playing. Thus, the Porter is authorized to (dis)figure what knocking "At the south entry" can be made to signify. In his double image, the Porter is a medium but also a producer of these signals. He can not only displace their locale and collapse their contextual meaning, but, remarkably, is made to produce a new meaning, one that in its turn reflects an imaginary, yet, for all that, theatrically charged reading. Hence, the represented location in the story of the play is supplemented by another location, that of "hell-gate," waiting to engulf the sinners of Jacobean London.

In other words, the hellish Porter is envisioned on the time-honored premises that the comic performer's own presence – not the "necessary question of the play" (*Hamlet* 3.2.42–43) – is authorized to determine locale. With his grim offer to usher spectators into "th'everlasting bon-fire," the performer's competence, though inscribed, gives him considerable control, if not authority, over the message and its meaning. This, I suggest, is what finally accounts for the sheer duration of the poundings away at the tiring house doors. The Porter, quite impervious to the perlocutionary force of these signals, is in command; he scarcely feels called upon, except at the end, to respond by opening the gate – be that the door to everlasting damnation or the entry to the castle of Inverness.

Thus, the act of deferral is sustained through the ambidexterous strength of a strange threshold position. Resolutely quibbling and juggling with the signifier, the Porter effectively delays what, through the primary representation, is signified. It is as though he prevaricates with the meaning of the message, so as to pursue his own equivocating authority on the threshold between presentation and representation. Again and again, the onomatopoeic echo in his voice provides the text (and pre-text) for a phantasmagoric game, a horrible, laughable show of hellish admittance. In his downstage position, the player's strong performative must have been associated with gestures of display and distribution, even by pointing at certain presumed sources and agents of stupendous evil and confusion. And as far as the Porter was one "of them that will themselves laugh" (*Hamlet* 3.2.40–41), this pointing must have been inseparable from grinning and laughing at the showing of the show. Surely, this was a "swelling scene" in its own right, where the "petty pace" in opening the gate for Macduff and Lennox contrasted, on the "unworthy scaffold," with "winged heels" in the duplicitous delivery of laughter and damnation.

By the time of the fifth stage direction, "*Knock,*" the Porter at long last desists. Note the need on the open platform space for him and the audience to "remember" (his own word) a modicum of his ties to the world of the play, with its represented locale that only now connotes, and is specified by, the "cold" of the North.

> *Port.* [. . .] But this place is too cold for hell. I'll devil-porter it no further. [. . .] (*Knock.*) Anon, anon! [*Opens the gate.*] I pray you remember the porter. *Enter* Macduff *and* Lennox.
> *Macd.* Was it so late, friend, ere you went to bed,
> That you do lie so late?
> *Port.* Faith, sir, we were carousing till the second cock; and drink, sir, is a great provoker of three things.
> *Macd.* What three things does drink especially provoke? (2.3.16–27)

Here, George Hunter's edition, following that of John Dover Wilson (1947), places the editorial stage direction "[*Opens the gate*]" where, if my reading is correct, it actually belongs, that is, *after* the player, turning to the audience, asks them to "remember" the role of "the porter." The momentary crossing of the threshold, the move from *platea* to *locus*, is carefully anticipated by what doubleness there is in "this place" which is "too cold for hell." For the audience to recall his position at Inverness castle is not to forget; it is to 'remember' that other space and the threshold on which the clown now can admit Macduff and Lennox. "I pray you remember the porter" – not unlike the knocking itself – exemplifies the doubleness in signs and locations. Small wonder, when the (un)localized gate now opens for an explanation. 'Explaining' the delay, the Porter readily grasps for the 'excuse' that, in a question coming from a represented character, now has to account for the delay in opening the gate. But far from altogether relinquishing the *platea* in search of a seamless motivation from cause to effect, this move is instrumental for a return to an open stage. In fact, the Porter, having snatched a brief corollary to the explanation ("we were carousing"), proceeds heartily to use and abuse it for a renewed display of mother-wit.

At this point to offer the impatient noblemen an obscene specimen of tavern talk is, after the self-expressed length of their wait 'outside,' as ludicrous as Macduff's willingness to play the game. This at least is so by the logocentric standards of verisimilar representation, such as would comply with the poetics of the *locus* rather than that of the *platea*. But for Macduff to take up the Clown's cue and placidly to ask the question, "What three things does drink especially provoke?" is blatantly to disregard the "necessary question of the play" (*Hamlet* 3.2.42–43). According to the space and mirror of their characterization, Madcuff and Lennox must have had a short and noisy night, described elsewhere as "unruly," and "Of dire combustion and confus'd events" (2.3.54; 58). Having "almost slipp'd the hour," they must have been concerned first and foremost to follow their instructions "to call timely" (46–47) on the king. But, instead, as they linger on a residual *platea*, it appears that closure and decorum are not operative in their representation. The sense of time and delay, even the pressure to oblige royal orders does not apply, at least as long as the authority of the *locus* in the represented world-of-the-play is relinquished to playing-in-the-world of the playhouse.

While important rules in high Renaissance poetics (to which I have drawn attention in chapter 6) are waived, the spatial measure of the *platea*-like place on Shakespeare's stage is wide enough and sufficiently authoritative to accommodate the advent of two noblemen. As they confront the Porter, cultural difference in the uses of theatrical space is awkwardly suspended. Even as the gate "At the south entry" is at long last opened, there is time enough for Macduff, unconditionally and uncondescendingly, to play the game of "rhyming mother-wits." "Game" here needs to be taken literally, because his complicity in the staging of the clown's "frivolous jestures" ("What three things does drink especially provoke?") is obvious. His readiness to ask the question (and provide the cue) makes him accessory to the delivery of the kind of riddling jest that the gravediggers in *Hamlet* excel at. In both scenes, the *platea* occasion holds sway, which foregrounds the time and place and the authority of spectatorship. In other words, the most pressing reason for the Thane of Scotland almost literally to rephrase the Porter's question is to lend clarity and emphasis for a riddle. The provocations that drink entails, especially in its equivocations with lechery, need to be considered, and that takes a moment when spectators are invited to participate in the solving of the conundrum. Their participation could be counted upon when, a few lines earlier, in the language of the chorus to *Henry V*, it was their "thoughts" that had to "deck" the sinful horror behind the rapping of invisible villains, treacherous contemporaries on their way to damnation. Here, the Porter goes one step further than the second gravedigger in *Hamlet*, whose riddling, quibbling question, again pronounced twice, shares the threefold structure of traditional oral lore ("What is he that builds stronger than either the mason, the shipwright, or the carpenter?" [5.1.41–42]). Along these lines, the legacy of the *platea* must have served *a fortiori* to make "theatrical meaning a participatory act" (Bulman, *Shakespeare, Theory, and Performance* 1), and a zestful affair full of game and sport at that.

Banqueting in *Timon of Athens*

If the reading of these two scenes from *Macbeth* teaches us anything, it is that we should not oppose the uses of *locus* and those of the *platea* or in the least minimize the enormous amount of reciprocity across the (altogether permeable) line of demarcation between them. A rare and short, but fully sustained *platea* occasion as in *Macbeth* (2.3) contains not only a representational underside but as a matter of fact presupposes, for the 'terrific' quality of its impact, an unrelenting "tragic glass." Nor can the range of interface and supplementarity be smaller where, as in most of the scenes with a mixed purpose of playing, the full spectrum of performance practices ranges from personation to presentation, from empathy to audience address. There the quality of incessant contact between the two types of theatrical space – *locus* and *platea* – is marked not by confrontation but intersection, not by separation but mutual engagement. As the dovetailing of three parties in *Troilus and Cressida* revealed, radically different uses of theatrical space – as those associated with Cressida/Diomedes and Thersites – can simultaneously be staged and yet further mixed with an intermediate position (Troilus and Ulysses – see chapter 3).

Such simultaneity is thoroughly inscribed in Timon's banquet, as spelled out in the Folio's opening stage directions.

> *Hoboys playing loud music. A great banquet serv'd in,* [Flavius *and others attending;*] *and then enter* Lord Timon, *the* States, *the* Athenian Lords, [Alcibiades, *and*] Ventidius, *which* Timon redeem'd *from prison. Then comes, dropping after all,* Apemantus, *discontentedly, like himself.* (SD 1.2)

Although the initial projection of temporal sequence and spatial order suggests a perfectly consistent, self-contained place of action, the stage direction in its last sentence, with its "Then" and "after all," hints at some temporal and spatial difference in the layout of the scene. Such differentiation is significant as a cue for actors; it invokes the theatrical process, not its imaginative product. Reflecting the author's draft or a scribal copy of it, the stage direction is written through an actor's eyes observing groupings and tempos in the movement of bodies. Nor is this angle of viewing unusual; as W. W. Greg notes, stage directions "write 'within' for what to the audience is without" (*Shakespeare's First Folio* 124), players enter "at several doors," even when, as imagined characters, they meet in a forest, and so forth.

Thus, the stage direction in *Timon of Athens* is in consonance with a *mise-en-scène* that, undaunted by high Renaissance principles of proportion, harmony, and tectonic order, accommodates meaningful gaps in space and time. Apemantus, "*dropping after all,*" breaks up unity both in the timing of the entrance and in the representation of social status and manners. If his appearance "*like himself*" does not read (again from a player's perspective), 'the actor playing Apemantus enters in his self-resembled show' – which reading is unlikely, though not completely out of the question – then at least his bearing differs from that of elevated Athenian characters, lords and senators. The difference in question is not nearly as sharp as in the case of Thersites who, discontentedly, again and again appears "like himself," that is, unlike the Athenian generals. Even so, the gap is pronounced enough to affect the representation of the banquet as a site of unquestioned splendor, lavish hospitality, and great matter of "worthiness." In spatial and verbal as well as socio-cultural terms, the difference residing in this gap unfolds gradually; initially bridged through genuine dialogue, the gap soon widens.

> *Tim.* O, Apemantus, You are welcome.
> *Apem.*   No;
>   You shall not make me welcome.
>   I come to have thee thrust me out of doors.   25
> *Tim.* Fie, th' art a churl. Ye have got a humor there
>   Does not become a man, 'tis much to blame.
>   They say, my lords, "*Ira furor brevis est,*"
>   But yond man is very angry. Go,
>   Let him have a table by himself,   30
>   For he does neither affect company,
>   Nor is he fit for't indeed.
> *Apem.* Let me stay at thine apperil, Timon.
>   I come to observe, I give thee warning on't.   34
> *Tim.* I take no heed of thee; th' art an Athenian,
>   therefore welcome. I myself would have no power;
>   prithee let my meat make thee silent.

Apem. I scorn thy meat, 'twould choke me; for I
should ne'er flatter thee. O you gods! what a number
of men eats Timon, and he sees 'em not! It grieves   40
me to see so many dip their meat in one man's blood,
and all the madness is, he cheers them up too.
I wonder men dare trust themselves with men.
Methinks they should invite them without knives:
Good for their meat, and safer for their lives.   45
There's much example for't: the fellow that sits next
him, now parts bread with him, pledges the breath of
him in a divided draught, is the readiest man to kill
him; 't 'as been prov'd. If I were a huge man, I should
fear to drink at meals,   50
Lest they should spy my windpipe's dangerous notes:
Great men should drink with harness on their throats.
Tim. My lord, in heart; and let the health go round.
2. *Lord.* Let it flow this way, my good lord.   54
Apem. Flow this way? A brave fellow! he keeps
his tides well. Those healths will make thee and thy
state look ill, Timon.
Here's that which is too weak to be a sinner,
Honest water, which ne'er left man i' th' mire.
This and my food are equals, there's no odds;   60
Feasts are too proud to give thanks to the gods.   (1.2.23–61)

Having first introduced himself with a sardonic "Ho, ho" and the twisting
of a proverb (22), Apemantus swiftly extricates himself from dialogic
exchange with his welcoming host. While his first and second utterances
are in direct response to Timon's invitation, his third already reveals, in
verbal as well as in spatial terms, a hybrid position. Whereas the second
person possessive pronoun (as in "I scorn thy meat") continues direct
address, the expletive "O" with its purely exclamatory gesture marks a
distinct move away from the use of dialogue. This movement culminates in
the emerging gulf between the action at the banquet table and Apemantus'
delivery. Once the discontented philosopher has ceased to *address* any of
the elevated characters at what is presumably a mid-stage location, the
scene harbors two radically different sites of action. In all likelihood
occupying a downstage position, Apemantus now refers to Timon in the
third person singular ("he sees 'em not!"). His speech has dissociated itself
from the central *locus* of representation, verbally as well as spatially and, as
it were, acoustically – firmly localized characters do not 'hear' *platea*-based
speech (or, for that matter, interjections coming from the pit).

There is, then, a significant correlation between language use and spatial
position on at least two levels. Timon's suggestion, to "Let him have a table
by himself" (29), does not result in the setting up of another *locus*; rather, it

acknowledges a physical (as well as of course social and cultural) differentiation between Apemantus' location and the main stage position of the
dominant characters. Even while the spatial differentiation is *motivated* in
representational terms (as a *character*, he is not "fit" for "company"), it
disrupts the high Renaissance poetics of discretion, verisimilitude, and
closure. Although the *locus* surrenders none of its consistency and function,
its self-contained status as a sovereign locale is seriously impaired. Confronted by an alien voice emerging from outside its discursive regime, the
banqueting party is suddenly enveloped in a dramaturgy not of unity but of
doubleness. Since the festive table as the major site in representation is
observed and questioned from within by an alien space – one that is a place
of chorus-like presentation – the banquet can be viewed at one remove, as a
precious, self-indulgent, but entirely untrustworthy occasion.

Thus, on a plane of simultaneity, there is an interplay between a localized space in the representation of "a great banquet" mid-stage and a
strongly liminal space for the presentation of the scene at large. Although
formally tied to the banquet, Apemantus' position is indebted to the legacy
of the *platea*. As such, it occupies in this scene an open type of space that,
defiantly, engages the unifying conventions of symbolically enclosed place
and dialogue. These of course persist throughout, even after "*the masque
of* Ladies, [as] *Amazons*" enters, "*with lutes in their hands, dancing and
playing*" (130–31). From within the main action, the dazzling occasion
unfolds with enhanced glamour, yielding a visual image rarely witnessed
by the vast majority of Elizabethan spectators. At this point Apemantus'
interpellation tends to be overwhelmed by the sheer force of the *locus*.
After the "*Lords rise from table* [. . .] *and all dance, men with women*"
(145–46), the forthright cynic has only one more line before Flavius and
"*another* Servant" (180–81) come into the picture.

However, before he becomes marginalized in this scene, Apemantus'
speech culminates in a highly presentational rhetoric. Sandwiched between
two rhymed couplets (44–45;51–52), the performer is almost certainly
made physically to point at a display of generous abundance, a rare
ceremony with pomp and select table manners. In doing so, Apemantus, as
an intervenient kind of presenter, goes to the length of singling out individual feasters: "the fellow that sits next him, now parts bread with him"
(46–47). At this juncture, the counterpointing performer is at more than
one remove from the represented occasion; he no longer shares the same
space or, for that matter, the fulsome language of those at the banquet
table.

Once the scene divides and the unity of place is ruptured, Apemantus'
position is not that of someone speaking 'aside,'[19] that is, *at the side* of
localized action. Rather, there is a bifold order of space – space represented

and a site (re)presenting – drawing on an openly accepted mode of simultaneity. Again, I use 'bifold' because the juxtaposition between the banquet table and Apemantus' "table by himself" does not implicate two entirely separate acts of staging, but rather the interface between a self-contained and an open site of action.

In each case, the order of theatrical space constitutes different rules and conventions. For instance, the open mode of simultaneity allows for a flow of signifiers from which the self-contained *locus* of the banquet isolates itself, being impervious to an awareness of foreboding disaster shared between Apemantus and spectators. In other words, while Apemantus can overhear and respond to what goes on center stage, the self-enclosed banqueting party remains deaf to the language of its own threshold and resists the smoldering premonition of imminent betrayal.

As a strictly imaginary and consistently iconic mode, the representation of the banquet safeguards, as it were, its own status of iconicity. The concomitant act of self-isolation goes hand in hand with a convention that, for better or worse, insulates the artificial persons from any contact with the "unworthy" institution of a common stage-as-stage. The "worthiness of the matter itself" goes unchallenged from within its own picturing premises. Whatever happens at the banquet table cannot unhinge the rules of iconicity. Nor does Apemantus invalidate the representation-as-representation. No matter how much privileged awareness or stubborn aggression reside in this *platea* angle, the *locus*-bound characters, and Timon in particular, must turn a 'deaf ear.' According to the new poetics of world-picturing, the rules of insulation are adamant enough to effect a regular sound barrier that shields the space *in* representation from the site of its production and performance. The elevated characters, one might say, are sheltered from, and yet exposed to, the noise and bustle, the common wisdom and the easy deprecation that *platea* figures like Thersites and Apemantus would share with the audience.

To point out the limits of representation in the banquet scene is not of course to underestimate the strength and complexity of the dramatic figuration mid-stage. In its in-depth iconography, the image of the banquet can suggest its liabilities from within, and because of, the intense self-coherence in its purely imaginary function. Thus, this scene and the banquet scene in *Macbeth* can in performance achieve that frightening, uncanny presence-in-absence which makes for an "imaginary puissance" unsurpassed by any *platea* action. In the teeth of the countervailing thrust of the latter, and despite the downstage force of presentation and mediation, the *locus* in Timon's house can be staged so as to convey the zest and pathos of a great occasion without obliterating the false glitter of its rewards. The banquet itself remains a precious object of display even while

Apemantus' speech, culminating in prose, uses indiscreet language entirely at odds with the culture of rhetorical hyperbole and decorum. In particular, the "fellow" that he points at is surely one of the "Athenian Lords" and senators. As such, the feaster is addressed not from within the parameters of dramatic representation but, rather, from a world without it. Throughout the scene, Apemantus' "table by himself" serves as a foil, not an alternative, to the falseness of unending abundance, which in itself provides a rare display of high hospitality and base ingratitude.

While Apemantus' separate table remains exceptional, the principles of spatial differentiation and detachment at work here are not. In the same scene, the positioning of Flavius, the Steward, is marked by a twofold capacity for both dialogic and nondialogic speech, as in the following exchange:

> *Tim.*   Flavius!
>   *Flav.* My lord?
> *Tim.*   The little casket bring me hither.
> *Flav.* Yes, my lord. [*Aside*] More jewels yet?
>   There is no crossing him in 's humor,
>   Else I should tell him well (i' faith, I should),
>   When all's spent, he'ld be cross'd then, and he could.
>   'Tis pity bounty had not eyes behind,
>   That man might ne'er be wretched for his mind. (1.2.157–164)

Preceding his editorially inserted 'aside,' the Steward's positioning is strictly representational. But as soon as he is made to leave the *locus* of his commission in pursuit of his errand, Flavius utters an uncomfortable question that already points beyond the confines of his station in the symbolizing space of Timon's household. Since in his reasoning Flavius proceeds to justify his silence about his master's plight, the suppressed concern is vented within the terms and effects of representation, as if the character utters a sorrowful sigh for himself. It is only when the so-called 'aside' winds up with a rhymed couplet that, almost unnoticeably, the utterance ceases to be in aid of the representation of either Timon's or the speaker's character. Instead, the language of "bounty" with "eyes" to see (recalling the moral play's allegorical personification), together with the drive and rhythm of the message, leads away from a purely dialogic stance. Delivered with verve, the couplet would at least momentarily presuppose a site that, from within a strictly self-contained representational poetics, is out of bounds.

In conclusion, then, these scenes from *Macbeth* and *Timon of Athens* exemplify some of the multiple uses of theatrical space in Shakespeare's theatre which, well into the tragedies, are unthinkable without the inscribed continuing strength of the player as both character and presenter.

As Albert Cook has noted, "the body orients space"; it is the body of the performer that, first and foremost, is absorbing audience attention on stage: "space is perceived from the body outward" ("Space and Culture" 554). If these "our body-bound perceptions of space" (551) yield, in Beckerman's phrase, a "double image," the reason is not exclusively that the Elizabethan stage, to "force a play," could ring the changes between the symbolic form of space as a landscape in representation and space as a ground for play and display. While in our approach the criteria of function, both the functioning of meaning and the performant function, are of course uppermost, ultimately these need to be complemented by larger parameters that can help historicize these notions of space themselves.

On this plane, the regime of writing and the craft of playing – although certainly quite relevant – cannot between them provide the crucial coordinates. When it comes to the great watershed in the modern spatial imagination, the differentiation between place and space gathers momentum all its own. While the profound cultural difference in this distinction helps us to understand the eventual triumph of the *locus* (paradoxically, a symbolizing abstraction) over the *platea* or place, the entire paradigm change implicates theatrical space only incidentally. According to the monumental work of Edward Casey, the Renaissance was the time of a double gaze: place as a vivid, lived site was easily perceived; it continued to be lumped together, even compounded with space as an increasingly boundless, expansive projection in the human mind. Early modern notions of space – and of course we think of Shakespeare – continued to resist "a forced choice between place and space" (Casey, *The Fate of Place* 136). There was, and again my reading of *locus* and *platea* conventions confirms this, a "more or less irenic cohabitation of place and space" – one that for a few precious years presented the King's Men with yet another platform for inclusion. A mere forty or so years later, William Gilbert can note, "place is nothing, does not exist, has no strength" (Casey, *The Fate of Place* 135).

In this bilateral use of theatrical space Shakespeare, however, is not simply conserving the rapidly vanishing grounds of a transitional situation in cultural history. There is an unprecedented expansion of space in dramatic representation; only, the "vasty fields" in a European landscape of "trafficke" and battle are made more potent rather than less by retaining a sense of theatrical place in the name of a "cockpit." At the same time, this expansiveness goes hand in hand with both an intrinsic dynamic and a spiritualization of newly appropriated space. Thus, the canopies of heaven and the skies meet in a grandiose image of wide-vaulting space when Faustus says, "See see where Christs blood streames in the firmament" (*Dr. Faustus* 1432). And further still, "O soule, be changed into little water drops, / And fal into the *Ocean*, nere be found" (1472–73).[20]

At this point Shakespeare, intertwining (represented) space and (representing) place, goes yet one step further. Using the same word ("firmament") he projects a site where the infinite space of the skies is perfectly confluent with 'the heavens' over the visible place of and on the stage. Hamlet addresses the "air," the invisible substance surrounding the earth, as a stately "canopy," only to expound further "this most excellent canopy, the air, look you, this brave o'erhanging firmament, this majestical roof fretted with golden fire" (2.2.299–301). Hamlet's phrase conjoins the global circumference of "this goodly frame the earth" with the protruding place of the stage as a "promontory" jutting out into the pit, surrounded by not altogether predictable waves of response. *Nomen* then was *omen*: in Shakespeare's Globe, space and place were jostling in one metaphor, just as in *mise-en-scène* the place of the stage and the space in the story could mutually engage one another somewhat like *platea* and *locus*.

Here, then, is another "scene individable" where space and place concur without contrariety; and yet must have carried with it a captivating, exhilarating tension for those onlookers thrust into an awareness of their own threshold position between the familiar unworthy place of a mere cockpit and the vast, unknown space imagined out there. The protagonist, who speaks these lines, himself exemplifies this doubleness in perception as a larger, crucially early modern experience. The tension is within the character's construction: "I could be bounded in a nutshell, and count myself a king of infinite space" (2.2.254–55). Hamlet has that within which enhances several dimensions of place and space, the space for and in representation. Moving between these, crossing thresholds again and again, his own register of space, "lying somewhere between action and production," is exemplary for what Joel Altman sums up in a profoundly suggestive phrase: "dramatic performance itself was a liminal category in early modern England" (Altman, "The Practice of Shakespeare's Text" 494). But these thresholds of playing and writing (and living) deserve to be studied in their own right.

8 Shakespeare's endings: commodious thresholds

Divided in its formative socio-cultural impulses, contrarious in its purposes of playing, unstable in the symbolism of its spatial conventions, the Elizabethan theatre harbored a pervasive need to digest the (ab)use of the distance between the world-in-the-play and the playing-in-the-world of early modern amphitheatrical scaffolds. To a certain extent, the "swift" and "swelling scene," the platform stage itself was commodious enough to accommodate, even thrive upon the social, cultural, spatial, and verbal differences in question. But when the performed play began and, even more so, when it came to an ending, the impromptu, pragmatic, and vulnerable interface between symbolic forms and material stages was most irrevocably in question. At this point, any sense of equivalence or any achieved form of contrariety between them must have found itself in a state of crisis. There must have been uncertainty about the untried, unfixed order of this interface, first of all in the process of the play's commencement, introduction, and unfolding. But there was an even greater incertitude in the phase of dissolution, when after a mere two or three hours' business, it was time to "untie the spell" (*The Tempest* 5.1.253) of this conjunction, to surrender unconditionally the world-in-the-play with its "so potent art" (50) to the circumstances of everyday existence. As "this insubstantial pageant faded" (4.1.155), all the grand Renaissance images, the "cloud-capp'd tow'rs, the gorgeous palaces, / The solemn temples" (152–53) came down, and the matter of "worthiness" itself, with its language of great passion, honor, and romance, its nobility and history, all came to nothing.

And yet, they did leave behind more than a "rack" (156), at least more than a mere wreckage of high Renaissance splendor. When the story and its "charms" were "all o'erthrown" (Epilogue 1), there remained the boards of a bare stage, the wooden bars and beams of "this unworthy scaffold," a mere "cockpit," a profitable structure, built down-to-earth for profit and a paying audience. But that audience, which had not come empty-handed, did not leave empty-minded. Their contribution, a profitable commodity, was rewarded with a volatile sense of "imaginary puissance." What remained in the theatre was the sum total of all the pennies paid, together with the desire and the need to have more of them from returning audiences. What at least some of the spectators must have retained and cherished was a memory, the remembrance of "these visions" (*A Midsummer Night's Dream*, Puck's epilogue 5.1.426), which, with

> all their minds transfigur'd so together,
> More witnesseth than fancy's images,
> And grows to something of great constancy;
> But howsoever, strange and admirable. (5.1.24–27)

While in the ending of the performed play a new kind of disparity – that between profit and pleasure – came to a head, the prologue by comparison constituted a somewhat different threshold. On this liminal site, there was space for various gestures, those of welcome, introduction, argument, apology, the assurance of entertainment, service, and the promise, if need be, to make amends. If some of these offerings were almost literally repeated at the end of the play (compare Puck's, "We will make amends ere long" [5.1.434]), the reason was that both prologues and epilogues implicated a peculiar type of contractual relationship between playhouse and spectators. These relations, again involving commodity and fantasy, could be negotiated as an article, respectively, of both aperture and closure for the (re)presentation itself. Implicit in these negotiations, there was the predication and acknowledgement of authority on either side, the unformulated readiness provisionally to authorize, and find legitimate, the part that each of the contracting parties, players and spectators, had engaged to play.

If, up to a time, the early modern playhouse went out of its way to paraphrase these contractual relations into prologues and epilogues, the reasons are complex. As Kierkegaard observed, there must have been "something seductive" about "the possibility of a beginning" that was at least not entirely "generated from previous conditions";[1] similarly, there was, perhaps, something intimidating about a conclusion that, when all was said and done, aimed at a hoped-for repetition, the return of audiences, renewed performances, a new beginning. A beginning is of course the more challenging when, as Edward Said has noted, it establishes "implicit rules of pertinence for itself" – rules which constitute "authority – both in the sense of explicit law and guiding force."

But at the end of the play, everything is in question, the "rules of pertinence" collapse, authority will need to be renegotiated, even while the issue of doubleness comes to a head. What, for a very few precious moments remains is the invisible but, in Shakespeare's theatre, commodious threshold. Again I use the unusual 'commodious' not just for its superficial jingle with 'commodity,' but because the space and, sometimes, the time of preparation for the execution of the play's ending requires ample room and deliberate strategy – especially when the Elizabethan threshold would constitute a final stage in the play's contrariety. Here is the ultimate juncture where the full diversity in the uses of theatrical space comes to the fore, offering a last opportunity, an undoubted climax, for the liminal site on which contrariety itself implodes. At this moment, the (in)dividable quality of the scaffold stage, housing real space and symbolic space in a very peculiar symbiosis, is about to vanish. But this vanishing point has its triumph; the inevitable destination of the two hours' traffic on this stage is not to be reached without a flourish that resounds with a message unheard of in Prologues. The latter prepare for the advent of actors, who, when initially entering, set out to chart and establish as symbolic the real space in which they move. But the conclusion of the play retracts the trail: the symbolism of theatrical space, always already vulnerable in any *platea* dimension, finally dissolves into air, into the thin air where "The best in this kind are but shadows." What Shakespeare's epilogues and endings do, among other things, is invest in the uncertain future of these "shadows," if only memory and "imagination amend them" (*A Midsummer Night's Dream* 5.1.211–12).

What, then, happens to a quasi-contractually shared authority when the Elizabethan play is over? Does its circulation come to a stand-still? Is it revoked or simply discontinued? The dissemination of this authority, never exclusively wielded by "author's pen or actor's voice," undergoes a supreme test, when its crucial hour humbly, perhaps too humbly for modern ears, is rehearsed in the epilogue. The process of reception is of course prefigured throughout the text (and the performance) of the play; but it is only in the ending of dramatic transactions that spectators are directly urged to endorse, even to remember and thereby keep alive, not only the work of "author's pen" but that of "actor's voice." For the audience itself to be acknowledged as the supreme court of appeal is an act of authorization that goes beyond that of the representation of dramatic fiction.

Elizabethan epilogues and endings pursued what in today's terminology is a "post performance reception" (Susan Bennett, *Theatre Audiences* 163). Since Shakespeare's endings have rarely, if ever been thought of in these terms, it may be helpful to illustrate this "important convention" in terms of our own experience. In the twentieth-century theatre at least, it is possible to address "the act of leaving the theatre" as providing, on the one hand, "a welcome release," even "the end of interpretative activity." On the other hand,

The buzz of an excited audience, slow to leave the theatre, continues the interpretative process and is likely to enhance the experience of that production in the individual's memory [. . .] In a publicly experienced cultural event, the opportunity to talk about the event afterwards is important socially. Theatre audiences, as has been noted, tend to consist of small groups of friends, family, and so on. Reception of a performance can be prolonged by group discussion of all aspects from general appreciation to specific questions to other group members about small details of the production (Bennett, *Theatre Audiences* 164–65).[2]

In Shakespeare's theatre, there was a different, though related convention, in fact a strategy inscribed into the text of the ending that was designed to help ensure the play's post-scriptural future. As I shall suggest, even before the circulation of authority in the playhouse collapses, there obtains an authorization of spectators to recollect, discuss, and reappropriate the performed play after its theatrical transaction is over. This extradramatic (though not necessarily extratheatrical) extension of authority raises a number of thorny questions. The endings of many plays cannot quite be understood without taking into account significant and partially contradictory ties between the socio-economic institution of the theatre and the more traditional elements in the story-telling culture of Elizabethan England. Although even at the turn of the century relatively viable, this culture of oral memory was already being undermined by variegated forces of change, among which the spread of print and literacy as well as an expanding market for cultural productions were foremost.[3] As, in the words of John Lyly, "trafficke and travell" came to affect the distribution and even the composition of entertainment, the story-telling propensity of Elizabethan spectators could innovatively be appropriated in the playhouse: it could be used as a medium for dispersing information about, and interest in, further performances, with a view to keeping the play's future alive, not only for the enjoyment of hoped-for audiences but for the benefit of those who depended on the continued showing of the play in the new cultural marketplace beyond the city gates.

Under these circumstances, the ending of the Elizabethan play, including the epilogue as a stylized mode of bringing its transaction to a close, inhabited a remarkably open, in many ways vulnerable, and, despite its genial tone and language, divisive site. Here was a liminal space in which the awareness of social occasion and the imaginary contours of dramatic discourse for one more time came to interact and affect one another in a particularly compelling fashion. To the extent that this site was inscribed in the dramatic text, it seems safe to identify it with the ultimate frontier between the representation of a textually inscribed dramatic story and the occasion of its theatrical production and reception. Since this was, in the full sense of the word, a threshold, to foreground it deliberately was one way of preparing for, and intercepting the collapse of, dramatic representations. In doing so, these conventions not only thrived upon the gap between scriptural representation and the public, socially mixed, but overwhelmingly oral response to its transaction; even more important, prologues as well as epilogues bore witness to a felt need to address, or even to bridge, this gap. They could do so by helping to assimilate the represented "matter" to the actual cultural purpose of its performance. Through this bridge-building, textualized representations were both reconciled to the site of their public transaction and marked in their distance from it.

Epilogues vs. closure

In this connection, the epilogue is especially revealing as it addressed some (though not to all) of the basic issues involved in the dramatic ending. The epilogue's appeal for applause offered the audience a space for response, even participation in, the presumably happy outcome of what, at least partially, remained a festive occasion. But in this occasion, increasingly, a residual sense of holiday must have grappled with a business-like sense of everyday. Especially in Shakespeare (but also in many other plays from the Tudor/ Stuart period to the Restoration), the artfully orchestrated transition between the two worlds inside and outside the theatre is as unmistakable as surely it was deliberate. As a rule, the imperfect closure of the play's ending is used both to cope with and delay the collapse of the represented figuration. As a glance at three of Shakespeare's more significant epilogues – those to *As You Like It*, *All's Well That Ends Well*, and *The Tempest* – may suggest, the epilogue gracefully helps to displace or at least tone down a sense of abruptness in the perception of an abiding gulf between represented roles and performing actors. Whatever rupture the trajectory from textualized fiction to cultural occasion may have involved is intercepted as long as the epilogue in its own conventional form rehearses (and condenses) the transition from dramatic script to theatrical institution. Through the use of this convention, Shakespeare's dramatic representations can, to a certain extent, organize and even celebrate their own successful collapse in the hoped-for applause of a judging audience.

Along these lines the language of Shakespeare's epilogues is particularly revealing in that their performance articulates and, at the same time, gracefully helps to displace a sense of contingency, vulnerability, and incertitude in confronting the gap between players and spectators; in fact, there is the attempt to stylize the desperate kind of pleasure to be derived from coping with the gap. Although, as Rosalind says at the end of *As You Like It*, "a good play needs no epilogue" (Epilogue 4–5), this function of the epilogue appears to be best served when that gap is playfully suspended. At that point the movement from the represented world of the dramatic fiction to the (re)presenting world of the Elizabethan playhouse is, through performance, turned into the awareness of a metamorphosis in whose achievement the audience is invited or even "conjured" to assist:

> It is not the fashion to see the lady the epilogue; [....] What a case am I in then, that am neither a good epilogue, nor cannot insinuate with you in the behalf of a good play! I am not furnish'd like a beggar, therefore to beg will not become me. My way is to conjure you, and I'll begin with the women. I charge you, O women, for the love you bear to men, to like as much of this play as please you; and I charge you, O men, for the love you bear to women (as I perceive by your simp'ring, none of you hates them), that between you and the women the play may please. If I were a woman I would kiss as many of you as had beards that pleas'd me, complexions that lik'd me, and breaths that I defied not; and I am sure, as many as have good beards, or good faces, or sweet breaths, will for my kind offer, when I make curtsy, bid me farewell. (Epilogue 1–23)

The transition is remarkably effected when the actor speaking as yet from within the role of Rosalind begins the epilogue by saying "It is not the fashion to see the lady the epilogue." But as he proceeds, he is gradually distancing the assimilated role, making his own cultural and sexual embodiment supersede whatever absent representation overlapped with the public dissolution of the dramatic fiction. So he begins the epilogue by associating himself one last time with the represented 'lady' only to end up pledging, "If I were a woman I would kiss as many of you as had beards that pleas'd me" (18–19). The transition, then, is from fictional representation to theatrical reality, from the assumed identity of the *role* of 'the lady' to the reality of the *body* of the boy actor who congenially establishes the true nonrepresentational identity of his gender by saying "If I were a woman." But since such statement involves the supreme irony of finally counterpointing, by rehearsing yet again, the comic changes of gender, the theatrical effect is so much more than that of a mere transition: in conclusion the play's threshold provides a precariously built-up tension between both worlds, the one associated with the fiction of the text, the other associated with its *actual use in society*. For one brief moment, before the illusion of the role vanishes and the world of the play finally surrenders to the world of existence, the arts of performance must confront and can playfully orchestrate the gulf between the two.

This threshold constitutes the site on which the sexual, social, and semiotic divisions in the performance of Shakespeare's boy-heroine are renegotiated at the end of the play. As a result, her/his representational status as some naturalized gendered subject finally explodes. The represented confusion involved in the fiction of cross-dressing stimulates, even as it is enhanced by, the actual histrionic energy of performance; it is an energy that in a young male actor inspires the art of performing highly complex images of continuity and discontinuity between who was represented and who was doing the representing. In this process of 'characterization,' the dominant notions of gendered difference are profoundly, and yet with great tact and charm, interrogated. As Jean Howard has noted, since the epilogue reminds us that Rosalind "is played by a boy, the neat convergence of biological sex and culturally constructed gender is once more severed" ("Crossdressing" 435). But when the language of the epilogue challenges the imagery not just of gendered but of social difference as well ("I am not furnish'd like a beggar"), the (dis)continuity between gentle role and the player's actual status (proverbially, though not invariably, referred to as 'beggarly') is left dangling in mid-air. After all, the represented signs of precious costume continue to so envelop some handsome representing body that, during the epilogue, they defer the social underside of the final metamorphosis of character back into actor.

However, the image of the beggar, so important in Lear's madness as a sign of limits in the representation of order, rank, and royalty, *can* be used to suggest the radical exhaustion of dramatic fiction. In the epilogue to *All's Well That Ends Well*, "The king's a beggar" (1), and the achieved stance of difference in this metamorphosis conveys at least a modicum of that actual social rupture between who was represented and who was doing the representing. Again, the play's ending conjures the ephemeral fantasia of the former by overthrowing the "charms" (as Prospero will call them) of the imagined represented images of authority. The trajectory is from the spell of the fiction of royalty to an awareness of the social reality of performance:

> *King.* Let us from point to point this story know,
>   To make the even truth in pleasure flow.
>   [*To Diana.*] If thou beest yet a fresh uncropped flower,
>   Choose thou thy husband, and I'll pay thy dower,
>   For I can guess that by thy honest aid
>   Thou kept'st a wife herself, thyself a maid.
>   Of that and all the progress, more and less,
>   Resolvedly more leisure shall express.
>   All yet seems well, and if it end so meet,
>   The bitter past, more welcome is the sweet. *Flourish.*
>   [EPILOGUE]
>   [*King. Advancing.*] The king's a beggar, now the play is done;
>   All is well ended, if this suit be won,
>   That you express content; which we will pay,
>   With strife to please you, day exceeding day.
>   Ours be your patience then, and yours our parts;
>   Your gentle hands lend us, and take our hearts.
>   *Exeunt omnes.* (5.3.325–334; Epilogue 1–6)

The King of France prepares for the ending on at least two of three levels. He sets out to provide for the play's post-scriptural future a sense of pleasurable recollection of the full canvas ("from point to point") of "this story." But the suggested cultural uses of hindsight and insight into the play from the point of view of its dénouement are made to coalesce with the final piece of dramatic fiction. So "the even truth" (326) derived from recollecting "point to point this story" combines with, even leads back to, the King's role as he (far from being a beggar yet) pays Diana's "dower." Even at this moment, the boundaries of representation, and within them the form of dialogue, vanish into thin air with the last "thou" in line 330. After "... thyself a maid," the speaker from his role of domineering donor makes a transition to a chorus-like utterance in two rhymed couplets. But again the 'transition' is most graceful; for now the last lines in the dialogue addressed to Diana are, as it were, *cited* as some exercise in the munificent uses of "leisure" and pastime ("Of *that* and all the progress...") after the play has virtually come to an end. At this point, the concluding fiction of this stage-business is already on tenuous grounds. This is one more reason why the final metamorphosis of the last vestiges of the dramatic role of the King into the common player's performance of the epilogue does not at all come as a surprise.

Even so, for G. K. Hunter and other modern editors to follow Rowe and insert the capitalized "EPILOGUE" in brackets (because not in Folio) while at the same time retaining for it italics (which *are* in the Folio) is to cope with the seeming (and somewhat shocking) abruptness of the collapse of a royal role into "The king's a beggar." If anywhere, here we have an element of rupture between the language of fictive representation and what now emerges as the player's "self-resembled" performance. Although one would wish to think so, it seems scarcely possible for the player to make this transition "in pleasure flow" and yet also accentuate the gulf involved in it. For the element of discontinuity appears especially pronounced after the ambivalent, even perhaps ominous fiction of "All yet seems well" is "Resolvedly" sheltered from doubt so as, not without effort, to culminate in "more welcome is the sweet." At the frontiers of these strenuous representations of harmony in what is no happy comedy, the king abruptly renounces the signs of his royal status.

As "the play is done," the vulnerable *locus* of royalty gives way to the *platea* occasion for nonrepresentational audience response. On this threshold between *locus* and *platea*, the "personator" (to use Thomas Heywood's term), performing still, steps forward from behind the 'personated.' Now the sign of signs, the symbols of status symbols, surrender their "little brief authority" (*Measure for Measure* 2.2.118), and the feigned image of the royal crown appears, in reality, as that piece of brass on the patient actor's head. At this point the performer stands naked except for the art of his delivery – but delivery with a difference: whatever the textually inscribed authority of a 'worthy' character's role may have constituted in a fiction, is no longer available. What is presumably the performer's tense anxiety boils down to an acknowledgement of his most basic task, his true legitimation: "With strife to please you, day exceeding day."

For all that, the theatre's readiness to provide a pleasurable conclusion appears as no servile or passive offering: the arts of performance achieve their final authority in the exchange of cultural labor with the audience. The performance, having outlived fictional representation, finally subsides, through an exchange of roles, in the performer's silence: "Ours be your patience then and yours our parts." "Imaginary puissance" in the uses of performance has now come full circle; the actors, in silent patience, confront the play's post-scriptural future. This future is thinkable as a space of mutuality only when the spectators "express content" and perform their own "parts," not only through their clapping hands but by rehearsing "this story" and by remembering it "from point to point."

Similarly, at the end of *The Tempest*, Prospero dislodges whatever boundary there was between the represented fiction in the text of the play and the representing agent in the real world of the playhouse:

> Now my charms are all o'erthrown,
> And what strength I have's mine own,
> Which is most faint. Now 'tis true,
> I must be here confin'd by you,
> Or sent to Naples. Let me not,
> Since I have my dukedom got,
> And pardon'd the deceiver, dwell
> In this bare island by your spell,
> But release me from my bands
> With the help of your good hands.
> Gentle breath of yours my sails
> Must fill, or else my project fails,
> Which was to please. Now I want
> Spirits to enforce, art to enchant,
> And my ending is despair,
> Unless I be reliev'd by prayer,
> Which pierces so, that it assaults
> Mercy itself, and frees all faults.
> As you from your crimes would pardon'd be,
> Let your indulgence set me free.   (Epilogue 1–20)

Having within the role of the enlightened magician finally abjured "this rough magic," having broken his "staff," drowned his "book" (5.1.54; 57), the imaginative figure of representation called Prospero collapses. But as this textual figuration is being released by the actual body of the actor, there is again, hovering over the play's ending, a precarious tension beween fictional representation and true embodiment. This informs some anxious interplay between the "bare island" in the text of *The Tempest* and the "unworthy scaffold" on which the actor is left behind, somewhat wary, lest his true "project fails/ Which was to please." Almost unnoticeably the "charms" in the text of the fiction turn into the past tense, once they are referred to the achieved cultural "project" of dramatic entertainment, which "was to please."

Again, the interaction of players and spectators is about to culminate in an exchange, almost, of roles: the past "charms" of dramatic fiction are surrendered to "the spell" which, finally, the audience has over the actor craving applause: "Let me not, / [. . .] dwell/ In this bare island by your spell, / But release me [. . .]" (5–9). Whatever authority the representation of Prospero may have enjoyed in the performed text of the play is now abdicated to that nonrepresentational realm in which the true pleasure of the audience serves as final arbiter of the fate of the drama in performance: "But release me from my bands/ With the help of your good hands" (9–10). The renegotiation of authority is effected through the interplay between what theatrical signs imaginatively represent (what "art" there is to "enchant") *and* what their representing function in society is. The underlying contradiction is between the fictional language of the text and its social history in the theatre.

Here to emphasize such interplay between language and history, text and theatre, is to suggest that dramatic representations, especially in the Elizabethan theatre, occupy a vulnerable space, opening themselves to the all-important 'part' of the audience. The authority of the text, as well as that of performance practice, explodes in an acute crisis when, between them, the ultimate voice of authorization, the cheering, hissing, clapping audience, finally declares itself. In such a situation, representational prac- tice, at least in the early modern commercial playhouse, is apt to refer beyond itself; the deconstructionist "*dis*linkage" between the signifier and the world (to which I shall return in the Afterword) never quite obtains. What now looms large is the nonfictional reality of performance as this performance self-consciously articulates its own existential need for being favorably received in the indulgent hands of its audience. The act of performance is thrown back on its own limited authority; for all that, its final legitimation is negotiated (and publicly evaluated) at the point of intersection between the actual place and institution of playing and the lingering impact of the playtext.

This point of intersection is symptomatic of the difference between two types of discourse and appropriation. The difference, as I have suggested, could be handled through "bifold authority" in the cultural uses and places of playing. But now that the play was about to end, the strategy of bifold authority can only serve as a playful mode of dissolution and discontinuity between the presence of the body of the actor and the 'absent' representation of his role. On the ingrained strength of this strategy, the subtly balanced movement from fictional text to cultural reality can be, as it were, arrested one more time, but only for the play to cancel its purely imaginary dimension, projecting itself into a nonrepresentational social occasion. The dramatic representation, in acknowledging its own limits and finiteness, opens itself beyond its ending and confronts the precarious nature of its own limited authority, spell-bound and asking for applause.

Thus, if we read Prospero's "strength" as the character's power, his self-contained capacity for expression in terms of his own representational figuration, then what "strength" remains to him in the epilogue is already situated beyond the boundaries of representation. Once his "charms are all o'erthrown," the actor's "strength" is to be found outside, no longer inside the representational framework of the text. As it appears, the 'I' (in "what strength I have's mine own") is that of the representer, not the represented. The actor steps forward, relinquishing his role and whatever signs and images of fictionality were associated with his representation. What remains, after these signs of authority are all "o'erthrown," is the actor's competence in the delivery of language and gesture. This competence needs to be endorsed according to the rules and effects of theatrical entertainment. The actor's "strength" is "most faint" indeed in that it is not (is no longer) enhanced by represented "spirits to enforce," by the great images of power, the verisimilitude of rank, the book of magic, the signs of sovereignty. Rather, the actor's strength (or what authority *he* has) needs to be acknowledged by success in the playhouse – which is as much to say that the authority of the actor, once it is nonrepresentational or "signifying nothing," is not that of the text but of the theatre itself. It is a "strength" achieved in the provision of pleasure, an authority authorized by the success of the institution in the fulfillment of its cultural function.

Ends of postponement: holiday into workaday

Although these three epilogues poignantly illustrate the staged quality in the scenario of transition between the represented play-world and the world of public entertainment, they cannot equally attest to what effect and by which strategy the Shakespearean ending can orchestrate its own threshold. For that, I propose to look at several other plays where liminality in the Shakespearean ending is turned to certain playful and profitable uses not developed in an epilogue. In at least eleven plays we have what Dennis Kay has called Shakespeare's "postponed endings" (207).[4] This strange element of deferment has been repeatedly observed but scarcely examined in the socio-cultural context of a "purpose of playing" that comprehends dramatic as well as extradramatic constellations of theatrical discourse and authority. At this point, it is an important but insufficient reading to associate Shakespeare's deferred endings with the dramatic strategy of an imperfect closure. The question is, how does the imperfect moment of closure relate to that larger purpose of playing that continues to be an issue once the play itself is over?

As a provisional answer, let us look at the threshold function of the play's ending in terms of its precarious relationship to Elizabethan uses of story-telling in and beyond the marketplace. In these endings, I suggest, there is evidence of an uneven kind of alliance between an appeal to some traditional form of oral memory and an early modern mode of calling attention to, and even advertizing, an extradramatic circuit of pleasurable exchanges, further engagements with, and distributions of news about, the play's events and figurations. Both the appeal to traditional uses of oral memory and the incipient circulation of exchange-value in the relation of cultural news and information come together in the projection of liminality in Shakespeare's imperfect closure.

The strategy in question, although contiguous with the represented play-world, clearly serves a purpose of playing that is dramatically neither cogent nor functional on the level of an intrinsic, self-contained representation. In the Shakespearean ending, this extradramatic move more often than not sets out with an impending change of place: characters resolve to retire to some other place with a promise made in no uncertain terms to share further information after the stage action proper has come to a conclusion. For example, take – with only three further lines to follow – the summons in: "Go hence to have more talk of these sad things" (*Romeo and Juliet* 5.3.307). But since such "talk" and knowledge is formally announced but never, in the text of the play itself, actually conveyed, communication as such is stimulated rather than provided in the representational context of an image or picture of that communication. The promise of further information is made in a liminal space, just before the symbolic use of *loci* on the platform stage gives way to an awareness of a mere "scaffold" (*Henry V*, Prologue 10) that is become even more "unworthy" once it is devoid of what represented meaning went into Richard Jones's matter of "worthiness." The postponed ending, therefore, is close to the same theatrical space and context in which epilogues find themselves. Resisting the closure of self-contained representations, both forms tend to dislodge, even as they move beyond, the dividing line between the represented fictions in the text of the play and their performing agency in the real world of the playhouse.

Here, the point is that the concluding pledge of characters "to have more talk of these sad things" and "answer all things" (*The Merchant of Venice* 5.1.299) may precipitate or even help constitute that transitional situation where the privileged position of a represented persona is relinquished to that of the (re)presenting actor. What is postponed in and through the ending relates to the same kind of passage that Prospero invokes between what "art" there is imaginatively "to enchant" and what in truth the "project" of performance ("which was to please") actually amounts to. The last lingering moments of performance, as far as its agents straddle the two worlds on either side of this threshold, would at least by implication acknowledge the circumstantial world of this "project," its political economy and future prospects. Anticipating a lively and responsive audience, the theatre would finally wish to assert not only its own need to be affirmed and applauded, but also its own potent role in the distribution of pleasure and knowledge, its hoped-for continuing impact on the "imaginary" faculties of spectators, their "quick forge and working-house of thought" (*Henry V*, Prologue 25; 5.0.23). In doing all this, the theatre would ultimately seek to provoke ways and means of memory in keeping the performed play alive.

In view of this liminal situation, dramatic representations of character and action could best cope with their own imminent collapse by being rechanneled into the circulation of a storytelling type of knowledge. As finally the theatre was confronted with the terms and durations of its own purpose and validity, the question was not only how to forestall an abrupt suspension of dramatic representations but, rather, how to retain at least a portion of what pleasure, insight, knowledge, vision, excitement, and satisfaction the performance had conveyed. How, then, was it possible for the audience to take home with them "something of great constancy" (*A Midsummer Night's Dream* 5.1.26)? An answer to this question, I suggest, could be found on the threshold of an imperfect closure, where there was space and precious time to mobilize spectators' faculties of assimilation through a show of probing recapitulation. The strategy was to stimulate both the audience's involvement and detachment, their readiness not to go hence without having "more talk" of these things.

In this respect, the ending of the Elizabethan play marked a site where a kind of engagement between textual meaning and performance practice, representation and existence, was played out in its final and crucial phase. Now the gap between the two worlds would be released into a future that was neither inscribed in the text of the play nor contained in any model of rhetorical performance practice. In these short-lived, vulnerable moments of conclusion it was not the actors, but "these our characters" who were in danger of "melting" into the thin air of forgetfulness. And while "the great globe itself" (*The Tempest* 4.1.153) could be assumed to follow in due time, "the baseless fabric of this vision" (151), the "insubstantial" *loci* of island, tent, and battlefield, were considerably more evanescent. At this crucial moment of dissolution, before the audience applauded, the concluding lines sent the play out into the world. The fleeting matter of fiction now was relegated to some sense of the actual circumstances of its survival through recapitulation and remembrance.

This, then, is what the strategies of deferment in Shakespeare's endings are most concerned with: one more time a glimpse of, or an interest in the "story" is offered to the audience as something to be completed or (re)told so that, like Prospero's "story of your life," it "must / Take the ear strangely" (5.1.313–14). As in *Timon of Athens*, the image of some memorable action or person ("of whose memory / Hereafter more" – 5.4.80–81) lives on in the process of its collective reproduction. "Hereafter," spoken so near the end of the play (there are only five more lines to follow), can only be read as referring to 'here,' 'after' the play is ended. In more than one sense, the public impact and the cultural potential of the Shakespearean text were inseparable from the mode of its incompleteness. The oral form of its delivery, as well as its reception in a cultural context of hearing and watching, combined to incite further interests and engagement with both the story and its figures. Over and beyond the textual version there was a "rest," and it seemed desirable "to hear the rest untold" (*Pericles* 5.3.84) – "untold," that is, unrevealed in the course of the staged representation.

Some of these pledges may of course connect with the need for the actors to withdraw. Thus, the move to clear the stage can be stylized in a gesture of withdrawal as best motivated by a desire to explore answers and raise further questions about the play once it is over. As Portia proposes in her concluding lines,

> Let us go in,
> And charge us there upon inter'gatories,
> And we will answer all things faithfully
> (*The Merchant of Venice* 5.1.297–99)

To be charged 'upon interrogation' is, in judicial language (here used most appropriately), to ask questions upon oath. The playful parameter is that of a truth publicly verifiable. In conjunction with Portia's finale, Cymbeline's final words, "Publish we this peace / To all our subjects" (*Cymbeline* 5.5.478–79) contain a characteristic emphasis.

The desire on the part of the players to withdraw may to a certain extent collide with the cultural uses of deferment. By the last scene, which often assembles a good many of the *dramatis personae*, the actors were presumably impatient of their own silent, lingering presence. Hence, Cymbeline's "Set we forward" (479) corresponds to Leontes' "Let's from this place" (5.3.146), which is taken up, again almost impatiently, in *The Winter's Tale*'s final lines:

> Lead us from hence, where we may leisurely
> Each one demand, and answer to his part
> Perform'd in this wide gap of time, since first
> We were dissever'd. Hastily lead away. *Exeunt.* (5 3.152–55)

Note how the text inscribes a gestus of recapitulation in withdrawal that is adverbially marked as both "leisurely" and "hastily." While "leisurely" can be read as a gesture of reintegrating the text in a story-telling culture, "hastily" responds to the dramatic need for a swift conclusion (and withdrawal) once the play was virtually over. The apparent contradiction has to do with the diversity of functions served by conclusions such as these. As the play metaphor struggles to mediate between the leisure conducive to an enduring response to the play and the desire to avoid wordiness and empty recapitulation, this metaphor itself turns characters into actors, into those who have "Perform'd" a "part." Thus, an oral culture demanding the leisure of listeners is reconciled, in a fashion, to the swiftness of actors in the economy of a Renaissance theatre. Assisting in the movement from representation to existence, the play metaphor suggests the willingness of the actors to look back upon and review their actual performance: in Portia's words, "to answer all things" or, in *The Winter's Tale*, to "demand and answer." Each "part" presupposes standards of histrionic competence that may well reflect the ensemble sense of responsibility for, and the shared circulation of authority in, the play's production.

While this loosely shared circulation combines the actors' and the audience's responses, the sense of a public, even perhaps semi-communal occasion is present too in other conclusions. For instance, the imagined scene to follow upon the ending of a comedy is sometimes envisioned as having a festive or ceremonious character involving, as early as *The Comedy of Errors*, "gossiping" – that is, drinking and chatting at a feast:

E. Dro. [. . .] Will you walk in to see their gossiping?
S. Dro. Not I, sir, you are my elder.
E. Dro. That's a question; how shall we try it?
S. Dro. We'll draw cuts for the senior, till then, lead thou first.
E. Dro. Nay then thus:

We came into the world like brother and brother;
And now let's go hand in hand, not one before another. (5.1.420–26)

Brotherly sentiment in the mutual self-discovery of the twins is an entirely appropriate mode of achieving comic identification in (and through) a show of unity. At the same time, the fraternal and convivial undertone may well have served an entirely pragmatic function. If this is so, my representational reading of the ending as contributing to the resolution of a comedy of confusion may perhaps have an extradramatic underside, a piece of advice to the audience as it is about to leave the theatre. Once we perceive the specular relationship between the actors "going in" ("Will you walk in...?") and the spectators going out, it seems not entirely impossible to read the "Nay then thus: ... let's go hand in hand" as a perlocutionary gesture urging the audience to avoid unnecessary thronging and pressing at the doors of the theatre.

Similarly, in *The Merry Wives of Windsor*, Mrs. Page in her final words offers a good-humored exit, inviting everyone to rehearse, and be further amused by, "this sport":

> Good husband, let us every one go home,
> And laugh this sport o'er by a country fire –
> Sir John and all. (5.5.241–43)

Again, the extrapolation is to something inclusive and conciliatory, a distinctly oral response in its relaxed *gestus* of recreation. This final representation of "every one" returning home may well unfold a more encompassing, extradramatic move, where every day is a kind of holiday, with "a country fire," on the boundaries between pastoral fiction and a city-dweller's own recreation. All those participating in the cultural event are invited, even beyond the threshold of theatrical representation, to continue to enjoy and recollect the play hours after they have left the theatre. A similar dynamic can be traced in *Measure for Measure,* where the concluding words of the Duke to Isabel combine a pledge of social (in this case, marital) unity with the suggestion that, even when the play is over, there remains something (or somebody?) that continues to satisfy questions:

> What's mine is yours, and what is yours is mine.
> So bring us to our palace, where we'll show
> What's yet behind, that['s] meet you all should know.
>   [*Exeunt*] (5.1.537–39)

Here as elsewhere the ending of the play must not, it seems, discontinue the circulation of pleasurable storytelling, which is extended from the holiday world of playing to the advent, in an everyday world, with at least a reminiscent potential of further mirth and playful recollection.

However, an ending which so straddles the threshold between the two worlds is not without its problems. For one thing, it may seek to prepare for a suppression of conflict in a purely wishful desire for communal harmony and nostalgic memories of unending "mirth." Take the Duke of Milan's summoning, in *The Two Gentlemen of Verona*:

> Come, let us go, we will include all jars
> With triumphs, mirth, and rare solemnity. (5.4.160–61)

As the outlaws (now "reformed, civil, full of good" [156]) are pardoned and Valentine is about to have "The story of [Proteus'] loves discovered" (171), the play ends in the expectation of "One feast, one house, one mutual happiness" (173). Here it may indeed seem difficult to establish a clear borderline between merely going through the motions of recuperating make-believe and a potentially utopian impulse leveling "all jars" and, perhaps, differences of rank and riches. The borderline becomes clearer on the more loaded plane of politics where, as early as *Richard III*, Richmond's epilogue-like speech performs a remarkable transposition of the eventual unity of the "White Rose and the Red" (5.5.19) onto the Elizabethan fruits of "this fair conjunction" (20). Anticipating "the time to come [. . .] / With smiling plenty, and fair prosperous days" (33–34) the speech in no uncertain terms dismisses as past the civil war that "divided York and Lancaster, / Divided in their dire division" (27–28) – while appropriating its lessons for the future.

There is no doubt about the persistence (and ambivalence) of some sense of inclusiveness at the closing of Shakespeare's plays. This unifying gesture in several important endings, however, does not preclude some entirely different uses of the dramatic finale. For instance, there is the spiteful curse of Pandarus' epilogue to *Troilus and Cressida* when he addresses the audience as "[traders] and bawds" (5.10.37) promising to "bequeath you my diseases" (56). If this is exceptional, there are plays in which the language of unity and decorum is dismissed so as to make room for communicating an awareness of tragic portent, which in its turn seems perfectly compatible with further talk and narration, after the play is ended. The tragedy of *Othello* lives on, and is best recollected, "When you shall these unlucky deeds relate" (*Othello* 5.2.341).

Again, the inducement to have "more talk of these sad things" helps constitute an opening beyond the play's closure in which the written text is either not explicit or is incomplete enough to be discussed and further probed into. "To hear the rest untold," as I have noted, suggests that there *is* a "rest" that has *not* been articulated – a dimension uninscribed in the dramatic text, even perhaps unrepresentable through its performance. What is crucial about this "rest" is its "hereafter," inseparable as that is from the play's afterlife, its appropriation by the minds and memories of the spectators. There is good reason to assume that this space for aperture was designed to empower those "untold" imaginary forces to which the prologue to *Henry V* appeals so eloquently.

Although, then, the need for the audience's response was again and again prefigured, its direction was not; in fact, there remained a remarkable margin for indirection and spontaneity in the play's reception by which spectators were allowed, and even urged, to speak for themselves. Such a margin for self-authorized directions in response is especially broad in both versions of *King Lear*:

> The weight of this sad time we must obey,
> Speak what we feel, not what we ought to say (5.3.324–25)

In these concluding lines, dramatic dialogue is suspended in the call for an unprescribed, immediate type of response. The spectators are indirectly summoned to speak their minds freely; they are authorized to avail themselves of an unusual license of expression. It is not entirely out of the question that such unadorned expression of "what we feel" was recommended as most appropriate (today we might say, most authentic) in coming to terms with the play as an exceptionally viable medium in the circulation of profoundly disturbing images of authority. The idea is to speak about or communicate what in modern parlance might be called a direct impression or experience of the play. In its ending, the tragedy constitutes an authorization of a type of discourse that itself is cause of further proliferation of discourses. The unprecedented questioning of "the great image of authority" (4.4.158) cannot properly be met by any given, previously authorized pattern of response in the reception of the tragedy.

The emphasis on unconventional sentiment may well have privileged a certain amount of empathy, as is the case in the conclusion to *Othello*. Here, the last word of the play – "relate" – is again couched between an eagerness for departure and an emphasis on the enduring, captivating quality of what is to be related. These are Lodovico's concluding words:

> Myself will straight aboard, and to the state
> This heavy act with heavy heart relate. (5.2.370–71)

Again, there is urgency in the project of narration, of handing on and making known the story. The text of the play, in positing an unconsummated act of narration, prefigures its own afterlife in the feeling 'hearts' of those who care to listen to what can be related about an extraordinary outcome of dramatic events.

A good many Shakespearean plays, in the *mise-en-scène* of their own reception, conclude with liminal metaphors of their relation (and recollection). Such *Rezeptionsvorgabe*, or "structured prefigurement"[5] helps organize a response that can be quite unambiguous where extraordinary action, courage, resolution, and passion make a character appear to deserve an afterlife. For instance, while in *Antony and Cleopatra* Octavius's final speech serves as a projection of the audience's response towards "their story" – involving "pity" as well as "glory" (5.2.361–62) – , spectators in *Coriolanus* are potentially even more directly involved in bringing about a conclusion conducive to the play's and its hero's future in the form of a "noble memory." The closing lines of the play, serving these mnemonic prefigurements, are both an object and an agent of such memory: "Yet he shall have a noble memory. Assist" (5.6.153–54). These concluding words are spoken by Aufidius; addressed to "three a' th' chiefest soldiers" (148), they have a liminal potential in that the final piece of staged action would have an impress "of great constancy" on a watching audience. While he is borne away with great solemnity, Coriolanus' body on an empty stage leaves "not a rack behind"; yet he shares the fate of "noble Timon, of whose memory / Hereafter more." Whatever authority the script retains at the moment of its ending is used to stimulate cultural involvement in the nonfictional world at the gates of the theatre. First and foremost, the call to "Assist" does of course provide a cue to carry the body offstage; still, in its conjunction with "a noble memory," the phrase may not be entirely unrelated to a call for an imaginary kind of audience participation. It is just possible that here, as elsewhere in Elizabethan theatrical practice, the conclusion of the text was achieved in collaboration with its 'assisting' audience.

Thresholds to memory and commodity

Once "the purpose of playing" in the ending of the Shakespearean play is conceived of as pointing beyond the confines of the platform stage, questions arise as to the uses of such suspension of discursive boundaries. Was there a design to appeal to "[th'] yet unknowing world" beyond the gates of the theatre? The phrase is from the ending of *Hamlet*; it is spoken by Horatio as part of a strange and somewhat sensationalized abstract of the play itself:

> *Hor.* And let me speak to [th'] yet unknowing world
> How these things came about. So shall you hear
> Of carnal, bloody, and unnatural acts,
> Of accidental judgments, casual slaughters,
> Of deaths put on by cunning and [forc'd] cause,

>   And in this upshot, purposes mistook
>   Fall'n on th' inventors' heads: all this can I
>   Truly deliver.
> *Fort.*   Let us haste to hear it,
>   And call the noblest to the audience. (5.2.379–87)

Horatio's promised act of recollection seems curiously distanced, lacking any sense of his own represented involvement in the story. There is a fanfare note in his speech that recalls the diction of a billboard or the language of a poster (or one of those lengthy sixteenth-century titles) designed to catch the eyes and ears of those who have not seen or read the thing itself. Horatio, as it were, climbs on a rostrum, not simply to address "Fortinbras *with the* [English] Embassadors [. . . *and Attendants*]" (361–62) but to send out a message to those who do not know the play. As Fortinbras hastens to reply, there is a readiness not just "to hear it," that is, the information about the play, but to "call the noblest to the audience." This is different from the Chorus in *Henry V*, who, towards the end of the play, suggests "to those that have not read the story" that he "may prompt them" (*Henry V* 5.0.1–2). For what Horatio pledges to "truly deliver" is designed to reach (inside the play) the ears of Fortinbras and attendants as well as – outside the theatre, one must surmise – those who have not as yet seen *Hamlet*. Horatio seems prepared to go into considerable detail ("Of that I shall have also cause to speak" – 5.2.391); but while the Chorus in *Henry V* delivers on his promise, providing the illiterate spectator with "the story," Horatio does not. His prompting is of another kind: it is to a potential interest in and a future engagement with the play.

For the remaining dozen or so lines, the solemn finale, culminating in Hamlet's "passage" (398), is made to "speak loudly for him," especially when "the rite of war," the "soldier's music" (399–400) and a *"peal of ordnance"* (final stage direction) launch a ceremonious exit. But at this point, the cultural uses of recollection are violently redesigned: the last word in the text of the play is "Go bid the soldiers shoot" (403). The "rite of war" makes for a ritualized passage of a kind; but the liminal occasion is full of doubleness when it goes hand in hand with those "rights, of memory" (389) which, militantly, Fortinbras claims. As this peculiar genitive suggests, these "rights" are primarily part of the represented world in the story. Unlike any purely cultural appropriation of the play, these "rights" apply to the fruits of acquisition and the "vantage" (390) of individual aggrandizement. The invocation of "memory" is turned into a medium serving ends that are quite remote from its communal uses in a more traditional type of culture.

And yet, fittingly, the *"peal of ordnance"* marks a threshold that, as Victor Turner suggests about liminality in preindustrial societies, may have "the effect of strengthening the bonds of communitas even as it dissolves antecedent structural ties" (*From Ritual to Theatre* 47). But the momentary sense, on the part of the audience, of a collective response to a great and imposing occasion is counteracted by a passage with a difference, one that subjects, in Turner's phrase, the liminal "betwixt-and-between" to no traditional purpose. On the contrary, the liminal space for "neither-this-nor-that, here-nor-there" (Turner, *From Ritual to Theatre* 37) is being redeployed in a manner that most forcefully reveals itself in Horatio's speech. Using an image from an archery contest (according to Philip Edwards, the "deciding shot"), Horatio "in this upshot" (384) re-presents the play as, simply, the story "Of carnal, bloody, and unnatural acts" (381). The shrill note in his address may well bear witness to an element of strenuousness in this transformation of mnemonic space into a site of appeal "to [th'] yet unknowing world" (379) inside and outside the play.

It is of course difficult to say whether and if so, to what degree, this gestus of dramatic self-advertising was designed to respond to an increasing traffic in news and stories (and a complementary bent for forgetfulness) in an early modern culture of commodified pleasure at large. But in this departure, in full view of a knowing audience, the traditional opening towards reciprocity in communication is given a decidedly modern note. Here, the imminent collapse of a dramatic representation is one more time intercepted by a presentation of what Horatio "can [. . .] / Truly deliver" (385–86). Only, the somewhat sensational delivery is made to serve the political economy of not so much a communal as a commercial design – reaching out, one may conjecture, to sections of an audience either late in attendance or as yet unsolicited and unrecruited to this play.[6] Whatever inroads the commercial status of the Elizabethan playhouse made on its public uses, memory in this context certainly had ceased to serve as an unquestioned, let alone a purely unifying, source of validity in cultural reproduction. Assuming an increasing multiplicity of social functions, cultural memory was made to serve an important role in the business of inducing audiences to (re)visit and respond fully to theatrical entertainments. Memory became a mixed resource of cultural energy, a not uncontaminated item in the political economy of circulating pleasure, knowledge, and the very stuff of telling stories – stories that could be appropriated at a price in the playhouses of early modern London.

In this rapidly changing environment, for a few precious years, collective memory and other constituents of an oral culture could be assimilated in a highly variable and dynamic manner, precisely because they had been or were about to be uprooted from their cultural matrix. Shakespeare, in using Horatio as a mouth-piece for advertising the play even before it was over, must have been well aware of how vulnerable the role of recollection had become, particularly so in those privileged play-goers' responses who bought a seat in the newly set up Globe. Hamlet himself provides a cue when, through a play metaphor, he promises to remember the ghost, "whiles memory holds a seat / In this distracted globe" (1.5.96–97). The imagery here thrives on the point where the world and the theatre together are exposed to forgetfulness and ephemerality. "Distracted" must not of course be read in Walter Benjamin's sense of "distraction" (*Zerstreuung*) – as marking the modern mode of reception in a mass culture of reproducible entertainment; yet the ambivalence hinted at seems unmistakable and is inseparable from a larger process of social change affecting and, possibly, blurring the boundary between popular traditions in the theatre and early modern consumer culture in a rapidly expanding marketplace.[7] In one of its dimensions, the theatre was, as Douglas Bruster notes, "a place of commercial exchange," operating "in the context of an early modern culture industry"; as such it participated in "the development of a consumer society in early modern England" (*Drama and the Market* 10).

The "distracted" cultural context of "memory" in Shakespeare's prolonged endings was at least partially consonant with some of the more striking innovations in dramatic representation. These could affect dramatic dénouements, especially in his comedies, where there was a marked degree of departure from classical tradition. For instance, in Hellenistic comedy as well as in Plautus and Terence (and of course in the Renaissance dramatic tradition derived from them), it was possible to achieve, in a much fuller sense than Shakespeare ever aimed at, a happy ending within the terms of the (not so distracted) world of the comedy itself. Comic conventions of emplotment – complications such as shipwreck, banishment, confusion or loss of identity, deception, misunderstanding, interference in love and happiness (inappropriate passion, vanity, the presumptuous claimant, the aging suitor, and so forth) – tended to be resolved on the level on which they unfolded. As Manfred Fuhrmann has shown in his reading of comic conclusions in the extant plays of Menander, Plautus, and Terence, the "social grammar" of dramatic reunion and recognition, aided by patience and forbearance, could ultimately and lastingly resolve all complications as a strictly temporary *malheur*.[8] But Shakespeare's comic resolutions, even in his early work, retain an element of incompleteness which precludes any full return to the *status quo*. Even when, as in *The Comedy of Errors*, all the topoi of comedy are reassembled, a grain of scepticism and questioning is unmistakable. Or, to take another example, in *Love's Labour's Lost* a happy dénouement, although impending, is delayed; appearing contingent and conditional, the ending comes not as a consummation of deferred passion and prosperity but as a provisional twist of events, culminating in a truce rather than a lasting peace. At the end of the play there is promise, hinged on a measure of self-control, rather than fulfillment in a clear vision of given options and circumstances.

The point here is not of course to minimize Shakespeare's profound indebtedness to classical and Renaissance comedy,[9] but to comprehend the ways in which these traditions intermingled with more innovative practices. The resulting mélange formed a complex cultural space to which Shakespeare's endings in their own way contribute. In this connection, the all too benign readings of C. L. Barber and Northrop Frye need to be revised; such a revision would seek to integrate the extent to which the element of semi-ritual "release" and the myth of the "green world" constitute a complicated watershed where traditional cultural practices and early modern representations uniquely merge and simultaneously drift asunder.

Here, as elsewhere, Shakespeare's endings can be at least as diverse and innovative as the purposes of playing informing the transaction of his plays in the theatre. Their thresholds, as we have seen, can harbor concluding visions of residual harmony that either rehearse traditional conventions of comedy or remain close to certain cultural practices in aid of festivity or popular and courtly forms of entertainment. At the same time his plays accommodate a strong element of 'distraction' (if I may shift its meaning somewhat) which is not nearly resolved at their endings. In the dark comedies, there is a great deal more division, perplexity, frenzy and amazement – a "most uneven and distracted manner" (*Measure for Measure* 4.4.3) – than is adumbrated at these endings. To take what is perhaps the most conspicuous level of difference, especially prominent in *Julius Caesar* and *Coriolanus*: ordinary people, as represented in dramatic fiction, more often than not tend to be depicted as "the distracted multitude" (*Hamlet* 4.3.4). But as participants in the theatrical occasion, ordinary playgoers would on extradramatic or liminal levels be addressed as "gentles all" and authorized to "make imaginary puissance" (*Henry V*, Prologue 8; 25).

If this juxtaposition, although striking, is much too static, it nevertheless points to the problem at hand: how was the dramatist to sustain his representational discourse up to and beyond the point where, as in epilogues, the scene was dominated by the player-as-performer? And vice versa: how, especially in comedy, could the writing cope with the enclosure of extradramatic cultural practices in the representation of a purely imaginary world? In many cases, the finale cannot, or at least can neither fully, nor exclusively, draw on the textualized "matter" inherent in the preceding representation. For one thing, the imaginary validity of the "green world," or for that matter, of other images of natural or social harmony is highly provisional; insofar as "clarification" does result, it cannot be an outgrowth of a traditional culture in which memories of old would as a matter of course be more valid than experimentation towards something new and vulnerable.

This, again, raises the question of the sources of cultural authority in the Elizabethan theatre; here, however, it must suffice to suggest that Shakespeare's return in his deferred endings to the largely oral story-telling culture of Elizabethan England is strangely at odds with the more searching, contestatory language of Renaissance representations, not to mention the rhetoric of early modern advertisement in the marketplace. There is a sense in which the dramatist, though fully prepared to adapt manifestations of popular lore and oral memory in the institutionalized practice of his own theatre, tends in his dramatic representations to go far beyond such traditional premises. True enough, in plays like *A Midsummer Night's Dream* there is sustained attention to the living memory of popular lore, especially in the case of Puck – the Elizabethan Robin Goodfellow – and the world of the fairies, which blend native folklore with classical and Germanic mythology. Here, Shakespeare was quite prepared to adopt and adapt in the theatre an as yet partially uninscribed repertoire of orally transmitted narrative. This memorial lore, however, was on the verge of being fatally threatened by a host of socio-cultural changes in the political economy of pleasure and the technology of its communication. The playhouse's continued uses of a seasonally organized structure of pleasurable perception, recollection, and 'game' could not presuppose an unchallenged continuity of age-old modes of telling and listening.

Thus, in Shakespeare's plays there were multiple and at least partially contradictory modes of authorizing memory and the comprehension of temporal sequence. On the one hand, there was still residual space for a traditional type of memory which blurred the boundaries between the processing of news and the celebration of rumor, between intuition and superstition, the analysis of the future and its 'prophecy.' Accordingly, representation of the course and outcome of events (a sense of their 'truth') was entirely reconcilable with anecdotes, riddles, dreams, oracles, all kinds of presentiment and *tribunaux d'arbitres*. These went hand in hand with pre-modern conventions of cultural and theatrical space.

On the other hand, these traditional uses of memory and temporal sequence were challenged by more modern dramatic uses of time, time past and time future, and causality; these involved more abstract concepts, using narratives which were no longer seasonally, let alone orally, sustained. An increasing awareness of contingency in temporal sequences was bound to make these narrative practices, together with the authorization of prophecy and presentiment, somewhat problematic. Traditional oral uses of prediction must have found themselves ill-equipped to cope with the sense of an unpredictable and unprecedented quality of change. Thus, the outcome of events and, by implication, the dénouement of a sequence of contingent actions in a history play such as *2 Henry IV* is marked by "necessities" (3.1.93) – a word emphatically underlined and, together with the adjective, repeated no less than three times in the scene where King Henry exclaims:

> how chance's mocks
> And changes fill the cup of alteration
> With divers liquors!   (3.1.51–53)

For any concept of memory to cope with the awareness of liquidity and a veritable hodge-podge of altering circumstances must have seemed difficult within an oral frame of reference. By contrast, the discourse of early modern historiography – itself in a state of flux – appeared better equipped than earlier models of interpretation and testimony.[10] In this situation, memory as of old could well be represented as inadequate in view of increasing gaps between past and future; at the same time, memories of revengeful nemesis and unchanging loyalty had to be discarded *vis-à-vis* the "all-changing" language of "commodity," with its "sway of motion" (*King John* 2.1.582; 578). Henceforth the traditional uses of memory could jar with "this vile-drawing bias" (577) in certain aims of representation, so much so that Henry, a politician keen "to busy giddy minds/ With foreign quarrels," feels called upon to "waste the memory of the former days" (*2 Henry IV* 4.5.213–15).

Highly diverse concepts of coming to terms with "former days" and remembered discourses thus existed side by side in Shakespeare's theatre. Memory as depicted in dialogue and dramatic action was and was not contiguous with the uses of memory entrusted by the theatrical event itself to its audience. And neither was identical with the *ars memorativa* as practiced in the work of the actors themselves. Hence, despite a significant area of overlap, there is a distinction to be made between memory as an object of representation and memory as an agency of both performances and their reception. In other words (and in line with important divisions of authority in the Elizabethan playhouse), memory could serve as both product and producer, as a (re)productive instance in Shakespeare's dramatic transactions.

Liminality: cultural authority 'betwixt-and-between'

In the last resort, however, such a general formula remains too abstract to do justice to the crucial element of (dis)continuity between image and agency in Shakespeare's endings. Since such (dis)continuity is central to the workings of the threshold in his plays, it seems best to return to the text of the plays where the crucial space of liminality between inscribed dramatic representation and cultural practices (in their material and performed dimensions) can more searchingly be explored as a site on which issues of authority and authorization are in question. If for a moment we recall the assimilation of the threshold in the stylized form of epilogues,[11] it seems possible against these wider contexts further to define relations between the images of representation and the agents of their performance. As in the case of *The Tempest*, Prospero on the one hand surrenders some of his most privileged matter of "worthiness," his "staff," his book of magic and his "charms," even before, in a downstage *platea* space, these articles of imaginative authority cease to be (to use Raymond Williams' phrase) "representative." Still, falling back on what "strength" is his own, the impersonating actor, even when finally seeing through the last piece of stage business, playfully refuses quite to forsake the imagery of the play-world: relinquishing the "bare island" in the text of the play, the speaker of the epilogue continues to inhabit a scaffold stage protruding, like an *isle*, into *waves* of clapping hands.

However, if the epilogue to *The Tempest* betrays a remarkably prolonged circulation of authority among stage practices and representations, the balance between them cannot, in the strategy of Shakespeare's endings, conceal an element of anxiety and ambivalence. As other epilogues confirm, the anticipation of applause is not entirely free from an element of uncertainty in the transference of authority in the playhouse. Applause in the theatre, as Balz Engler has recently noted, must not be viewed as primarily a unifying gesture; what it serves to convey is first and foremost a "distantiation," if not a kind of liberation from an emotional pressure and a cultural self-disciplining which spectators submit to temporarily, under a strictly limited contract (98). Applause ends this contract; it breaks the "spell," under which spectators could be as 'spell-bound' by the play as actors would be tongue-tied by its text. The ensuing shift in the circulation of authority can of course only tentatively be reconstructed. Still, it seems safe to assume that dramatists at this point were in no position to assert the literate authority of their text as against a largely oral, physically immediate concurrence of players and spectators.[12]

The epilogue, then, in projecting the space and motivation for applause, is itself a catalytic agent of liminality serving the redistribution of authority in the playhouse. Playing down the contestatory moment in the realignment of playwright, actors, and spectators, Shakespeare – himself an actor – was close enough to the profession to make the ultimate space for writing subserve a strictly theatrical use of diabasis.[13] The conventional form provides a congenial protocol of changing relations of authority. Ambivalence and anxiety are displaced in favor of an attempt to intercept whatever rupture or collision the trajectory from dramatic fiction to cultural occasion may have to cope with. Shakespeare's dramatic representations can thus, to a certain extent, organize and even celebrate their own successful collapse in the hoped for applause of a judging audience.

At this final point, the gesture of authorization in the epilogue again comes close to what happens in Shakespeare's postponed endings: the flow of authority in the playhouse is effectively recirculated. The performer, whether asking for applause or suggesting post-scriptural sources of further information, is about to be no longer at the service of the script, but at that of his spectators. What retains validity in this situation is the audience's pleasure, knowledge, and engagement. The theatre's readiness "to please" is, ultimately, crucial; the arts of performance achieve their greatest authority in the *circulation* of cultural signs with the audience, either in response to clapping hands or further talking after the play is ended. It is in this context that, as I have noted, the performance culminates in an *exchange* of roles, in the performers' silence and the audience's applauding, memorizing, and talking. If I may quote again:

> Ours be your patience then, and yours our parts;
> Your gentle hands lend us, and take our hearts.
> (*All's Well That Ends Well*, Epilogue 5–6)

Now the flow of authority has come full circle on what is a site of perfect liminality. The audience has their cue: spectators are expected to play their "parts," are even encouraged to let "pleasure" (as well as "truth" and, by implication, knowledge and authority) "flow." But while the audience is about to perform their "parts," the actors in their turn "will *pay*, / With strife to please you" (Epilogue 3–4); in silent patience, they confront the play's post-textual future. This future is thinkable as a space of mutuality only, in which "imaginary puissance" and memory are two sides of the same coin in keeping alive a meaningfully entertaining theatre. The uses of the epilogue and those of narrative deferment coalesce in the extradramatic celebration of a threshold to profitable memory.

Once the liminal space in Shakespeare's endings can be seen as a site on which the interplay of diverse modes of cultural production and authorization comes to a head, certain questions arise that in conclusion call for an answer. These questions relate to both the significance of Shakespearean liminality in the present revaluation of performance practices and the way thresholds on Elizabethan stages can further be studied as a significant moment in the history of the early modern theatre. Strangely ignored by generations of Shakespeare editors and scholars,[14] cultural uses of theatrical thresholds present us with an underestimated practice of performance at the point of intersection where an undiminished interest in a classical text is amplified as well as, potentially, enhanced by an awareness of countervailing nonclassical, noncanonical socio-cultural forces and circumstances. In Shakespeare's dramatic endings, the difference in social interests and cultural pursuits deep down in provenance and function of the Elizabethan theatre finally asserts itself in an intrinsic/extrinsic, partially extradramatic form. Conjoining literate standards of dramatic composition with the peremptory need for a public acclaim of its histrionic delivery, the endings culminate in a new version of doubleness – one dominated by the authority and the sheer presence of players applauded, or otherwise, by spectators. At the end of the dramatic transaction, the force of contrariety is spent; there is no need further to "digest" either the "abuse of distance" or the gap between "author's pen" and "actor's voice." Nor can this gap be entirely displaced when the circulation of cultural authority has come full circle.

In the play's finale, representational form and, in Alter's terms, "referential" function find themselves suspended in, and finally predicated on, a strictly performative, strongly presentational purpose of playing. The epilogue in particular serves as a vessel with which to deliver (one might say, salvage) the represented condition of players abandoned to the bare, nonsymbolic boards of the stage. Still, in most of these postponed endings, images of further talk and communication appear to be part of the dramatic, imaginary world in the play. These, however, are "representative" with a difference. What they in fact stand for is not a dramatic fiction but a need for actors on the stage-as-stage to withdraw and / or a scenario for a prolonged audience response outside the gates of the theatre.

As I have suggested in an earlier chapter, the scope and dynamic of these liminal practices are subjected to change and contingency in the relations of the referential and the performative. But while there is considerable need for further historicizing thresholds on Elizabethan stages, their historicity borders on anthropological grounds. Although there is good evidence that a conjunction of history, theatre, and anthropology can yield fruitful results,[15] theatrical uses of liminality have scarcely begun to be considered under the latter aspect. But as Arnold Van Gennep's *Rites de passage* suggested many decades ago, liminality is a condition of profound transformations; often enough, these are contiguous with all sorts and conditions of play and performance. A systematic study of liminality in Western – or, for that matter, world – theatre would, I suspect, wish to view related performance strategies in connection with tangential transitions in ritual, gendered, and biological types of cultural practice. Here we have a host of socially significant activities relating to transformations in a wide range of vital experiences such as accompany age, sex, work, and leisure.

As van Gennep and other anthropologists have shown, thresholds are constituted by a passage which, in its mid-liminal process, is socially marked by association, dissociation, and reassociation of individuals.[16] Although the anthropological field is far more inclusive and encompassing than any purely theatrical or performative 'passage', both have in common certain basic parameters. For instance, in the context of the early modern theatre, performers in the play's ending share certain attributes with "liminaries" (Victor Turner's phrase for those on the threshold) in secular rituals. The latter, according to Turner, are in their passage marked by "neither-this-nor-that" (*From Ritual to Theatre* 37). In their liminal position, they enjoy a brief moment of indeterminacy (and of course incertitude); they undergo a "symbolic status-reversal" (39) through which "new ways of acting, new combinations of symbols, are tried out" (40). Altogether the space for liminality in secular ritual "is particularly conducive to play"; it provokes and helps constitute a "spontaneous, 'performative,' ludic quality" (40–41) of action.

In view of these obvious correlatives in the field of anthropology, the study of thresholds on Shakespeare's stage can be rewarding on more than one level. There can be little doubt that the element of liminality helps enhance the ludic and the performative dimensions in Elizabethan stage plays, as far as these go beyond, or are not necessarily limited by, the written text. Not unlike liminaries in secular ritual, actors-characters, being *both* this *and* that, are propelled "into thinking hard about the elements and basic building blocks of symbolic complexes they had hitherto taken for granted as 'natural' units" (Turner, *From Ritual to Theatre* 38). The passage from elevated status-symbol to the unadorned state of common player, processed in the midst of a cheering multitude, must have promoted a strange familiarity with greatness, a sense of preeminence on radically different and abruptly changing levels of authority. In fact, the ephemeral experience of an 'as / if' must have contributed to an uncommon awareness of what "little brief authority" players *through their office*, or work, enjoyed. Nor was this threshold experience limited to the ending of the performed play: a spell of liminality, as I have suggested, thrived in the play's opening but also in transitions between different uses of theatrical space and, last not least, in divergent projections of temporality, when the move from time represented to the time of and for representation was at least by implication a liminal act.

Thus, as far as the study of liminality in Shakespeare's theatre can throw new light on the strength and authority of the performant function, it may serve to underline that the crossing of thresholds, momentarily at least, was implicit in most versions of contrariety and disfigurement. It was latent wherever doubleness informs characterization, and "bifold authority" serves as an impulse in dramaturgy. If anywhere performance practice comes into its own and can, by indirection through its textual traces, be studied in its own right, liminality is not far to seek. Most important of all, thresholds stand for a two-way traffic. In today's Shakespeare criticism, they present us with a challenge to reconceive "the purpose of playing" in its doubleness, which implicates its double reference to the world-in-the-play and to playing-in-the-world.

Afterword: thresholds forever after

I cannot resist the temptation to conclude with an epilogue that takes up on the very threshold where the last chapter has broached a discussion about the postscriptural future of verbal artifacts. What a good many Shakespearean endings aimed at was to suspend the play, after it had ended, in an off-stage action of a sort, in speech acts which, more than anything, rehearsed the memory of what was seen and heard, pointing beyond the time and place of the theatrical occasion. The recollection – derived as it was from performance of persons and stories, not from a printed playtext – harbored knowledge of a particular kind. It was a knowledge 'of' rather than a knowledge 'that.' Such knowledge had some of the immediacy of what was felt, a resonance that invited response. The idea was for spectators to take away images of the story-world and the thrill over the work of "our Actors" which, in John Webster's phrase, would "give them [the "Actors"] authority to play."[1] The audience, as Terence Hawkes notes, left the playhouse with "the speech of the play on the stage as part of the oral reality of the speech of life off-stage" (*Shakespeare's Talking Animals* 56). Such postscriptural uses of the products of writing and playing entertained what Homi Bhabha in *The Location of Culture* calls "a priority of eye over inscription, or voice over writing, that insists on the 'image' of knowledge as confrontation between the self and the object" (127).

At this stage to inflect the theme of the book's last chapter, ending with reflections on endings, is perhaps the best way for an afterword to articulate its own sense of liminality. To recall the culture of thresholds in the early modern theatre offers a remarkable foil, in fact, an inducement to look at the thresholds of what culture we can hope to invoke, or even share, through and beyond writing in our own cultural history. To do so is particularly appropriate, even perhaps a matter of some urgency, to the present undertaking where, in retrospect, the gap between my subject (playing and writing then) and its treatment through writing now is quite formidable; in fact, it is daunting when I come to think of this book's performance – or should it be, reception – beyond the time and place of its composition. At this liminal juncture, the dilemma must be confronted that, when separated by four centuries, the distance between player's voice and historian's pen would grow infinite.

Having felt the dilemma throughout the writing of this volume, I ask myself (and invite readers to join me in asking), how best to bear the burden of this altogether different type of threshold. Is it at all possible to intercept in writing the incongruity between a critical text and an orally delivered, lived practice of performance? Perhaps an answer to this question is significant over and beyond the present discrepancy between subject-matter and medium. Could it be that the Elizabethan theatre, i.e. my subject-matter itself, at least in one crucial aspect *does* anticipate, even participate in the beginnings of, a deep-going "division" between "writing" and "action" in our modern civilization?

These words are Raymond Williams', taken from the citation prefixed to the Introduction to this volume. For one thing, the idea was right at the outset of the book, to set readers thinking about the problem at hand or, more generally, to instigate a subtext that would preclude both facile and disparaging responses to relations of past significance and present meaning in this cultural history. To say this is not after all to deny the depth of the abyss between what richness then made a great theatre tick and the poverty in a latter-day endeavor through mere thinking and writing to come to terms with it. Nor would I ever wish to suggest that what is wanted is a retrieval of some kind of activism in order to take care of the gap between thought and action. Or, worse still, to insinuate that Williams had any such 'solution' in mind when, in his own *Drama in Performance*, he so memorably voiced the larger contours of the dilemma. In all likelihood he did so, I suspect, because he knew full well that critical and scholarly writings constitute some of the "indirect, conventional and reacting forms" of response – unless of course such writings degenerate into propaganda.

There is, then, no acceptable alternative for critical and historical work in the humanities to severely delimiting its own thresholds. The one thing which can be hoped for is that "the attachment of writing to this static form, away from the human voices and movements" can be defied by indirection or, even, from within a new conception of our subject-matter itself. In other words, the attempt should be made from within the argument to *connect* performance in the theatre with cultural practices outside the theatre, and to do so in relation to our "most serious interests."

Along these lines, several questions need to be taken further: for instance, which circumstances helped enhance or resist the linkage between actually practiced performance and the more and more self-contained enclosure of *imitatio vitae*? What actually was, in Williams' sense of the word, "representative" in this conjunction? If there was a connection between the politics of what then was "representative" and the form and purpose of theatrical representation, how can we best hope to unravel the sociocultural dynamic in that connection? Questions such as these address "representative" but also non-representative activities within and without the doors of the theatre. Implicit but not necessarily pursued in the present project, these questions point to a larger and potentially more viable range of cultural practices that went into the making (and may best stimulate the reception today) of Shakespeare's theatre.

To say this is not to plead for another, correct version of cultural politics (which I find just as crippling as, in my younger days, I found the precepts of socialist realism). Rather, the question is whether we can revitalize a legacy in ways different from either its traditional or its deconstructionist reception. Of course it is true that poststructural theory, simply by challenging the notion of an unmediated identity of the player or of playing, helpfully precludes any facile idealization of an alternative to the cult of the bard. Whether it is playing or writing, there is in the Elizabethan theatre no one mode of cultural practice that is not somehow informed by what it seems to exclude. These differential premises, pointing beyond the now-dated metaphysical notions of fixed opposites, do not, however, resist – in fact, they can make dynamic – the attempt to historicize relations of "author's pen" and "actor's voice."

To a certain extent (which I have hinted at in the Introduction), it seems possible for a historicizing project to turn the tables on the deconstructionist "*dis*linkage," in the theatre, "of cause and effect between the signifier and the world" (Parker and Sedgwick *Performativity and Performance* 2, italics *ibid.*). The rupture in question cannot be denied; and yet there is a linkage behind the dislinkage allowing for separate and sometimes incompatible practices to convolve and communicate. It is, in Webster's definition, an 'interface' between the material/imaginary doubleness informing the use of *both* the signifier in the imaginary world of the play and the perceived signified, mediated between text and playing, in the actually performed play. On each of these two levels the linkage is between what producing/receiving agents are actually performing and perceiving and what represented *imitatio vitae* is spoken/shown and meant. Across the full scope of this (dis)linkage there obtains in the Elizabethan theatre a crisscrossing of cultural differences between "author's pen" and "actor's voice" which, as we have seen, subsists right onto the threshold of Shakespeare's endings.

There is probably no better way to assimilate to Shakespeare studies the enormous cultural energies inherent in recent practices and theories of performance. Let us not forget that, as Erika Fischer-Lichte recently noted, theatre "is always a performative medium," in fact "the performative genre *par excellence*" ("Performance as Art" 71). To dispute this is, in most cases, to predicate a traditional, narrow concept of theatre, one that tends to reduce "the purpose of playing" to representation. Ironically, it is performance itself that through this reduction can be impoverished. In the present project, the emphasis in Shakespeare's playhouse on doubleness and bifold authority is designed to foreground performance in its difference from, but also its confederation with, the dramatic text. The idea is to view performance in its own right and yet to counter "its drift away from theatre" (Diamond, *Unmaking Mimesis* 12, note 22) as diagnosed by Elin Diamond and William Worthen.

As by implication this study suggests, Shakespeare's stage uniquely challenges this drift. Today more than ever his theatre is, in Bristol's sense of the word, a great "gift" in that it bestows upon us an unsurpassed paradigm in artful communication. As such it is profoundly relevant in an age of electronic information where it presents us with a cultural horizon of the fullest spectrum in relations of the aural and the visual, but also, and more generally, of language and show. On early modern stages in England, but particularly on Shakespeare's, these relations in their scope and balance have a supple, resilient strength. This strength is maintained despite certain readjustments and, even, erosions in the face of impending differentiations, imminent exclusions, and nascent withdrawals. As Jonathan Baldo suggests, the initial pattern of competition between image and word leads to "increasingly strained relations between the visual and the verbal" so that in the Jacobean years there emerges on both political and theatrical levels a "preference for discourse, particularly texts" (*The Unmasking of Drama* 135; 144). Still, at the turn of the century relations of the senses continue to be marked by an ease of interaction that allows the emerging preference for textual articulation to be at least partially criss-crossed. Thus, as long as the Renaissance mirror is held up to antic distraction, the "very faculties of eyes and ears" (*Hamlet* 2.2.566) continue to be conceived as mutually supportive. As we know from *Troilus and Cressida*, it is possible through a kind of "credence" (5.2.120) to "invert th' attest of eyes and ears" (122). Between them, vision and hearing – thriving in the proximity of "bifold authority" (144) – continue to respond to both friction and alignment in convolving relations of "author's pen" and "actor's voice." I say *between them* because it is only in their fair conjunction that eyes and ears can fully comprise, and simultaneously receive, the process of playing and the products of writing. In doing so, they cannot of course provide more than a semblance of a link between (Williams' phrase) "writing and action"; but the relation, however precarious, is not of an "abstract" kind. It is, as I have suggested, most full-blooded and dramatic where, to this day, "writing and action" come together, as in a play.

Conjoining the material and the imaginary in the teeth of their difference, performance and text constitute, on a threshold to be crossed forever after, the inexhaustible terrain of *and* between present players' bodies and absent, verbally certified representations.

Notes

1 Today I might wish to revise several of the terms and concepts but not the basic statement of these issues, as first set forth in "Past Significance and Present Meaning"; for a substantially augmented version, see my *Structure and Society in Literary History* 51–56.

2 According to Herbert Blau, "it was Brecht who virtually initiated the discourse on ideology and performance" (*To All Appearances* 28). For this project, especially helpful later twentieth-century perspectives are provided by Rouse, "Textuality and Authority in Theater and Drama"; Bharucha, *Theatre and the World* 211–19; Phelan, *Unmarked* 146–64; Kershaw, *The Politics of Performance* 25–29; Martin, *Voice in Modern Theatre* 23–32; and others cited *passim*.

3 See, in connection with this, several of the studies contained in Bulman (ed.), *Shakespeare, Theory, and Performance*.

4 Graff, *The Labyrinths of Literacy* 243; see 63–65, 114–17.

5 McLuhan, *Understanding Media: The Extension of Man*; Ong, *The Presence of the Word*; Ong, *Interfaces of the Word*; Havelock and Hershbell, *Communication Arts in the Ancient World*; Goody, *The Logic of Writing and the Organization of Society*.

6 See Havelock, *The Literate Revolution in Ancient Greece and its Cultural Consquences*. Even more relevant is Havelock's discussion of orality in Greek drama in *The Muse Learns To Write*, esp. 14, 21–22.

7 See Barroll, *Politics, Plague and Shakespeare's Theater* esp. 7–16.

8 Here, the phrase ironically refers to the gallant "planted valiantly (because impudently)" on stage (2:248).

9 Bristol, *Big-time Shakespeare* 144; cf. 123–46.

10 *Authority and Representation in Early Modern Discourse*, esp. 23–99.

11 Here, to give only one example, a collection like Zarrilli (ed.), *Action (Re)considered* provides an absolute host of illustrations, verbal and visual, of how performance practice can go beyond any subservience to the text and its representational function.

12 Although there is an encouraging emphasis on "the craft of showing" ("presentational acting long outlasted the architectural division of actors and audience"), Thomson continues to focus on the "style" of performance. See his "Rogues and Rhetoricians," esp. 324. See also Hattaway on "Acting Styles," in his otherwise remarkable study of *Elizabethan Popular Theatre* 72–79; for

further literature on the subject see note 10, chapter 4.

13 While "place implies constriction and delimitation," as "always tied to the specificities of a given locale," it "was in exploring the extensiveness of space, its seemingly undelimitable outspread, its unendingness, that the coordinate but distinguishable notions of spatial absoluteness and infinity began to seem irresistible" (Casey, *The Fate of Place* 134). As Casey notes, "the more or less irenic cohabitation of place and space" continues to be "a viable option" (135), until "space is no longer situated in the physical world but in the subjectivity of the human mind that formally shapes this world" (136) – not unlike those imaginary, world-picturing representations on the late Renaissance stage.

14 Paradoxically, "despite all appearances, *différance* is itself a powerful principle of unity" (Dews, *Logics of Disintegration* 43), serving *de facto* as a ubiquitous master-key "'older' or 'more originary' than presence and identity" (25).

15 Looking back at his *History of Sexuality*, Foucault in his Preface to the German edition (1983) of *La volonté de savoir* (Paris: Gallimard, 1976), discussing *relations* between power and knowledge (and sexuality), refuses to subsume these under "repression" or "displacement." The use of "subject" and "truth" in volumes 2 and 3 of his *History* is actually prepared for in volume 1 where there is an unambiguous differentiation between "discursive production," "the production of power," and "the productions of knowledge," as in the conclusion to chapter 1.

16 I have made related distinctions in the chapters on mimesis and ritual in my *Shakespeare and the Popular Tradition in the Theater* 1–48.

17 Dollimore, *Radical Tragedy* 70–82. The gulf between these two important concepts of mimesis could be bridged and used to very remarkable effects in both popular Renaissance narrative and drama; see my essay, "*Fabula* and *Historia.*"

18 Cf. Bristol, *Carnival and Theater*, esp. 197–202.

I PERFORMANCE AND AUTHORITY IN *HAMLET* (1603)

1 Scoloker, "Epistle to *Daiphantes*"; cited by Chambers, *William Shakespeare* 2: 215.

2 Among recent attempts at a revaluation of Q1 *Hamlet*, see Urkowitz, "Well-sayd olde Mole" 37–70; Clayton (ed.), *The 'Hamlet' First Published (Q1, 1603)*; but also the cautious Introduction to Irace (ed.), *The First Quarto of Hamlet*, and others.

3 My text is *The Tragicall Historie of Hamlet Prince of Denmarke*, as reproduced in the *Bodley Head Quartos* series. For modern editions that, for systematic comparison, conveniently assemble all variants, see Mowat and Werstine (eds.), The Folger Shakespeare *Hamlet*; or, even more complete, Bertram and Kliman (eds.), *The Three-Text Hamlet*. Unless otherwise noted, as here, my Shakespearean text throughout is *The Riverside Shakespeare*. Citation of Folio material follows *The Norton Facsimile*, ed. Hinman.

4 See e.g., Werstine, "The Textual Mystery of *Hamlet.*"

5 This socially acute awareness is not to be confused with the politics in the representation of the Elsinore part which is conventional throughout. The

ending of Q1, for instance, has none of the troubling overtones that in Q2 are associated with Fortinbras; rather, there is a conclusion that "promises a full break with the past, a new beginning" (McGuire, "Which Fortinbras" 171).

6 Jenkins (ed.), *Hamlet*; see the editor's note to 3.1.62, defining "shocks" in the "primary sense of 'clashes of arms.'"

7 As against "editorial practice in mainstream editions of *Hamlet*," Marcus in her provocative chapter "Bad Taste and Bad *Hamlet*" (*Unediting the Renaissance* 132–76) provides an important new perspective on "the strong movement [. . .] to rehabilitate Q1" (135) in terms of the play's remarkable "position on the register between orality and literacy" (176).

8 In critically reassessing both the piracy and the memorial reconstruction theories for Q1 *Hamlet* I have especially profited from Weiner's critique of "the theory of Elizabethan play reporting" in his edition of *Hamlet. The First Quarto, 1603*, esp. 8–45. I am even more strongly indebted to Maguire, *Shakespearean Suspect Texts*, and Werstine, "A Century of 'Bad' Shakespeare Quartos." The latter is complementary to Maguire's study in that it systematically re-examines "the memorial-reconstruction-by-actors hypothesis" in the terms in which, since the days of W. W. Greg and A. W. Pollard, it was (un)critically perpetuated right into the highly sophisticated quantitative approaches of John Jordan, Gary Taylor, and Kathleen Irace.

9 Jenkins (ed.), *Hamlet* 289.

10 Duthie 232–37. But note John Dover Wilson's repeated opinion that "this addition must be a personal attack upon a particular clown" (The New Cambridge *Hamlet* 197), which appears to modify somewhat his earlier assumption, upon discovering the Tarltonic source of two of the clown's "cinkapase of jests," that the passage in question was the dramatist's attack on Tarlton himself (*The Library*, esp. 240–41). As against Dover Wilson, Chambers argued that the passage "can only be a theatrical interpolation" (*William Shakespeare* 1:418–19). Duthie, however, at some length considers Nicholson's suggestion that the attack was leveled at William Kempe. Although, as Albert Furnivall in his response to Nicholson's 1880 paper noted, the latter contains several "ingenious may-bes" (Nicholson, "Kemp and the Play of *Hamlet*" 65), Hamlet's sneers in Q1 may well have been "aimed at some special clown, who would naturally be Kemp" (65). At least there is no evidence that contradicts Nicholson's assumption that Hamlet's "bitterness against the Clown" must have been due to "his extemporizing and non-attention to and interference with the proper business of the scene" (60). At this point, we are strongly indebted to Wiles for pursuing this question further.

11 The phrase is taken from Richard Jones' Preface to *Tamburlaine the Great*; see Cunningham (ed.) 111.

12 Cf. lines 151, 701, 744.

13 Irace (ed.), *The First Quarto of Hamlet* 18. While this edition does not pursue the issue of dramaturgy, it offers what I believe are helpful suggestions towards a conjectural reconstruction of the play's provenance. See esp. 7–8, 17–21. See also note 14.

14 Irace, "Origins and Agents of Q1 *Hamlet*" 100: According to her conjectural reconstruction, which is of course highly speculative, "a few of Shakespeare's

colleagues, including 'Marcellus', may have had an unexpected need for a *Hamlet* playtext while on tour; it might have been quicker – or safer – to reconstruct the play rather than return to plague-ridden London for the promptbook" (100).

15 Cf. MacLean, "Tour Routes" esp. 10–12, who traces many positive responses to regular touring well into the 1620s.

2 A NEW AGENDA FOR AUTHORITY

1 Worthen, *Shakespeare and the Authority of Performance*, blurb; see especially chapter 1, "Authority and Performance" 1–43.

2 *Monthly Review,* 50 (1774), 144; cited in Dobson, *The Making of the National Poet* 209. For Jones' use of histrionic "deformities," see the *Tamburlaine* section in chapter 3.

3 For an even more searching critique of Malone's concept of "authenticity," see de Grazia, *Shakespeare Verbatim*, esp. 49–93.

4 As Gondris notes, "the essence of Shakespeare is perceived as locked into the syntactic, lexical, and graphic properties of the printed text," even to the degree that the writing in its printed medium "codifies performance" (*Reading Readings*, xiv–xv).

5 The best study that we have of this emerging new authority in the theatre is Murray, *Theatrical Legitimation*. See also Barish's important *Antitheatrical Prejudice*, and Mowat, "The Theater and Literary Culture," who pertinently observes that "relationships among performance, playscript, and printed text are thus more fluid, more disturbed, than scholars have tended to imagine and describe them" (216).

6 See chapter 5, "Jonson and the Loathéd Stage" (131–54).

7 For some of the answers towards these questions, see the last 3 chapters of this project as well as those essays that I have listed in "Works Cited" in order to document further readings and perspectives alluded to but, for reasons of space, not incorporated in this study (see Preface). Together, these published essays contain material which I propose to use in further exploring forms and functions of representation in the Elizabethan theatre, taking account of, among other things, its "functioning as a significant cultural intervention in a process of political reformation" (Kastan, *Shakespeare after Theory* 111).

8 In the case of the recent Oxford edition, for example, this leads to "whole passages of additional dialogue," and to "revamping the wording for clarification." It may well be said that "even the boldest of eighteenth-century versifying editors are not this intrusive" (Bevington, "Determining the Indeterminate" 505; 507).

9 These observations are drawn from, respectively, Hibbard (ed.), *Hamlet* 69; and Chambers, *William Shakespeare* 1: 415.

10 See Marcus, *Unediting the Renaissance* 1–37, especially chapter 5 (132–76) where she recasts the discussion about Q1 *Hamlet* by approaching the play in terms of the differing expectations created by orality and literacy as "competing forms of communication within the Renaissance playhouse" (131).

11 In *Shakespearean Suspect Texts*, Maguire establishes only three plays out of

forty-one bad quartos in this category and another four where "a strong case can be made for memorial reconstruction"; see her listing, 324.

12 Pettitt, "Formulaic Dramaturgy" 167–91, esp. 175–80. Drawing attention to oral formulaic material, Pettitt advances the "concept of the dramaturgical formula" (180) as an element in both performance practice and *mise-en-scène*, thereby recalling Hattaway's comparison between textual instability of early ballads and verbal fluidity in the popular theatre (Hattaway, *Elizabethan Popular Theatre* 54–55).

13 For a magisterial account especially of printing and writing in the 1590's, see Bruster, "The Structural Transformation of Print in Late Elizabethan England," who traces in these years an "extensive habituation to print."

14 On the difference between orality and literacy in the Elizabethan playhouse, see also Pettitt, who states that oral formulas, interjections, and stock phrases occur "particularly (and probably significantly) in 'bad' play-texts" (169).

15 See Gurr, "The Bare Island" 30.

16 See my *Authority and Representation* (68–82), where Foxe's record of Gardiner's concern about the "anchor-hold of authority" is further discussed.

17 As Sir Thomas Smith in 1565 wrote about "the justices of the peace": "Each of them hath *authority* upon complaint to him made of any theft, robbery, manslaughter, murder, violence, complots, riots, *unlawful games, or any such disturbance of the peace and quiet* of the realm, to commit the persons whom he supposes offenders to the prison" (cit. Elton [ed.], *The Tudor Constitution* 469; my emphasis). JPs, then, always already were authorized to control public "games" and help "rule the people, whereby they are kept always as it were in a bridle of good order" (470).

18 On the crucial role of 'interpretation' in early modern discourse, see the searching study of Lambropoulos, *The Rise of Eurocentrism*.

19 See Knutson, *The Repertory*, who persuasively suggests similarities in business practices between Shakespeare's company and Henslowe. See esp. 2–5, 58–60.

20 Carroll (ed.), *Greene's Groatsworth of Wit. Bought With a Million of Repentance*. In his Preface, the editor suggests that Henry Chettle had more than a finger in the composition of the tract. About Chettle's participation, see also Jowett, "Johannes Factotum: Henry Chettle and *Greene's Groatsworth of Wit*."

21 See also Miller, *Poetic License* 6 *et passim*.

22 I cite from Carroll's edition of the text. My reading is indebted to Greenblatt who first approached the underlying "extended borrowings, collective exchanges" (7) in terms of stringently defined "types of symbolic acquisition" and "appropriation" (9–10) without thereby downplaying "the overwhelming importance and immediacy of material interests" (14) in Shakespeare's theatre. See his *Shakespearean Negotiations*, where the relevant concept of a "circulation" of authority is shown to implicate a "blend of appropriation and aggression" (113).

23 Perhaps, as Honigmann suggests, not unjustifiably: the "*Tygers hart*" (line 940) is part of considerable evidence of an ungentle Shakespeare, "sharp and businesslike." See *Shakespeare's Impact on His Contemporaries* 7, 9, 11, 22.

3 PEN AND VOICE: VERSIONS OF DOUBLENESS

1 My text for this play is Cunningham's edition.

2 Carroll (ed.), *Greene's Groatsworth of Wit*, lines 935, 951, and 955, respectively.

3 See Foakes and Rickert, *Diary* 24–37.

4 The printer, who "was not working from a theatre manuscript," may actually have been Thomas Orwin printing for Richard Jones; see Cunningham (ed.) 89–90. But, since the latter is named in the Stationers' Register entry for the play (14 August, 1590), I shall continue to refer to Jones as Marlowe's printer.

5 This preface is printed in Cunningham's edition, 111–12.

6 Of all the modernizing editions I have consulted, Cunningham's is the only one that faithfully follows the Octavo text of 1590 and prints "frivolous jestures" (instead of the usual "gestures") because justifiably, I think, this word here is "clearly associated with jest" (111).

7 But in no case would the printer's disapproval of those "fond and frivolous" elements have referred to the scornful taunts addressed to Mycetes or Bajazeth in Part I, as F. P. Wilson once suggested (*Marlowe and the Early Shakespeare* 28). Rather, these "graced deformities" have their origins in the demands of the playhouse, not the culture of humanistic literacy; as David Bevington notes, "Marlowe's company would hardly have countenanced a public renunciation of its popular Vice comedy in *Tamburlaine*, only to return to it in *Doctor Faustus*" (*From "Mankind" to Marlowe* 201).

8 See also McMillin, *The Elizabethan Theatre* 21.

9 In dating *Troilus and Cressida* I follow Honigmann in the assumption that Shakespeare "probably composed the play in the later or middle months of 1601" when the "prologue arm'd" must have been a fresh gibe at the armed prologue in *Poetaster* (certainly dated mid-1601). Honigmann's argument, though conjectural, is highly plausible in that his dating embraces stage-history, transmission, genre, and interpretation, except that his reading of "not in confidence," current since the days of E. K. Chambers, is exclusively explained as a reference to the armed prologue in *Poetaster*, "who begs not to be accused of arrogance" (*Myriad-minded Shakespeare* 112–29; cit. 114.) But this reference, I submit, does not satisfy.

10 See my essay, "Textual Authority and Performative Agency."

11 For some detailed and closely argued reconstructions of this scene, see Sprigg, "Shakespeare's Visual Stagecraft"; and Shurgot, *Stages of Play* 183–88, with graphic material on the staging of our scene, 197–98. While both studies persuasively underline the demanding multiplicity of perspectives, they ignore or underestimate the localizing force of both tent and "torch" (5.2.5) as well as Thersites' presentational *gestus*.

12 My reading here is based on the assumption that, against Sir Thomas Hanmer's emendation, followed in the Arden and the Oxford editions, we should adhere to Q and F and give this line, which both these early texts set as prose, to Thersites.

13 Nor does this necessarily conflict with the assumption that, by a few months, even weeks, "the weight of the evidence excludes *Henry V*" from the Globe plays (Beckerman, *Shakespeare at the Globe* xiv).

4 PLAYING WITH A DIFFERENCE

1 David Williams in his *Deformed Discourse* revealingly illuminates the poetics of the monstrous in terms of its etymology: *monstrare* is to "show forth," as distinguished from *(re)praesentare*. As "aesthetic deformations also propose a fundamental critique of rational discourse," the use therein of "the sign is incommensurable with the signified, form cannot contain being" (6). In other words, "signs so deformed and so transgressive of the process of signification itself" annihilate the potential for copy, in that "confusion of the real with its language construct" becomes "impossible, even scandalous" (7). Here, I read "copy" for (neo)-Aristotelian mimesis or representation, which Williams appears to have in mind when, emphasizing "threshold" positions (17) and "nonreferentiality" (102), he notes that the "factor common to all aesthetic expressions of deformity appears to be that they take mimesis as their target" (79). For a nonrepresentational reading of the sources of mimesis, see Koller, *Die Mimesis in der Antike* esp. 12, 75, 119. There is an unsuspected link between Koller's historical/etymological readings and some more recent poststructuralist criticism, as when Philippe Lacoue-Labarthe, invoking Nietzsche and René Girard's *La Violence et le sacré*, postulates that "mimesis [. . .] is anterior, in some way or other, to representation" ("Mimesis and Truth" 17). Among the most helpful nondeconstructionist discussions, see Ricoeur, "Mimesis and Representation," esp. 15–17.

2 The strength of the performance element in the early history of mimesis – as in Koller's emphasis on its sources in ritual dance (see preceding note) – has an epistemological correlative which helps illuminate the performative component in the play of contrariety and disfigurement, especially its distance from representation. Here I cannot of course document the remarkable extent to which the notion of knowledge as accurate mode of representation has in our century been discarded by major thinkers like Wittgenstein, Dewey, and Heidegger. But the by now commonplace critique of representation ("We must get the visual, and in particular the mirroring, metaphors out of our speech altogether" [Rorty, *Philosophy*] 371) presents us with a crucial foil against which the preoccupation with play and performance needs to be seen in a historical and critical perspective. Take only Jacques Derrida's famous celebration of play as "the Nietzschean *affirmation*, that is the joyous affirmation of the play of the world and of the innocence of becoming, the affirmation of a world of signs without fault, without truth, and without origin" (*Writing and Difference* 292 – in an essay which concludes with an invocation of "the formless, mute, infant, and terrifying form of monstrosity" [293]). In the present project I positively seek to overcome the traditional repression of play and the suppression of the sign without however underestimating the indelible role of representations in shaping the modalities of social and cultural articulation and their contribution to "accommodating," then and now, "writers, performers, readers, and audiences to multiple and shifting subject positions within the world that they themselves both constitute and inhabit" (Montrose, "New Historicisms" 396). For an important attempt to redefine representation on the strength of a performative investment in play and playing, see Iser's Epilogue to *The Fictive and the Imaginary*.

3 See, as among the best that we have, Faas, *Shakespeare's Poetics* and Kiernan, *Shakespeare's Theory of Drama*. For an important study of "the daemonic element in Renaissance drama," in particular of Harlequin and the comic poetics of "where there is naturalness there is artifice," see Cope, *Dramaturgy of the Daemonic* xi; 145. But there is to my knowledge no sustained reconsideration of the presentational mode in Elizabethan performance; for some helpful suggestions see Shephard, *Marlowe and the Politics of Elizabethan Theatre*, who notes the "duality of presentation/mimesis" (108), in particular "the tension between mimesis and presentation in the signaling of the subjectivity of an individual" (74). See also Thomson, "Rogues and Rhetoricians," esp. 329.

4 Referring to "a cultural divide [. . .] in opposed styles of architecture and in opposed legal systems, as well as in different modes of pageantry and poetry" ("Barbarous Tongues" 289), Helgerson here has in mind the broader division between the native, 'barbarous,' 'gothic' tradition and neoclassical innovation.

5 These quotations are from the York mystery cycle (XVI, 234, 240) and the Chester cycle (VIII, 377, 187), respectively. For further discussion of Herod and Pilate in the mystery cycles, see my *Shakespeare and the Popular Tradition in the Theater* 64–72.

6 I cite *King Cambises* from *Chief Pre-Shakespearean Dramas*, ed. Adams.

7 John Webster, *Academiarum Examen*; the analogy refers to the "performance" of "scholastic exercises" (91).

8 As Latham notes, Shakespeare in his own turn inverts "the fairies' passion for stealing human children from their cradles and their known practice of disfiguring them with withered arms and elvish marks" (*The Elizabethan Fairies* 183).

9 See Bradbrook, *The Rise of the Common Player*, as well as Wiles, *Shakespeare's Clown* and Mann, *The Elizabethan Player*.

10 See Harbage, "Elizabethan Acting" 692; also Joseph, *Elizabethan Acting*; Rosenberg, "Elizabethan Actors, Men or Marionettes?"; Goldstein, "On the Transition from Formal to Naturalistic Acting in the Elizabethan and Post-Elizabethan Theatre"; Foakes, "*The Player's Passion*"; Marker, "Nature and Decorum in the Theory of Elizabethan Acting"; Seltzer, "The Actors and Staging"; Cohen, *Acting in Shakespeare*; Russell Brown, *Shakespeare's Plays in Performance* 16–41; Gurr *The Shakespearean Stage* 95–102; Skura, *Shakespeare the Actor and the Purposes of Playing*; Thomson, "Rogues and Rhetoricians."

11 While Goldstein's approach to Elizabethan acting stands alone as an elaborate, though somewhat rigid attempt to historicize changes in performance practice in terms of feudal/bourgeois formations in economics and class structure, Seltzer's is among the most persuasive among those emphasizing a "'mixed' style" ("The Actors and Staging" 37).

12 See Beckerman's chapter 4 (*Shakespeare at the Globe* 109–156).

13 Bentley, *The Profession of Player in Shakespeare's Time, 1590–1642*; in addition to *The Shakespearean Stage* and *Playgoing in Shakespeare's London*, see also Gurr's early articles, "Who Strutted and Bellowed?" and "Elizabethan Action."

14 Skura acknowledges her indebtedness to Michael Goldman's work and other studies of "the actor's experience" (*Shakespeare the Actor* 236), including

Worthen's *The Idea of the Actor*.

15 See Carlson, *Performance* 81–85.

16 Also in Issacharoff and Jones (eds.), *Performing Texts* 75. Parts of the passage cited are eliminated from the chapter that reproduces this essay in *A Sociosemiotic Theory of Theatre*. Today's Shakespeare criticism, in coming to terms with this "performant function" in its historicity, may wish to compare two rather different recent developments, as briefly mentioned in the Introduction: (1) the advent of performance arts, embracing "a myriad of performance practices, ranging from stage to festival" (Parker and Sedgwick, *Performativity and Performance* 2).These performance practices constitute "an open-ended medium with endless variables" (Goldberg, *Performance Art* 9) with(out) text. At the same time, this recent willingness to credit a performative dimension in all ritual, festive, ceremonial, circus and of course theatrical occasions is intriguingly linked to (2) the poststructuralist emphasis on "a radical estrangement between the meaning and the performance of any text" (de Man, *Allegories of Reading* 298). Parker and Sedgwick refer to this trend as "the nonreference of the performative," as informing a questionable opposition between "the *extroversion* of the actor" and "the *introversion* of the signifier" (*Performativity and Performance* 2; italics *ibid.*) While my own project does not subscribe to such immanence of the illocutionary signifier, the proposed "torsion, the mutual perversion, as one might say, of reference and performativity" (3) is of vital consequence wherever the doubleness of pen and voice tends to be assimilated to what I prefer to call the uses of contrariety and disfigurement on, often enough, grounds exterritorial to representational writing.

5 HISTORIES IN ELIZABETHAN PERFORMANCE

1 For the cultural semiotics behind John Lyly's uses of these terms, see my essay, "Scene Individable, Mingle-Mangle Unlimited."

2 See Astington, "The London Stage in the 1580's" 1; Bradley, *From Text to Performance in the Elizabethan Theatre*; William Ingram, *The Business of Playing*; Loengard, "An Elizabethan Lawsuit." For Paul White, *Theatre and Reformation*, see below, note 12.

3 See Loengard, "An Elizabethan Lawsuit." The Red Lion was not actually at Stepney but "at Myle End," i.e. "within a thirty- or forty-minute walk from St. Paul's" (Astington, "The Red Lion Playhouse" 456–57).

4 Stockwood, *A Sermon* 137.

5 But this date is considered by Chambers to be an error; he proposes 1594 as the correct year. See *The Elizabethan Stage* 2:14.

6 Bradley (*From Text to Performance* 253, n. 19) reads the satirical verses cited by Chambers as evidence that the Duttons led a troupe of primarily "fiddlers and rope-dancers."

7 See Chambers, *The Elizabethan Stage* 2:98.

8 Greenfield, "Professional Players at Gloucester"; see Table 1, 75.

9 Together with Axton's Introduction to her edition of *Jack Juggler*, White's reading (*Theatre and Reformation* 123–29) establishes the (carefully concealed) Protestant slant of the play most convincingly.

10 Axton (ed.), *Jack Juggler* 18–19.

11 I cite from Axton's edition of the play in *Three Tudor Classical Interludes*.

12 For the earlier Tudor period, see Westfall, *Patrons and Performance: Early Tudor Household Records*; Blackstone, "Patrons and Elizabethan Acting Companies"; see also Paul White, *Theatre and Reformation*, esp. 61–66, 68–72.

13 See also Sisson, *Le Goût public et le théâtre élisabéthain jusqu'à la mort de Shakespeare*, esp. 35–51.

14 I have read and documented the Tudor socio-cultural mingle-mangle at length in my dissertation (Humboldt University, 1955) *Drama und Wirklichkeit in der Shakespearezeit* 13–180, and more briefly in *Shakespeare and the Popular Tradition in the Theater*, especially the chapters "Toward the Culture of a Nation" and "Sociology of the Elizabethan Stage" 161–77. In more recent social and political historiography, among studies addressing the political, social, and cultural relations behind the Elizabethan Settlement, I have found particularly helpful, in addition to what has been already cited: Elton, *Policy and Police*; Hurstfield, *Freedom, Corruption, and Government in Elizabethan England*; MacCaffrey, *The Shaping of the Elizabethan Regime*; Hassell Smith, *Gentry and Court*; James, *Family, Lineage, and Civil Society*; Collinson, *The Elizabethan Puritan Movement*; Wrightson, *English Society, 1580–1680*.

15 Helgerson, in *Forms of Nationhood*, proceeds to view Shakespeare's position in the theatre as more or less marked by a strategy of "exclusion."

16 The most persuasive assemblage of evidence is still Ferguson's *The Articulate Citizen and the English Renaissance*.

17 Cit. by Hill, "The Pre-Revolutionary Decades," *The Collected Essays* 1:10.

18 Visiting the "Rose, / Or Curtaine" and going on "An idle Citty-walke," the satirist must "Witness that hotch-potch of so many noyses" and the rough music "of so many seuerall voyces" (Guilpin, *Skialetheia* 5: 28–29; 38; 41–42) that he thinks "the *Genius* of antiquitie, / [has] come to complaine of our varietie" (90–91). In other words, inclusiveness may present problems on several levels for a neoclassical departure in satire.

19 In ascribing the play to the early John Marston, I follow Kernan, "John Marston's play, *Histriomastix*," and Finkelpearl, "John Marston's *Histrio-Mastix* as an Inns of Court Play: A Hypothesis." See further on the play's sources, the same, *John Marston of the Middle Temple* 119–24. Finkelpearl's dating (*ibid.* 265) of the play (1598/99) is by now well accepted by R. W. Ingram, *John Marston* 11, 59; and Geckle, *John Marston's Drama* 34. For my discussion of the play, see the text above.

20 On Jonson, I am obviously indebted to the work of Jonas Barish and Timothy Murray but also, and despite differences in theme and approach, to the distinguished reinterpretation of Jonson's cultural politics by Don Wayne, in his "Drama and Society in the Age of Jonson."

21 Here and throughout my text is Herford and Simpson (eds.), *Ben Jonson*, with page references in the text.

22 This reference to Hobbes must not obscure that, paradoxically, Jonson's enhanced pride in solitary authorship went hand in hand with both some altogether traditional, anti-acquisitive and some fairly inclusive positions in economics and politics respectively. For the former, see Knights' *Drama and Society*

in the Age of Jonson, esp. 12, 22; for the latter, see among other recent work Perry's study of *Bartholomew Fair*, especially of the fair as "a microcosm" of "social and geographical heterogeneity," inspired by the "play's interest in the alienation and circulation of authority" (Perry, *The Making of Jacobean Culture* 224; 227).

23 Cit. Bradbrook, *The Rise of the Common Player* 124.

24 Leo Salingar, "Jacobean Playwrights and 'Judicious' Spectators" 233, n. 5.

25 But not only that colleague; according to Bentley (*The Profession of Player in Shakespeare's Time* 5) "perhaps twenty out of approximately one thousand performing in the time are known to have accumulated respectable estates."

26 Jonson, Preface to *The New Inn* (Herford and Simpson, *Ben Jonson* 6:397).

27 Beaumont's own response provides further evidence of socio-cultural division in the early Jacobean theatre: "But multitudes there are whose judgements goes/ Headlong according to the actors' clothes" (Bowers, *The Dramatic Works* 3:491). The appeal to "judgement" and the "judicious" throughout serves as an all-important parameter of differentiation, even threatened withdrawal from "the public stage." Says Beaumont,

> Why should the man, whose wit nere had a staine,
> Upon the publike stage present his vaine,
> And make a thousand men in judgement sit. (Bowers 3:490)

28 For authorship and date of the play, see above, note 19. According to Finkelpearl, *John Marston of the Middle Temple*, we are dealing, then, with a singeing attack of student or (near)adult amateur actors on common players in "the free-spoken, irreverent, independent atmosphere of the Inns" (69).

29 Cook's study, *The Privileged Playgoers*, provides valuable evidence that, by implication, documents the ongoing stratification, even though her claim cannot, I think, be upheld for the earlier period.

30 Florio and Harvey are cited in Cook, *The Privileged Playgoers of Shakespeare's London* 125–26.

31 See James, *Family, Lineage and Civil Society* 104f.; and Stone, *The Crisis of the Aristocracy, 1558–1641* 672; 702–24.

32 See also McIntosh, *A Community Transformed* 406–11.

33 W. A. Armstrong, although giving Blackfriars "the central place in the overall development" of the Elizabethan theatre, first noted that there is an overwhelming amount of structural affinity in the *mise-en-scène* at private and public stages (17). Harbage in his *Shakespeare and the Rival Traditions* sought to establish a series of social, moral, and thematic differences between public and "coterie" stages; although the book continues to be valuable in its consideration of socially distinct audience expectations, this mode of differentiation was too narrow to permit for developments in staging, performance, and writing.

34 For instance, if "therle of Derby his players shall playe in this cittie contrary to Mr. Maiors commanndmt then they shalbe committed to prison" (Norwich, June 9, 1602).

35 More general background can be found in Elton, *The Tudor Revolution in Government*. Deeply indebted to the historians named in the text above, I have discussed the historiography of both division and "Integrating Difference" at

somewhat greater length in my *Authority and Representation in Early Modern Discourse*, esp. 1–22, 190–207.

36 Perry Anderson, *Lineages of the Absolutist State*; Elton, *Policy and Police*, and Clark, *English Provincial Society from the Reformation to the Revolution* 111, 142, 144; Hassell Smith, *County and Court* 277.

37 Collinson, *The Birthpangs of Protestant England* 8; Hill, *The Collected Essays* 2:28–29. But the same Protestantism that enhanced the unifying sense of English patriotism was a major force in both "staging reform" and "reforming the stage" (to adapt the title of Huston Diehl's study; see, esp., 3, 80–85, 213).

38 Harbage, *Shakespeare's Audience* 38 n.35; cf. Bevington, *Tudor Drama and Politics* 294–97.

39 After the "gentry's withdrawal from armed political demonstrations in alliance with the people" was by 1600 irrevocable, "Control of the people" became "a key issue of county politics" (Fletcher and Stevenson, *Order and Disorder* 11).

40 See Münz, *Das "andere" Theater*; Haider-Pregler, *Des sittlichen Bürgers Abendschule*, among others. The countervailing *Literarisierung* may well be said both to culminate and be transmuted in Friedrich Schiller's early pamphlet on the theatre as a "moralische Anstalt" – *Theater as a Moral Institution*.

6 *HAMLET* AND THE PURPOSES OF PLAYING

1 For recent exceptions to this rule, see several of the contributions to Cox and Kastan (eds.), *A New History of Early English Drama*; Kiernan, *Shakespeare's Theory of Drama*; Worthen, *Shakespeare and the Authority of Performance*, esp. 1–43; but also, by implication, the work of Alvin Kernan, and others.

2 Here I am indebted to Benno Besson's production of the play at the Berlin Volksbühne.

3 Cf. Berger, *Imaginary Audition* 157; 159. This reading is in reference to *Richard II*.

4 Reiss has recently studied the rise of this discourse as "a rational aesthetics" (15), or an "aesthetic rationalization" (197), in response to that crisis in Renaissance humanism which saw "the failure of language as a tool for discovery" (xiv). See his *Knowledge, Discovery and Imagination in Early Modern Europe*, which, in the present context, raises the question of how far the widespread "awareness of responding to a breakdown in the authority of language" (127) is at least partially inflected in the crisis in which Hamlet, the Wittenberg humanist, finds himself (and for whose articulation, among other factors, the antic legacy potentially provides a theatrically viable, appropriately discordant instrument – one that helps expose the liabilities of both humanism and humanistic study).

5 Cf. also Sidney, *Prose Works* 3:17, 29.

6 *The Shepherd's Calendar*, Epistle to Gabriel Harvey 417: "Even so doe those rough and harsh terms enlumine and make more clearly to appear the brightnesse of braue and glorious words."

7 For the uses of deformity and disfigurement, see above chapter 4.

8 Compare: "So he [Amleth] chose to feign dulness, and pretend an utter lack of wits. This cunning course not only concealed his intelligence but ensured his safety. Every day he remained in his mother's house utterly listless and unclean,

flinging himself on the ground and bespattering his person with foul and filthy dirt. His discoloured face and visage smutched with slime denoted foolish and groteque madness" (Bullough, *Narrative and Dramatic Sources* 7:62).

9 The qualification – before 1600 – is crucial when we come to think that Erasmus' *Praise of Folly* with its humanistic use of *stultitia* as abundant vehicle of hetero-glossia, was unthinkable among the new generation of humanists (Marston, Hall, Guilpin, and others); see my *Authority and Representation in Early Modern Discourse* 133–46.

7 SPACE (IN)DIVIDABLE: *LOCUS* AND *PLATEA* REVISITED

1 My distinction between the (imaginative) space *in* representation and the (ma-terial) space *of* theatrical (re)presentation seeks to assimilate but also to qualify such a definition of theatrical space as provided by Eli Konigson, *L'espace théâtral médiéval* 9: "Les représentations de l'espace et leur réalisation technique concernent donc à la fois les textes et les différents aspects des lieux théâtraux durant les spectacles." While I remain reluctant to use concepts like "réalisa-tion," this relationship between the "representations of space" and the material site of its transaction is vital in that it constitutes, in Bakhtin's parlance, a "chronotope." Together these (non-identical) spatial and temporal dimensions constitute an all-important structuring force shaping any theater event. The interface between the time/place represented and the time and place of what practices are doing the representing is absolutely crucial to any theatrical articu-lation. As Patrice Pavis says, it is "like a magnet" that is "drawing the rest of the performance to it" ("Performance Analysis" note 22). In what follows I can consider the temporal dimension only in passing.

2 Here I adopt a phrase from the title of Kirby's *Indifferent Boundaries: Spatial Concepts of Human Subjectivity*. This study reminds us that "metaphors of space," or simply the "language of space is everywhere in theory today" and that, in particular, the concept of 'difference' when opposed to 'reference' is "a spatial concept, unimaginable or just barely imaginable outside the register of space" (1,3). This is not the place to reassess the current critical investment in the concept of space except to acknowledge the intriguing impact of a contemporary perspective that, as in Saussure and Derrida, Kristeva and Jameson, has resulted in a sense of 'indifferent boundaries' between 'space' as a target and as a category of perception. See, in this connection, Pollock, *Vision and Difference: Femininity, Feminism, and the Histories of Art*, who attempts to view together not only "the spaces represented, or the spaces of representation, but the social spaces from which the representation is made and its reciprocal positionalities" (66).

3 In the Introduction to his essay, Berger refers to a then unpublished work on "text versus performance in Shakespeare" ("Bodies and Texts" 146) that is now accessible in his *Making Trifles of Terrors* 50–69; 98–125; for an illuminating view of "the crucial difference between text and performance" (68) that largely but not entirely runs counter to my own, see esp. 99–111.

4 In revisiting the distinction between *locus* and *platea* in the (pre)Shakespearean theatre (see my *Shakespeare and the Popular Tradition in the Theater* 73–85), I still believe that Southern, in *The Medieval Theatre in the Round* provides us

with extremely helpful evidence on the uses of *platea* or "place" (219–36). It is of course true that his reading of the diagram contained in the manuscript of *The Castle of Perseverance* (cf. Mark Eccles [ed.], *The Macro Plays*, facsimile opposite title page) has undergone a considerable amount of revision. But, for example, as used by Glynne Wickham, it appears perfectly possible to distinguish the "*platea* or acting area, and *locus* or symbols for identification of place" in the medieval theatre (*Early English Stages, 1300–1575* 160). However, as Pamela M. King notes, if "we can look at the diagram freed from the idea that it presents an area marked out as a theatre, we can begin to look at how as a set design it delimits different types of space" ("Spatial Semantics" 48). For further revisionary criticism, see Schmitt, "Was There a Medieval Theater in the Round? A Re-examination of the Evidence," and Neuss, "The Staging of *The Creacion of the World,* '" esp. 191–94. My own approach to the interaction of *locus* and *platea* has meanwhile been taken further by Michael Mooney in his *Shakespeare's Dramatic Transactions*; it has been (re)conceived so as to chart theatrical space in the modern theatre by Colin Counsell, *Signs of Performance*, 16–18; and developed further, critically as well as constructively, by Harry Berger in his recent essay in *Shakespeare Quarterly* (1998). See also the helpful study of Shurgot, *Stages of Play*, 195–202; 228 – although this author, unfortunately, misreads my use of *locus* and *platea* as constituting a rigid "dichotomy" (195).

5 See, for example, Hussey, *The Literary Language of Shakespeare*, esp. the emphasis on "semantic density" in chapter 2, "The Expanding Vocabulary" (10–33).

6 John Foxe's phrase; see my *Authority and Representation in Early Modern Discourse* 133–89.

7 Although this emphasis, I think, needs to be qualified in its exclusiveness, Kernan does remind us, as J. S. Smart did decades ago (*Shakespeare: Truth and Tradition*, 130, 157, 167–68), that the image of the native bard has definitively been replaced by that of a conscious, ambitious, deliberate writer of plays in consonance with a good many Renaissance endeavors of art.

8 Carlson, *Places of Performance*, esp. 20–26; 38–49.

9 See Kernodle, *From Art to Theatre* 130–53. For a trenchant critique of the spatial implications of Kernodle's preoccupation with visual arts, see Konigson, *L'espace théâtral médiéval* 275–80, where the notion of "linéarité spatiale," especially in "la frise-procession comme principe general" (278), is convincingly, I think, questioned.

10 *The First Booke of Architecture*, made by Sebastian Serly, entreating of "geometrie." Translated out of Italian into Dutch, and out of Dutch into English. Note that books 2–5 have separate title pages and foliation.

11 The fresco in the lobby of the theatre shows the opening scene of *Oedipus*; I owe the knowledge of it to Stephen Orgel.

12 Thorndike, *Shakespeare's Theater* 102 ff.; cit. by Beckerman, *Shakespeare at the Globe* 66.

13 I have explored further this scene in "Performing at the Frontiers of Representation," esp. 107–09.

14 In this connection, see the early specifications of an Elizabethan "double

consciousness," by Bethell, *Shakespeare and the Popular Dramatic Tradition*; Cope, *The Theater and the Dream*; and others.

15 The way "stage space" and "dramatic space," i.e. the space "symbolized in the text," can be seen to "overlap, interact," creates "transitions between them" (Pavis, "Performance Analysis" 14) which, in a strictly localized action, can be assumed to be immanent rather than explicit. Again, the threshold quality, the element of fluidity, among these demarcations cannot very well be conceived in terms of a purely structural analysis. This becomes apparent as soon as the three distinctions in the remarkable work of Anne Ubersfeld (*Lire le théâtre*, *L'Ecole du Spectateur*, *L'Espace théâtral*, together with Georges Banu) are applied to a pre-modern type of culture. For instance, her differentiation between "theatrical space" (the theatre building or location) "scenic space" (the acting area), and "dramatic space" (in the represented story) are, in Greek tragedy, blurred among the first two terms. See David Wiles, *Tragedy in Athens*: "it is hard to make any useful distinction between 'theatrical space' and 'scenic space' since the acting area is merely a function of the building" (16). The same cannot quite be said about the Elizabethan theatre, but there an important element of overlapping persists in any adaptation of a *platea*-like space. As against the structuralist notion 'to read' theatrical space, I prefer to follow Lefebvre's and Casey's emphases on the historicity and materiality as well as on the 'constructedness' of space; see my Introduction, p. 12.

16 On metalanguage, among others, see Pfister, "Kommentar, Metasprache und Metakommunikation in *Hamlet*."

17 Glynne Wickham in his essay, "Hell-castle and its Door Keeper," certainly goes too far when saying that the story of *The Harrowing of Hell* "provided Shakespeare with his model for the particular form in which he chose to cast Act II, scene iii of *Macbeth*" (68). Nor can Macduff be viewed, in the light of the apocryphal Book of Nicodemus, as "the triumphant Christ-figure of early Christian and medieval legend" (Harcourt, "I pray you" 401). In the thoroughly orthodox gospel of Nicodemus it is Satan, master of Hell, who orders the porter to "open wyde yhour endeles yhates here" to allow Jesus to enter (Hulme's edition, lines 1347–48). Nicodemus is the fundamental source of the entire Harrowing of Hell tradition, and both in its nondramatic and dramatic forms it is worlds apart from what happens in *Macbeth*, 2.3.

18 Here, "sound scenery" is coined in analogy to a term for which I remain indebted to Rudolf Stamm, *Shakespeare's Word Scenery*. Pfister, in *The Theory and Analysis of Drama*, makes a distinction between "implicit stage-directions in the primary text" (16) and a "word scenery" that, as one of the "verbal localization techniques," is equated, in Heinz Kindermann's phrase, with "spoken space" (cited by Pfister, *Theory and Analysis* 267). I find these distinctions helpful in that they point to "the semantic structuring of space" (261). What I have in mind is a 'structure' of theatrical space as, for instance, outlined in Halpern's study of the political struggle in *Julius Caesar*. There, space in the play is viewed as "largely a contest between the material, rhetorical, theatrical, and even interpretive practices of its two public spaces." In this connection, the brilliant suggestion is made that both the site of the Senate-house and that of "the plebeian milieu" "embody different characteristics of the early modern

theater, and leave it poised between two distinct (but, in a sense, simultaneous) historical trajectories" (*Shakespeare Among the Moderns* 79).

19 For a more specific and quite comprehensive overview of differing uses of 'aside,' see Pfister, *The Theory and Analysis of Drama*, 137–40.

20 The old-spelling text of *Doctor Faustus* (1604) is cited from C. F. Tucker Brooke's edition of Marlowe's works.

8 SHAKESPEARE'S ENDINGS: COMMODIOUS THRESHOLDS

1 *The Concept of Irony: With Constant Reference to Socrates*, cited by Said, *Beginnings* 88.

2 If the chronology of my argument were of any interest, perhaps it should be noted that I came across this modern "Theory of Production and Reception" after the present chapter was first published in *Representations* 53 (Winter 1996), 1–20.

3 The conjuncture of oral uses of memory in the Elizabethan story-telling culture, although obvious, harbors problems that can scarcely be hinted at in the present context. For one thing, the functions of memory in oral and in literate types of articulation need to be differentiated, especially as far as in each case diverse modes of authorization were involved. Over long periods in early medieval history, two distinct ways of verification and legitimation of past 'truth' existed side by side. As M. T. Clanchy has cogently demonstrated, there was, on the one hand, the "simple and personal" use of recollection, "the living memory voiced by wise men of age and experience" and, on the other hand, "the literate preference for the artificial memory of written record" (*From Memory to Written Record* 233). But in imaginative types of discourse, the uses of memory and the grounds of its validity and efficacy were even more intricate and encompassing. As Hans-Georg Gadamer reminds us, "Mnemosyne ist die Mutter aller Musen" ("Unterwegs zur Schrift?" 19). The goddess of Mneme, more ancient than most deities, sanctions a cultural practice that mothers all the muses, that precedes writing and yet is constitutive of its use as a memorial aid to those who know – which contradiction is at the heart of Plato's *Phaedrus* 274–78. In view of these distinctions it seems unacceptable to talk of 'memory' as a unified cultural phenomenon and to treat it *tout court* as "a child of the alphabet" designed "to fix the flow of speech in phonetic transcription" (Illich and Sanders, *ABC* 15).

4 There are a number of further studies in Shakespeare's endings, such as R. S. White, *Shakespeare and the Romance Ending*; Craik, "'You that way; we this way'"; and Jensen, *Shakespeare and the Ends of Comedy*, but these do not pursue the question of the threshold – one is tempted to say surprisingly so, when for instance Craik views the epilogue to *The Tempest* as "a subtle amalgam of Prospero and Actor-of-Prospero" (54) or when Jensen emphatically objects to both the thematic and the festive "preoccupation with the endings of the romantic comedies" (2) and resists "a critical emphasis on closure" (6), refusing to locate meaning "primarily in closure" (9).

5 To use Iser's rendering of the concept of *Rezeptionsvorgabe*, as developed by Naumann, Schlenstedt, and Barck, *Gesellschaft Literatur Lesen. Literatur-*

rezeption in theoretischer Sicht 35. In Shakespeare criticism, the most searching study of such theatrical "prefigurements" is, despite its somewhat narrow, intrinsic focus, *Sympathielenkung in den Dramen Shakespeares*, Habicht and Schabert (eds.).

6 A further explanation – necessarily conjectural – could be offered if we assume that spectators were free to enter the playhouse late in the course of the performance. For them (as well as for inattentive listeners) a fanfare argument of the play in conclusion might stimulate a desire to return.

7 See Thirsk, *Economic Policy and Projects* 8, 13, 176–77, who suggests that economic data, including Gregory King's estimate of "the annual consumption of apparel" and similar goods in 1688 (ten million pairs of stockings, eight million pairs of gloves and mittens, almost five million hats and caps were bought per year) can be used to illuminate corresponding patterns of an early consumer culture in Elizabethan England. For important links between the theatre and the expanding market for consumption, see Agnew, *Worlds Apart*; Bruster, *Drama and the Market in the Age of Shakespeare*.

8 Fuhrmann, "Lizenzen und Tabus des Lachens," esp. 101.

9 This indebtedness is strongly underlined by critics such as Salingar, *Shakespeare and the Traditions of Comedy* 76–174; and more recently, Riehle, *Shakespeare, Plautus, and the Humanist Tradition*.

10 For these earlier models of recollection see Stock, *The Implications of Literacy*; further Assmann, "Der Kampf der Erinnerungen in Shakespeares Historien" 56. Again, the point is that in the history plays there are diverse and partially antagonistic patterns of recollection (see note 3 to this chapter): "Feudal memoria," whose self-destructive vehicles are *nemesis* and *fama*, gives way to an "impulse of recollection" that surrenders the murderous self-perpetuating memories of victimage and revenge in favor of a larger national (no longer lineage-tied) and personalized function of 'memoria.'

11 Again, this is not an exhaustive listing of the uses of Elizabethan epilogues, as Elam has perceptively sketched them; see *Shakespeare's Universe of Discourse* 37–40.

12 For the ensuing "field of tension" between the text and its reception, see Engler, "Über den Applaus bei Shakespeare" 93 and his reference (*ibid.*) to Hawkes' pioneering study, *Shakespeare's Talking Animals*.

13 Cope, *The Theater and the Dream*. Against the background of Florentine Platonism, Cope suggestively relates the "double vision" in "theatrical space" to a concept of diabasis: a transition, an action of crossing over – where "process and product fuse," – is made to "turn inside out" (2) so as to bridge, through the theatrical transaction, the verbal and the non-verbal. For a further development of the dialectic in question, see Mooney, *Shakespeare's Dramatic Transactions*.

14 Whatever critical interest thresholds have recently received is predominantly in aid of the cultural politics associated with performance art, artists, and theoreticians. See, for example, the stimulating collection *Of Borders and Thresholds*, Kobialka (ed.), which – despite "Theatre History" in its subtitle – has virtually nothing to say about pre-eighteenth-century drama and, with the exception of Roach's "Territorial Passages" (110–24), not too much about liminality in the

theatre. As McKenzie notes in another recent collection, "In the beginning of performance studies was limen, and in its end(s) as well" (*The Ends of Performance*, Phelan and Lane [eds.], 219). The trouble with these uses of liminality is that by now they constitute something normative, what McKenzie calls "the liminal-norm": "the liminal-norm refers to any situation wherein the valorization of transgression itself becomes normative" (*ibid.*). For a further collection relevant in this context, see *Border Theory*, Michaelsen and Johnson (eds.).

15 Among the most influential, see Turner, *From Ritual to Theatre*, esp. 20–60, and Schechner, *Between Theater and Anthropology, passim*. In Shakespeare studies, see Montrose's brilliant foray, subtitled "Reflections on a Shakespearean Anthropology," and Iser's essay on *As You Like It* in his highly suggestive *Prospecting. From Reader Response to Literary Anthropology*, 98–130.

16 See van Gennep, *The Rites of Passage*, esp. chap. 1.

AFTERWORD

1 John Webster, "To his beloved friend, Master Thomas Heywood" in Lucas (ed.), *The Complete Works of John Webster* 2:260.

Works cited

PRIMARY LITERATURE

The Acts and Monuments of John Foxe, Cattley, Stephen Reed (ed.), London: Seeley and Burnside, 1838

Bancroft, Richard, *A Sermon Preached at Paul's Cross*, London,1588

Beaumont, Francis, *The Knight of the Burning Pestle*, Sheldon P. Zitner (ed.), Manchester University Press, 1984

The Dramatic Works in the Beaumont and Fletcher Canon, Bowers, Fredson (ed.), 4 vols., Cambridge University Press, 1976

Brome, Richard, *Antipodes*, Ann Haaker (ed.), Lincoln: University of Nebraska Press, 1966

Castiglione, Baldassare, *The Book of the Courtier*, Hoby, Thomas (trans.), Whitfield, J. H. (ed.), London: Dent, 1975

The Castle of Perseverance, The Macro Plays, Eccles, Mark (ed.), EETS, 262 (1969)

Chapman, George, *The Plays of George Chapman: The Tragedies. A Critical Edition*, Holaday, Allan (ed.), Cambridge: D. S. Brewer, 1987

Chief Pre-Shakespearean Dramas, Adams, Joseph Quincy (ed.), Boston: Houghton Mifflin, 1924

The Civile Conversation of M. Steeven Guazzo, Pettie, George (trans.) (the first three books) and Young, Bartholomew (the fourth), Sullivan, Edward (ed.), repr. New York: AMS Press, 1967

Dekker, Thomas, *The Gull's Horn Book, The Non-Dramatic Works of Thomas Dekker*, 5 vols., Grosart, Alexander B. (ed.), New York: Russell and Russell, 1963

Florio, John, *First Fruites*, London: Printed by Thomas Dawson for Thomas Woodcocke, 1578

Gayton, Edmund, *Pleasant Notes Upon Don Quixote*, London: William Hunt, 1654

Greene's Groatsworth of Wit. Bought With a Million of Repentance, Carroll, D. Allen. (ed.), Binghamton: Medieval and Renaissance Texts and Studies, 1994

Guilpin, Everard, *Skialetheia or A Shadowe of Truth in Certaine Epigrams and Satyres*, Carroll, D. Allen (ed.), Chapel Hill: University of North Carolina Press, 1974

Hall, Joseph, *Virgidemiarum* (1597), *The Works*, Philip Wynter (ed.), vol. 9, Oxford, 1863, AMS Press repr., 1969

Harvey, Gabriel, *Letter Book*, Scott, E. J. L. (ed.), Camden Society Publications,

33, (1884)

Henslowe's Diary, Foakes, R. A. and Rickert, R. T. (eds.), Cambridge University Press, 1968

Heywood, Thomas, *The Golden Age, The Dramatic Works of Thomas Heywood*, vol. 3, London: J. Pearson, 1874, rpt. New York: Russell & Russell, 1964, 1–79

An Apology for Actors, facsimile edition, New York: Garland Publishing, Inc., 1973

Hobbes, Thomas, *Leviathan* (1651), New York: Dutton, 1950

Three Tudor Classical Interludes, Marie Axton (ed.), Cambridge: Brewer, 1982

Jones, Richard, Preface to *Tamburlaine the Great*, Cunningham, J. S. (ed.), Manchester University Press, 1981

Jonson, Ben, *Ben Jonson*, 11 vols., Herford, C. H. and Simpson, Percy and Evelyn (eds.), Oxford: Clarendon Press, 1925–52

Lupton, Thomas, *All for Money*, London: Roger Warde and Richard Mundee, 1578

Lyly, John, *The Complete Works of John Lyly*, 3 vols., Bond, Warwick R. (ed.), Oxford: Clarendon Press, 1902

Marlowe, Christopher, *The Complete Works of Christopher Marlowe*, 2 vols., Bowers, Fredson (ed.), Cambridge University Press, 1973

The Works of Christopher Marlowe, Tucker Brooke, C. F. (ed.), Oxford: Clarendon Press, 1925

Tamburlaine the Great, Cunningham, J. S. (ed.), Manchester University Press, 1981, 111

Tamburlaine. Parts One and Two, Dawson, Anthony B. (ed.), London: A & C Black, 1997

Marston, John, *Histriomastix. Or, The Player Whip't*, London: T. Thorpe, 1610

Jacke Drums Entertainment, The Tudor Facsimile Texts, London: Printed for Richard Olive, 1601

The Middle-English Harrowing of Hell and Gospel of Nicodemus, Hulme, William Henry (ed.), EETS, E.S. 100 (1907)

Milton, John, *Samson Agonistes, The Poems of John Milton*, Carey, John and Fowler, Alastair (eds.), London: Longmans and Green, 1968

More, Thomas, *The History of King Richard III*, Sylvester, Richard (ed.), Yale Edition, vol. 2, New Haven: Yale University Press, 1963

New and Choise Characters, of seueral authors: together with The Wife, written by Syr. T. Overburie, London: T. Creede for L. Lisle, 1615

North, Thomas, *Plutarch's Lives of the Noble Grecians and Romans. Englished by Sir Thomas North* (1579), Wyndham, George (ed.), New York: AMS Press, 1967

Peacham, Henry, *The Complete Gentleman* [etc.], Heltzel, Virgil B. (ed.), Ithaca: Cornell University Press, 1962

Prynne, William, *Histrio-Mastix. The Player's Scourge or, Actor's Tragedy* (1633), 2 vols., New York: Jonson repr., 1972

Puttenham, George, *The Arte of English Poesie*, Arber, Edward (ed.), London: Murray, 1869

Read, Conyers (ed.), *William Lambarde and Local Government: His "Ephemeries" and Twenty-nine Charges to Juries and Commissions*, Ithaca: Cornell University Press, 1962

The Return from Parnassus, The Three Parnassus Plays (1598–1601), Leishman, J.B. (ed.), London: Nicholson & Watson, 1949

The School of Shakespeare, 2 vols., Simpson, Richard (ed.), London: Chatto and Windus, 1878

Serlio, Sebastiano, *The First Booke of Architecture*, London: Printed by Simon Stafford and Thomas Snodham for Robert Peake, 1611

Riverside Shakespeare, 2nd edn., Evans, Blakemore (ed.), Boston: Houghton Mifflin, 1997

The First Folio of Shakespeare, Hinman, Charlton (ed.), 2nd. edn., New York: W. W. Norton, 1996

Shakespeare, William, *All's Well that End's Well*, Hunter, G. K. (ed.), "The Arden Shakespeare," London: Methuen, 1959

The Tragicall Historie of Hamlet Prince of Denmarke (1603), London, printed for N. L. and Iohn Trundell, *Bodley Head Quartos* series, London: John Lane, 1922

Hamlet. The First Quarto, 1603, Weiner, Albert (ed.), Great Neck, N. Y.: Barron's Educational Series, 1962

The First Quarto of Hamlet, Irace, Kathleen O. (ed.), Cambridge University Press, 1998

Hamlet, Wilson, John Dover (ed.), "The New Cambridge Shakespeare," Cambridge University Press, 1934

Hamlet, Jenkins, Harold (ed.), "The Arden Shakespeare," London: Methuen, 1982

Hamlet: Prince of Denmark, Edwards, Philip (ed.), "The New Cambridge Shakespeare," Cambridge University Press, 1985

Hamlet, Hibbard, G. R. (ed.), Oxford: Clarendon Press, 1987

Hamlet, Mowat, Barbara and Werstine, Paul (eds.), "The Folger Shakespeare," New York: Washington Square Press, 1992

The Three-Text Hamlet, Bertram, Paul and Kliman, Bernice W. (eds.), New York: AMS Press, 1991

King Henry V, Gurr, Andrew (ed.), "The New Cambridge Shakespeare," Cambridge University Press, 1992

King Richard III., Antony Hammond, (ed.), Arden Edition, London: Methuen, 1981

Macbeth, Hunter, G. K. (ed.), Harmondsworth: Penguin Books, 1967

Measure for Measure, Gibbons, Brian (ed.), Cambridge University Press, 1991

Troilus and Cressida, Palmer, Kenneth (ed.), "The Arden Shakespeare," Methuen: London, 1982

Sidney, Philip, *The Prose Works of Sir Philip Sidney*, 4 vols., Feuillerat, Albert (ed.), Cambridge University Press, 1912

Spenser, Edmund, *The Poetical Works of Edmund Spenser*, Smith, J. C. and de Selincourt, E. (eds.), London: Oxford University Press, 1912

Stephens, John, *Satyrical Essayes Characters and Others*, Second Impression, London: Printed by E. Allde for Phillip Knight, 1615

Stockwood, John, *A Sermon Preached at Paules Crosse*, London: Henry Bynneman for George Byshop, 1578

The Towneley Plays, England, George and Pollard, A. W. (eds.), EETS, E.S. 71 (1897)

Wapull, George, *The Tide Tarrieth No Man*, Rühl, Ernst (ed.), *Shakespeare Jahrbuch* 43 (1907), 1–52

Webster, John (*c.* 1580–*c.* 1634), *The Complete Works of John Webster*, 4 vols., Lucas, F. L. (ed.), London: Chatto and Windus, 1927

Webster, John (1610–1682), *Academiarum Examen* (1653), *Science and Education in the Seventeenth Century: The Webster-Ward Debate*, Debus, Allen (ed.), London: Macdonald, 1970

Wever, Richard, *An Enterlude Called Lusty Juventus*, ed. Helen Scarborough Thomas ("The Renaissance Imagination," vol. 2), New York: Garland, 1982

York Plays, Smith, L. T. (ed.), Oxford: Clarendon Press, 1885

SECONDARY LITERATURE

Agnew, Jean-Christophe, *Worlds Apart: the Market and the Theater in Anglo-American Thought, 1550–1750*, Cambridge University Press, 1986

Alter, Jean, *A Sociosemiotic Theory of Theatre*, Philadelphia: University of Pennsylvania Press, 1990

Altman, Joel B., "The Practice of Shakespeare's Text," *Style* 23 (1989), 466–500

Anderson, Perry, *Lineages of the Absolutist State*, London: New Left Books, 1974

Armstrong, Paul B., "Play and Cultural Difference," *The Kenyon Review* 13 (1991), 157–71

Armstrong, W. A., *The Elizabethan Private Theatres: Facts and Problems*, London: Printed for the Society of Theatre Research, 1958

Assmann, Aleida, "Der Kampf der Erinnerungen in Shakespeares Historien," *Shakespeare Jahrbuch*, 1994, 44–46

Assmann, Aleida, et al. (eds.), *Schrift und Gedächtnis. Beiträge zur Archäologie der literarischen Kommunikation I*, München: Fink, 1983

Astington, John H. "The Red Lion Playhouse: Two Notes," *Shakespeare Quarterly* 36 (1985), 456–57

"The London Stage in the 1580s," *The Elizabethan Theatre* 11 (1990), 1–18

Astington, John H. (ed.), *The Development of Shakespeare's Theater*, New York: AMS Press, 1992

Aston, Elaine and Savona, George, *Theatre as Sign-System: A Semiotics of Text and Performance*, London: Routledge, 1991

Auslander, Philip, *From Acting to Performance: Essays in Modernism and Postmodernism*, London: Routledge, 1997

Bakhtin, Mikhail, *The Dialogic Imagination*, Holquist, Michael and Emerson, Caryl (trans.), Austin: University of Texas Press, 1981

Baldo, Jonathan, *The Unmasking of Drama: Contested Representation in Shakespeare's Tragedies*, Detroit: Wayne State University Press, 1996

Barber, C. L., *Shakespeare's Festive Comedy: A Study of Dramatic Form and its Relation to Social Custom*, Princeton University Press, 1959

Barish, Jonas, *The Antitheatrical Prejudice*, Berkeley: University of California Press, 1981

Barroll, Leeds, *Politics, Plague and Shakespeare's Theater: The Stuart Years*, Ithaca: Cornell University Press, 1991

Baskerville, C. R., *The Elizabethan Jig*, University of Chicago Press, 1929

Beckerman, Bernard, *Shakespeare at the Globe, 1599–1609*, New York: Macmillan, 1962

Belsey, Catherine, *The Subject of Tragedy*, London: Methuen, 1985

Benjamin, Walter, "The Work of Art in the Age of Mechanical Reproduction," *Illuminations*, Arendt, Hannah (ed.), Zohn, Harry (trans.), New York: Harcourt, Brace & World, 1968, 217–251

Bennett, Susan, *Theatre Audiences: A Theory of Production and Reception*, second ed., New York: Routledge, 1997

Bentley, G. E., *The Profession of Player in Shakespeare's Time, 1590–1642*, Princeton University Press, 1984

Berger, Harry, Jr., "Bodies and Texts," *Representations* 17 (1987), 144–166
  Imaginary Audition: Shakespeare on Stage and Page, Berkeley, University of California Press, 1989
  Making Trifles of Terrors, Peter Erickson, (ed.), Stanford University Press, 1997
  "The Prince's Dog: Falstaff and the Perils of Speech-Prefixity," *Shakespeare Quarterly* 49 (1998), 40–73

Bethell, S. L., *Shakespeare and the Popular Dramatic Tradition*, Durham, N. C.: Duke University Press, 1944

Bevington, David, *From "Mankind" to Marlowe: Growth of Structure in the Popular Drama of Tudor England*, Cambridge, MA: Harvard University Press, 1962
  Tudor Drama and Politics: A Critical Approach to Topical Meaning, Cambridge, MA: Harvard University Press, 1968
  "Determining the Indeterminate: The Oxford Shakespeare," *Shakespeare Quarterly* 38 (1987), 501–519

Bhabha, Homi K., *The Location of Culture*, London: Routledge, 1994

Bharucha, Rustom, *Theatre and the World: Performance and the Politics of Culture*, London: Routledge, 1993

Blackstone, Mary A., "Patrons and Elizabethan Acting Companies," *Elizabethan Theatre* 10 (1988), 112–32

Blau, Herbert, *To All Appearances: Ideology and Performance,* London: Routledge, 1992

Boose, Lynda E. and Burt, Richard (eds.), *Shakespeare, the Movie: Popularizing the Plays on Film, TV, and Video*, London: Routledge, 1997

Bradbrook, Muriel, *The Rise of the Common Player: A Study of Actor and Society in Shakespeare's England*, London: Chatto & Windus, 1962

Bradley, David, *From Text to Performance in the Elizabethan Theatre: Preparing the Play for the Stage*, Cambridge University Press, 1992

Braider, Christopher, *Refiguring the Real: Picture and Modernity in Word and Image, 1400–1700*, Princeton University Press, 1993

Bristol, Michael D., *Carnival and Theater: Plebeian Culture and the Structure of Authority in Renaissance England*, London: Methuen 1985
  Shakespeare's America / America's Shakespeare, London: Routledge, 1990
  "The Festive Agon: The Politics of Carnival," *Twelfth Night: New Casebooks*,

White, R. S. (ed.), New York: St. Martin's Press, 1996

Big-time Shakespeare, London: Routledge, 1996

Brown, John Russell, *Shakespeare's Plays in Performance*, rev. edn., New York: Applause, 1993

Brownlee, Marina S. and Gumbrecht, Hans Ulrich (eds.), *Cultural Authority in Golden Age Spain*, Baltimore: Johns Hopkins University Press, 1995

Bruster, Douglas, *Drama and the Market in the Age of Shakespeare*, Cambridge University Press, 1992

"Local *Tempest*: Shakespeare and the Work of the Early Modern Playhouse," *The Journal of Medieval and Renaissance Studies* 25 (1995), 33–53

"The Structural Transformation of Print in Late Elizabethan England," *Print and the Other Media in Early Modern England,* Marotti, Arthur and Bristol, Michael (eds.), Columbus: Ohio State University Press, 2000, forthcoming

Bullough, Geoffrey (ed.), *Narrative and Dramatic Sources of Shakespeare*, 8 vols., London: Routledge and Kegan Paul, 1973

Bulman, James (ed.), *Shakespeare, Theory, and Performance*, London: Routledge, 1996

Burke, Peter, *Popular Culture in Early Modern Europe*, rev. edn. repr., Hants: Scolar Press, 1994

Bush, Douglas, *English Literature in the Earlier Seventeenth Century, 1600–1660*, Oxford History of English Literature, vol. 5, Oxford: Clarendon Press, 1962

Butler, Judith. *Gender Trouble: Feminism and the Subversion of Identity*, London: Routledge, 1990

Carlson, Marvin, *Places of Performance: The Semiotics of Theatre Architecture*, Ithaca: Cornell University Press: 1989

Theatre Semiotics: Signs of Life, Bloomington: Indiana University Press, 1990

Performance: A Critical Introduction, London: Routledge, 1996

Casey, Edward S., *Getting Back into Place: Toward a Renewed Understanding of the Place-World*, Bloomington: Indiana University Press, 1993

The Fate of Place: A Philosophical History, Berkeley: The University of California Press, 1997

Castoriadis, Cornelius, *The Imaginary Institution of Society*, Blamey, Kathleen (trans.), Cambridge, MA: MIT Press, 1998

Chambers, E. K., *The Elizabethan Stage*, 4 vols., Oxford: Clarendon Press, 1923

William Shakespeare: A Study of Facts and Problems, 2 vols., Oxford: Clarendon Press, 1930

Charney, Maurice (ed.), *'Bad' Shakespeare: Revaluations of the Shakespeare Canon*, Rutherford: Fairleigh Dickinson University Press, 1988

Chartier, Roger, *The Cultural Uses of Print in Early Modern France*, Cochrane, Lydia G. (trans.), Princeton University Press, 1987

Clanchy, M. T., *From Memory to Written Record*, London: Arnold, 1979

Clark, Peter, *English Provincial Society from the Reformation to the Revolution: Religion, Politics, and Society in Kent, 1500–1640*, Hassocks, Sussex: County Council, 1977

Clayton, Thomas (ed.), *The 'Hamlet' First Published (Q1 1603): Origins, Form, Intertextuality*, Newark: University of Delaware Press, 1992

Clemen, Wolfgang, *A Commentary on Shakespeare's Richard III*, Bonheim, Jean (trans.), London: Methuen, 1968

Clopper, Lawrence M. (ed.), *Records of Early English Drama: Chester*, University of Toronto Press, 1979

Cohen, Philip, Introduction, *Devils and Angels: Textual Editing and Literary Theory*, Cohen, Philip (ed.), Charlottesville: University of Virginia Press, 1991, ix–xviii

Cohen, Philip and Jackson, David H., "Notes on Emerging Paradigms in Editorial Theory," *Devils and Angels: Textual Editing and Literary Theory*, Cohen, Philip (ed.), 1991, 103–123

Cohen, Robert, *Acting in Shakespeare*, Mountain View, CA: Mayfield, 1991

  "'Be Your Tears Wet?': Tears (and Acting) in Shakespeare," *Journal of Dramatic Theory and Criticism*, 10 (1996), 21–30

Cole, Richard G., "The Dynamics of Printing in the Sixteenth Century," *The Social History of the Reformation*, Buck, Lawrence P. and Zophy, Jonathan W. (eds.), Columbus: Ohio State University Press, 1972, 93–105

Collinson, Patrick, *From Iconoclasm to Iconophobia: The Cultural Impact of the Second English Reformation*, The Stetson Lecture, 1985, University of Reading Press, 1986

  The Birthpangs of Protestant England: Religious and Cultural Change in the Sixteenth and Seventeenth Centuries, London: Macmillan, 1988

  The Elizabethan Puritan Movement, Oxford: Clarendon Press, 1990

Cook, Albert, "Space and Culture," *New Literary History* 29 (1998), 551–72

Cook, Ann Jennalie, *The Privileged Playgoers of Shakespeare's London, 1576–1642*, Princeton University Press, 1981

Cope, Jackson I., *The Theater and the Dream: From Metaphor to Form in Renaissance Drama*, Baltimore: Johns Hopkins University Press, 1973

  Dramaturgy of the Daemonic, Baltimore: Johns Hopkins University Press, 1984

Counsell, Colin, *Signs of Performance: An Introduction to Twentieth-Century Theatre*, London: Routledge, 1996

Cox, John D. and Kastan, David Scott (eds.), *A New History of Early English Drama*, New York: Columbia University Press, 1997

Craik, T. W., "'You that way; we this way': Shakespeare's Endings," *Mirror up to Shakespeare: Essays in Honor of G. R. Hibbard*, University of Toronto Press, 1984, 44–54

Crary, Jonathan, *Techniques of the Observer: On Vision and Modernity in the Nineteenth Century*, Cambridge, MA: MIT Press, 1990

De Certeau, Michel, *The Practice of Everyday Life*, trans. Steven F. Rendall, Berkeley: University of California Press, 1984

De Grazia, Margreta, *Shakespeare Verbatim: The Reproduction of Authenticity and the 1790 Apparatus*, Oxford: Clarendon Press, 1991

De Grazia, Margreta and Stallybrass, Peter, "The Materiality of the Shakespearean Text," *Shakespeare Quarterly* 44 (1993), 255–83

De Man, Paul, *Allegories of Reading: Figural Language in Rousseau, Nietzsche, Rilke, and Proust*, New Haven: Yale University Press, 1979

De Marinis, Marco, *The Semiotics of Performance*, O'Healy, Aine (trans.), Bloomington: Indiana University Press, 1993

De Quincey, Thomas, "On the Knocking on the Gate in *Macbeth*," *Shakespeare: 'Macbeth.' A Casebook*, Wain, John (ed.), Nashville: Aurora, 1969, 90–93

Derrida, Jacques, *Writing and Difference*, Bass, Alan (trans.), University of Chicago Press, 1978

Dews, Peter, *Logics of Disintegration: Post-structuralist Thought and the Claims of Critical Theory*, London: Verso, 1987

Diamond, Elin (ed.), *Performance and Cultural Politics*, London: Routledge, 1996
 Unmaking Mimesis: Essays on Feminism and Theater, London: Routledge, 1997

Diehl, Huston, *Staging Reform, Reforming the Stage: Protestantism and Popular Theater in Early Modern England*, Ithaca: Cornell University Press, 1997

Dobson, Michael, *The Making of the National Poet: Shakespeare, Adaptation and Authorship, 1660–1769*, Oxford: Clarendon Press, 1992

Dollimore, Jonathan, *Radical Tragedy: Religion, Ideology and Power in the Drama of Shakespeare and his Contemporaries*, Brighton: Harvester Press, 1984

Drakakis, John, "'Fashion it thus': *Julius Caesar* and the Politics of Theatrical Representation," *Shakespeare Survey* 44 (1992), 65–73

Duthie, G. I., *The 'Bad' Quarto of Hamlet: A Critical Study*, Cambridge University Press, 1941

Dutton, Richard, "The Birth of the Author," *Texts and Cultural Change in Early Modern England*, Brown, Cedric C. and Marotti, Arthur F. (eds.), Basingstoke: Macmillan, 1997, 153–78

Elam, Keir, *The Semiotics of Theatre and Drama*, London: Methuen, 1980
 Shakespeare's Universe of Discourse: Language Games in the Comedies, Cambridge University Press, 1984
 "The Wars of the Texts," *Shakespeare Studies* 24 (1996), 81–92

Elton, G. R. *The Tudor Revolution in Government: Administrative Changes in the Reign of Henry VIII*, Cambridge University Press, 1953
 Policy and Police: The Enforcement of the Reformation in the Age of Thomas Cromwell, Cambridge University Press, 1972

Elton, G. R. (ed.), *The Tudor Constitution*, second edn., Cambridge University Press, 1982

Engler, Balz, "Über den Applaus bei Shakespeare," *Shakespeare Jahrbuch* 1993, 85–98

Evans, Malcolm, *Signifying Nothing: Truth's True Contents in Shakespeare's Text*, Brighton: Harvester Press, 1986

Ewbank, Inga-Stina, "The Word in the Theater," *Shakespeare, Man of the Theater*, Muir, Kenneth, Halio, Jay L., and Palmer, D. J. (eds.), Newark: University of Delaware Press, 1983, 55–76

Faas, Ekbert, *Shakespeare's Poetics*, Cambridge University Press, 1986

Ferguson, Arthur B., *The Articulate Citizen and the English Renaissance*, Durham: Duke University Press, 1965

Finkelpearl, Philip, "John Marston's *Histrio-Mastix* as an Inns of Court Play: A Hypothesis," *Huntington Library Quarterly* 29 (1966), 223–34
 John Marston of the Middle Temple: An Elizabethan Dramatist in his Social Setting, Cambridge, MA: Harvard University Press, 1969

Finnegan, Ruth, *Literacy and Orality: Studies in the Technology of Communication*, Oxford: Blackwell, 1988

"Literacy as Mythical Charter," *Literacy: Interdisciplinary Conversations*, Keller-Cohen, Deborah (ed.), Creskill, NJ: Hampton Press, 1994, 31–48

Fischer-Lichte, Erika, "Performance as Art – Art as Performance," *Interart Poetics: Essays on the Interrelations of the Arts and Media*, Lagerroth, Ulla-Britta, Lund, Hans, and Hedling, Erik (eds.), Amsterdam: Editions Rodopi, 1997, 69–84

Fletcher, Anthony and Stevenson, John (eds.), *Order and Disorder in Early Modern England*, Cambridge University Press

Foakes, R. A., *"The Player's Passion:* Some Notes on Elizabethan Psychology and Acting," *Essays and Studies* 7 (1954), 62–77

Forte, Jeanie, "Focus on the Body: Pain, Praxis, and Pleasure in Feminist Performance," *Critical Theory and Performance*, Reinelt and Roach (eds.), 248–62

Friedenreich, Kenneth et al. (eds.), *"A poet and a filthy playmaker": New Essays on Christopher Marlowe*, New York: AMS Press, 1988

Frye, Northrop, *A Natural Perspective: The Development of Shakespearean Comedy and Romance*, New York and London, 1965

Fuhrmann, Manfred, "Lizenzen und Tabus des Lachens: Zur sozialen Grammatik der hellenistisch-römischen Komödie," *Das Komische*, Preisendanz, Wolfgang and Warning, Rainer (eds.), München: Fink, 1976, 65–101

Gadamer, Hans-Georg, "Unterwegs zur Schrift?," *Schrift und Gedächtnis. Beiträge zur Archäologie der literarischen Kommunikation*, Aleida and Jan Assmann (eds.), Munich: Fink, 1983, 10–19

Garber, Marjorie, "Descanting on Deformity: *Richard III* and the Shape of History," *The Historical Renaissance: New Essays on Tudor and Stuart Literature and Culture*, Dubrow, Heather and Strier, Richard (eds.), University of Chicago Press, 1988, 79–103

Geckle, George L., *John Marston's Drama: Themes, Images, Sources*, London/Toronto: Associated University Presses, 1980

Gennep, Arnold van, *The Rites of Passage*, Vizedom, Monika B. and Caffe, Gabrielle L. (trans.), University of Chicago Press, 1960

Gildersleeve, Virginia Crocheron, *Government Regulation of the Elizabethan Drama*, New York: Burt Franklin, 1908

Girard, René, *La Violence et le sacré*, Paris: Grasset, 1972

Goldberg, Rose Lee, *Performance Art: From Futurism to the Present*, New York: Harry N. Abrams, 1988

Goldman, Michael, *The Actor's Freedom: Towards a Theory of Drama*, New York: Viking Press, 1975

"Acting Values and Shakespearean Meaning: Some Suggestions," *Shakespeare: Pattern of Excelling Nature*, Bevington, David, and Halio, Jay L. (eds.), Newark: University of Delaware Press, 1978, 190–97

Goldstein, Leonard, "On the Transition from Formal to Naturalistic Acting in the Elizabethan and Post-Elizabethan Theatre," *Bulletin. New York Public Library* 62 (1958), 330–49

Gondris, Joanna (ed.), *Reading Readings: Essays on Shakespeare Editing in the Eighteenth Century*, Fairleigh Dickinson University Press, 1998

Goody, Jack, *The Logic of Writing and the Organization of Society*, Cambridge University Press, 1987

Graff, Harvey J., *The Labyrinths of Literacy: Reflections on Literacy Past and Present*, London: The Falmer Press, 1987

Greenblatt, Stephen, *Renaissance Self-Fashioning: From More to Shakespeare*, University of Chicago Press, 1980

Shakespearean Negotiations: The Circulation of Social Energy in Renaissance England, Oxford: Clarendon Press, 1988

Greenfield, Peter H., "Professional Players at Gloucester: Conditions of Provincial Performing," *The Elizabethan Theatre* 10 (1998), 73–92

Greg, W. W., *Shakespeare's First Folio: Its Bibliographical and Textual History*, Oxford: Clarendon Press, 1955

Grudin, C. F. Robert, *Mighty Opposites: Shakespeare and Renaissance Contrariety*, Berkeley: University of California Press, 1979

Gurr, Andrew, "Who Strutted and Bellowed?" *Shakespeare Survey* 16 (1963), 95–102

"Elizabethan Action," *Studies in Philology* 63 (1966), 144–56

The Shakespearean Stage 1574–1642, third edn., Cambridge University Press, 1992

"The Bare Island," *Shakespeare Survey* 47 (1994), 29–43

Playgoing in Shakespeare's London, second edn., Cambridge University Press, 1996

Habicht, Werner and Schabert, Ina (eds.), *Sympathielenkung in den Dramen Shakespeares. Studien zur publikumsbezogenen Dramaturgie*, Munich: Fink, 1978

Haider-Pregler, Hilde, *Des sittlichen Bürgers Abendschule. Bildungsanspruch und Bildungsauftrag des Berufstheaters im 18. Jahrhundert*, Wien: Volk und Jugend, 1980

Halpern, Richard, *Shakespeare Among the Moderns*, Ithaca: Cornell University Press, 1997

Hanmer, Sir Thomas, "Preface to 'The Works of William Shakespeare,'" *Eighteenth Century Essays on Shakespeare*, Smith (ed.), 85–88

Harbage, Alfred, "Elizabethan Acting," *PMLA* 54 (1939), 685–708

Shakespeare and the Rival Traditions, New York: Macmillan Press, 1952

Shakespeare's Audience, New York: Columbia University Press, 1961

Annals of English Drama 975–1700, S. Schoenbaum, rev.; third edn., Sylvia S. Wagonheim, rev., London: Routledge, 1989

Harcourt, John B., "I Pray You, Remember the Porter," *Shakespeare Quarterly* 12 (1961), 393–402

Hattaway, Michael, *Elizabethan Popular Theatre: Plays in Performance*, London: Routledge and Kegan Paul, 1982

Havelock, E. A., *The Literate Revolution in Ancient Greece and its Cultural Consquences*, Princeton University Press, 1982

The Muse Learns to Write: Reflections on Orality and Literacy from Antiquity to the Present, New Haven: Yale University Press, 1986

and Hershbell, J. P., *Communication Arts in the Ancient World*, New York: Hastings House, 1978

Hawkes, Terence, *Shakespeare's Talking Animals: Language in Drama and Society*, London: Edward Arnold, 1973

Haynes, Jonathan, *The Social Relations of Jonson's Theatre*, Cambridge University Press, 1992

Hegel, G. F. W., *Ästhetik*, Bassenge, Friedrich (ed.), Berlin: Aufbau, 1955

Heidegger, Martin, "The Age of the World Picture," *The Question Concerning Technology and Other Essays*, Lovitt, William (trans.), New York: Harper and Row, 1977, 115–54

Helgerson, Richard, "Barbarous Tongues: The Ideology of Poetic Form in Renaissance England," *The Historical Renaissance: New Essays on Tudor and Stuart Literature and Culture*, Dubrow, Heather and Strier, Richard (eds.), University of Chicago Press, 1988, 273–92

Forms of Nationhood: The Elizabethan Writing of England, University of Chicago Press, 1992

Hibbard, G. R., "From 'iygging vaines of riming mother wits' to 'the spacious volubilitie of a drumming decasillabon'," *The Elizabethan Theatre* 11 (1990), 55–73

Hill, Christopher, *The Collected Essays of Christopher Hill*, 2 vols., Brighton: Harvester Press, 1985

Hillman, David, "Puttenham, Shakespeare, and the Abuse of Rhetoric," *Studies in English Literature* 36 (1996), 70–93

Hilton, Julian (ed.), *Performance*, London: Macmillan, 1987

New Directions in Theatre, London: Macmillan, 1993

Honigmann, E. A. J., *Shakespeare's Impact on His Contemporaries*, Totowa, NJ: Barnes and Noble, 1982

Myriad-minded Shakespeare, London: Macmillan, 1989

Howard, Jean, "Crossdressing, the Theatre, and Gender Struggle in Early Modern England," *Shakespeare Quarterly* 39 (1988), 418–40

The Stage and Social Struggle in Early Modern England, London: Routledge, 1994

Hurstfield, Joel, *Freedom, Corruption, and Government in Elizabethan England*, London: Cape, 1973

Hussey, S. S., *The Literary Language of Shakespeare*, London: Longman, 1982

Hutton, Ronald, *The Rise and Fall of Merry England: The Ritual Year 1400–1700*, Oxford University Press, 1994

Illich, Ivan and Sanders, Barry, *ABC: The Alphabetization of the Popular Mind*, New York: Random House, 1988

Ingram, Martin, *Church Courts, Sex and Marriage in England, 1570–1640*, Cambridge University Press, 1990

"Ridings, Rough Music and the 'Reform of Popular Culture' in Early Modern England," *Past and Present* 105 (1984), 79–113

Ingram, R. W., *John Marston*, Boston: Twayne Publishers, 1978

Ingram, R. W. (ed.), *Records of Early English Drama: Coventry*, University of Toronto Press, 1979

Ingram, William, *The Business of Playing: The Beginnings of the Adult Professional Theatre in Elizabethan London*, Ithaca: Cornell University Press, 1992

"The 'Evolution' of the Elizabethan Playing Company," *The Development of Shakespeare's Theater*, Astington (ed.), 13–28

Irace, Kathleen O., "Origins and Agents of Q1 *Hamlet*," *The 'Hamlet' First

Published, Clayton (ed.), 90–122

Reforming the 'Bad' Quartos: Performance and Provenance of Six Shakespearean First Editions, Newark: University of Delaware Press, 1994

Iser, Wolfgang, *Prospecting: From Reader Response to Literary Anthropology*, Baltimore: Johns Hopkins University Press, 1989

The Fictive and the Imaginary: Charting Literary Anthropology, Baltimore: Johns Hopkins University Press, 1993

Issacharoff, Michael and Jones, Robin F. (eds.), "Postscript or Pinch of Salt: Performance as Mediation or Deconstruction," *Performing Texts*, Philadelphia: University of Pennsylvania Press, 1988, 138–43

James, Mervyn, *Family, Lineage, and Civil Society: A Study of Society, Politics and Mentality in the Durham Region, 1500–1640*, Oxford: Clarendon Press, 1974

Jardine, Lisa, *Still Harping on Daughters: Women and Drama in the Age of Shakespeare*, New York: Columbia University Press, 1989

Jensen, Ejner J., *Shakespeare and the Ends of Comedy*, Bloomington: Indiana University Press, 1991

Johnson, Samuel, "Preface to 'The Works of William Shakespeare,'" *Eighteenth Century Essays on Shakespeare*, Smith (ed.), 104–50

Joseph, B. L., *Elizabethan Acting*, second edn., Oxford University Press, 1964

Jowett, John, "Johannes Factotum: Henry Chettle and *Greene's Groatsworth of Wit*," *Papers of the Bibliographical Society of America* 87 (1993), 453–86

Kastan, David Scott, "The Mechanics of Culture: Editing Shakespeare Today," *Shakespeare Studies* 24 (1996), 30–37

"Shakespeare after Theory," *Textus*, 9 (1997) pp. 357–74

Shakespeare after Theory, New York: Routledge, 1999

Kay, Dennis, "'To hear the rest untold': Shakespeare's Postponed Endings," *Renaissance Quarterly* 37 (1984), 207–27

Kearney, Richard, "Dialogue with Emmanuel Levinas," *Dialogues with Contemporary Continental Thinkers*, Manchester University Press, 1984, 47–70

Kendall, Ritchie D., *The Drama of Dissent: The Radical Poetics of Nonconformity, 1380–1599*, Chapel Hill: University of North Carolina Press, 1986

Kernan, Alvin, "John Marston's Play, *Histriomastix*," *Modern Language Quarterly* 19 (1958), 134–140

The Playwright as Magician: Shakespeare's Image of the Poet in the English Public Theater, New Haven: Yale University Press, 1979

Kernodle, G. R., *From Art to Theatre: Form and Convention in the Renaissance*, Chicago University Press, 1944

Kershaw, Baz, *The Politics of Performance: Radical Theatre as Cultural Intervention*, London: Routledge, 1992

Kiefer, Fredrick, *Writing on the Renaissance Stage: Written Words, Printed Pages, Metaphoric Books*, Newark: University of Delaware Press, 1996

Kiernan, Pauline, *Shakespeare's Theory of Drama*, Cambridge University Press, 1996

King, Pamela M., "Spatial Semantics and the Medieval Theatre," *The Theatrical Space*, "Themes in Drama" 9, Cambridge University Press, 1987, 45–58

Kirby, Kathleen M., *Indifferent Boundaries: Spatial Concepts of Human Subjectivity*, New York: The Guilford Press, 1996

Knapp, Robert S., *Shakespeare: The Theater and the Book*, Princeton University Press, 1989

Knights, L. C., *Drama and Society in the Age of Jonson*, Chicago: Northwestern University Press, 1971

Knutson, Roslyn L., *The Repertory of Shakespeare's Company 1594–1613*, Fayetteville: University of Arkansas Press, 1991

Kobialka, Michal (ed.), *Of Borders and Thresholds: Theatre History, Practice, and Theory*, Minneapolis: University of Minnesota Press, 1998

Koller, Hermann, *Mimesis in der Antike*, Bern: Francke, 1954

Konigson, Eli, *L'espace théâtral médiéval*, Paris: Editions du CNRS, 1975

Lacoue-Labarthe, Philippe, "Mimesis and Truth," *Diacritics* (March 1978), 10–23

Lamb, Charles, "On the Tragedies of Shakespeare, Considered with Reference to their Fitness for Stage Representation," *English Critical Essays: Nineteenth Century*, Jones, Edmund D. (ed.), London: Oxford University Press, 1934, 81–101

Lambropoulos, Vassilis, *The Rise of Eurocentrism: Anatomy of Interpretation*, Princeton University Press, 1993

Lancashire, Ian, *Dramatic Texts and Records of Britain: A Chronological Topography*, University of Toronto Press, 1984

Lanier, Douglas, "Drowning the Book: Prospero's Books and the Textual Shakespeare," *Shakespeare, Theory, and Performance*, Bulman (ed.), 187–209

Latham, M. W., *The Elizabethan Fairies: The Fairies of Folklore and the Fairies of Shakespeare*, New York: Columbia University Press, 1930

Law, R. A., "The Choruses in *Henry the Fifth*," *University of Texas Studies in English* 35 (1956), 11–21

Leech, Clifford, *Christopher Marlowe: Poet for the Stage*, Lancashire, Anne (ed.), New York: AMS Press, 1986

Lefebvre, Henri, *The Production of Space*, Nicholson-Smith, Donald (trans.), Oxford: Blackwell, 1991

Leggatt, Alexander, *Jacobean Public Theatre*, London: Routledge, 1992

Levenson, Jill L., "'Working Words': The Verbal Dynamic of *Tamburlaine*," *"A Poet and a filthy play-maker": New Essays on Christopher Marlowe*, Friedenreich et al. (eds.), 99–115

Levine, David, and Wrightson, Keith, *Poverty and Piety in an English Village: Terling, 1525–1700*, New York: Academic Press, 1979

Loengard, Janet S., "An Elizabethan Lawsuit: John Brayne, his Carpenter, and the Building of the Red Lion Theater," *Shakespeare Quarterly* 34 (1983), 298–310

Loughrey, Bryan, "Q1 in Recent Performance: An Interview," *The Hamlet First Published,* Clayton (ed.), 123–136

MacCaffrey, Wallace, *The Shaping of the Elizabethan Regime*, Princeton University Press, 1968

MacLean, Sally-Beth, "Tour Routes: 'Provincial Wanderings' or Traditional Circuits?" *Medieval and Renaissance Drama in England* 6 (1993), 1–14

Maguire, Laurie E., *Shakespearean Suspect Texts: The 'Bad' Quartos and Their Contexts*, Cambridge University Press, 1996

Mahood, M. M., *Shakespeare's Wordplay*, London: Methuen, 1957

Malone, Edmund, "A Life of the Poet," *The Plays and Poems of William Shake-*

speare, vol. 2, repr., New York: AMS Press, 1966

Manlove, Colin N., *The Gap in Shakespeare: The Motif of Division from "Richard II" to "The Tempest,"* London: Vision Press, 1981

Mann, David, *The Elizabethan Player: Contemporary Stage Representation*, London: Routledge, 1991

Marcus, Leah, "Shopping-Mall Shakespeare: Quartos, Folios, and Social Difference," *Huntington Library Quarterly* 58 (1996), 161–78

Unediting the Renaissance: Shakespeare, Marlowe, Milton, London: Routledge, 1996

Marker, Lise-Lone, "Nature and Decorum in the Theory of Elizabethan Acting," *The Elizabethan Theater* 2 (1970), 87–107

Martin, Jacqueline, *Voice in Modern Theatre*, London: Routledge, 1991

Maus, Katharine Eisaman, *Inwardness and the Theater in the English Renaissance*, University of Chicago Press, 1995

May, Todd, *Reconsidering Difference: Nancy, Derrida, Levinas, Deleuze*, Penn State University Press, 1998

McAlindon, Thomas, *Shakespeare and Decorum*, London: Macmillan, 1973

McGann, Jerome J., *A Critique of Modern Textual Criticism*, University of Chicago Press, 1983

McGuire, Philip C., "Which Fortinbras, Which *Hamlet?*" *The 'Hamlet' First Published*, Clayton (ed.), 151–78

McIntosh, Marjorie Keniston, *A Community Transformed: The Manor and Liberty of Havering, 1500–1620*, Cambridge University Press, 1991

McKenzie, Jon, "Genre Trouble: (The) Butler Did It," *The Ends of Performance*, Phelan and Lane (eds.), 217–35

McLuhan, Marshall, *Understanding Media: The Extensions of Man*, London: Sphere Books, 1967

McMillin, Scott, *The Elizabethan Theatre and 'The Book of Sir Thomas More,'* Ithaca: Cornell University Press, 1987

Michaelsen, Scott and Johnson, David E. (eds.), *Border Theory: The Limits of Cultural Politics*, Minneapolis: University of Minnesota Press, 1997

Miller, Jacqueline T., *Poetic License: Authority and Authorship in Medieval and Renaissance Contexts*, New York: Oxford University Press, 1986

Mitchell, W. J. T., *Iconology: Image, Texts, Ideology*, University of Chicago Press, 1986

Picture Theory: Essays on Verbal and Visual Representation, University of Chicago Press, 1994

Montrose, Louis, "The Purpose of Playing: Reflections on a Shakespearean Anthropology," *Helios* 7 (1980), 51–74

"New Historicisms," *Redrawing the Boundaries: The Transformation of English and American Studies*, Greenblatt, Stephen and Gunn, Giles (eds.), New York: Modern Language Association, 1992, 392–418

The Purpose of Playing: Shakespeare and the Cultural Politics of the Elizabethan Theatre, University of Chicago Press, 1996

Mooney, Michael E., *Shakespeare's Dramatic Transactions*, Durham: Duke University Press, 1990

Mowat, Barbara, "The Theater and Literary Culture," *A New History of Early*

English Drama, Cox and Kastan (eds.), 213–30

Muchembled, Robert, *Popular Culture and Elite Culture in France 1400–1750*, Cochrane, Lydia (trans.), Baton Rouge: Louisiana State University, 1984

Mullaney, Steven, *The Place of the Stage: License, Play, and Power in Renaissance England*, University of Chicago Press, 1988

Münz, Rudolf, *Das "andere" Theater: Studien über ein deutschsprachiges teatro dell'arte der Lessingzeit*, Berlin: Henschel, 1979

Murray, John Tucker, *English Dramatic Companies, 1558–1642*, 2 vols., New York: Russell & Russell, 1910

Murray, Timothy, *Theatrical Legitimation: Allegories of Genius in Seventeenth-Century England and France*, New York: Oxford University Press, 1987

Naumann, Manfred, Schlenstedt, Dieter, and Barck, Karl-Heinz, *Gesellschaft – Literatur – Lesen. Literaturrezeption in theoretischer Sicht*, Berlin: Aufbau, 1973

Nelson, Alan H. (ed.), *Records of Early English Drama: Cambridge*, 2 vols., University of Toronto Press, 1989

Neuss, Paula, "The Staging of *The Creacion of the World*," *Medieval English Drama: A Casebook*, Happé, Peter (ed.), London: Macmillan, 1984

Nicholson, Brinsley, "Kemp and the Play of *Hamlet* – Yorick and Tarlton – A Short Chapter in Dramatic History," *The New Shakspere Society's Transactions (1880–82)*, London: Trübner and Ludgate Hill, Part 1, 57–66

Ong, W. J., *The Presence of the Word*, New Haven: Yale University Press, 1967

Interfaces of the Word, Ithaca: Cornell University Press, 1977

Orgel, Stephen, "The Authentic Shakespeare," *Representations* 21 (1988), 1–25

Impersonations: The Performance of Gender in Shakespeare's England, Cambridge University Press, 1996

"What is an Editor?" *Shakespeare Studies* 24 (1996), 23–29

Orrell, John, "The Theaters," *A New History of Early English Drama*, Cox and Kastan (eds.), 93–112

Padel, Ruth, *Whom Gods Destroy: Elements of Greek and Tragic Madness*, Princeton University Press, 1995

Panofsky, Erwin, *Perspective as Symbolic Form*, Kwinter, Stanford (ed.), Wood, Christopher S. (trans.), Cambridge, MA: Zone Books, 1991

Parker, Andrew and Sedgwick, Eve Kosofsky (eds.), *Performativity and Performance,* "Essays from the English Institute," New York: Routledge, 1995

Patterson, Annabel, "Back by Popular Demand: The Two Versions of *Henry V*," *Renaissance Drama* 19 (1988), 29–62

Pavis, Patrice, "Performance Analysis: Space, Time, Action," *Gestos* 11:2 (1996), 11–32

Perry, Curtis, *The Making of Jacobean Culture: James I and the Renegotiation of Elizabethan Literary Practice*, Cambridge University Press, 1997

Pettitt, Thomas, "Formulaic Dramaturgy in *Doctor Faustus*," *"A poet and a filthy playmaker,"* Friedenreich et al. (eds.), 167–91

Pfister, Manfred, *Studien zum Wandel der Perspektivstruktur in elisabethanischen und jakobäischen Komödien,* München: Fink, 1974

"Kommentar, Metasprache und Metakommunikation in *Hamlet*," *Shakespeare Jahrbuch* (West), 1979, 132–51

The Theory and Analysis of Drama, Halliday, John (trans.), Cambridge University Press, 1988

"Reading the Body: The Corporeality of Shakespeare's Text," *Reading Plays: Interpretation and Reception*, Scolnicov, Hanna and Holland, Peter (eds.), Cambridge University Press, 1991, 110–22

Phelan, Peggy, *Unmarked: The Politics of Performance*, London: Routledge, 1993

Phelan, Peggy and Lane, Jill (eds), *The Ends of Performance*, New York University Press, 1998

Pollock, Della (ed.), *Exceptional Spaces: Essays in Performance and History*, Chapel Hill: University of North Carolina Press, 1998

Pollock, Griselda, *Vision and Difference: Femininity, Feminism, and the Histories of Art*, London: Routledge, 1988

Pope, Alexander, "Preface to Shakespeare," *Eighteenth Century Essays on Shakespeare*, Smith (ed.), 44–58

Rasmussen, Eric, "Setting Down What the Clown Spoke: Improvisation, Hand B, and *The Book of Sir Thomas More*," *Library* 13 (1991), 126–36

Reinelt, Janelle G. and Roach, Joseph R. (eds.), *Critical Theory and Performance*, Ann Arbor: University of Michigan Press, 1992

Reiss, Timothy J., *Knowledge, Discovery and Imagination in Early Modern Europe*, Cambridge University Press, 1997

Ricoeur, Paul, "Mimesis and Representation," *Annals of Scholarship: Metastudies of the Humanities and Social Sciences* 2 (1981), no. 3, 15–32

Riehle, Wolfgang, *Shakespeare, Plautus, and the Humanist Tradition*, Cambridge: D. S. Brewer, 1990

Righter, Anne, *Shakespeare and the Idea of the Play*, London: Chatto and Windus, 1962

Roach, Joseph, "Territorial Passages: Time, Place, and Action," *Of Borders and Thresholds*, Kobialka (ed.), 110–24

Rorty, Richard, *Philosophy and the Mirror of Nature*, Princeton University Press, 1979

Rosenberg, Marvin, "Elizabethan Actors, Men or Marionettes?" *PMLA* 69 (1954), 915–27

Rouse, John, "Textuality and Authority in Theater and Drama: Some Contemporary Possibilities," *Critical Theory and Performance*, Reinelt and Roach (eds.), 146–157

Said, Edward, *Beginnings: Intention and Method*, New York: Columbia University Press, 1985

Salingar, Leo, *Shakespeare and the Traditions of Comedy*, Cambridge University Press, 1974

"Jacobean Playwrights and 'Judicious' Spectators," *British Academy Shakespeare Lectures, 1980–89*, E. A. J. Honigmann (ed.), Oxford University Press, 1993, 231–53

Schechner, Richard, *Between Theater and Anthropology*, Philadelphia: University of Pennsylvania Press, 1985

"A New Paradigm for Theatre in the Academy," *Tulane Drama Review* 36 (1992), 7–10

Schmidt, Alexander, *Shakespeare-Lexicon: A Complete Dictionary of all the Eng-*

lish Words, Phrases and Constructions in the Works of the Poet, 2 vols., Berlin: G. Reimer, 1874–75

Schmitt, N. C., "Was There a Medieval Theater in the Round? A Re-examination of the Evidence," *Medieval English Drama: Essays Critical and Contextual*, Taylor, Jerome and Nelson, Alan H. (eds.), University of Chicago Press, 1972, 292–315

Schoenbaum, S., *William Shakespeare: A Documentary Life*, New York: Oxford University Press, 1975

Schwarz, Henry, "'He is no unlettered man': *King Lear*, 'The Courier's Tragedy' and the Historical Agency of Postage," *Shakespeare Jahrbuch* (Weimar) 127 (1991), 63–76

Scolnicov, Hanna, "Theatre Space, Theatrical Space, and the Theatrical Space Without," *The Theatrical Space*, Redmond, James (ed.), Cambridge University Press, 1987, 11–26

Seltzer, Daniel, "The Actors and Staging," *A New Companion to Shakespeare Studies*, Muir, Kenneth and Schoenbaum, S. (eds.), 35–66

Sharpe, Jim, "Social Strain and Social Dislocation, 1585–1603," *The Reign of Elizabeth I: Court and Culture in the Last Decade*, Guy, John (ed.), Cambridge University Press, 1995, 192–211

Shepard, Simon, *Marlowe and the Politics of Elizabethan Theatre*, Brighton: Harvester Press, 1986

Shurgot, Michael W., *Stages of Play: Shakespeare's Theatrical Energies in Elizabethan Performance*, Newark: University of Delaware Press, 1998

Sinfield, Alan (ed.), *Macbeth*, "New Casebooks," London: Macmillan, 1992

Sisson, C. J., *Le Goût public et le théâtre élisabéthain jusqu'à la mort de Shakespeare*, Dijon: Darantiere, 1922

Skura, Meredith Anne, *Shakespeare the Actor and the Purposes of Playing*, University of Chicago Press, 1993

Smart, J. S., *Shakespeare: Truth and Tradition*, London: Arnold, 1928

Smith, A. Hassell, *County and Court: Government and Politics in Norfolk, 1558–1603*, Oxford Clarendon Press, 1974

Smith, David Nichol (ed.), *Eighteenth Century Essays on Shakespeare*, New York: Russel and Russell, 1962

Smith, Warren D., "The *Henry V* Choruses in the First Folio," *Journal of English and Germanic Philology* 53 (1954), 38–57

Somerset, Alan, "'How Chances it they Travel?' Provincial Touring, Playing Places, and the King's Men," *Shakespeare Survey* 47 (1994), 45–60

Southern, Richard, *The Medieval Theatre in the Round*, London: Faber & Faber, 1957

Sprigg, Douglas, "Shakespeare's Visual Stagecraft: The Seduction of Cressida," *Shakespeare: The Theatrical Dimension*, McGuire, Philip C. and Samuelson, David A. (eds.), New York: AMS Press, 1979, 149–63

Stamm, Rudolf, *Shakespeare's Word Scenery*, Zürich: Polygraphischer Verlag, 1954

Stock, Brian, *The Implications of Literacy: Written Language and Models of Interpretation in the Eleventh and Twelfth Centuries*, Princeton University Press, 1983

Stone, Lawrence, *The Crisis of the Aristocracy, 1558–1641*, Oxford: Clarendon Press, 1965

Styan, J. L., *Shakespeare's Stagecraft*, Cambridge University Press, 1967

Drama, Stage and Audience, Cambridge University Press, 1975

The Shakespeare Revolution: Criticism and Performance in the Twentieth Century, Cambridge University Press, 1977

"Stage Space and the Shakespeare Experience," *Shakespeare and the Sense of Performance: Essays in the Tradition of Performance Criticism in Honor of Bernard Beckerman*, Thompson, Marvin and Ruth (eds.), Newark: University of Delaware Press, 1989, 195–209

Thirsk, Joan, *Economic Policy and Projects: The Development of a Consumer Society in Early Modern England*, Oxford: Clarendon Press, 1978

Thomas, Keith, "The Place of Laughter in Tudor and Stuart England," *TLS* 21 Jan. 1977, 77–81

Thomson, Peter, "Rogues and Rhetoricians: Acting Styles in Early English Drama," *A New History of Early English Drama*, Cox and Kastan (eds.), 321–35

Shakespeare's Professional Career, Cambridge University Press, 1992

Thorndike, Ashley, *Shakespeare's Theater*, New York: Macmillan, 1916

Turner, Victor, "Variations on a Theme of Liminality," *Secular Ritual*, Moore, Sally F. and Myerhoff, Barbara E. (eds.), Assen / Amsterdam: Van Gorcum, 1977, 36–52

From Ritual to Theatre: The Human Seriousness of Play, New York: PAJ Publications, 1982

Ubersfeld, Anne, *Lire le théâtre*, Paris: Éditions sociales, 1977

L'école du Spectateur, Paris: Éditions sociales, 1981

Ubersfeld, Anne and Banu, Georges, *L'Espace théâtral recherches dans la mise en scène d'aujourd'hui*, Paris: Centre national de documentation pédagogique, 1982

Urkowitz, Steven, "'Well-sayd olde Mole': Burying Three *Hamlets* in Modern Editions," *Shakespeare Study Today*, Ziegler, Georgianna (ed.), New York: AMS Press, 1986, 37–70

Walch, Günter, "Tudor-Legende und Geschichtsbewegung in *The Life of King Henry V*: Zur Rezeptionslenkung durch den Chorus," *Shakespeare Jahrbuch* (Weimar) 122 (1986), 36–46

Walker, Greg, *The Politics of Performance in Early Renaissance Drama*, Cambridge University Press, 1998

Warburton, William, "Preface to 'The Works of William Shakespeare,'" *Eighteenth Century Essays on Shakespeare*, Smith (ed.), 89–103

Watt, Tessa, *Cheap Print and Popular Piety, 1550–1640*, Cambridge University Press, 1991

Wayne, Don, "Drama and Society in the Age of Jonson: An Alternative View," *Renaissance Drama* 13 (1982), 103–29

Weimann, Robert, *Shakespeare and the Popular Tradition in the Theater*, Schwartz, Robert (ed.), Baltimore: Johns Hopkins University Press, 1978

"*Fabula* and *Historia*: The Crisis of the 'Universall Consideration' in *The Unfortunate Traveller*," *Representations* 8 (1984), 14–29

"Performing at the Frontiers of Representation: Epilogue and Post-Scriptural Future in Shakespeare's Plays," *The Arts of Performance in Elizabethan and Early Stuart Drama: Essays for G. K. Hunter*, Biggs, Murray et al. (eds.), Edinburgh University Press, 1991, 96–112

"Textual Authority and Performative Agency: The Uses of Disguise in Shakespeare's Theater," *New Literary History* 25 (1994), 789–808 (See chapter 2, note 7.)

"'Moralize two Meanings' in one Play: Divided Authority on the Morality Stage," *Mediaevalia* 18 (1995), 427–50

Authority and Representation in Early Modern Discourse, Baltimore: Johns Hopkins University Press, 1996

"Performance-Game and Representation in *Richard III*," *Textual and Theatrical Shakespeare: Questions of Evidence,* Pechter, Edward (ed.), University of Iowa Press, 1996, 66–85

"Scene Individable, Mingle-Mangle Unlimited: Authority and Poetics in Lyly's and Shakespeare's Theaters," *European Journal of English Studies* 1 (1997), 310–28

Werstine, Paul, "The Textual Mystery of *Hamlet*," *Shakespeare Quarterly* 39 (1988), 1–26

"A Century of 'Bad' Shakespeare Quartos," *Shakespeare Quarterly* 50 (1999), 310–33

Westfall, Suzanne R., "'A commonty a Christmas gambold or a tumbling trick': Household Theater," *A New History of Early English Drama*, Cox and Kastan (eds.), 39–58

Patrons and Performance: Early Tudor Household Records, Oxford: Clarendon Press, 1990

Whigham, Frank, *Ambition and Privilege: The Social Tropes of Elizabethan Courtesy Theory*, Berkeley: University of California Press, 1984

White, Paul Whitfield, *Theatre and Reformation: Protestantism, Patronage, and Playing in Tudor England*, Cambridge University Press, 1993

White, R. S., *Shakespeare and the Romance Ending*, Newcastle upon Tyne: School of English, 1981

Wickham, Glynne, "Hell-Castle and its Door-Keeper," *Shakespeare Survey* 19 (1966), 68–74

Early English Stages, 1300–1575, London: Routledge & Kegan Paul, 1980

Wiles, David, *Shakespeare's Clown: Actor and Text in the Elizabethan Playhouse*, Cambridge University Press, 1987

Tragedy in Athens: Performance Space and Theatrical Meaning, Cambridge University Press, 1997

Williams, David, *Deformed Discourse: The Function of the Monster in Medieval Thought and Literature*, McGill: Queen's University Press, 1998

Williams, Raymond, *Drama in Performance*, London: Watts, 1968

Wilson, F. P., *Marlowe and the Early Shakespeare*, Oxford: Clarendon Press, 1953

Wilson, John Dover, "The 'Hamlet' Transcript, 1953," *The Library* 9 (1918), 217–47

Wölfflin, Heinrich, *Renaissance and Baroque*, Simon, Kathrin (trans.), Ithaca: Cornell University Press, 1966

Worthen, W. B., *The Idea of the Actor: Drama and the Ethics of Performance*, Princeton University Press, 1984

Shakespeare and the Authority of Performance, Cambridge University Press, 1997

"Drama, Performativity, and Performance," *PMLA* 113 (1998), 1093–107

Wrightson, Keith, *English Society, 1580–1680*, London: Hutchinson, 1982

Zarilli, Phillip B. (ed.), *Acting (Re)considered: Theories and Practices*, London: Routledge, 1995

Zimansky, Curt A. (ed.), *The Critical Works of Thomas Rymer*, New Haven: Yale University Press, 1956

Zimmerman, Susan, Afterword to Forum: "Editing Early Modern Texts," *Shakespeare Studies* 24 (1996), 71–74

Index

Cambridge Studies in Renaissance Literature and Culture

General editor
STEPHEN ORGEL
Jackson Eli Reynolds Professor of Humanities, Stanford University